D0225363

THE BUSINESS OF WINE

THE BUSINESS OF WINE

An Encyclopedia

Edited by
Geralyn Brostrom and Jack Brostrom

Foreword by
Robert Smiley

GREENWOOD PRESS
Westport, Connecticut · London

Library of Congress Cataloging-in-Publication Data

The business of wine : an encyclopedia / edited by Geralyn Brostrom and Jack Brostrom ;
   foreword by Robert Smiley.
      p. cm.
   Includes bibliographical references and index.
   ISBN 978-0-313-35400-7 (alk. paper)
   1. Wine industry—Encyclopedias. 2. Viticulture—Encyclopedias. 3. Wine and wine making—
Encyclopedias. I. Brostrom, Jack. II. Brostrom, Geralyn, 1961-
HD9370.5.B868   2009
338.4´7663203—dc22   2008032965

British Library Cataloguing in Publication Data is available.

Library of Congress Catalog Card Number: 2008032965
ISBN: 978-0-313-35400-7

First published in 2009

Greenwood Press, 88 Post Road West, Westport, CT 06881
An imprint of Greenwood Publishing Group, Inc.
www.greenwood.com

Printed in the United States of America

The paper used in this book complies with the
Permanent Paper Standard issued by the National
Information Standards Organization (Z39.48–1984).

10 9 8 7 6 5 4 3 2 1

Contents

Foreword

Why is the wine industry so interesting? It is a business that is unique and has a mystique all its own. Many people have a personal relationship to the industry —primarily as wine drinkers. Behind the labels, the wine trade is full of fascinating characters and companies.

The global wine industry differs from other industries in several respects. First, the wine business is more vertically integrated than virtually any other. With the possible exception of farmer's markets, no other industry grows its own raw material (winery-owned vineyards grow grapes), produces the product, and sells to the consumer as wineries do. The bottom line is that wineries must master many skills to be successful.

Wine also is a lifestyle choice for many producers. Fortunes made elsewhere are often invested in Napa, Bordeaux, or Tuscany. This flow of funds floods the industry with excess capital, leading to an oversupply of quality wine grapes and wine, and a perennial global wine glut. With growers—especially in Europe —reluctant to switch from grapes to other crops as their markets decline, the global surplus of wine can occasionally paralyze the industry.

The global wine industry is quite cyclical, as well. For example, periods of grape shortages will lead to higher prices. Growers flush with cash will plant new vineyards, and four or five years later, those vineyards mature and produce substantial amounts of new grapes, which leads to an oversupply. This results in falling prices, bankruptcies by some growers, and financiers pulling the plug, leaving fewer vines. A strategic decision by one grower can—when combined with thousands of similar decisions—spark a cycle. From peak to peak, this grape cycle lasts about 10 years.

Diverse ownership structures also distinguish the wine industry. Many of the leading wineries are privately owned, including the E.&J. Gallo Winery, the Wine Group, and the Bronco Wine Company. A few are publicly traded corporations, such as Constellation Brands, Inc. Others are divisions of much larger conglomerates, such as Domaine Chandon, a division of LVMH; Fetzer Brothers, a division of Brown-Forman; and Diageo Chateau & Estate Wines, producer of Sterling and BV, which is a division of Diageo PLC, the world's largest spirits company.

The business has its fair share of innovative trailblazers. In the United States, these entrepreneurs include Fred Franzia of Bronco, Robert Mondavi, Ernest Gallo, and Randall Grahm of Bonnie Doon Vineyard. They are pioneers and iconic personalities of the industry.

From an economist's standpoint, the wine market is intriguing because quality and price are so highly variable. No other industry I can think of has such high variability in price. Almost no other product category contains both commodities (jug wine) and aspirational luxury brands such as Napa's Screaming Eagle or Bordeaux's Château Margaux. Consumers may choose wine in one price range, but desire a higher-priced wine in the future. Wine is also an "affordable" luxury. We can enjoy an expensive wine on rare occasions, even if we cannot afford a $10 million home on the coast.

Finally, wine presents a conundrum for the consumer because quality is difficult to discern. No other product category in a retail market has so many facings or SKUs (stock-keeping units), which makes it hard for consumers to make informed choices.

Why an encyclopedia of the business of wine? From airlines to Zinfandel, this first-of-its-kind reference source offers detailed and up-to-date information about today's wine business. The sections range from comments about such industry luminaries as Robert Mondavi and Robert Parker to some of the most influential powerhouses in the wine industry: E.&J. Gallo, Constellation Brands, Inc., and the Wine Group.

You will find information about grape-growing techniques, the art and science of winemaking, and characteristics of grape varieties. The book also covers legal issues, such as regulation, direct shipping, and drinking age. Featured, too, are such current issues as the French paradox and flying winemakers (of *Mondovino* fame), getting wine to consumers through distributors, and sustainability and environmental trends. This book will educate the general public and practitioners, too, about a fascinating and mysterious industry. Just settle in with a glass of your favorite wine and enjoy.

Robert Smiley
Professor of Management
Director of Wine Industry Programs
Graduate School of Management
University of California, Davis

Preface

This encyclopedia focuses on the everyday business aspects of the wine world, both to give outsiders a glimpse of some of the issues and structure of the industry and to serve as a general reference for people in the wine trade. Rather than being a source of basic wine knowledge on such topics as regions and grape varieties or a description of specific wines or producers, it provides authoritative information about why certain regions, grapes, wine styles, and issues are important to the wine industry as a whole. It is, to some extent, a peek beneath the surface to see the working parts in operation.

The encyclopedia, written by a host of knowledgeable wine business professionals, contains more than 140 entries on a variety of subjects of interest for everyone from casual browsers to wine aficionados to those in the industry. Among the entries, the reader will find most of the individual segments of the wine industry, from grape growing to consumers, including some segments that are not on the typical flowchart of the industry such as auction houses, cruise lines, and wine tourism. Another large group of entries focuses on business topics, with entries on such current controversial issues as consolidation and direct shipping; innovations that have changed the industry, such as mechanization and varietal labeling; economics-related subjects such as exchange rates and supply and demand; and profiles of major wine companies. Other entries cover more familiar ground, including wine grapes, wine regions, and wine styles. Entries on historical periods of great importance for the development of the trade (Ancient Mediterranean, Prohibition, religion), legal issues (control states, direct shipping), and such key people as winemaker Robert Mondavi round out the encyclopedia.

Terms that appear in boldface in the text are cross-references to other entries in this volume. Additional cross-references may appear at the end of the entry.

An alphabetical list and a topical list of entries are provided in the front matter to help readers quickly find information of interest, and an index at the end will help locate topics that do not have individual entries. Sidebars and an appendix with wine data are added value.

In general, most entries provide some historical context, an overview of current trade statistics, and an outlook for the future, as appropriate; issues-oriented entries explain the main arguments of both sides of the discussion. In order to keep the focus on trade and business aspects, no attempt has been made to provide complete basic information—this information is readily available in many other books, including those listed in the selected bibliography.

An encyclopedia such as this is inevitably a snapshot in time, and in an industry as dynamic as wine, everything is a moving target. However, it presents a broad picture that will remain useful for years to come. Most of the statistics are from the 2006 calendar year or 2006 vintage, which is the most recent year for which data are widely available at this writing. In some cases, especially for the Southern Hemisphere, 2007 data have been released, and these are included where possible.

For comparison purposes, statistics have been converted into U.S. measures, such as acres and degrees Fahrenheit; metric conversions are included in a Conversions appendix in the back matter. Exceptions to this general policy were made for volume measures of wine, since the standard worldwide is the 750-milliliter (ml) bottle. Small volumes are therefore given in liters or milliliters so they can quickly be compared to number of bottles. Large volumes are given in cases, often millions of cases, based on the standard nine-liter case (typically, twelve 750-ml bottles or six 1.5-liter double bottles). Obviously, this makes less sense when talking about bulk wine, which by definition is not in cases at all, but it is nevertheless useful for comparative purposes between entries and can be converted to liters or gallons if necessary.

Sources often disagree on even the simplest statistics, perhaps due to different assumptions or definitions of what to include, different time frames, or preliminary estimates that were later updated. We have tried to make sense of the statistics and use the most accurate sources. For production and consumption statistics, we have used national official sources where available, including the U.S. Department of Commerce and the Alcohol and Tobacco Tax and Trade Bureau for U.S. data. Where national statistics were unavailable or unreliable, we have generally used data from the OIV (International Organization of Vine and Wine). For U.S. domestic statistics especially, data for comparison and analysis came from *Adams Wine Handbook 2007,* the Alcohol and Tobacco Tax and Trade Bureau, the California Department of Food and Agriculture, *Impact,* MKF Research, the New York Wine & Grape Foundation, the Oregon Wine Board, the U.S. Department of Agriculture, the U.S. Department of Commerce, Vines.org, the Washington Wine Commission, *Wine Business Monthly,* and the Wine Institute, along with various corporate Web sites and industry experts.

We would like to express our sincere appreciation to all the people who contributed entries and added their valuable insights to this book. In particular, we thank Doug Frost for being the first person to agree to contribute and Roger Bohmrich for his early and enthusiastic support of the project. We would also like to acknowledge the assistance of Markus Bokisch, Jeff Cohn, Jennifer Frighetto, Colleen LeMasters, and Zelma Long on various entries. Those entries not otherwise attributed are the responsibility of the editors.

Introduction

The history of the wine trade is as long as the history of wine itself, going back as far as eight millennia to the discovery in the Caucasus region of Asia of the process for controlling grape fermentation and producing an alcoholic beverage. It cannot have taken long from the time winemaking began before someone realized that this product could be traded for other valuable goods and the first wine merchant appeared. As this new beverage that tasted so interesting and caused great euphoria among imbibers became better known, demand for it increased, and vineyards were planted farther and farther from the grapes' homeland, at the same time being improved by a slow process of selection of the best vines for further propagation.

By 5,000 years ago, wine was well known in Mesopotamia and Egypt, the major civilizations of the Western world. Over the next couple of millennia, the rise of the Phoenicians, a mercantile culture based in present-day Syria and Lebanon, carried wine and vines as trade goods throughout the length of the Mediterranean's African coast, to most of the Mediterranean islands, and to Greece and Turkey. Wine was a staple of cuisine in the Near East at that time and, consequently, was adopted as part of ritual celebrations and formal meals by the Jews in Palestine, among others.

By the first millennium BC, the Greeks warmly embraced grapevines and wine, raising winemaking to new heights and spreading the wine culture to their colonies on the south coast of Europe, notably in Enotria—the "land of wine" in the southern Italian Peninsula. Amphorae of wine were commonly shipped back and forth between Greek colonies and the homeland, as well as to other Mediterranean markets.

The Romans then took the wine baton from the Greeks and ran with it throughout Europe. Wine was hugely popular in the Roman world, requiring the production of wine on an unheard-of scale to supply the Roman metropolises and the armies and garrisons in faraway lands. Southern Italy was the breadbasket for Rome, and it was the largest source of wine as well. Because wine did not necessarily travel well, however, it was necessary to develop additional supply sources as the empire spread. With Roman control stretching from the Atlantic to the

Near East, the Romans planted vineyards everywhere they could, from Portugal to Eastern Europe, as well as throughout Italy and much of France, which both seemed perfectly suited to the production of the best wine yet made. Importantly, wine remained a part of the Near Eastern culture, too, taking on a whole new significance when Jesus equated wine with his own blood at the Last Supper.

The popularity of wine survived the decline, division, and eventual disappearance of the Roman Empire. Even as the Western world took several steps backward in most fields of technology and trade, the production of wine continued almost everywhere it had been established by the Romans. To some extent, this was because of the need for wine in the Christian Mass, and therefore the wine knowledge often resided most strongly in the religious communities of the day; wine, however, was also imbibed extensively as a thoroughly secular beverage, and most production, even from ecclesiastical vineyards, was consumed outside the church.

Wine merchants were already well established, carrying wine from the source to eager consumers, especially in the cities, where water was generally scarce or unsanitary and wine therefore a much more healthful beverage. Because the wine would spoil if it had to be carried very far in warm temperatures, it became common to add brandy, which was developed in the Middle Ages, to create a fortified wine that would stay drinkable much longer.

Over the course of more than 1,000 years, random crossings and mutations resulted in myriad varieties of wine grapes that were unlike anything that had existed in Roman times or earlier. Through trial and error, winegrowers in Europe matched grape varieties with the areas and even specific plots of land where they grew best, creating the Old World structure of vine-and-region correspondences that have become today's appellations. This system still drives price setting in such places as Burgundy and Piedmont and is responsible for the dear prices of wines from the best sites.

After the Norman conquest of England, members of the new English aristocracy found themselves in a land that was generally inhospitable for vineyards and therefore nurtured a vibrant cross-Channel wine trade with France, particularly the Bordeaux region that was under English domination for centuries. This was the start of the modern wine trade, with vineyards in southwestern France, as well as in Portugal and Spain (which were so far away that their wine required fortification to make the voyage, thus creating Port and Sherry), sending much of their output to London merchants. As the feudal system broke down and barter was replaced by money, the wine trade began to resemble the organization of producers, shippers, and merchants that it has today.

With the discovery of the Americas and the rush to found colonies in distant lands, wine was introduced to the New World. The first vines were taken to the Americas by missionaries, who needed a source of wine in order to consecrate the Mass among their converts and colonists. These plantings did not turn into the commercial enterprises that the medieval monasteries did, but in some cases they did act as nurseries for secular vineyards that came later. In most of the colonies, growing grapes either proved nearly impossible or was forbidden by authorities who stood to lose out on a monopoly on supplying alcohol if they allowed colonists to develop an indigenous industry. Thus, global trade on a scale exceeding that of even the Silk Road developed, and wine was one of the commodities that was shipped from producers and merchants in Europe across the oceans to the Americas and to the outposts in South Africa and the South Pacific.

Before the nineteenth century, almost all of the world's wine was made in Europe, but the New World slowly founded its own domestic wine industry after locating suitable winegrowing regions and acquiring quality *Vitis vinifera* vine cuttings from European vineyards—many brought by immigrants from Old World winegrowing regions, who also brought technical skills. California, Chile, and Argentina moved beyond their missionary cottage industry backgrounds to develop large commercial vineyards. Australia, South Africa, and New Zealand, too, found areas not far from some of their larger cities where grapes would grow well. All these areas began to produce wines that, even if they did not yet rival those of France, were at least of decent quality and were much cheaper and more readily available than French or other European wines.

One New World area that was not successful in wine production was the eastern United States, where, among other lesser problems, the root louse phylloxera made the cultivation of European grape varieties impossible. The phylloxera problem went unrecognized until after the insect had inadvertently been exported to most of the rest of the wine-producing world on sample cuttings of native American grapevines. Phylloxera ravaged the defenseless vinifera vines almost everywhere in the late nineteenth century, causing massive upheaval in the wine industry.

Eventually, it was discovered that grafting vinifera cuttings onto native American rootstocks would keep the phylloxera plague in check, but by the time the solution had been effected, much had changed. For one thing, almost every grapevine in the world had to be uprooted and replaced with grafted vines. In the process, lesser varieties and vineyards were abandoned, resulting in a higher-quality but somewhat less diverse viticultural world that has to a large extent carried through to today. Another effect of phylloxera was that, with the European, especially French, wine industry temporarily sidelined by phylloxera damage and replanting, New World regions were for a time able to take the spotlight and demonstrate their potential (until they, too, were struck by phylloxera). Even in Europe, the French hiatus sent French winemakers to other countries in search of work, raising the bar of quality in many regions.

The first part of the twentieth century saw serious economic hurdles for the wine industry, including two world wars that wreaked havoc in the vineyards of Europe, as well as dampening world trade in general, and Prohibition in the United States, which largely removed the United States from the wine trade as both producer and consumer for a dozen years. Beginning with the postwar prosperity of the 1950s, though, the wine trade has grown and diversified steadily. A milestone was reached in 1976, when California wines bested French wines in a high-profile blind tasting, symbolically signaling the New World's coming of age. That opened the door for not only California wines but also those of Washington, Oregon, Australia, New Zealand, Chile, and others to take their places on wine shelves and wine cellars everywhere. It also forced the Old World wine producers to reevaluate their products and strategies, causing an upsurge in wines that compete in the New World style and a renewed focus on quality in the top wine regions.

Today, wine is no longer a dietary staple as it once was. Rather, it is a beverage of choice. In most countries, it competes with not only beer and spirits but also a wide range of soft drinks and safe-to-drink water—not to mention bottled waters that in some cases cost almost as much as wine. In the southern half of Europe, where wine drinking was once a defining part of the culture, health and legal concerns over alcohol, coupled with the availability of cheaper nonalcoholic alternatives, have reduced wine to an option, and wine consumption continues to drop, albeit from quite high levels. In most of the rest of the world, however, wine drinking is becoming more popular, so overall the world's wine consumption is increasing.

Wine competes with other drinks on the strength of its taste and quality, as well as on its reputation as the most civilized of beverages, and it appears to be holding its own against the competition. Nevertheless, because wine is no longer an automatic choice even in its southern European strongholds, the wine industry needs to continue to refine its quality, find new markets, and broaden its appeal in mature markets. Nowhere is this more apparent than in the United States, where wine-versus-wine and wine-versus-other-drink competition is fierce because of the huge potential of the American market. With its wine consumption increasing as France's and Italy's decline, the United States is expected to become the world's largest wine-consuming nation by 2010—yet almost two-thirds of the population reports not drinking wine at all, and half of the wine drinkers drink only occasionally. Thus, the United States represents a dichotomy of both a mature market that has the capacity to consume more and a new market full of people who might be interested in wine if they knew more about it. In both instances, quality and the quality–price ratio will determine success for the wine industry in general and for individual countries or producers that are after the American consumer.

This encyclopedia presents useful information on the wine industry to provide readers with a behind-the-scenes look at the commercial wine world. In fact, a point that is well known to people who make a living in the wine industry, but is typically lost on the general public and often on those who have just entered this line of work, is that the wine business is actually a *business*. Many people outside the trade think that working in the wine business must be one long party, sort of like being in the movies or working on a cruise ship. They do not realize that there is a great deal of hard work involved in growing grapes, making wine, and selling wine (as there is in making movies or being part of a cruise ship's crew) and furthermore that when these things are not done well—and even sometimes when they are but the market conditions are unfavorable—employees lose their jobs and companies go bankrupt in the wine industry just as in any other type of business.

The wine industry is a complex network of interrelated businesses that collectively serve to produce wine and get it into the hands of consumers. In its simplest form, the industry consists of a producer—a person who grows grapes and makes wine out of them—and a consumer—someone who then drinks that wine. Historically, this producer–supplier relationship existed between the local farmer and villagers. As the world of commerce has expanded exponentially since those times, so too has the wine world. Today's global wine business is an interconnected system of middlemen that serves to get wine from the source to the consumer in often far-flung locations.

Although agricultural in nature, the wine industry can be broken down into large segments, each of which comprises numerous companies and individuals who perform support roles between the grape grower/winemaker and the consumer. There are basically four segments: production, distribution, sales, and consumption. Since consumers are usually considered separately, this arrangement is often known as the *three-tier system*.

The *production tier* is the heart and soul of the wine industry. Its two main functions are grape growing and winemaking. In some instances, these two functions are performed by the same business—the estate winery—and occasionally even by the same people. In most cases, however, the two are fairly independent even when part of the same company. Grape growers are supported by nurseries, viticultural consultants, manufacturers of vineyard equipment and tools, and any number of vineyard workers who prune, pick, and perform other duties in the field. Ideally, the winemaker who will be taking the crop also works with the grape grower to ensure that the fruit characteristics match with the style of wine to be made. Other times, a broker may be involved in finding a purchaser for the fruit.

In very small commercial operations, the winemaker may be the only person directly involved in the day-to-day activities, but in a large winery, the winemaker may be supported by dozens or even hundreds of other individuals in producing, aging, and handling the wine. Other businesses that are involved in the production phase include those that supply the equipment used: tanks, presses, crushers, forklifts, hoses, pumps, and so on; or in some cases, all of this may be part of a custom crush facility. If the wine is aged in oak, a cooperage or broker of used barrels is involved. Assistance may be required from enologist consultants and from laboratories. Bulk wine brokers may be needed either to help sell the wine to someone else or to help acquire additional must or wine to fill out the volume desired. Once the wine is ready to be released, glass from a factory and case boxes are usually needed, along with a bottling line that may be owned or rented; if alternative packaging such as bag-in-box is used, the equivalent materials and system are required.

The *distribution tier* takes the wine from the winery and gets it to consumers who are too far away or otherwise unable or unwilling to get the wine directly from the winery. This typically involves the tasks of transporting and warehousing the wine, deploying sales personnel to convince retail outlets to put the wine on their shelves or wine lists, and dealing with the paperwork required by national and local regulators. In addition, if the wine is being sold in another country, an importer or agent is normally required to process the extra paperwork and to transport the wine perhaps halfway around the world before handing it over to a distributor or retailer in the destination country. The distribution tier is strong and well entrenched in the United States and a few other countries, requiring regulatory and legal personnel to get involved in the mix. Conversely, this tier is relatively weak in Europe, where a substantial amount of wine moves directly from supplier to retailer.

The *retail tier* is the usual interface with the actual wine consumer. This segment is divided into *off-premise,* also known as the off-trade or simply as retailers—businesses that sell wine that people take away and drink at home or elsewhere—and *on-premise* (the on-trade), which are businesses that sell wine for people to consume on the spot. Off-premise wine sales take place at dedicated wine retailers, general wine and spirits stores, supermarkets, big-box superstores, convenience stores, and some on-premise establishments that have an "on-and-off" license, as well as at many wineries and their tasting rooms or outlets. Some of these venues have sales staff specifically geared toward wine sales, but others may have no one with wine knowledge at all, perhaps relying on distributor reps for help in selecting the wines to stock. Another off-premise channel that is becoming a bigger factor is e-commerce, where customers order wine online and have it delivered directly to their homes via a shipping service. Wineries also often sell directly to customers at a distance via e-commerce or mail order.

On-premise wine outlets include restaurants, wine bars, bars, hotels, catering companies, airlines, cruise lines, and other food and/or drink establishments. These may have specialized staff, such as sommeliers, whose job specifically involves the sale and service of wine, or the sale of wine may be a collateral duty for employees whose main responsibilities are unrelated. Obviously, the more focused and interested the individual is regarding wine, the more effective he or she will be in selling it.

The *consumption tier* is the level at which someone actually pays for the labor of all the people who work in the other three tiers, then hopefully opens the wine and enjoys it. This tier includes hundreds of millions of people who drink wine worldwide, along with a small group of speculators who purchase wine more as an investment than a beverage. Supporting this tier, along with the army of producers and salespeople in the other tiers, are a number of people who do not make or sell wine directly but instead work to make the consumer's experience more rewarding. These include producers and vendors of wine accessories such as books and corkscrews, people who work in wine tourism, organizers of wine festivals and competitions, auction houses that facilitate wine sales between individuals, and a cadre of wine writers, critics, and educators.

Thus, it is apparent that the wine industry is a far-reaching web of businesses and people whose livelihoods are governed by the forces of nature, yet depend to a greater or lesser degree on the purchase and enjoyment of wine by consumers. This encyclopedia endeavors to show how those different segments work together to bring wine to the public and describes the trade in wine and its related subsidiary elements. Consumers and interested readers need to appreciate the work that has gone into their glass of wine, and industry professionals, too, need to understand their roles in the great clockwork mechanism of wine production, distribution, and sales.

Alphabetical List of Entries

Topical List of Entries

Companies
Banfi Vintners
Bronco Wine Company
Constellation Brands
Diageo
Foster's Group
Gallo
Kendall-Jackson
Mondavi, Robert
Shanken Communications
Trinchero Family Estates
The Wine Group
Yellow Tail

Economics
Exchange Rates
Profit and Profitability
Promotion
Supply and Demand
Trade Barriers

Grape Varieties
Cabernet Sauvignon
Chardonnay
Merlot
Pinot Grigio/Pinot Gris
Pinot Noir
Riesling
Sauvignon Blanc
Syrah/Shiraz
Varietal Labeling
Zinfandel

History
Ancient Mediterranean
Colonial Era
Monasteries
Phylloxera
Prohibition
Religion

Industry Segments
Airlines
Auction Houses
Barrels and Oak Alternatives
Bulk Wine/Juice Trade
Consumers
Control States
Cruise Lines
Custom Crush Facilities
Distillation
Distributors
E-Commerce
Festivals, Trade Shows, and Competitions
Grape Growing
Hospitality Industry
Importers
Négociants
Nurseries
Personnel
Promotion
Restaurants
Retailers
Sommeliers
Supermarkets
Virtual Wineries
Wine Clubs

A

AIRLINES

Wine sales to airline companies represent tens of millions of dollars spent in the **United States**, as well as many more millions in Europe and **Asia**. These sales exist in two straightforward categories: inexpensive wines in single-serve sizes intended to be sold to economy-class customers, and more expensive and exclusive wines to be given at no charge to each airline's business- and first-class passengers. Only a few years ago, most airlines still offered wines for free to economy-class fliers on transcontinental flights, but recent financial challenges have ended many of those giveaways.

Within the upper classes of airline service, free high-quality wines continue to provide a method whereby airlines hope to differentiate themselves from their competition. Of course, it is misleading to talk about these wines as giveaways: the price of business- and first-class tickets is higher than ever and can be four or five times the price of a standard-fare ticket. For these far greater sums, upper-class customers receive a wider seat, a bit more legroom, quicker boarding—and little else that is tangible, other than free drinks and a better meal. Still, dedicated flight attendant service, enhanced frequent-flyer programs, greater comfort, and sexy wine selections are embraced by most global carriers as tools for creating customer loyalty among the upper and expensive classes of service. Most of the top airlines employ dedicated consultants to help plan their purchases.

Almost all carriers offer at least one **red wine** and one white in economy class. Most of these wines come from a handful of large, global wine companies that can offer pleasant wine in great volumes and at very affordable prices to airlines. In the United States, these wines usually hail from California, **Chile**, or **Argentina**. Despite the fact that most carriers charge around $5 (depending on the currency) for these 187-milliliter (ml) wines, and despite the low prices paid for most of them, airlines do not see their wine programs as providing a **profit** center. With worldwide shipping (in many cases), advanced purchasing, and plenty of inventory losses (for a myriad of reasons), airlines simply post any revenues against their multimillion-dollar wine giveaways for the upper classes of service.

U.S.-based global carriers, such as United Airlines, Delta Air Lines, American Airlines, Northwest Airlines, and Continental Airlines, all have similar wine programs. These airlines offer inexpensive wines for sale in economy class, with occasional giveaway coupons for frequent flyers, and they offer aggressive wine programs in business and first class on domestic as well as international flights. For long international flights, in business class, carriers routinely give away expensive and exclusive **Champagnes** and offer red and white wines that would typically sell for $8–$15; wines in first class would often sell for even more.

The U.S. airline industry has been roiled for years by consolidation, low-cost competition, a changing regulatory environment, aging workforces and consequent increasing labor costs (especially pensions), ever-changing security demands, terrorism fears (if not occasional panic), and perhaps, most importantly, skyrocketing oil prices. At times, *low-cost carriers* have been able to take advantage of some of these challenges. While some have made brief forays into wine programs, few of these carriers remain focused on wine for long. One exception might be JetBlue Airways, which gained some media exposure by teaming with Best Cellars whiz founder Josh Wesson to select wines. But other airlines, such as Southwest Airlines, have based their corporate images upon their perceived low prices; highly considered wines would work against that image, and many of these airlines have only one class of service.

Not so with most *European carriers;* many of these have moderate- to high-level wine selections. If the airline's country of origin has a developed wine industry, it serves its own national wines. Economy-class wines are sometimes free, but are most often comparable selections to U.S. carriers' economy-class wines. Upper classes of service may see very exciting offerings.

Some *Asian airlines* are legendary for their wine selections. Carriers such as Singapore Airlines offer what might reasonably be considered to be the world's best wines in the air. And while carriers in other regions leave flight attendants more or less to their own devices, some Asian airlines offer basic wine training for their staffs.

For *carriers throughout the rest of the world,* the wines served are most often from the resident country of the airline, at least when those countries have a wine industry. Most wines served represent pleasant, relatively inexpensive offerings.

Doug Frost

ALCOHOL AND TOBACCO TAX AND TRADE BUREAU (TTB)

The Alcohol and Tobacco Tax and Trade Bureau (TTB) is the U.S. government agency responsible for the oversight of wine and the wine industry in the United States. It was created in 2003 when the responsibilities of the Bureau of Alcohol, Tobacco, and Firearms (BATF or ATF) were divided between the Department of Justice and the Department of the Treasury. The BATF has roots that go as far back as the first tax on whiskey under President George Washington. Over the next two centuries, the organization and responsibilities of the division, part of the Treasury Department, changed and grew, taking on the administration and enforcement of not only all forms of alcohol but also tobacco, guns, and explosives. It was at its zenith, or nadir, during **Prohibition**. As part of the massive government reorganization of 2002, the enforcement and intelligence duties of BATF—along with the name—were moved into the Department of Justice, leaving the regulatory functions in the Department of the Treasury in the newly minted TTB.

The TTB is charged with collecting the federal taxes levied on wine, as well as with generally supervising the wine industry in the public interest. It approves wine labels; licenses **wineries**, **importers**, **distributors**, and others involved in making or transporting wine; issues permits for wine **retailers**; and designates American viticultural areas (AVAs), among other duties. The basic laws are contained in Title 27 of the U.S. Code.

While the TTB takes care of compliance with federal laws, all states and many smaller jurisdictions have parallel organizations that enforce and oversee state and local laws and regulations, such as **drinking age** restrictions, hours of sale, location of premises, and so forth. Licensing of on- and off-premise retail sales is primarily a local function in most states. *See also* Appellations; Dessert Wine; Direct Shipping; Table Wine; Varietal Labeling.

Further Reading
TTB. www.ttb.gov.

ALTERNATIVE PACKAGING

A current hot topic in the wine trade, *alternative packaging* refers to the use of alternatives to glass bottles as a means of storing wine from the vineyard, through the transit process, and then on to the place of consumption. Glass bottles themselves are a relatively recent innovation in the 7,000-year history of wine, dating back only to the eighteenth century. Prior to this, wine was transported in **bulk** and sold from a **barrel** or clay amphora, moving to more temporary storage media at its destination, such as the wineskin. Much of today's wine still never sees a bottle, but is drunk close to the source.

Glass is ideally suited for storing wine because it is excellent at protecting against the ingress of oxygen. However, it is heavy and has a tendency to break. Indeed, two of the driving forces behind the current search for alternatives to glass bottles are concern over the environmental impact of the logistics of moving wine around in these heavy bottles and the desire for the wine industry to have a lower carbon footprint. Current alternatives to glass include bag-in-box, polyethylene teraphthalate (PET), cans, pouches, and Tetra Paks.

Bag-in-Box.   Putting wine in a plastic bag with a tap suits those consumers who drink modestly or infrequently. As a serving is drawn from the wine box, the internal bag collapses so no air enters to fill the gap left by the vacated wine. This avoids any oxygen ingress and subsequent oxidation, with the consequence that the residual wine is kept fresh for some time. Bag-in-box is also an economical way to ship wine, because a pallet of bag-in-box wine holds 80 percent more wine and is less than two-thirds the weight of the equivalent volume of glass-bottled wine. Further, boxes appeal to retailers because they are easy to merchandise.

The drawback of bag-in-box is the high oxygen transmission of the bag material, which can result in rapid product evolution and short shelf life. There are two main bag materials: metalized polyester and coextrusion with ethyl vinyl alcohol (EVOH). Both have drawbacks. The metalized polyester bag suffers from flex cracking during transport, which can quadruple the oxygen transmission level; EVOH does not have this problem, but it works less well at higher temperatures and humidities. Another source of oxygen transmission is the tap, which is plastic, and there is frequently some extra oxygen pickup during filling. All this results in a shelf life of just nine months or so, which has resulted in a move toward filling the bags at their destination market. In addition, the sulfur dioxide levels of bag-in-box products are usually elevated to counter the higher oxygen transmission.

Bag-in-box is particularly popular in Sweden, **Australia**, and Norway and is growing in popularity in Denmark. In other countries, such as the United Kingdom, France, and the **United States**, bag-in-box also continues to be a strong presence in the market. The most common sizes are the three- and five-liter casks, with the three-liter size seeing the greatest growth.

Plastic Bottles.   The latest development in packaging is the appearance of 750-ml PET bottles on **supermarket** shelves. PET has been used for wine before, most commonly with small 250-ml bottles, and also with 1.5-liter bottles of inexpensive wine from the south of France. But this current move to PET is significant because it is the first time that wine in standard-size 750-ml bottles has been presented in plastic in stores.

The main advantage of PET is its weight (a 750-ml glass bottle weighs around 14 ounces; the same size in PET weighs just 2 ounces, making transport more efficient), durability, and smaller size. The main driving force behind the adoption of PET is the potential environmental benefit of shipping lighter, smaller bottles, which reduces their carbon footprint through savings in the transport chain. If this is coupled to bottling in the target market with bulk shipment of the wine, then the savings are magnified because around double the volume of wine per container can be shipped in bulk compared with bottled wine.

The main disadvantage with PET, as with bag-in-box, is in preserving wine quality. As with all plastics, PET allows diffusion of oxygen, and thus the wine has a shorter shelf life, losing freshness more quickly. To counter this, barrier technologies and oxygen scavengers are incorporated into the PET construction. The barrier technologies lose their effectiveness at higher temperatures, however, which is one of the reasons that it is inadvisable to ship PET bottles over long distances.

Tetra Prisma.   A radically "alternative" option is the Tetra Prisma, from Tetra Pak. While the company's Tetra Brick has been around for quite a while as a way of packaging wine, it has not really caught on. The better-looking Prisma is a new development and is proving much more popular. The French company Boisset has been the market leader with this packaging: its French Rabbit **brand** of Vin de Pays d'Oc wines, launched in August 2005, has been designed with the Tetra Prisma as an intrinsic component. Technically speaking, the Prisma has aluminum foil sandwiched between polyethylene layers, with an outer cardboard skin.

The barrier properties of this foil are good because the flex cracking that occurs in the foil layer of bags is unlikely to occur here. Boisset claims that the Prisma reduces packaging by 90% compared with glass and is fully recyclable.

Other Options.   A variation on the bag-in-box theme that has recently shown promise is the wine pouch, which is effectively the bag without the box. Two prominent brands, Arniston Bay of **South Africa** and Palandri of Australia, have been released in the ''E-Pak,'' which is a foil/plastic pouch. In the **British market**, the Tesco supermarket chain has recently listed the Arniston Bay 1.5-liter E-Pak. Ring-pull cans are also available and are widely stocked by supermarkets, but this remains a niche, involving cheap wines, and shows little sign of growth.

The Future.   While the glass/cork combination looks set to stay, it seems that alternative packaging will become increasingly important for the wine trade, with environmental considerations a key driver of this transition. For inexpensive wines, it is becoming common to ship in 25,000-liter Flexitanks and to bottle—in glass or whichever alternative packaging format is desired—in the destination country. The main drawback of these alternative packaging formats—the increased oxygen transmission levels, leading to reduced shelf life—is then moderated to the point where it is not really an issue, providing decent stock control measures are in place. As yet, many of the more exciting alternative packaging formats, such as Tetra Prisma, PET bottles, and pouches are in their infancy; the extent to which they are adopted will depend on **consumer** reaction and so is likely to differ by market. *See also* Closures; Scandinavian Market.

Jamie Goode

ANCIENT MEDITERRANEAN

Modern winemaking owes much to the ancient Mediterranean world, where wine first achieved a place as a dietary staple. In antiquity, wine was central to **religious** functions and private social gatherings, a legacy bequeathed to the Christian church and Roman secular elites that they then passed on to the medieval world and thence to modern Europe. Phoenicians, Egyptians, **Greeks**, Carthaginians, and Romans added to a rich wine matrix that still influences taste and expression today.

Vitis vinifera originated in the Caucasus region, and by the Bronze Age (c. 3500–1100 BC) had spread to the Aegean and Mediterranean regions. Under the care of early Phoenician growers, at least by the ninth century BC, fine wines were produced along the coast of present-day Lebanon and Israel and traded widely throughout the Middle East in distinctive two-handled clay jars called *amphorae*. These were commonly sealed with clay, lime, or gypsum and lined with pitch, which allowed wine to keep for a considerable period, as the porosity of the clay permitted gentle oxidation over time. During the period of extensive Phoenician contacts and colonization throughout the Mediterranean (twelfth through sixth centuries BC), colonists spread wine-grape production to North Africa and **Spain**, and probably into parts of southern **France** as well.

Greek colonies began in the eighth century BC in mainland **Italy**, Sicily, and southern France and around the Black Sea coast, and Greek vine husbandry preferences and skills spread to these regions. By the Classical period (fifth century BC), the Greeks had developed a technical vocabulary for wine and thoroughly enjoyed wines of different types and origins. Wine drinking formed the centerpiece of the Classical Greek *symposium,* the gathering of the intelligentsia for entertaining, social networking, and political debates, and was drunk by all members of society.

As Greek influence spread, their wine tastes and habits followed. The pan-Mediterranean wine trade was especially active in the Hellenistic period (fourth through first centuries BC) that followed the Macedonian and Greek conquest of the Middle East. It is during this era that the Greeks began to rationalize and systematize agricultural improvements. The screw press, an efficient device initially developed in the Hellenistic period, has remained little changed into modern times. The remains of a fourth-century BC shipwreck contained not only amphorae but also grapevine cuttings. The desire and ability to ship vine stock around the ancient world shows the Greeks' dedication to viticulture, but also hints at the vast spread of different ancient varieties over much of Europe between the first century BC and the fifth century AD.

The best ancient Greek wines were those from the islands of Kos and Thasos, while the most popular vintages came from on and around Rhodes. The wine amphorae from such active production centers bore control stamps that ensured the jars were standard in size and that their origin could be guaranteed and appropriately taxed. The former Phoenician colony of Carthage in North Africa also developed a thriving wine industry and exported its production to Sicily, Sardinia, the Balearic Islands, and Spain.

By the time of Pliny the Elder in the first century AD, the Romans had developed a taste for Greek wines and developed their own distinctive wine types and local grape varieties. Roman merchants traded Italian wines extensively throughout Gaul (France), and it is likely, but remains to be proved, that many old French varieties came from Italy and farther east with Roman conquest and colonization.

While it is difficult to state with precision which modern cultivars are most closely related to ancient wine grapes, there are some descriptions of popular wines. Varieties known under the name Apianis are believed by some to be close relatives of Fiano, which today is witnessing a commercial revival. Falernian wine, a beverage famous in Italy for centuries and served at the table of Roman emperors, was sought after around the Mediterranean world and traded as far away as Arabia and India. A grape called Aminean rendered sweet, highly alcoholic wine that could be kept for years, and it probably became the most commonly grown variety in the ancient Mediterranean. Like famous varieties of today, it was known by name in the marketplace and sold for about four times the value of common wines.

Wine was a universal beverage drunk by all adults, and though **women** were discouraged from drinking, they also enjoyed it. Wine was customarily drunk mixed with water—to drink it neat in Greece or Rome was considered barbaric. Adding honey to it was fashionable. Modern imbibers would also find strange the tendency to resinate or heavily salt wines, generally by a suffusion of seawater, in order to stabilize them for transport. Raisin wine pressed from sun-dried grapes was another popular type of wine in the Roman Empire. In addition, wine was a common medicine; certain potent vintages were viewed as particularly helpful in digestive complaints.

The ability of the vine to flourish over a wide range of conditions, the pleasure wine offered, and the array of its uses meant that there was enormous demand. Since the masses of the city of Rome alone needed as much as 75 million liters (the equivalent of 8 million cases) of undiluted wine per year to fulfill their basic consumption, it is easy to see why Italian viticulture flourished during the empire. Estate vineyards were geared toward the markets that the thriving cities of the empire provided. While the average individual Roman vineyard block was fairly small (three acres or so), large estates had scores or even hundreds of such discreet blocks, planted with different varieties and spread over large areas to minimize the potential damage of pests, hail, and disease. Vineyards focused on high-volume production. Wine presses found in excavation in Israel reveal complex installations designed for speedy processing; some of these gargantuan presses held as much as 60,000 liters of must.

In the third century AD, Rome's economic and political woes caused disruptions to viniculture, a situation exacerbated by the barbarian invasions of the fourth and fifth centuries. Cultivation survived in Gaul, Italy, and Spain, but the famous vintages, such as Falernian, fell on hard times. Most northern barbarians favored beer, although many came to appreciate wine. Nevertheless, Western wine exports dissolved and vineyards declined in the fourth through sixth centuries. By then, upper-class tastes had changed to favor those wines then in fashion in the imperial court at Constantinople—primarily strong white wines from Gaza and Ascalon on the southern Palestinian coast. The arrival of Islam ended this golden age for Eastern wines, and the West took centuries to recover its preeminent skills in winemaking.

Michael J. Decker

Further Reading
Fleming, Stuart James. *Vinum: The Story of Roman Wine*. Glen Mills, PA: Art Flair, 2001.
Lambert-Gócs, Miles. *The Wines of Greece*. London: Faber & Faber, 2002.
McGovern, Patrick. *Ancient Wine: The Search for the Origins of Viniculture*. Princeton, NJ: Princeton University Press, 2003.
Pliny the Elder. *Natural History,* books XII–XVI.

APPELLATIONS

Grape growers and winemakers throughout the world rely on appellations to identify wine origin. Although not all wines are sold on the basis of origin, appellations have become an increasingly important means of differentiating wines, along with **brand**, variety, and vintage.

The appellation systems of the Old World and the **New World** are strikingly different. Although both systems delimit specific areas of production (provenance) based on distinguishing, viticulturally relevant, natural features such as soil, climate, and geography, the Old World systems also regulate human factors, including viticultural and winemaking practices. The so-called controlled appellations, such as the French *appellations d'origine contrôlée* (AOC) and the **Italian** *denominazioni di origine controllata* (DOC), indicate to consumers not only where the grapes were grown but also the type of grapes grown there and many of the wines' defining characteristics—minimum alcohol strength, degree of sweetness, clonal selection, trellis system, and so on. Often the wines are tasted blind by a tasting panel before they can be sold under the appellation name. This is intended to weed out wines that are defective or that do not express the basic character of the appellation (*goût de terroir*).

The New World appellation systems like those of the **United States**, **Australia**, and **South Africa** indicate provenance only. There are no associated viticultural or winemaking controls. For example, although the **Napa Valley** American Viticultural Area (AVA) may be best known for its **Cabernet Sauvignon** wines, any grape variety can be planted there and carry the appellation name so long as 85 percent of the grapes used to make that wine were grown within the AVA boundaries; the remaining 15 percent can come from anywhere. By contrast, a **Burgundy** AOC wine must be made with 100 percent Burgundy grapes.

Appellations have their detractors in both the Old and New Worlds. In Europe, some producers believe that the appellation standards have become so lax that the **consumer** no longer can be assured of the distinguishing characteristics (*typicité*) or quality that the appellation should represent. Others contend that the controls are too rigid and inhibit innovation. This led certain Italian producers in Tuscany in the 1970s to abandon the DOC system in favor of a *vino da tavola* (**table wine**) designation. Free from the appellation's restrictions, the **wineries** were able to blend in grape varieties that otherwise would have been prohibited, such as Cabernet Sauvignon. Subsequently, a new category of appellation known as *indicazione geografica tipica* (IGT) was established that authorized the use of the nontraditional varieties. Similarly, Mas de Daumas Gassac, a winery in the Languedoc AOC of southern **France**, chose to use a *vin de pays* (country wine) designation in order to blend in varieties that were outside the AOC specifications.

The New World appellations offer the consumer little by way of taste or quality guarantees. In the United States, growers and vintners have turned to private means, outside of the government-run AVA system, to offer consumers the value added that the best appellations represent. By researching and **promoting** specific grape varieties grown in specific appellations—Walla Walla **Merlot** and Willamette Valley **Pinot Noir**, for example—private vintner-grower appellation associations promote the notion of typicity that the Old World appellations mandate. For example, for many years, the Carneros Quality Alliance (now the Carneros Wine Alliance) produced an archetypical Pinot Noir under the association's own label from grapes grown in the finest sites within the Carneros AVA to showcase the unique attributes of the district's Pinot Noir—red berry, jam, and spicy aromas and flavors without the leather, smoke, tar, or vegetal character of Pinots grown elsewhere. Ultimately, this effort was abandoned. Interestingly, today many critics believe that Carneros's Merlot is more distinctive than its Pinot Noir, attesting to the lack of established tradition in the New World and the need for continued experimentation.

Appellations are not only about establishment and promotion but also protection and defense. The enforcement function is generally assigned to a national administrative agency, such as the *Direction de la Concurrence, de la Consommation, et de la Répression des Fraudes* in France or the **Alcohol and Tobacco Tax and Trade Bureau (TTB)** in the U.S. Treasury Department. These agencies can take action to halt label fraud, including the use of appellations on nonqualifying wines. But usurpation also takes other forms. The appellation name may be appropriated for a grape variety (for example, Gamay Beaujolais or Johannesburg Riesling) or a familiar type of wine ("**California** Champagne" or "Australian Port"). In some countries, the generic use of geographic names has been phased out, often as part of a bilateral agreement, such as the 1994 Agreement between the European Community and Australia and on Trade in Wine. In other countries, only new uses of those names have been disallowed, as occurred in the 2006 Wine Accord between the **European Union** and the United States.

An appellation also may appear as part of a winery's brand name (for example, Château Margaux or Napa Ridge), with local regulations governing whether the wine must meet the appellation requirements for the named area. Different countries have established different rules about the primacy of geographic brand names or appellations. Some follow the principle of "first in time, first in right," affording priority to whoever first used the geographic name. Under this rule, a winery owner who had long used a geographic name as part of his brand could prevent the designation of that name as an appellation, and vice versa. Other countries give precedence to the appellation whether or not it existed before the brand name. In this case, the brand name generally is not invalidated by a later established appellation, but it must be used only on wines that meet the appellation requirements. For example, "Château Margaux" can be used only on wines that qualify for the Margaux AOC. Finally, certain countries have more elaborate conflict resolution rules that take into account such factors as the length of usage of the brand name and appellation, consumer recognition, and the good faith of the brand owner and appellation petitioners.

The World Trade Organization's Agreement on Trade-Related Aspects of Intellectual Property Rights (TRIPS) has its own set of rules that apply to trade in wine between its members. The basic tenet is that a wine cannot carry a geographic designation if it is not of that origin, whether or not it is modified by words such as "style," "kind," or "type" and regardless of whether consumers are, in fact, deceived [Art. 23(1)]. Since 1996, under TRIPS rules, no brand owner has been able to register a geographic mark unless the wine originates from that place. However, TRIPS also establishes exceptions for geographic names that, by virtue of their long use in a country, have become generic [Art. 24(6)] or that were used in good faith before the appellation was protected in the country of origin [Art. 24(5)].

Many countries have complicated rules and procedures governing the internal market. The 2004 case of *Bronco Wine Company v. Jolly* (33 Cal.4th 943) is illustrative. In 1986, the TTB's predecessor (the Bureau of Alcohol, Tobacco, and Firearms) prohibited the use of geographic brand names that do not qualify for the named appellation, but established an exception for brands named in Certificates of Label Approval issued before July 7, 1986 [27 CFR 4.39(i)]. The **Bronco Wine Company** availed itself of this grandfather clause by buying pre-1986 brand names that refer to various Napa appellations, including Napa Ridge and Rutherford Vintners, and using those names on non–Napa Valley wines. The State of California then passed a law banning the use of Napa brand names, including those grandfathered under federal law, unless the wine was made from at least 75 percent Napa County grapes. This law survived a constitutional challenge in which Bronco alleged that it was preempted by federal law, interfered with interstate commerce, violated Bronco's free speech rights, and constituted a taking of Bronco's property without just compensation. The California Supreme Court upheld the law and the right of the state to regulate the labeling of wines produced or sold there.

Another example of a thorny name conflict is Great Western, which is a brand and an appellation in Australia, both of which had been in use since the mid-1800s. Not only was the actual first-use date difficult to determine, but it would have been a harsh result indeed to preclude one or the other on that basis following more than a century and a half of coexistence. Ultimately, both uses were allowed. Today, Seppelt's Great Western is not required to source the wines sold under that name from the Great Western appellation.

These conflicts have important economic consequences. Whenever the brand or the appellation becomes well known, there is the potential for free riding and tarnishment. The widespread principle of territoriality (limiting protection to the place where the name is known) further complicates the matter in an increasingly **global wine industry** where a geographic brand may be started literally overnight in a country far away from the appellation area. For this reason, a multinational register of appellation names is essential. Additionally, procedures to resolve conflicts must allow for due process, including notice and an opportunity for all concerned parties to be heard.

Richard Mendelson

Further Reading
TTB. "Wine Appellations of Origin." www.ttb.gov/appellation/index.shtml.

ARGENTINA

Argentina is currently the fifth largest wine producer in the world, with the ninth largest surface area under vine. Throughout most of its history, Argentine vintners have been predominantly inward focused, dedicated to supplying a very large domestic market. Like many other wine **consumers** in the world, today's Argentines are drinking less wine, but what they are drinking is much higher in quality and price. A gradual drop in domestic consumption, coupled with the favorable **exchange rate** that followed the financial crisis of 2001 and an appealing flavor profile appreciated by many consumers around the world, has led to double-digit rates of growth in exports over the last five years. Today, Argentine Malbec is the fastest-growing import varietal in the **United States**. Argentina's privileged high-elevation desert **terroir** at the foot of the Andes, where cool climate, intense sunlight, and controlled irrigation make for intensely colored, aromatic, and well-ripened wines, bodes well for the country's winemaking future. Argentina is poised to become a major player in the international premium wine market.

History.   The Argentine wine industry dates back to the 1500s and the arrival of Spanish missionaries. As in other **New World** wine regions, winemaking began primarily to supply these missionaries with the sacramental wine necessary for **religious** use. The Argentine wine industry continued in a rather undeveloped state, producing wine for local inhabitants, mainly in the province of Mendoza, for several hundred years. Then in the late nineteenth century, two important developments caused rapid growth in both grape and wine production, transforming Argentine winemaking into a true mature industry.

The first factor was a wave of European immigration arriving in Mendoza from **Spain** and **Italy** in the 1880s. Many of these new arrivals had experience in vineyard management and winemaking, and they began to apply their knowledge to the nascent winemaking activity in Mendoza, laying the foundation for explosive growth in the next 20 years.

The second factor was the completion of the transnational railroad that connected Mendoza to Buenos Aires, the largest city and main port of Argentina. This enabled the shipment of wine to a huge market of thirsty European immigrants, as well as the importation of European technology and machinery that would drastically increase production.

Production and Trade.   Currently, Argentina produces more than 15 million hectoliters of wine, the equivalent of 170 million cases (mc), from almost 550,000 acres of vineyards. More than two-thirds of this wine is consumed domestically, with a per-capita consumption of 39 liters, making Argentina the eighth largest wine-consuming market. Wine exports for 2007 totaled 56.1 mc for a total value of $665 million—up more than 70 percent from 2006 (32.6 mc, $380 million). Argentina's top export destinations are the United States, followed by the **British**, **Canadian**, **Brazilian**, and **Dutch** markets. There is very little imported wine sold in Argentina.

The province of Mendoza is by far the largest winegrowing region in Argentina. With 70 percent of the country's vines, Mendoza accounts for 76 percent of the total wine production. Its high-altitude desert climate is ideal for growing premium quality grapes, especially its signature varietal, Malbec. Due to the presence of the Andes and the influence of altitude on temperature and sunlight intensity, there are a multitude of microclimates throughout the province, accounting for a vast array of wine styles. The highest-altitude vineyards (between 3,000 and 8,000 feet above sea level), with their extremely cool temperatures and elevated levels of sunlight intensity, produce the highest-quality, most age-worthy, and most concentrated wines.

San Juan, Mendoza's neighboring province to the north, is the second most important wine region of Argentina, with 25 percent of the country's vineyards producing 16 percent of its wine. Smaller amounts of wine come from the provinces of La Rioja, north of San Juan; Salta, the most northerly wine region in Argentina; and more recently Río Negro and Neuquén in cooler Patagonia to the south of Mendoza.

Wines of Argentina is a national organization of exporting **wineries** that coordinates efforts to **promote** Argentine wine abroad. It is funded through dues paid by participating wineries and funds from the national government from a tax levied on grapes harvested and wine produced. Its main activities include managing advertising campaigns, national participation in wine fairs, and national tastings in different wine markets throughout the world.

Outlook.   The Argentine wine industry has experienced a quality revolution in the last 15 years. Argentina is in the process of transforming its entire industry from **table wine** production to the vinification of high-quality ultrapremium wines capable of competing on the international stage. This process has been aided by an influx of French, U.S., and Italian **flying winemakers** and by local visionaries, such as Nicolás Catena Zapata, who is credited with pioneering high-end Malbec production in Mendoza's upland wine country, much as **Robert Mondavi** did for **Cabernet Sauvignon** in the **Napa Valley**. The focus on quality has led to higher-elevation, cooler-climate plantings and to significant reductions in vineyard yields. Although recently Malbec has taken the spotlight as the most popular and highest-rated Argentine variety, Argentina also produces outstanding whites from **Chardonnay** and Torrontés and **red wines** from Cabernet Sauvignon and Bonarda. *See also* Branding.

Laura Catena

Further Reading

Rolland, Michel, and Enrique Chrabolowsky. *Wines of Argentina* [in Spanish]. Buenos Aires: Mirroll, 2006.

Tapia, Patricio. *Descorchados* [in Spanish]. Santiago, Chile: Planeta, 2004.

Waldin, Monty. *The Wines of South America*. London: Mitchell Beazley, 2003.

AROMATIZED WINE.   *See* Vermouth

ASIA

The continent of Asia, despite being the birthplace of wine, has not been a major participant in the **global wine industry** for thousands of years. However, that has begun to change.

Asia is the largest continent and is tremendously diverse in culture, politics, **religions**, topography, and climate. From a wine standpoint, though, it is possible to break it down into four zones.

Northern Asia, mostly consisting of the vast swath of Asian Russia, is for the most part too cold for **grape growing** and too sparsely populated to be of significance as a consumer. Russia is an important player in the industry, but mainly from the part of the country in **Eastern Europe**, not Siberia.

Southwest and Central Asia, from the Arabian Peninsula to Turkey to Kazakhstan to Pakistan, is dominated by Islamic culture, which disapproves of, and in many places bans, alcohol. Thus, wine is not widely drunk or even available in this zone. The primary exceptions to this are the Jewish state of Israel, the Christian nations of Georgia and Armenia, and multicultural Lebanon. None of these is a particularly large country, but all produce wine. Georgia, on the south side of the Caucasus Mountains, is considered the home of winemaking 8,000 years ago and still produces the equivalent of about 11 million nine-liter cases (mc) annually, keeping it within the top 25 in the world. Turkey and Iran are, respectively, the fourth and seventh largest grape-growing countries in the world, but the vast majority of this fruit goes to making raisins rather than wine.

Southeast Asia and most of South Asia have a tropical and monsoonal climate that is too hot year-round and far too wet for successful winegrowing. It also has a strong Islamic influence in many places. This zone has neither wine production nor consumption of note.

This leaves a fourth zone that has wine exporters around the world excited and in some cases a little worried. The temperate band that runs from Japan through central China and, skipping over the vast barren Tibetan Plateau, takes in the highlands of India has an enormous population that is just beginning to become interested in wine, as well as large areas that are suitable for grape growing. India and China together are home to nearly half of the world's population, but their per-capita wine consumption is very low. However, with economies that are growing robustly and cultures that are opening up to much greater participation on the world stage, they have the potential to become top-tier wine-consuming countries for the **globalizing** wine industry. At the same time, they could also become major wine producers, which would blunt the hoped-for growth in imports to serve the increasing demand and could even become strong competition for wine producers in other countries that live by exporting.

China.   Although many Westerners still see China as virgin territory for wine, they are misguided. China is already the seventh largest wine-producing country in the world, with an output estimated at about 135 mc for 2005, although only about 35 percent of this (48 mc) is grape wine. The majority of Chinese "wine" is made from fermented millet or rice, similar to Japanese sake. This beverage, also known as *huang jiu* or "yellow wine," has been brewed in China for thousands of years. Grape wine, or *putao jiu,* though not quite as long historied as huang jiu, has been made and enjoyed in China off and on for more than 2,000 years. However, it did not become a large-scale industry until the 1980s after Deng Xiaoping's "Four Modernizations" program opened the country to foreign investment. The Chinese government entered into joint ventures with French and other partners to develop commercial winegrowing along an international model. Given this connection, it is not surprising that French varieties, especially **Cabernet Sauvignon**, account for nearly all wine-grape plantings.

China has roughly 1.25 million acres of grapevines, placing it fifth globally. Of these, half go into wine production; the rest are primarily table grapes. More than 80 percent of the wine grapes are grown in Shandong, Hebei, and Tianjin provinces to the south of Beijing. However, Xinjiang Province in the dry northwest of the country may have the greatest long-term potential for quality wine grapes.

There are more than 400 **wineries** in China, but a handful of very large producers—led by Great Wall, Changyu, Dynasty, and Dragon Seal—control most of the market. Ten facilities have the capacity to make more than a million cases a year. These wineries stretch the Chinese grape harvest several times over with significant amounts of **bulk wine** from **Chile**, **Australia**, and **Spain**, as well as huang jiu, water, or other fruit juices. Foreign bulk wine accounts for around 10 mc of domestic production.

Despite a per-capita consumption rate of less than a liter per year, China, with its 1⅓ billion people, manages to consume 150 mc of wine (including huang jiu) annually, essentially tying it with Spain for fifth place worldwide. While some fine wine is drunk in China, the majority of Chinese **consumers** are still developing a taste for wine, rather like the American consumer of a half-century ago, and therefore have a general preference for wines that are either sweet or high in alcohol (many make little distinction between wine and brandy, both called *jiu*). However, the government has also promoted the **health** benefits of red wine, resulting in lopsided sales in favor of reds, which may then be drunk with some fruit juice, liquor, or a splash of soda added to make them more palatable.

Because China is nearly able to cover its demand for wine, imports of bottled wine to China are a relatively small category, but many producers worldwide dream of getting a toehold in the burgeoning Chinese market. Imports in 2006 amounted to just 2.3 mc. **France** was the largest foreign source of bottled wine, with a third of the market, followed by Australia, the **United States**, and **Italy**. Red wine overshadows other categories four to one.

With China's acceptance into the World Trade Organization (WTO) in 2001, tariffs on wine dropped to just one-fifth of their previous protectionist level. In February 2008, Hong Kong—the former British colony that is now a special autonomous region of China—abolished the import duty on wine altogether in a bid to firmly establish itself as Asia's center for the fine wine trade. Sales of wine can be expected to skyrocket there. These developments, combined with the growing levels of disposable income, the maturing Chinese palate, and the cachet of being seen as cosmopolitan—boosted by the internationalism engendered by the 2008 Summer Olympics in Beijing—hint at a potential rosy future for imports into China. By the same token, as Chinese producers expand, their output will be largely absorbed by the growing domestic demand, and despite their ambitions, it will be several years before China will become a significant exporter.

India.   India is still a question mark for the wine industry. Many exporters and producers are excited by the fact that India, with a population over a billion, has seen wine consumption grow by 25 to 30 percent annually for the last several years. Added to this are the promising facts that domestic wine production is very small, the ranks of the upper classes and professionals with disposable income are growing, and tariffs on wine imports—formerly as high as 550 percent—were reduced in July 2007 to a still punishing 150 percent, the maximum allowed under WTO rules.

However, the reality is that, while the potential is enormous, the size of the market at present is minuscule. Despite the recent growth, consumption measured a meager 600,000 cases in 2006, a per-capita rate of just 0.006 liters per adult. Expansion at triple-digit rates would be required to turn this into a major market anytime soon. Currently, the majority of wine consumed in India is sold at hotels and **restaurants** in the major cities, such as New Delhi, Mumbai, and Chennai. A good portion of this can be assumed to be purchased by tourists and visiting businesspeople rather than by the Indians themselves. Government-run liquor stores do not focus on wine, but some **supermarkets** are beginning to offer wine on the shelves, which could boost consumption. About half of the wine consumed is imported from France.

India is in the process of developing a domestic wine industry, although the climate of the country makes this difficult. The majority of the vineyards are in the state of Maharashtra in central India on the Deccan Plateau at elevations above 2,500 feet. The slopes of the Himalayas in Punjab and Kashmir are considered to have potential as well. Three wineries—Sula, Indage, and Grover—account for most of the production, about 500,000 cases. Most of the wine grapes are international vinifera varieties, including Chenin Blanc, **Sauvignon Blanc**, **Chardonnay**, Cabernet Sauvignon, and **Merlot**, although some table grapes are used in wine production as well.

Japan.   While China and India have the potential to far outweigh it someday, Japan is currently the largest market for imports in Asia, bringing in about 16.7 mc in 2006, seven times more than China. Japan's largest source for bottled wine imports in 2006 was France, with a 42 percent share, followed by Italy (19 percent) and the United States (14 percent). Bulk wine imports, one-tenth the volume of bottled wine, were led by Chile and **Argentina**.

Sake—the traditional rice beverage that is often included in the wine category—is four times as popular as wine in Japan, although the gap has been slowly closing. Combining sake and wine, Japanese per-capita consumption is higher than the U.S. level and 11 times higher than that of the Chinese. However, wine consumption remains quite low at 2.0 liters. Consumers embraced red wine for its health aspects in the late 1990s, increasing its share of the market from around 20 percent to nearly 60 percent, where it remains.

Total grape wine consumption in Japan in 2005 was almost 28 mc. The difference between this amount and the imports is filled by wine made domestically in Japan, estimated at 12.3 mc in 2005. The primary varieties used are hybrids, such as Delaware and Muscat Bailey A, and unique vinifera varieties, such as Koshu and Zenkoji, that are descended from vines carried along the Silk Road. Some international varieties are being tried, but the humid conditions make them very difficult to grow successfully. For the most part, Japanese domestic wine fills the price points below the imports, which monopolize the higher price and quality levels. Five producers, led by Mercian and Sapporo Beer, make 96 percent of the domestic wine.

It will be several years before China can overtake Japan's leading import position in Asia. Even though the Japanese market has seen only slow growth in recent years, it should improve now that a backlog of imports is disappearing and as the number of retail outlets increases due to the recent deregulation of liquor licensing. Japanese wine is unlikely to find a significant overseas market, and it will increasingly be supplanted by higher quality, low-price wine from the United States and the Southern Hemisphere.

Further Reading

Rozelle, Scott, Daniel Sumner, and Jikun Huang. *Wine in China*. 2006. http://aic.ucdavis
 .edu/research1/Wine_in_China.pdf.
USDA Foreign Agricultural Service. *Japan Wine Report 2006*. 2007. www.fas.usda
 .gov/gainfiles/200701/146280024.pdf.

AUCTION HOUSES

Auction houses generally operate as a secondary market for wine sales, selling wines that have already been purchased by private collectors to other private collectors, as well as the trade (wine merchants, **restaurants**, hotels, and others). Collectors may wish to sell for a variety of reasons, including the four *d*'s—death, debt, divorce, and doctor's orders—but most find that since wine is a readily available commodity and they desire a wide range of drinking options, they buy more than they can **consume** and at some stage wish to sell some of their collection (usually to make room for new purchases).

The wine auction market has existed for around 300 years, with both the major international houses, Sotheby's and Christie's, holding auctions in the United Kingdom. The market was mostly confined to a small group of knowledgeable collectors. The major change in wine auctions occurred in 1994, when **New York** changed its laws to permit wine auctions (prior to 1994, auctions were permitted in **California** and Illinois, but were again mostly confined to a small group of collectors). This change had a dramatic effect on the global wine market and prices for fine and rare wines (defined here as wine priced over $50 per bottle and not in mass distribution). In New York, Sotheby's and Christie's teamed up with the top **retailers**, Sherry-Lehmann and Zachys, and provided a secondary market for wine that immediately became international in nature. Collectors now had a legitimate resale market, which opened up the opportunity for wine buyers to collect wine for both investment and drinking. The timing was also fortuitous, as interest in wine and food was experiencing enormous growth, with such publications as the *Wine Spectator* and **Robert Parker**'s *Wine Advocate* fueling consumers' appetites. Auction sales have since increased by 770 percent, from $23 million in 1995, the first full year of wine auctions in the **United States**, to more than $200 million in 2007.

The major auctioneers worldwide remain the two international houses, Sotheby's and Christie's, with combined sales of $121 million in 2007. However, in New York, they have been joined by two other retailers turned auctioneers, Zachys and Acker Merrall & Condit, which had combined sales of $108 million in 2007.

The wines offered at auction range from $25 per bottle upward, with the majority of the value of the sales coming from first-growth **Bordeaux** and **Burgundy**'s Domaine de la Romanée Conti (DRC). At Sotheby's, Bordeaux represents 72 percent of auction sales and Burgundy another 16 percent. The average lot price over the last three years was $5,242 (or an approximate bottle price of $500). The top lots naturally tend to get the most attention from the press. For example, Sotheby's sold a jeroboam (4.5-liter bottle) of 1945 Château Mouton Rothschild for $310,700 and a case of 1990 DRC for $262,900, while in September 2006, Christie's sold six magnums of 1945 Mouton Rothschild for $345,000. Nevertheless, there are many lots of excellent mature drinking wine that sell for between $25 and $100 per bottle.

The collectors who *sell* wines in the United States are mostly (95 percent at Sotheby's) American private collectors, with the balance being restaurants, hotels, or **wineries**. The size of these consignments varies from $20,000 to

$20 million. In 1994, it was unthinkable for a collector to have a $10 million wine collection; by 2008, some collections were approaching the $100 million level. The enormous growth in the size of collections and demand for the greatest wines (the best wines from the top producers in the greatest vintages) has led to a significant increase in the number of fraudulent wines appearing on the market, so collectors should exercise caution when buying such "trophy" wines and seek the counsel of trusted experts who can verify the provenance and authenticity of these wines.

The *buyers* at auction include some who buy wines to drink them and others who solely invest in wine, though generally it is a marriage of the two. The North American market has been driving the increase in prices, with very strong demand over the past decade. However, in the last two years, many more international buyers have been coming into the market, particularly from **Asia** (Hong Kong, India, Taiwan, and South Korea, among others), South America, and all over Europe. Since the late 1990s, the average age of buyers has also decreased, from around 60 to nearer 40 years old.

Jamie Ritchie

Further Reading
Hermacinski, Ursula. *The Wine Lover's Guide to Auctions: The Art and Science of Buying and Selling Wines.* Garden City Park, NY: Square One, 2007.

AUSTRALIA

Although wine has been made in Australia for more than 200 years, it was not until the late twentieth century that most of the world started to take notice. The reasons for this apparent sudden renown were many. Internationally, there were **phylloxera** outbreaks in **California** and less-than-stellar vintages in Europe. Meanwhile, Penfolds Grange from South Australia received the number-one spot on the *Wine Spectator*'s Top 100 in December 1995. When Australia started to come on, it came on strong. Suddenly, Australia appeared to be leading the way in wine research, breaking records for growth, and focusing on world domination.

For decades now, Australia has been known as an industry leader in viticulture, winemaking, and wine marketing. The country's early acceptance of **mechanical** harvesting helped keep prices down, just as rotofermenters kept flavors forward. Australia's commitment to screw-cap **closures** started a world trend. And with the launch of **Yellow Tail** in 2000, Australia created the "lifestyle wine" category that quite possibly changed the way Millennials think about wine.

The Early Years.   When Capt. Arthur Phillip sailed from England into what is now Sydney Harbor with the First Fleet in 1788, he had the vine cuttings that were used to establish Australia's first vineyard. These cuttings came from **South Africa** (thus the Australian use of *Shiraz* rather than **Syrah** for this variety). With no viticulturalists and very few farmers, those first vines did not survive, but others soon did.

Gregory Blaxton arrived in Australia in 1806 from England. He experimented in viticulture and was the first to export wines back to England. In 1828, his "tawny red" received a gold medal in Europe. Around the same time, James Busby, who had studied viticulture in **France**, published a guide to winemaking in New South Wales. He then embarked on a European tour from which he returned in 1832 with 570 French and Spanish vine cuttings. It was not long after that that wine grapes were planted across Australia. There were hardships along the way— depression and phylloxera in the late 1800s, but thankfully no **Prohibition**. Today, Australia can boast some of the oldest vines in the world.

After World War II, a wave of immigration brought many newcomers from wine-producing countries—**Italy**, **Spain**, **Portugal**, and **Greece**—along with their wine-drinking habits and viticultural know-how. Australia's new winemakers cared little for traditions or regulations. With grapes of all kinds being grown in adjacent vineyards—even side by side in the same vineyard—winemakers would blend to their own tastes. The practice of blending varieties that never mixed in their home countries or juice from different regions became the new tradition.

Geographic Indications.   Geographical indications (GIs) were introduced in 1993 to allow Australia to fulfill its agreements with the European Community on wine-labeling laws. As the name implies, a GI simply defines the border of a region, as with the American viticultural areas in the **United States**. Much less restrictive than the **appellation** systems of Europe, the only qualification for a wine to carry the regional name is that it must contain at least 85 percent of its fruit from that region. No viticultural or winemaking guidelines are imposed.

Australia is a big country—about 14 times the size of France and only 4 percent smaller than the United States. Scattered mostly along the coasts in the southeast and the southwest, the 64 different wine regions have very diverse climates, elevations, and soil types. Five of the best known follow:

- *Hunter* (New South Wales): With an unbroken history of winemaking back to 1825, Hunter's most acclaimed wine is the long-lived Semillon, though **Chardonnay** is, statistically, the most important.
- *Yarra Valley* (Victoria): First planted in 1838, it fell into obscurity during the depression era only to regain recognition and production levels in the 1990s. Quite cool, with many hills and valleys, the Yarra is known for **Pinot Noir** and Chardonnay.
- *Barossa Valley* (South Australia): Founded in 1847, Barossa prizes its century-old bush-trained vines of Shiraz and Grenache.
- *McLaren Vale* (South Australia): With the Mount Lofty Ranges on one side and the ocean at its feet, McLaren Vale offers a variety of microclimates, as well as breathtaking vistas. Growers rely on evening breezes to keep the temperatures down.
- *Margaret River* (Western Australia): Relatively new, first planted in the 1970s, Margaret River catapulted into fame for Chardonnay and **Cabernet Sauvignon**. Surrounded on three sides by the seas, it is truly maritime in climate.

In addition to the GIs, labeling regulations allow "zones." Zones include several regions combined. For example, a wine labeled "Limestone Coast" can include fruit from Coonawarra, Wrattonbully, Padthaway, and Langhorne Creek. Also, wines can be labeled for a state and include juice from any region in the state.

The ultimate blend, "Southeastern Australia," includes all the vineyards in the states of New South Wales, Victoria, and Tasmania, as well as most of Queensland and South Australia. This blending provides consistency of style, year in and year out, which is a big part of Australia's international success.

Importance of Exports.   Since the early days, Australia's wine industry has relied on exports. Although Australia is ranked sixth in the world for total wine production—amounting to 159 million nine-liter cases (mc) in 2006—it is ranked higher, at the fourth position, for its export success. In 2007, Australia exported more than 87 mc, worth close to A$3 billion, to over a hundred nations around the world.

Australia's original export market is still number one: the United Kingdom. However, the United States is a close second (23.5 mc), now representing about 26 percent of all exports in volume and over 30 percent in value. As recently as 2005, when Australia had an oversupply of fruit, Australia shipped a lot of **bulk wine** to the United States. With the oversupply quickly turning into undersupply because of severe drought conditions, bulk shipments have since fallen significantly. Bulk red wine shipments are down 63 percent and whites decreased by 52 percent. With 2008 expected to be the fifth largest on record, bulk wine volumes should increase again.

In addition to the U.S. and the **British market**, Australia's principal export destinations are **Canada**, **Germany**, **New Zealand**, the **Dutch market**, and Denmark.

The Marketing Mix: Cooperation and Collaboration.   With an eye to expanding the opportunities for Australian exports, a broad industry-funded **promotional** office, the Australian Wine Bureau (AWB), opened in London in the 1980s. An office in the United States (originally called the Australian Wine Importers Association) followed in 1989. In 2006, an industry review changed the name of the AWBs worldwide to Wine Australia and modernized the logo.

The Australian wine industry's understanding of the benefits of collaboration has helped its growth in immeasurable ways. Heads of wine corporations and boutique winemakers come together regularly at conferences and colloquiums. Industry bodies, such as the Winemakers Federation of Australia and the Australian Wine and Brandy Corporation, listen to them, too. Since 1996, three major initiatives have been published by the industry: *Strategy 2025* (1996) outlined sales goals, which were surpassed by 2005. *The Marketing Decade* (2000) defined the concept of market development and the importance of **branding**. *Directions to 2025,* released in May 2007, identifies challenges and strategies for the industry, divides the category into brand "personalities," and outlines the possibilities for sustainable growth.

In Country.   The development of "cask wine," or bag-in-box **alternative packaging**, in the mid-1960s helped Australia become a wine-drinking nation. Though consumption numbers are not near Europe's highs, Australians do consume an average of 26 liters per adult, making it the highest major country outside of Europe with the exception of **Argentina**. And Australia's wine consumption is still growing.

As noted, exports have long been a part of the Australian wine industry, but in the past several years, imports have become more important as well. In 2007, imports totaled almost 5 mc. Although half of that amount is from neighboring

New Zealand, the other imports have more than doubled since 2001, with the largest volumes coming from Italy, France, **Chile**, and Spain.

Future Focus.   Australia has added interest and intrigue to the story of wine in many ways: **flying winemakers** and unique characters; research, experimentation, and innovation; the vine pull scheme and the show system; the Len Evans tutorial; the **sustainability** issue; the new and innovative educational program *Australia: World Class;* and so much more. All of these have helped to shape Australia's current wine industry and point to much more intrigue and activity in the future.

Jan Stuebing Smyth

Further Reading

Australian Wine Research Institute. www.awri.com.au.

Clarke, Oz. *Oz Clarke's Australian Wine Companion*. Orlando, FL: Harcourt, 2005.

Grapegrower and Winemaker. www.grapeandwine.com.au.

Halliday, James. *Wine Atlas of Australia*. Berkeley: University of California Press, 2006.

Mattinson, Campbell. *Why the French Hate Us: The Real Story of Australian Wine*. South Yarra, Victoria, Australia: Hardie Grant, 2007.

WBM: Australia's Wine Business Magazine. www.awbm.com.au.

Wine Australia. www.wineaustralia.com.

AUSTRIA

Wine has been part of Austria's culture since Roman and maybe even Celtic times. Austrian viticulture was brought to excellence by the many **monasteries** along the Danube River and south of Vienna, but the tragic events of the first half of the twentieth century with the fall of the Habsburg Empire and the two world wars destroyed many economic hopes, including those of many of the country's wine producers. Then in 1985, just as the industry was recovering, a wine adulteration scandal shattered the rebuilding of the image. Austrian wines disappeared for years from many export markets.

Since then, a little miracle has happened. A strict new wine law supported dramatic quality improvements, and a new generation of quality-oriented winemakers was able to sell wine at prices that paid back their efforts. Austria has always had excellent **terroirs**, especially for great white and sweet wines. But with just 125,000 acres under vine, less than 1 percent of the **global wine** production, and more than 75 percent local consumption, Austria has not been perceived as a leading wine producer. Nevertheless, in the last 20 years, Austria has achieved international acclaim for quality.

Austrian wine law allows 22 white and 13 red grape varieties for **quality wine**. The flagship grape is the white Grüner Veltliner, which represents two-thirds of total production. It is mainly grown in the Niederösterreich (Lower Austria) quality wine area. Austria's leading red grape varieties are the indigenous Zweigelt (12.5 percent of Austria's total acreage) and Blaufränkisch (6.5 percent). Burgenland, the second biggest wine region, is prime red grape territory, as well as one of the world's finest sources for sweet **dessert wines** from grapes affected by botrytis. International varieties such as **Sauvignon Blanc**, Pinot Blanc, **Chardonnay**, and especially **Riesling** are also grown in Austria. Sauvignon Blanc is a focus in the southernmost quality wine area, Steiermark (Styria). The fourth wine area is Vienna, the federal capital, which has more than 1,700 acres under vine.

The Austrian *Prädikat* grading system, based on the sugar concentration in the grape, ranges from slightly sweet Spätlese and Auslese to the richly sweet Beerenauslese, Ausbruch, and Trockenbeerenauslese. Eiswein (made from naturally frozen grapes) and Strohwein or Schilfwein (made from sun-dried grapes) complete the spectrum.

Recently Austria has developed a new **appellation** system, the Districtus Austriae Controllatus (DAC). Currently there are four delimited DACs: Weinviertel (for Grüner Veltliner), Traisental and Kremstal (Grüner Veltliner and Riesling), and Mittelburgenland (Blaufränkisch).

In an average year, Austria produces around 2.2–2.5 million hectoliters of wine (about 25 million cases [mc]), 70 percent of it white and 30 percent red. More than three-quarters is sold domestically: 58 percent in restaurants, 38 percent at retail (**supermarkets**, wine shops, and direct sales), and 4 percent to tourists. It exports the equivalent of 5.5–9.0 mc per year, depending largely on harvests, with a total export value of €75–€120 million. The most important export market has always been **Germany** (65 percent by volume and 56 percent by value in 2006). Next are Switzerland (3 percent/13 percent) and the **United States** (2 percent/10 percent), both with modest quantities but high-value imports. The Czech Republic and **Italy** are traditional **bulk wine** buyers.

Austria produces only a fifth as much wine as **Australia**, but has three times more bottling estates (6,000). The average estate in Austria covers less than seven acres, although the trend goes toward bigger, more **profitable** units. Family ownership is the driving force, and the young generation is dynamic, motivated, and innovative. Austrian estates work with great respect for nature. **Organic** wine production has recently doubled to 8 percent of total production. With its low yields, controlled use of treatments, and small family estates where most of the crop is handpicked, Austria is one of the most environmentally friendly wine economies in the world.

The Austrian Wine Marketing Board (AWMB), a nonprofit organization funded by the wine industry, **promotes** Austrian wine at home and abroad. Its goal is to keep local consumption as high as it is, while shifting more and more exported wine from bulk business to reasonable sales of bottled quality wines. The official aim of the AWMB was to double 2000's bottled wine sales within 10 years—a goal reached in just 5 years. It is now looking to increase exports to €100–€150 million over the next 5 years.

Willi Klinger

Further Reading
Austrian Wine Marketing Board. www.winesfromaustria.com.
Blom, Phillip. *The Wines of Austria.* Rev. ed. London: Mitchell Beazley, 2006.

B

BANFI VINTNERS

Banfi Vintners is a producer of **Italian** wine and an **importer** of primarily Italian and South American wine. Founded in 1919, Banfi Vintners rose to prominence importing Lambrusco in the 1970s and 1980s. It is currently the seventh largest wine company and the second largest importer in the **United States**, with a 2006 volume of 6.85 million cases (mc), a 2.3 percent share of the U.S. market. Sales in 2007 reached $250 million. Banfi's leading **brands** are Concha y Toro from **Chile** (2.7 mc in 2006) and Riunite from Italy (2.3 mc); other well-known brands include Walnut Crest (Chile), Villa Banfi (Italy), and Placido (Italy). The company owns winemaking properties in Italy, Castello Banfi in Montalcino and Vigne Regali in Piedmont. The U.S. headquarters are in Old Brookville, **New York**. Co-CEOs James W. Mariani and Cristina Mariani-May are the grandchildren of the founder.

BARRELS AND OAK ALTERNATIVES

Nearly all of the top **red wines** in the world are aged for some length of time in oak barrels, and many premier dry white wines are also aged or even fermented in oak. The barrels provide an ideal slow maturation for wine, and oak imparts desirable flavors as well. The use of barrels is almost essential for wines intended to age rather than to be drunk young, but barrels add considerable expense and are part of the reason such wines cost as much as they do. As a result, there have been various attempts to find ways of getting the same benefits of oak barrel-aging at a lower cost.

History of Barrels. In the early days of winemaking, barrels were used in many places mainly because they were one of the easiest and cheapest ways to store wine. Initially, the wood used to make the barrels was whatever was abundant in the regions where the wines were produced—chestnut, oak, cherry, and so on. Barrels were made in many different sizes and shapes. Some were huge and were permanently housed in wine cellars, but barrels of around 225-liter

(60-gallon) capacity became popular because they were the largest size that was manageable by a single person for filling, emptying, and moving and were a practical container for shipping the wine by boat.

Later on, it was discovered that storing the wine in barrels gave the wine positive attributes—more color, flavor, and complexity—due to the wood's natural porosity. The micro-oxygenation of the wine through the wood made the tannins softer and the color more stable. It also became apparent that, of the different types of wood used, oak was the one that complemented the wine flavor best and made it more interesting. Others, such as chestnut, were a little bitter and not as elegant, so oak became the standard material for barrels.

With further experimentation, it was found that not all oaks were the same. The characteristics imparted to the wine depended on the type of oak (among the different species and subspecies of American, French, Slovenian, and other oaks), the age of the tree, and the forest where it was grown—which affected the grain (tight or loose) and, consequently, the degree of micro-oxygenation— and the length of seasoning of the wood after cutting. Also, in the barrel-making process, in which oak staves were heated over fires to allow them to be shaped into the proper curvature, the degree of toasting of the staves had a marked effect on flavor.

Cooperages.   Barrel makers, known as *coopers,* are found in all the main wine-producing countries. However, the major companies are French, because the huge oak forests of the Massif Central in the middle of **France** are generally considered to be the best source of wood for wine barrels. Some of these companies have set up cooperages in other countries; Demptos and Seguin Moreau both have facilities in the **Napa Valley** making barrels with French and other types of oak. Barrels are typically made to order, using the customer's preferences for oak source and the degree of toasting of the barrel staves and ends (heads). The barrel size and shape are selectable as well, although the classic **Bordeaux**-style barrel of 225 liters and the somewhat shorter and wider **Burgundy**-style barrel of 228 liters are by far the most popular. Still, lately there has been a certain trend back to larger barrels (400–700 liters) to lower the impact of the oak flavor in the wines.

The world's largest cooperage firm is World Cooperage, a division of Independent Stave Company, based in Missouri. It produces more than a million barrels a year, although most are for the whiskey industry. The largest wine barrel maker is Oeneo, the parent of Seguin Moreau and Tonnellerie Radoux, followed by François Frères. Almost 2 million barrels a year are sold in the United States alone.

Cost of Barrels.   Depending on the source and the characteristics of the barrel itself, new barrels vary in price from a few hundred dollars to more than a thousand. French barrels made in France are the most expensive, due to the high demand for them, as well as the poor **exchange rate** with the U.S. dollar. They can run $1,000–$1,200 each. American-made French barrels—that is, barrels made from lumber cut and seasoned in France but manufactured in the United States—cost around $650–$850.

If a **winery** purchases new French oak barrels at, say, $750 each, that adds $2.50 to the cost of each bottle of wine aged in those barrels (not counting the additional labor involved in barrel-aging a fine wine). Thus, if the entire lot was aged in new barrels, around $5 of the **retail** cost of a bottle of wine would be directly attributable to the barrel purchases. For this reason, only high-end wines are likely to be aged in a substantial amount of new French oak.

Less expensive options include American oak, which comes mostly from forests in Missouri and elsewhere in the Midwest, with barrels available for $300–$400, as well as oak from Russia, Slovenia, Hungary, and elsewhere in **Eastern Europe**, which cost $500–$600 due to the added shipping costs. Some of these other oak sources can have spicier and stronger flavors than French oak and can therefore introduce a more pronounced oak character; early experiments have shown that others could be considered fair substitutes for French oak. In the end, however, the choice of oak source depends upon the desired style of the finished wine.

Another option for reducing cost is to buy (or to continue to use after the first season when they were new) used barrels. These cost about half the price of new barrels for one-year-used ones to as little as $50 for older ones. They have little of the flavor left in them compared to new barrels, but they still provide the micro-oxygenation that helps the wine age properly. Wineries often use a combination of new and used barrels from a variety of wood sources and cooperages both to keep costs down and to add complexity to the final blended wine.

Oak Alternatives.   About 20 years ago in some of the **New World** countries, wineries started experimenting with alternatives to oak barrels as a technique to give wines some of the advantages of the barrel-aging at a much lower cost that would be affordable for medium- and even low-priced wines. These products include oak staves that are suspended inside stainless-steel tanks and oak chips (available in many shapes and sizes) that are added to wines in tanks.

The Old World initially reacted to this idea with a lot of resistance because these oak treatments were seen as something nontraditional that would have a negative impact on the image of the wine because they were considered an adulteration or unnatural flavoring of the wine. As a result, in Europe, until a few years ago, it was illegal to use these products, as it still is for some **quality wines** of specific **appellations**.

The point of using oak barrels for wine aging is basically twofold: to add to the wine some components from the oak, including flavor, some polysaccharides, and oak tannins responsible for an improvement in the wine's structure, complexity, and roundness; and to micro-oxygenate the wine, allowing a better tannin and color development over time. The first of these goals can be accomplished equally well with the use of oak staves and chips—possibly even better, because the surface area in contact with the wine may be greater with staves and chips. The second goal can be achieved through the use of an artificial, induced micro-oxygenation that is simply done by injecting into the tank or vat through a porcelain cartridge a predetermined amount of oxygen, which basically replicates the same environment as in the barrels.

Winemakers who widely use these techniques say that there is no difference between putting the wine into oak or the oak into wine. There is no doubt that the use of oak alternatives—if properly done, using good-quality oak in the right amount and at the proper stage (that is, during fermentation or right after pressing), along with proper micro-oxygenation—can improve wine quality at a much lower cost. In addition, there is very little handling required compared with the use of barrels, which provides further savings. Those concerned with the environment are more accepting of oak alternatives. Since coopers can use only about 25 to 30 percent of a tree for barrels, waste-conscious producers and consumers alike are happy to hear that the rest of the tree can be used for oak alternatives.

In addition to staves and chips, such products as oak extract, tannin powder, and oak shavings are now available. The use of these products has expanded the oak supplier segment of the industry. Many long-time international cooperage houses, such as Seguin Moreau, Radoux, Nadalie, and Canton, sell these alternatives alongside their barrels. Entirely new companies have been created that sell only these products, such as Innerstave located in **Sonoma County**, California. Others such as StaVin, located in Sausalito, California, focus on oak alternatives, but offer barrels as well.

Oak alternatives are not designed to replace the use of barrels and never will be. They represent a viable, less expensive option and are tied to the price point and style of the wine; $4 worth of chips can be used to flavor 225 liters (300 bottles) of wine, as can a $400–$1,200 barrel. The result of a barrel-aged wine is not the same as that from an alternative oak treatment. Barrels give the wines more elegance, complexity, and balance, and the impact of the oak on the wine is not as strong and invasive as with the alternatives. Furthermore, barrels, of different sizes and shapes, are part of the tradition and charm of many premium wines and wineries in both the New and Old Worlds—something that oak staves and chips cannot provide. Nevertheless, alternative oak treatments can improve the wine quality in many good, medium-priced wines that cannot support the cost of expensive barrel-aging.

Alberto Antonini

Further Reading

Caputo, Tina. "Winemaking with Oak Alternatives." *Wines & Vines,* July 2006, www.winesandvines.com/template.cfm?section=features&content=49681.

Fleming, Chris. "A Refresher Course on Barrels." *Wines & Vines,* February 2007, www.winesandvines.com/template.cfm?section=features&content=47804.

Work, Henry. "Saving Money on Cooperage." *Practical Winery & Vineyard,* January/February 2003, www.practicalwinery.com/janfeb03/janfeb03p13.htm.

BATF. *See* Alcohol and Tobacco Tax and Trade Bureau (TTB)

BIODYNAMIC VITICULTURE

The current biodynamic movement has its roots in the writings and beliefs of Austrian philosopher and scientist Rudolf Steiner (1861–1925), who in turn was influenced by Johann Wolfgang von Goethe's literary works. Biodynamic farmers believe in **organic** principles and see the land as a complete ecosystem, but take measures a step further by introducing a spiritual aspect to their activities.

They look after the health of their farms using methods similar to homeopathic remedies, striving to improve the overall health and fertility of the land they farm by applying natural preparations (made from such substances as medicinal herbs, minerals, and cow dung) to restore and enhance the ecosystem in which they operate. The biodynamic concept that has attracted most of the attention to this group, however, is their belief that farming activities should be aligned with the phases of the cosmos and that there are planetary effects on agricultural crops. Subscribing winemakers believe that only under biodynamic conditions does the true **terroir** of a site show itself.

Even most skeptics agree that biodynamic farming has an overall positive effect on the health of the vines and subsequent quality of those wines, though scientific evidence that the cosmic applications of biodynamic farming are responsible is quite slim. It is more widely held that the healthier farming techniques lead ultimately to higher-quality and possibly better-tasting wines.

The organization that certifies biodynamic practices is Demeter-International e.V. (www.demeter.net), with 18 member organizations in Europe, the **United States** (www.demeter-usa.org), **Canada**, **New Zealand**, and elsewhere. Demeter certifies both vineyards and **wineries**, and, as in the case of organic wines, there can be "biodynamic wine" and (nonbiodynamic) "wine made from biodynamic grapes." Biodynamic winemaking, among other things, requires the use of only native yeast and forbids most **must and wine adjustments**.

Further Reading

Joly, Nicolas. *Biodynamic Wine, Demystified.* San Francisco: Wine Appreciation Guild, 2007.

Waldin, Monty. *Biodynamic Wines.* London: Mitchell Beazley, 2004.

BORDEAUX

The Bordeaux region of France is often described as the world's largest fine-wine producing area. Not only is it impressive in size (307,000 acres of **appellation**-quality vines in 2005), but its top properties make much greater quantities of wine than do most other producers of similar renown around the world—an average of 220,000 bottles per year for Château Latour, 230,000 bottles for Château Lafite Rothschild, and 300,000 for Château Mouton Rothschild are but three examples of this. Nonetheless, Bordeaux's traditional economic prominence has been severely challenged in the past several years due to a confluence of long-standing conditions within the region and relatively new circumstances from without.

Bordeaux's weather has never been ideal for winemaking, fine or otherwise. Its proximity to the Atlantic Ocean gives the area a cool maritime climate that makes it extremely difficult to obtain optimally ripe grapes. Naturally enough under such conditions, a proportion of each year's production is inevitably of poor quality, and due to the region's large size, this proportion can represent a significant volume. This has greatly contributed to the region's "two-speed" economy composed of producers whose wines have always been in great demand (around 5 percent of

Bordeaux's total production of 60–70 million cases) and the others who must actively work at selling what they make. Historically, however, practically everyone has been able to find a buyer thanks to the commercial entity known as the Bordeaux marketplace.

This institution evolved over many generations to sell each year's substantial volume of wine in a timely manner, thus avoiding a bottleneck in **distribution** when the following vintage became available. The marketplace depends on Bordeaux's three main actors: the producers, who make the wine; the **négociants**, who buy it; and the brokers, who arrange its sale. Even though this system is hundreds of years old and much about Bordeaux has changed during this time, each of these actors still remains essential, and the absence of any one of them would seriously degrade the smooth operation of business.

Among its other effects, the local marketplace divides Bordeaux's total production into three main types: château wines made by individual producers, **branded** wines made in larger quantities by blending grapes or finished wine from individual producers, and cooperative wines produced by a collective of small-size individual producers.

Until recently, the Bordeaux marketplace's efficacy made it possible to sell all three types, a task made significantly easier by the relatively limited sources for wine throughout the world. Although fine-quality vineyards have existed far beyond Bordeaux for centuries, their output and reputations were often too modest to attract much interest from the average wine drinker. However, over the past several decades this has changed, much to Bordeaux's detriment.

New World wine regions have one great advantage over Bordeaux: their vineyards have been planted purposefully in areas where the existing climate will guarantee ripe grapes. By contrast, Old World vineyards were situated to satisfy the needs of a thirsty local population, regardless of the prevailing weather. Thus, even though they may use such grapes as **Cabernet Sauvignon** and **Merlot** that are synonymous with Bordeaux, New World vineyards have developed a popularity surpassing that enjoyed by these varieties' home region. This is largely because these areas can grow great quantities of consistently ripe grapes to produce satisfying wines at a lower cost than is possible in Bordeaux. Simply put, wine drinkers seeking a decent bottle of basic **red wine** used to look to Bordeaux; today they have many other choices that are often more attractive—both to their tastes and their budgets.

The traditional arguments that have contributed to Bordeaux's success (and that of French wine in general), such as the importance of **terroir** and the resulting abundance of appellations, are no longer persuasive. Thus, a number of measures have been introduced that Bordeaux hopes will help restore its fortunes.

Regulatory reforms adopted in 2005, falling into line with **European Union** rules, now allow producers to incorporate up to 15 percent of wine from a different year and still qualify for vintage status. While relatively few châteaux are likely to take advantage of this, it will probably be embraced by branded wine producers to increase their production to levels that can compete with the large-scale output of companies from **California** and **Australia**. Another major change is the introduction of **varietal labeling**, explicitly naming grape varieties on wine labels to satisfy **consumers**' preferences for such information when making their purchases.

Since the late 1990s, an increasing number of producers have adopted the practice of moving mandatory legal information such as alcohol degree, bottle size, and the official *appellation contrôlée* designation to a secondary label (which is technically therefore the "front label"). This offers the consumer a cleaner, less complex presentation usually comprising just the château name, the vintage, and the basic area of production.

Recent efforts have attempted to simplify Bordeaux's offering by reducing its number of appellations from the current 57. The project among the region's Côtes appellations to unite in the creation of a single "Côtes de Bordeaux" designation is the most prominent example of this.

Finally, the local application of a national program for uprooting vines from areas of marginal quality was instituted in 2005, but the winemakers' tepid response is not likely to yield significant results. In any event, it has been suggested that once Bordeaux's current economic difficulties are resolved, there will be a lot fewer vines left anyway—market forces will eliminate those that produce lower-quality, unsalable wines. However, this is not certain.

There may well be a **consolidation** of smaller vineyards as struggling owners sell out to financially secure neighbors or enter into long-term contracts with major *négociants* seeking control and access to more grapes. In both cases, greater investment may bring out these vines' unrealized potential for making better wine.

What is certain is that Bordeaux's overall quality will improve over the coming years; the only question is exactly how this will be achieved. *See also* Auction Houses; Futures.

Dewey Markham, Jr.

Further Reading

Bordeaux Wine Bureau. www.bordeauxwinebureau.org, www.bordeaux.com.
Brook, Stephen. *Bordeaux: People, Power and Politics*. London: Mitchell Beazley, 2001.
Faith, Nicholas. *The Winemasters of Bordeaux*. London: Carlton Books, 2005.

BRANDING

A brand represents a value proposition to the **consumer**. The very mention of the brand's name or sight of its logo engenders trust in the mind of the buyer and the feeling that this item is better than other branded or generic alternatives. Brand loyalty is demonstrated when consumers are willing to pay more or search harder for a particular product than for any other because of the perception of its superior quality and value relative to all competing brands. From a producer's point of view, "branding" one's product—that is, creating a brand identity for it—and building up brand loyalty among consumers is an essential path in establishing large-volume and/or high-**profit** sales.

Wine brands represent a particular subset of consumer goods brands, and like brands in general, there is a variety of different types of brands. At one end of the spectrum are commodity or mass-market brands, which compete on high volume and low price point. At the other end are luxury brands, which compete on the basis of reputation, name recognition, and a perception of exclusivity and are able to command higher, sometimes much higher, prices. In theory, quality improves as one moves along the continuum from commodity to luxury brands, although it is really the perception of quality (which, up to a point, may be attained through the higher price itself) that is more crucial. There are also niche brands, filling the needs or desires of a specific subset of consumers and may be found anywhere in the spectrum, and **cult** brands, which are the most exclusive of the luxury brands.

Many wines—the vast majority, by volume—are commodity brands. They are made specifically with the goal of consistency. Regardless of what impels the consumer to try the brand in the first place, the branded wine seeks to ensure that if the consumer likes what he or she had the first time, the second and all future experiences will be identical. Another implied promise of a brand is availability; within reason, consumers expect a major brand always to be available when they want to buy it. Some of the largest commodity brands include Franzia, E&J Wine Cellars, Carlo Rossi, **Yellow Tail**, Beringer, Concha y Toro, Almaden, and Sutter Home.

Luxury brands command a high price, but they are not always produced in small quantities. One very famous luxury brand, **Bordeaux** estate Château Mouton Rothschild, produces some 30,000 cases of wine in the best vintage years— hardly low volume. Cult and niche brands, however, are typically small. Screaming Eagle, a cult **Cabernet Sauvignon** from the **Napa Valley**, offers only about 500 cases a year. Yet both Mouton and Screaming Eagle enjoy fierce brand loyalty from their customers and have built up substantial marketable equity in their brand names.

It is difficult, if not impossible, for an estate winery of whatever size to be commodity brand in the truest sense. Variations in weather from year to year inevitably mean differences in the quantity and quality of the harvested grapes, which poses significant challenges to making a wine consistent. Large estates may be able to select fruit from different parcels to blend into a familiar taste, and vineyards in many **New World** regions normally have far less variation to deal with between growing seasons than the typical Old World vineyard does, but complete consistency is still difficult to achieve. Indeed, estate wineries are more likely to emphasize the *distinctions* between vintages, relying on such attributes as steady quality rather than uniformity of characteristics as their brand's hallmark. In this sense, the opposite of a brand is a "**terroir** wine"—a wine that seeks to channel nature's every whim to make each vintage, and each parcel of land, show off its unique individuality. Because of this, many producers who follow this brand strategy have chosen to promote their terroir, their history, and their own uniqueness as a point of differentiation.

For commodity brands, the twin goals of consistency and availability require a different strategy. The primary focus is usually on sourcing of grapes. A brand ideally will search out grapes of a particular flavor profile wherever they might be grown in a given year—subject, of course, to legal restrictions. For this reason, brands usually carry broad **appellations**, allowing them to seek out fruit in a large area with many different local growing conditions without being forced to relabel the wine. In the **United States**, for example, brands might carry a county appellation, such as Monterey County, but they are even more likely to be identified with a multicounty superappellation, such as the Central Coast American Viticultural Area (AVA) or simply as "**California**" or even "American" wine. These allow much greater freedom in sourcing—in the case of "American wine," allowing the use of grapes from anywhere in the United States plus up to 25 percent grapes, juice, or **bulk wine** from anywhere else in the world. With so many sources from which to choose, it is quite possible to produce a dependable wine year after year even though the place of origin and perhaps even the grape varieties used differ every time.

Even when it is not feasible to get compatible grapes every year, there are many techniques that can be employed by the winemaker to steer the final product toward a specific style. Adjustments of alcohol or tannin, for example, may bring the wine into line with the desired flavor profile. Large brands typically have winemaking teams rather than individual winemakers, again helping to ensure a continuity of style.

Today's wine consumers can be fickle at the commodity end of the spectrum. Many consumers at this level do not stay with a product very long before moving on to the next big thing. Large brands require a constant influx of new customers to improve their market share, and this is the job of marketing. Savvy brand marketers know that they can never stop investing in innovation in their brands. Like so many other aspects of the business world, brands are subject to a life cycle. The job of the brand manager is constantly to be aware of where the brand is in its cycle and to strive to show new benefits and meanings for the brand in order to maintain brand loyalty.

Whether it is an internal department or an agency hired to take care of **promotion**, major brands need a marketing team to help plant the seed in the minds of the public that the brand is desirable. This may be accomplished through advertising, special events, attractive **labels**, **wine education** activities, product placements, or other means. If the job is done right, consumers will be willing to try a whole new line of products—or extension—launched by their favorite brands, based solely on the brand name.

Mass-market brands may compete largely on a price basis, using economies of scale and aggressive **distribution** and **retail** strategies to be the lowest priced and most prominent wine. Because these brands must sell huge volumes of wine to make a profit, the biggest brands all fall into this category. The largest brand in the United States, Franzia, sold 22.8 million cases in 2006 (half again as much as all the wine made in **New Zealand** that year). These wines are typically generically labeled (for example, "White" or "Blush") **table wine** with a national origin (for example, "Product of **Chile**") and are usually seen in large-format **alternative packaging**, such as five-liter boxes.

At higher price points, brands must create an image of quality or prestige that justifies the extra cost. These brands will normally have a well-regarded place of origin—for example, Columbia Valley AVA or South Eastern **Australia** or something even more specific—are often **varietally labeled**, may use some oak **barrels** or alternatives to oak, and are sold for the most part in 750-milliliter bottles, although they may be available in both larger and smaller sizes.

Needing to maintain a relatively high volume of sales, few brands can venture very far into the superpremium category over, say, $15 a bottle. One exception is in **sparkling wine**, which has higher costs to begin with and also has a built-in reputation for luxury and festivity that validates a higher price. Nonvintage **Champagne** can be considered the earliest case of branding because it was here that the idea of blending multiple grapes, areas, and vintages to get a consistent product was first developed. Moët & Chandon, the largest Champagne house, produces 2.85 million cases annually, much of it nonvintage, with an average bottle price at retail in the United States of $50. *See also* E-Commerce; Globalization; Must and Wine Adjustments; Négociants.

Further Reading

Aaker, David A. *Building Strong Brands*. New York: Free Press, 1996.

Davis, Scott M., and Michael Dunn. *Building the Brand-Driven Business: Operationalize Your Brand to Drive Profitable Growth*. San Francisco: Jossey-Bass, 2002.

Ries, Al, and Laura Ries. *The 22 Immutable Laws of Branding: How to Build a Product or Service into a World-Class Brand*. New York: HarperBusiness, 2002.

BRAZIL

As the world's fifth most populous nation, Brazil is a significant potential market for wine. With a large populace descended from European immigrants and no **religious** barriers to alcohol, there is every reason to expect Brazil's wine consumption to grow as its economy expands.

Per-capita wine consumption in Brazil is currently quite low, at about three liters per adult (a quarter that of the **United States**), which can be attributed to the combination of widespread poverty and the typical reduced interest in wine in tropical climates. Brazilian wine consumption in 2006 totaled 39.5 million nine-liter cases (mc). Brazilians have a particular taste for **vermouth**, which comprises more than 5 percent of sales. However, they drink much more beer and cachaça sugar cane–based spirits than wine, and growing problems with underage drinking and alcohol-related **health** issues have brought calls for stricter controls on alcoholic beverages. This movement's effect on wine will depend on the extent to which wine is included with the efforts against beer and spirits abuse.

Brazil is also a fairly substantial producer of wine, the third largest in South America and among the top 15 in the world. Despite the country's position straddling the equator, it is large enough to stretch into the temperate zone as far as 33° south latitude, making **grape growing** quite feasible. Brazil has about 215,000 acres of wine grapes, about 55 percent of them in the southernmost state of Rio Grande do Sul; São Paulo State has another 21 percent. Another area that has garnered interest in recent years is in the states of Bahia and Pernambuco, a relatively dry (for Brazil) region just 8° south of the equator, where rigorous vineyard management can produce harvests year-round.

Not surprisingly, winegrowing in Brazil began not long after the beginning of colonization by **Portugal** in the sixteenth century. A true wine industry did not develop until the nineteenth century, however, and was mostly built around native American grapes and hybrids such as Concord and Isabel due to the country's generally high rainfall and humidity. Major European varieties were introduced by immigrants in the twentieth century, especially from **Italy**. Native American varieties and hybrids still predominate, but several international varieties are grown, including **Cabernet Sauvignon**, **Chardonnay**, Malbec, **Merlot**, **Riesling**, and **Syrah**, along with Trebbiano, Pinotage, Tannat, and for **sparkling wine**, Prosecco.

Brazil's total annual wine production averages around 34 mc, of which 5 mc is vinifera, but had a poor harvest in 2006 and produced only 24 mc. The largest **winery**, the Aurora cooperative, produces about a quarter of production. Brazil has made strides in exports. It was the source for the Marcus James **brand** in the 1980s and 1990s until the demand outstripped production capacity. The primary markets for Brazilian exports outside South America are the United States, **Canada**, and **Germany**.

Further Reading

União Brasileira de Vitivinicultura [in Portuguese]. www.uvibra.com.br.
Wines from Brazil. www.winesfrombrazil.com.

BRITISH MARKET

In many ways, the British wine market is *the* wine market. Historically, it was the English love of wine, and the lack of suitable conditions for producing wine in the British Isles, that spurred the development of the international wine trade and made London its hub. If the English had been less interested in drinking wine or if the British Empire had not been the dominant force that it was, the center of the international commerce in wine would eventually have situated itself in Amsterdam or Paris or perhaps later New York.

The United Kingdom is the seventh largest wine-consuming country at 130 million nine-liter cases (mc) in 2006. However, it is the only country among the top 10 wine consumers that does not produce a significant amount of wine itself, thus making it a major importer of wine—the biggest in the world by value, and second only to **Germany** by volume. British per-capita consumption, 24.6 liters per adult in 2006, is toward the low end of the scale among European countries, but is still ahead of the rest of the world apart from **Argentina**, **Australia**, and Uruguay. Significantly, while consumption has been declining in category leaders such as **Italy** and **France**, Britain's consumption is growing at 5 to 6 percent annually at the expense of the beer and spirits industries. Two-thirds of Britons at least occasionally drink wine.

In 2006, Britain imported about 141 mc of wine, worth £2.3 billion (about $4.2 billion). For centuries (except in the not infrequent periods when England and France were at war with one another), the primary flow of wine has come across the English Channel from France, but Australia, a source of wine in Britain since the early nineteenth century, has stolen the top spot in recent years, rising in sales volume as France's volume has shrunk. Australia's exports to the United Kingdom reached almost 30 mc in 2006, a 21 percent market share, while France fell below 25 mc. Nevertheless, the scales remain tipped heavily in France's favor in terms of value (£802 million to Australia's £445 million) due to sales of expensive **Bordeaux**, **Burgundy**, and other high-priced French imports, and French import volume rebounded by 4 percent in 2007. The next tier of imports includes Italy, **Spain**, the **United States**, **Chile**, and **South Africa**. The **New World** surpassed the Old in volume among British imports for the first time in 2003 and now claims about 55 percent market share. U.S. exports to the United Kingdom in 2006 totaled 13.3 mc and have been increasing in both volume and value, although the dollar's weak **exchange rate** with the pound has helped the former and hurt the latter. **Branded** wines are very important in the British market, and **Gallo** Family Vineyards and **Diageo**'s Blossom Hill represent more than half of the U.S. wine volume; Hardys from Australia is the top brand overall.

While the image of the upper-crust British wine connoisseur with huge stacks of old Bordeaux in the cellar of the manor house still has some validity, the average British wine buyer is mad for value. The **retail** trade ("off-trade") is dominated by **supermarkets**, which have competed with one another to provide decent drinkable wine at rock-bottom prices. Discounts and **promotions** are the rule, with the grocery chains able to turn a **profit** thanks to huge volume and major concessions from their suppliers. The retail sector accounts for 79 percent of wine sales in Britain, but only 54 percent of revenues due to the low prices. Of this, supermarket sales dwarf those of traditional wine retailers by a factor of six to one. The Tesco chain alone sells more than £1.5 billion of wine annually, giving it at least a third of the British market and making it the world's largest wine retailer. Supermarkets once relied greatly on their own-label wines to keep the prices low, but their clout in the trade now allows them the leverage to drive hard bargains with the big brands as well.

The median price of a bottle of wine in supermarkets has fallen to £3.86 ($7.70), which is all the more remarkable given that more than half of that is taxes. In March 2008, the British government raised the duty on imported wine by 14 pence per bottle, to £1.46 ($2.90), with further increases planned annually for four years. For a wine at the popular price point of £3.99 per bottle, this means that—including the 17.5 percent value-added tax—£2.16 goes to the government, leaving just £1.83 to be shared by the retailer, producer, and anyone in between. (By comparison, the total federal import duty and tax on a bottle of **table wine** imported into the United States from most countries is $0.26.) Britain's tariffs are now the highest in Europe.

Wine being shipped to the United Kingdom must pass through an **importer**, often referred to as an agent. Because the tiers can overlap in this relatively free system, the importer may be an off-license retailer; it may also be a wholesaler, who usually sells to the on-trade (**restaurants**, bars, and the **hospitality industry**), or a third party who simply facilitates the passage from supplier to retailer for a fee. Wine from outside the **European Union** faces a small additional tariff.

Besides Tesco, the major supermarket chains for wine sales are Sainsbury's, Waitrose, and Asda. Supermarkets and independent grocers capture three-quarters of the off-trade. However, their ever-diminishing range of choices (due to the cutthroat pricing that can be endured only by the major suppliers) may be opening the door for a return of the wine specialist store. After years of

consolidation, the largest wine retail chain is the Thresher Group (Threshers, The Local, Wine Rack, and Haddows), with 1,500 stores; others include Majestic Wine Warehouses Ltd. (144 stores), which sells wines only by the (mixed) case, and Oddbins (161 stores). There are a number of single-store (or small-chain) fine wine specialists in London and other large cities that account for an outsized proportion of the upper-end wine purchases. Some of these, such as Berry Bros. & Rudd, have been in operation for centuries. It is estimated that about 8 percent of the wine trade is conducted via **e-commerce**, mail order, and **wine clubs**. Half of the online trade is claimed by Tesco.com, and much of the rest is controlled by Direct Wines and its Laithwaites online storefront.

Despite the British love of claret (red Bordeaux), white wine outsells **red wine** in the United Kingdom 48 percent to 44 percent. **Rosé** (and blush) accounts for the remaining 8 percent and has seen strong growth recently. **Chardonnay** is the most popular variety, and **Sauvignon Blanc** has been second for many years, but may be displaced by **Pinot Grigio**, whose sales increased 74 percent in 2006. Among red **varietally labeled** wines, **Syrah**—more likely Shiraz from Australia or South Africa—is in the lead, followed by the ever-popular **Merlot** and **Cabernet Sauvignon**; **Pinot Noir** is far behind, though gaining. **Alternative packaging** is making inroads, with bag-in-box wine now up to 10 percent of sales.

The amount of wine made in Britain is negligible compared to the demand. In 2006, about 3.7 mc was produced in the United Kingdom, but almost all of that was "British wine"—wine made in Britain from grapes or juice grown outside the country. "English wine" and "Welsh wine" are the products of grapes actually grown in the British Isles, and this totaled just 281,000 cases in the bumper crop year of 2006; 180,000 cases is more typical. The 100-plus **wineries**, with less than 2,000 acres in production, make mostly white still and **sparkling wine**, primarily from hybrid grape varieties. It is interesting to speculate how global **climate change** might change the British domestic wine industry, however; warmer temperatures could provide opportunities for substantially more production and greater use of vinifera varieties, if the disease problems caused by rain and humidity can be kept under control. *See also* Colonial Era.

Further Reading

Decanter. www.decanter.com.

Drinks Business. www.thedrinksbusiness.com.

U.K. Department for Environment, Food and Rural Affairs. "Wine." www.defra.gov.uk/foodrin/wine/index.htm.

Wine & Spirit. www.wine-spirit.com.

Wine and Spirit Trade Association. www.wsta.co.uk.

BRONCO WINE COMPANY

The Bronco Wine Company is the producer of "Two Buck Chuck." Bronco Wine was started in 1973 by brothers Fred and Joseph and cousin John Franzia, from the family that established (and sold) the Franzia **brand**. It is now the fourth largest wine company in the **United States**, with 2006 sales of 22 million cases (mc).

Its annual sales are approximately $250 million. Much of the production is sold as **bulk wine** or bottled for other labels, but the company also has some 30 brands of its own. Bronco's best-known brand is Charles Shaw, launched in early 2003 and sold exclusively by Trader Joe's **supermarkets**; priced at $2 per bottle in **California** for the **Chardonnay** ($3 in other states), the brand became a sensation known as Two Buck Chuck, which has sold 25 mc in five years. Other labels include Crane Lake, ForestVille, and Forest Glen, and its **restaurant**-only Salmon Creek brand is one of the top on-premise wines.

Bronco Wine bought a **winery** in Escalon, California, from **Constellation** in 2003 with the capacity to produce about 33 mc; it also owns a production facility in the **Napa Valley** and plans a bottling plant adjacent to it. The company is the largest vineyard owner in California, with more than 35,000 acres of vineyards, mostly in the Central Valley, although it also buys grapes and wine from all over the state. Bronco's headquarters are in Ceres, California, south of Modesto. *See also* Appellations.

BULK WINE/JUICE TRADE

The voyage of all wines begins as bulk wine from the time the grape sugars have been converted by yeast to alcohol. Bulk wine, like any bulk product, is defined as a commodity that has yet to find its way into the package sold to **consumers**—in this case, wine not yet in a bottle, bag, or other **alternative packaging**. In the past, consumers were able to purchase bulk wine directly from **wineries** in their own containers, but time and the human condition have made this practice far less common. Today, bulk wine is actively traded primarily between countries or regions and among wineries.

The bulk wine industry is as old as wine itself. Some 3,000 years ago, the **Greeks** traded their wines throughout the **ancient Mediterranean** by ship inside sealed *amphorae*. The wine amphorae were tall and pointed at the base, allowing for efficient storage and transportation. By medieval times, **barrels** became the bulk wine vessel of choice, and merchants traveled great distances to find new wines to sell. During the **colonial era**, barrels of wine were shipped from European wine producers to colonies all over the world, as well as to such nonproducer countries as England and Holland.

In modern times, bulk wines continue to be traded globally by ship, as well as by rail and trucks. Totes, using stainless steel and rubber bladders to protect the wine, are the modern replacement for barrels. **Temperature control** is often employed when high heat may damage the wine, as when moving wine across country during summer or through the tropics.

While some countries produce more wine than they can consume, others consume considerably more wine than they make. In addition, the volume of wine that flows annually is dependent on the global supply of fruit, and being an agricultural product, there can be booms and busts depending upon the year and country of origin. In general, bulk wine fills the gaps between countries' output and needs. Thus, **importers**, exporters, and various brokers and agents conduct trade to match **supply and demand** through the international trade in wine. Bottled wine is the most visible form of this trade, but for long-distance trade, the most economical way to transport the wine is in bulk, saving the extra weight and volume and inevitable breakage of packaged, especially bottled, wine. As time goes by, more and more wine is being shipped in bulk to bottlers in the country of **distribution**.

The nations of northern Europe have long been the destination for wine from warmer climates to the south, and with the **globalization** of the wine industry, the network has spread to the farthest corners of the Earth in search of good-quality, low-price wines for everyday drinking. The **British**, **Dutch**, and **Scandinavian markets** are large importers of bulk wines, particularly from **Chile** and **South Africa**. **Germany** and Russia are also big importers, but they tend to prefer sources closer to home—**Italy** and **France** in the case of Germany; **Eastern Europe**, especially Bulgaria and Belarus, for Russia.

Argentina has become a bulk wine supplier to China—which may one day become a significant exporter itself. **Australia**, whose wine industry depends heavily on exports, has at least temporarily become an importer of bulk wine from Argentina, Chile, South Africa, and even the **United States** as its recent measures to deal with a huge overproduction problem have left it undersupplied. The bulk wine is being used for inexpensive domestic wines so that the top-quality fruit can continue to go into high-value exports.

The United States imported some 22 million gallons of bulk wine in 2006—the equivalent of 9.1 million nine-liter cases—which is more than double the amount of 2005 and quadruple that of 2004, although this market naturally fluctuates wildly. More than half of this wine came from Australia, with Argentina and France also being large contributors; together, these three represented 93 percent of the U.S. bulk wine market. The primary grape varieties imported were **Chardonnay**, **Cabernet Sauvignon**, **Pinot Noir**, and **Pinot Grigio**. Much of this wine was used to blend into low-priced wines with an "American wine" designation; up to 25 percent of the content of these wines can legally be sourced from other countries. On the flip side of the coin, about 18 percent of U.S. exports went out in bulk. One notable example is Blossom Hill, a **brand** vinified in **California** but almost entirely shipped in bulk to Italy and bottled there.

Virtually all established wineries, **négociants**, **grape growers**, and members of other food industries at least occasionally engage in the bulk wine trade. Other uses for bulk wine are the vinegar and **distillation** (brandy, grappa, and industrial ethanol) industries, which require wine as an input. Nor is the bulk trade restricted to wine. Some grape juice enters the bulk market even before it becomes wine. Wineries can hold juice until after harvest to determine their exact needs and then either ferment and sell it or sell the juice outright to another processor for fermentation and blending. Also, some grapes are crushed and concentrated to be used in wine and other products requiring the use of grape concentrate.

There are many advantages for wineries entering into the bulk wine trade. While many may initially use the bulk wine market for disposing of excess or mediocre inventory, the vast majority of bulk wine traded around the globe is intended for and utilized by big brands. In fact, without the bulk wine trade, brands as we think of them—wines known for their consistent style and price year in and year out—could not exist.

From a financial perspective, using bulk wine, the barriers to entry in the wine industry are dramatically lowered. A winery that wants to expand without waiting for vineyards to develop or without needing to input thousands of dollars in capital expenditures can do so with very little effort. For the winery selling bulk wine, it is an opportunity to increase short-term cash flow, reduce inventories acquired during a bumper harvest, and balance inventory based on sales in a given year.

As the wine industry embraces globalization, the bulk wine trade will play a critical role in helping emergent wine producers, such as China, to develop strong business models. It will continue to feed such countries as the United Kingdom and the United States, where the consumers' desire for different and varied wines continues to develop. And as wine companies continue to **consolidate**, the bulk wine trade will help to define the brands that exist today and create the brands of tomorrow.

Steve Dorfman

BURGUNDY

The wine production of Burgundy in France—approximately 1.5 million hectoliters, equal to 16.7 million nine-liter cases (mc)—is less than 1 percent of world output, yet its wines account for 5 percent of **global** wine transactions by value, reflecting the luxury prices commanded by the finest Burgundies. These wines remain the classic benchmarks for **Pinot Noir** and **Chardonnay**, despite competition from many other countries. White wines constitute 61 percent of total output, **red wines** (and a small volume of **rosé**) 32 percent, and *crémant* (**sparkling**) 7 percent.

The three most important **appellations** in sales volume are red and white Bourgogne (1.9 mc), Chablis (1.9 mc), and Mâcon-Villages (1.3 mc). About half of Burgundy's output, valued at €550 million on average, is exported, primarily within the **European Union**. Great Britain is by far the largest export market by volume, followed by the **United States**, although the two countries account for a similar value.

History.   While winegrowing may have existed earlier, organized vineyards were first planted in Burgundy by Gallo-Romans in the third century. The Catholic Church succeeded the Roman Empire, and **religious** orders actively cultivated and expanded vineyards. The Benedictine Abbey of Cluny, in the Mâconnais, was established in 910. The Cistercians at Citeaux (founded 1098) constructed the Clos de Vougeot on the Côte d'Or in 1110. They also took up residence in Chablis at the Abbey of Pontigny in 1118. Monks took cuttings, studied vines, and tasted wines from different vineyards, identifying unique traits from certain parcels and thereby advancing the *cru* concept that is integral to modern French appellations.

The Valois dukes of Burgundy further developed viticulture in the fourteenth and fifteenth centuries. The French Revolution (1789–1799) led to the dissolution of large estates belonging to the aristocracy and the Church, and the Napoleonic Code dictated that land be divided equally among all heirs. Together, these factors resulted in extensive fragmentation, reinforced by the devastation caused by **phylloxera** in the late 1800s. Consequently, one vineyard was often divided among many individual proprietors. Fragmented holdings within a total of 100 appellations make it challenging to comprehend and to market Burgundy wines.

Industry Structure.   There are more than 4,000 individual wine estates or *domaines* in Burgundy; a third of them bottle the wine from their holdings. Direct sales by estates comprise 30 percent of the total, a share that has grown over the last 30 years. Growers, sometimes with brokers as intermediaries, also sell their grapes, juice, or wine to *négociants*, who perform such functions as vinification, maturation, and bottling and account for half of sales. Négociants may also own substantial vineyards, as do leading houses such as Maison Bouchard Père et Fils, Maison Joseph Drouhin, Maison Louis Jadot, and Maison Louis Latour. Growers sometimes belong to cooperatives that process the fruit from their members' vineyards; these account for 15 percent of sales volume.

Regions.   *Chablis* is an island far removed from the rest of Burgundy, with 11,700 acres under vine. The grape for Chablis is Chardonnay, grown on slopes of clay and marls over limestone. The *Appellation d'Origine Contrôlée* (AOC) legislation establishes a hierarchy of quality: from lowest to highest, Petit Chablis; Chablis, representing two-thirds of production; Chablis *premier cru* from 79 named sites (17 percent of volume); and Chablis *grand cru*, coming from seven vineyards covering 255 acres and producing just 58,000 cases on average (less than 2 percent of volume). The Chablis name—like that of Burgundy itself—has been widely abused in other countries, appearing on labels of wines that have nothing in common with authentic Chablis.

The *Côte d'Or* is the most glamorous of all the subregions of Burgundy, producing 2.8 mc annually of red and white wines. The finest Côte d'Or bottlings are prized for their rarity, complexity, and ability to improve with age. The Côte is a narrow strip of vineyards, less than a mile in width, that is divided into two halves: the Côte de Nuits and Côte de Beaune. The variations of limestones and clays are partly responsible for a mosaic of vineyard parcels and, it is argued, **terroir** characteristics. The decisive elements in the delimitation of Côte d'Or vineyards are orientation, slope, soil permeability, and historical patterns of vineyard cultivation and ownership. Côte d'Or wines include blends such as Côte de Beaune-Villages, communal or *village* appellations (Volnay, Vosne-Romanée, Meursault, and so forth), premiers crus (usually labeled with a vineyard name), and grands crus, of which there are 33 producing a total of 185,000 cases per vintage. These ''great growths'' are among the most expensive and collectible wines in the world and bear such legendary place names as Romanée Conti, Chambertin, Corton-Charlemagne, and Montrachet. The smallest grand cru is La Romanée at 2.1 acres, yielding less than 500 bottles a year, while the largest is Corton (248 acres, 40,000 cases).

The *Chalonnais* is the least known subregion due in part to its limited output. The vineyards and soils are more variegated than elsewhere in Burgundy, and the Chalonnais wines resemble the lighter and faster maturing ones of the Côte de

Beaujolais

The Beaujolais region is often considered part of **Burgundy**, yet many features set it apart: a warmer, more southerly location; mainly acidic rather than alkaline soils suited to its dominant grape variety, Gamay Noir á Jus Blanc; and its distinctive wine styles. The annual production of 14.5 million cases nearly matches the total of Burgundy. More than a third is exported to leading markets such as Japan, the **United States**, **Germany**, and the **British market**. **Grape growing** is in the hands of smallholders, while 75 percent of sales pass through *négociants*. Beaujolais is divided into three categories: the 10 *crus,* which are marketed under their individual names (for example, Fleurie or Brouilly) and account for one-fourth of production; Beaujolais-Villages; and basic Beaujolais, accounting for half of production. A large share of the annual harvest is sold as Beaujolais Nouveau, which is fermented by a special technique (carbonic maceration) to obtain a grapey, soft red wine to be drunk young. Released each year just after the harvest, on the third Thursday of November, Nouveau became a modern marketing phenomenon—and a liability; the image of Nouveau has tarnished Beaujolais as a whole, exacerbated by overproduction and quality concerns. Total exports have declined by one-third since the late 1990s. This has led to mandatory **distillation** of unwanted wine and economic hardship for growers. The long-term viability of the Beaujolais "**brand**" will depend on cuts in production and greater emphasis on traditional wines, particularly the crus, supported by a regional marketing effort relying on image-building initiatives.

Beaune. There are four main appellations: Rully, Mercurey, and Givry, producing both whites and reds, and Montagny, solely white.

The *Mâconnais* is the southernmost subregion of Burgundy, adjoining Beaujolais (see the sidebar). Chardonnay dominates, with much smaller amounts of Gamay and Pinot Noir. The mainstay of Mâcon wines is a basic, tank-fermented Chardonnay intended for early consumption. Common appellations are Mâcon, Mâcon-Villages, or Mâcon hyphenated with the name of a village such as Lugny or Igé. This subregion also produces St. Véran and Pouilly-Fuissé, which obtains the highest price of Mâconnais whites.

Outlook. Burgundy is faced with commercial competition from the **New World**, particularly in Chardonnay. The region's iconic wines, however, produced in finite quantities, are likely to experience demand pressure from new global markets, and these luxury products will tend to increase further in price. **Climate change** could have profound effects. If temperatures continue to rise, Burgundy may no longer be within the range of optimal maturity for Pinot Noir, which would threaten the assumptions on which appellation rules are founded and could lead to such fundamental changes as the introduction of new grape varieties and wine styles.

Roger C. Bohmrich

Further Reading

Burgundy Wines. www.burgundy-wines.fr.

Coates, Clive. *Côte d'Or*. Berkeley: University of California Press, 1997.

Norman, Remington. *The Great Domaines of Burgundy*. 2nd ed. New York: Henry Holt, 1996.

Ribéreau-Gayon, Pascal, ed. *The Wines and Vineyards of France*. New York: Penguin, 1990.

C

CABERNET SAUVIGNON

Cabernet Sauvignon is arguably the king of red grape varieties. It is probably the source or at least an ingredient in more great **red wines** of the world than any other variety, most notably the wines of **Bordeaux** and many top wines from **California**, **Italy**, **Australia**, and elsewhere. Its longevity, depth of flavor, average price, and geographic scope cannot be matched by any other variety.

Cabernet Sauvignon has a recognizable flavor and aroma profile that is to a large extent independent of its place of origin. Black fruit (blackberries, black currants, boysenberries, black cherries) makes up the core, surrounded by accents that may be more origin dependent (eucalyptus, leather, tar, chocolate, bell pepper). Its small berries give a high skins-to-pulp ratio that results in intense flavor and color. The wines are usually quite tannic when young, with fairly **high alcohol content**. The acidity level, as usual, varies with the climate, decreasing for hotter regions. Top-quality Cabernet is often aged in oak **barrels**, gaining additional tannin and an overlay of vanilla and spice that melds well with the variety's own profile. In addition, it is common to blend in at least a small proportion of **Merlot** and perhaps Cabernet Franc to smooth some of Cabernet Sauvignon's hard edges and add further complexity (conversely, Cabernet Sauvignon is frequently added to Merlot wines to add backbone).

Bordeaux is Cabernet Sauvignon's hometown, and its lead role in the blends of most Médoc wines and all the first-growth châteaux of Bordeaux is by itself sufficient to place it near the front ranks of the red grape varieties. It is present in greater or lesser amounts in most red Bordeaux wines, but it is in the stony soils of the Médoc that it reigns supreme. About one-quarter of Bordeaux's vineyards, 68,800 acres, is planted with Cabernet Sauvignon. A similar amount is planted outside Bordeaux in the rest of **France**, mainly in the Languedoc. Altogether, France has 145,400 acres of Cabernet Sauvignon, a little less than a quarter of the world's total.

Because of Cabernet's importance to Bordeaux, it was transplanted to many new winegrowing areas around the world, and it has proven to be remarkably tolerant of different **terroirs**. Cabernet Sauvignon is one of the latest-ripening varieties and therefore thrives in places with warm to hot climates and long growing seasons. In Bordeaux, it is the last of the grapes harvested, and in some years, ripening the Cabernet Sauvignon can be a challenge (which is part of the reason the Bordelais hedge their bets with plenty of early-ripening Merlot). In places with warmer, sunnier climates, however, it flourishes, and it has become the most important red grape variety in most of the **New World** countries. **Chile** is particularly fond of Cabernet: its 101,000 acres represent almost a third of all of Chile's wine grapes.

Even in the Old World, the lure of Cabernet Sauvignon is strong. **Eastern Europe** has more than 85,000 acres of it, and it is what makes many Super Tuscans in Italy "super." **Spain** has had Cabernet in Ribera del Duero for well over a century, and it is now becoming more common in innovative regions in Catalunya and Navarre.

In the **United States**, Cabernet Sauvignon covers at least 85,000 acres, including 76,000 in California and 6,000 in **Washington**. The **Napa Valley** is renowned for its Cabernet and is considered the New World benchmark for this variety. The majority of the most expensive U.S. bottlings are of Cabernet Sauvignon or a Cabernet-led blend. According to *Adams Wine Handbook 2007*, Cabernet was the third most purchased **table wine** variety in the United States in 2006 (after **Chardonnay** and Merlot), with a 12 percent market share, but it climbed past Merlot in 2007. **Varietally labeled** Cabernet sales amounted to 26.8 million cases (mc), plus 1.1 mc of red Bordeaux. *See also* Cult Wines; Ratings and Scores.

CALIFORNIA

California has long been considered the epicenter of the U.S. wine industry—not surprisingly, considering that the state produces as much as 90 percent of the wine of the **United States** and that if California were a nation unto itself, it would rank fourth in world production. The pioneering nature of its early inhabitants spawned an industry full of innovation with the ideals of creating a wine industry that would rival anything else in the country and perhaps the world. California's growers and vintners were not content to produce average products, and as a result the industry has thrived in many ways.

History. Spanish missionaries brought viticulture to California's Catholic missions in the 1700s for production of sacramental wine, but the influence of some of the early immigrants to California after it became U.S. territory was more important to the wine industry. In the nineteenth century, Agoston Haraszthy brought cuttings to California's **Sonoma County** from Europe, and Gustave Niebaum was integral in introducing **Bordeaux** grapes to the California scene. Many immigrants from **Italy**, **Germany**, and elsewhere who were familiar with the quality of European wines used their resources to produce wines that had a foundation in traditional methods and grape varieties, but with a fresh face. Ties to these forefathers of the California wine industry run deep, as many venerable **wineries** still exist today; for example, the Wente family's fifth generation is now involved in the winery that was started in 1883 by German immigrant Carl H. Wente.

California forged ahead despite such crises as **phylloxera**, which devastated the vineyards—twice—and **Prohibition**. While the number of wineries was decreased dramatically by Prohibition, the dream of making exceptional wine from California did not die. **Robert Mondavi** was vital as a proponent of the quality of California wines, convincing many of his colleagues and neighbors to follow his lead and strive for quality. Aided by European winemakers such as André Tchelistcheff, vintners were able to revitalize the stagnant industry. The quality of California's wines was famously demonstrated at the Paris Wine Tasting of 1976 organized by Steven Spurrier, at which French judges gave their top votes to California wines in a blind tasting, proving that they rivaled the best that **France** had to offer.

Regions.   While California may inspire thoughts of sunshine and beaches, the diverse expanse of the state is significantly moderated not only by latitude, which ranges from 32° to 41°, but also by proximity to the ocean. Coastal ranges, valleys large and small, and the Sierra Nevada mountain range all combine to create a multitude of diverse aspects, geology, and microclimates that result in diversity and complexity from north to south.

The Central Valley, California's agricultural breadbasket, produces two-thirds of the state's wine grapes, as well as almost all of its table grapes and raisins. Most of this production goes into the large amount of inexpensive generic wines labeled as "California" or "American" wine—any wine labeled as being from California or any smaller region within California must contain 100 percent grapes from the state—or, as **bulk wine**, is blended in small quantities with other California American viticultural areas (AVAs), shipped to other states, or exported to other countries.

Within the state, several large AVAs exist; the huge Central Coast **appellation**, for example, covers 4 million acres and produces an eighth of California's grapes within its boundaries. However, California producers are now fine-tuning their **grape growing** and vinification to their specific vineyard conditions, and most producers are opting to use appellations that are more representative of their specific **terroir**. California currently has 107 recognized viticultural areas, with many more pending. There is an increased effort to designate AVAs by climatic boundaries, soil series, and moderating influences. For example, the Santa Rita Hills AVA encompasses the cooler parts of the Santa Ynez Valley AVA, and Mendocino Ridge is a unique discontinuous AVA delimited by elevation. In addition, a trend toward recognizing vineyards that consistently produce high-quality fruit has developed, as producers without their own land vie for the best lots of grapes—establishing names like Pisoni, Hyde, and Hudson as California's *crus*.

To ensure cohesiveness, allow for marketing opportunities, and create meaningful distinctions between AVAs, many regional trade organizations have popped up throughout California. **Napa Valley** Vintners (NVV), created in 1943, has even initiated an international program to protect place names globally, the "Joint Declaration to Protect Wine Place and Origin." It was also able to garner geographic indication status from the **European Union** to further protect the Napa Valley name.

California Wine Industry.   Wine is big business in California. The Wine Institute, an advocacy group for California wine, estimates that the wine industry's direct and indirect economic impact on the state is $45.4 billion and declares that "wine is California's most valuable finished agricultural product" (www.wineinstitute.org/resources/consumerfeaturedstories/article336). California had 475,000 acres under vine in 2006, 62 percent of that with red grape varieties.

The grape harvest in 2007 provided 3.24 million tons of wine grapes, led by **Chardonnay** (18 percent), **Cabernet Sauvignon** (13 percent), **Zinfandel** (12.5 percent), French Colombard (10 percent), and **Merlot** (9 percent).

Wine production in 2006 was 592 million gallons, the equivalent of 249 million nine-liter cases (mc), 181 mc of which was purchased by U.S. **consumers**; 65 percent of wine consumption in the United States is California wine, with a retail value of about $16.5 billion. A growing proportion of this wine goes straight to consumers via **direct shipping** and **e-commerce**. The state dominates U.S. wine exports as well, with 95 percent of the market. Furthermore, California is by far the largest wine-consuming state; home to 10 percent of the U.S. population, it accounts for about 50 mc or 18 percent of U.S. retail purchases, more than double second-place Florida.

While extremely **profitable**, the California wine industry is generous and is estimated to donate $73 million annually to charitable causes. Auction Napa Valley alone has raised nearly $78 million since its inception in 1981.

California's vintners and growers increasingly focus on "green" agriculture. Whether **sustainable**, **organic**, **biodynamic**, or a combination of the three, there is more and more emphasis on farming with consideration for the environment. The Wine Institute and the California Association of Winegrape Growers created the California Sustainable Winegrowing Alliance to encourage producers to self-assess their sustainability, and there are numerous local efforts like the Lodi-Woodbridge Winegrape Commission's Sustainable Viticulture Program. Many regions have made dramatic inroads into organic viticulture; Mendocino County is a leader in this category, holding 36 percent of the state's certified organic vineyard acreage. NVV has established the Napa Valley Green Winery initiative, a program to manage winery waste and reduce the use of natural resources; founded the nation's first agriculture preserve to protect open space and prevent development; opted to provide farmworker housing with monies from a self-assessed tax on vineyard acreage; and created a task force to address the threat of global **climate change**.

The 2,687 California wineries and their related support businesses generate substantial revenues through **wine tourism**, estimated at more than $1.3 billion spent by 14.8 million tourists annually. Recently the Wine Institute and the California Travel and Tourism Commission partnered to **promote** California wine and food. Regional organizations do more than just provide maps and tasting room guides; they also co-promote wine and tourism with such events as the Great Wine Escape Weekend hosted by the Monterey County Vintners and Growers Association.

Wine is further mingled with culture as producers combine wine and the arts, such as concerts at Robert Mondavi Winery and the Staglin Music Festival for Mental Health. Copia: The American Center for Wine, Food, and the Arts in Napa has many events and wine-related exhibits. Professional **wine education** classes are held at the Culinary Institute of America at Greystone, and Copia presents both professional and consumer courses. California also promotes the industry with viticulture and enology programs at its universities, such as the University of California at Davis, Sonoma State, and Fresno State.

California **cult wines** have made names for themselves internationally. And the wines are not the only stars—there are also celebrities who have become winemakers, such as filmmaker Francis Ford Coppola; iconic winemakers, such as Randall Grahm and, of course, Robert Mondavi himself; and even winemakers who have been turned into celebrities, such as Chateau Montelena's James L. Barrett, portrayed by actor Bill Pullman in *Bottle Shock,* a film about the 1976 Paris tasting.

The real reason behind the success of the California wine industry and the example it sets for other regions is the people. Too many to mention, the incredible richness of those who work in the industry in California is imbued with a spirit of camaraderie. Perhaps it derives from the trailblazing tradition of the West: in order to survive and succeed, incredible commitment was necessary, but even more important was cooperation. Amazingly diverse in many ways, California has uniquely managed to laud diversity while working as a team. *See also* Branding; Direct Shipping; High Alcohol Content; New World versus Old World; Ratings and Scores; Varietal Labeling.

Rebecca Chapa

Further Reading
Wine Institute. www.wineinstitute.org.

CANADA

Canada's importance to the **global wine industry** is largely based on its imports, 2.87 million hectoliters in 2006, the equivalent of 31.9 million nine-liter cases (mc). This made Canada the seventh largest wine-importing country in the world. Canada is also a small but rising wine producer, renowned especially for its ice wine.

Consumption.   In 2006, Canadians consumed 42.1 mc of wine, a per-capita rate of about 15 liters per adult—not a particularly high rate, but better than the level of the **United States**. **Table wine** preferences ran toward **red** (57 percent) over white (40 percent) and **rosé** (3 percent). **Sparkling wine** made up only about 3.1 percent of consumption, less than half the worldwide average.

Imported winemakes up three-quarters of the wine consumed and 61 percent of bottled wine sales. **France** has the largest market share, with 16.5 percent of all imported wine in 2006; French wines, which are particularly popular in Francophone Quebec, represented almost a quarter of bottled wine imports. **Italy** has traditionally been second, but **Australia** has been gaining fast and was able to overtake Italy in 2006. The United States was fourth in the import market at about a 10 percent share. Conversely, Canada was the United States' second largest destination for exports, amounting to more than 18 percent of U.S. wine shipments to other countries.

Market Structure.   Canada is essentially a monopoly market, although the monopolists are the provinces rather than the federal government. With the exception of Alberta, which privatized its alcohol retail and distribution sectors in 1993, each provincial government is the sole **importer** and **distributor** within its jurisdiction. The liquor control board of Quebec, as the largest wine-consuming province, is one of the largest wine-purchasing entities in the world, with wine sales of C$1.6 billion in fiscal year 2006/2007. **Wineries** from other countries must apply to each provincial liquor control board, normally through a Canadian agent, in order to get listed as being available for possible orders by retail outlets (similar to the way many U.S. **control states** operate).

The provinces (other than Alberta) control not only importation and wholesaling but also liquor retailing. However, wine is often not as strictly controlled as spirits. Wine may be available through both government stores and private **retailers**, such as **supermarkets**, grocery stores, convenience stores, and sometimes licensed wine shops. In addition, Canadian wineries can generally sell their own wines at the winery or in winery stores.

Some provinces, such as Quebec, also control a significant portion of production, importing and bottling **bulk wine** to compete with both bottled imports and domestic Canadian wine. Nationally, wine sales in 2006 amounted to C$4.61 billion, of which 69 percent was almost evenly split between Quebec and Ontario, with British Columbia adding another 15 percent.

Production.   Canada's winemaking history parallels that of the United States, minus the Spanish influence in **California**. Early attempts to make wine with imported European cuttings during the **colonial era** were generally unsuccessful, but subsequently a thriving local trade developed in the eastern provinces around native American and hybrid grape varieties, for the most part in sweet and/or **fortified** styles. In more recent times, cool-climate vinifera grapes were reintroduced and, with **phylloxera**-resistant rootstocks and proper vineyard management, were successful.

The primary **grape-growing** region is the southernmost part of Ontario, especially the Niagara Peninsula between lakes Erie and Ontario. Ontario has 16,000 acres of wine grapes and is the source of 80 percent of Canada's total grape production, including table and juice grapes. Some 63 percent of the province's grapes are vinifera, of which the principal varieties are **Chardonnay**, Cabernet Franc, and **Riesling**. Harvests in Ontario can be extremely variable due to weather. For example, the very cold winter of 2004/2005 resulted in serious crop damage and a harvest only a third the size of the 2006 vintage. About 700 acres of vineyards are also found in Quebec and Nova Scotia.

The rest of Canada's wine is made in British Columbia. As with **Washington** just to the south, only a small fraction of British Columbia's wine grapes come from the cool, rainy west of the province; some 97 percent are from across the Coast Mountains range (the northward continuation of the Cascades), where conditions are much drier. The Okanagan Valley in south-central British Columbia is an extension of the Columbia Valley of eastern Washington, with similar growing conditions. Grapes were introduced here in the mid-nineteenth century, but there were only 13 wineries in the valley by 1984, growing mostly hybrids. Twenty years later, however, there were 90 wineries, and thanks to a massive replanting program in the early 1990s that replaced most of the hybrids with international vinifera varieties, the Okanagan Valley has since earned a reputation for fine wines, especially reds. The valley had almost 5,500 acres of vines planted as of 2004. British Columbia's production is overwhelmingly vinifera, with the primary varieties being **Merlot**, Chardonnay, **Pinot Gris**, Pinot Blanc, **Pinot Noir**, **Cabernet Sauvignon**, and Gewürztraminer.

Altogether, Canadian wineries produced a little over 10 mc of wine in 2006. However, because a wine labeled as "Canadian" wine may contain up to 75 percent imported bulk wine content, the amount of Canadian wine sold was officially 16.4 mc.

Canada has a **quality wine** certification program based on standards set by the Vintners Quality Alliance (VQA). The VQA standards are in effect a voluntary **appellation** system that is closer to the European model than most **New World** systems. In order to be allowed to put the VQA logo on a wine, the wine must be from grapes grown in a designated Canadian quality wine region, follow stipulations for harvest and winemaking, meet higher standards of **varietal labeling** and content, and be screened for quality by a tasting panel. VQA wines account for about 20 percent of Ontario's wine and perhaps half of British Columbia's.

If any one wine defines Canadian production, it is ice wine—in Canada, typically spelled *icewine*—a sweet **dessert wine** made from late-harvest grapes that freeze on the vine and are picked and pressed while still frozen. In 2006, about 150,000 cases of ice wine was produced, roughly half of that qualifying as VQA. The majority of Canadian ice wines are made from the hybrid Vidal.

Exports are a relatively small category, around 800,000 cases total in 2006, valued at C$32 million. The United States is the destination for two-thirds of these wines, and most of the rest goes to **Asia**, particularly Taiwan.

Further Reading

Schreiner, John. *Wines of Canada*. London: Mitchell Beazley, 2005.
Vintners Quality Alliance Ontario. www.vqaontario.com.
Wines of British Columbia. www.winebc.com.

CHAMPAGNE

Champagne is the standard against which all **sparkling wines** are measured. Currently, the production of Champagne represents the equivalent of more than 25 million nine-liter cases (mc), about 15 percent of the global sparkling wine category. In 2006, Champagne sales amounted to 26.8 mc, valued at €4.12 billion. Champagne's boom of the early 2000s has led to changes in the **appellation**'s yield, as well as to a probable moderate increase of the appellation area. In 2006, the area in production was 79,900 acres. Meanwhile, the price of Champagne on the shelves has been rapidly increasing.

History.   The first mentions of sparkling Champagne are provided by late seventeenth-century English literature. At first completely haphazard, the production of Champagne slowly improved by trial and error. The advent of cork and heavy glass bottles in the late 1660s made it possible to bottle the spirited wine, leading to its adoption by the royal courts first of **France** and England and then of the rest of Europe. At the time, sparkling Champagne was considered a disgrace by some of the local wine brokers and merchants, and it took a while for it to become the mainstay of the local trade. Nevertheless, the fashion of drinking sparkling Champagne spread from the royal courts to all those who could afford it. By the late nineteenth century, Champagne was being shipped around the world.

Vineyards.   Three grape varieties dominate Champagne's vineyards and wines: **Pinot Noir** (38 percent of plantings), Pinot Meunier (33 percent), and **Chardonnay** (28 percent). In 2007, there were 319 villages in the Champagne appellation. Based on the current appellation review program, another 40 villages will be added and 2 dropped. However, it is not clear at this writing how much acreage will be added. In any case, this program will not have an impact on the production area until 2017.

The vineyards are rated along an *échelle des crus*. In Champagne, unlike **Burgundy**, a *cru* is a village. Among these villages, 17 are recognized as *grands crus* and 44 as *premiers crus*. With a few exceptions, vineyards in the grands crus are planted only with Chardonnay or Pinot Noir.

The Champagne Trade.   Historically, the growers used to cultivate the vineyards and sell their grapes to **négociants**, usually with brokers facilitating the exchange. During a severe crisis in the 1920s, a few growers started to produce their own Champagnes, and others pooled their strengths together to establish the first growers' cooperatives. In the 1950s and 1960s, many more growers applied themselves to producing Champagne and many new cooperatives came to life.

As of 2006, there were 15,300 *vignerons* or growers. Altogether, the growers own 90 percent of the vineyards and sell a little over half of the harvest to the négociants. The wines are produced by 284 négociants or Champagne houses and 140 cooperatives.

The Champagne houses sold 18.1 mc in 2006, though they own only about 8,000 acres of vineyards. They buy the majority of their grapes from multiple growers with whom they have contracts. They also purchase bottles from growers and cooperatives. The five largest houses are responsible for close to 25 percent of total sales. All the houses were family owned until the 1950s, but today only a handful are, and a few large corporate groups dominate the trade. The largest, LVMH (Moët Hennessy Louis Vuitton), was responsible for almost a fifth of global Champagne sales in 2006.

The domestic French market accounted for 56 percent of Champagne's sales in 2006. The largest export market was the United Kingdom (2.45 mc, or 11.4 percent of total sales), followed by the **United States** (1.92 mc), **Germany** (1.02 mc), Belgium (775,000 cases), **Italy** (774,000 cases), and Japan (668,000 cases). Growth has been particularly strong in the United States and Japan.

Nonvintage Champagne, made with wines from several grape varieties and including a variable amount of reserve wine, is the mainstay of production and comprises 87 percent of export sales. Prestige cuvées, which can be nonvintage or vintage, make up 4.8 percent of exports. Most Champagnes are brut or drier—less than 15 grams per liter of residual sugar. The slightly sweeter, "extra dry" category accounts for just 3.3 percent of export sales, nearly all of which goes to the United States, where it represents almost 20 percent of the market.

Champagne benefits from a very well-organized, active, and powerful trade association, the Comité Interprofessionnel du vin de Champagne (CIVC). Established in 1941, the CIVC's status was revised and strengthened by law in 2007. Its role is extensive and includes relations between growers and houses, pursuit of quality, and **promotion** and protection of the Champagne appellation.

Outlook.   The challenges of the future for Champagne are many. One is the limited supply of grapes. Champagne has been caught for years in a volume growth strategy. The region will need to find a balance between expansion and quality, or else the divide will widen between the houses and growers who are devoted to producing wines that are truly characterful and exciting and those whose wines are characterless, mass-produced, and commercial. As this gap grows, the price spectrum will also increase between the former and the latter, and many of the mass-market Champagnes will be relying on **supermarket** sales.

The postmillennium crash in demand has been followed by a quick-paced rebound, with much interest in prestige cuvées and **rosés**. However, with the many woes affecting global markets, the U.S. economy in particular, demand for luxury products is likely to be affected. As Champagne prices have increased— at an even faster pace in the United States due to the **exchange rate** weakness of the dollar—sparkling alternatives have become more attractive to consumers. Many think these wines provide better value for the money, especially since more and more sparkling wines deliver a level of quality that is close and occasionally superior to that of ordinary Champagnes.

The future success of Champagne relies on quality—not just technical quality, which by and large is achieved by all, but an ability to express **terroir** and cause emotions—to remain the standard for all sparkling wines and preserve its place in the hearts and minds of consumers. This pursuit of quality needs to be unrelenting and sustainable.

Jean-Louis Carbonnier

Further Reading
CIVC. www.champagne.com.
Juhlin, Richard. *4,000 Champagnes*. Paris: Flammarion, 2005.
McCarthy, Ed. *Champagne for Dummies*. Foster City, CA: IDG Books, 1999.

CHARDONNAY

The most widely planted quality white grape in the world, Chardonnay is grown in almost every wine-producing country. It is the mainstay of white wine production in the **New World**. Chardonnay is a relatively hardy grape variety that is fairly tolerant of growing conditions. It produces a fairly neutral wine that takes particularly well to oak aging.

There are three archetypes of Chardonnay. First, Chardonnay is renowned as the white grape of **Burgundy**, where it produces some of the most respected— and most expensive—white wines in the world. White Burgundies are typically medium- to full-bodied and dry, with medium acidity and alcohol. With some bottle age, their aromas can become quite complex, featuring earthy notes along with the characteristic aromas of apples and citrus. Wines from Chablis in the north of Burgundy tend to be a bit sharper in acid and more austere. The great *grand cru* Burgundies from the Côte de Beaune are unusually long-lived for a white wine and over time develop tremendous complexity that makes them among the most sought after of wines.

Also in the Old World, Chardonnay is the white grape of **Champagne**, where the cool climate results in grapes with much higher acidity and less flavor development. Blanc de Blancs Champagne, made from only Chardonnay, is creamier, paler, and more delicate than the other styles made partially or entirely from red grapes. The majority of **sparkling wine** producers throughout the world use Chardonnay as one of their primary blending grapes.

The third archetypical Chardonnay is the New World style made in **California** or **Australia**. Produced in warmer, sunnier climates, these Chardonnays are fuller bodied, deeper colored, higher in alcohol, and just generally bolder than most Old World Chardonnays. More often than not, these wines are aged for a time in oak **barrels** or with alternatives to oak barrels, such as wood chips, to absorb flavor components from the wood; in such wines, the oak-induced vanilla, caramel, and butterscotch aromas tend to dominate the mild natural aromas of the Chardonnay itself. New World Chardonnays tend to have lower natural acidity and produce a rich, buttery, creamy style of wine. A marginally perceptible amount of residual sugar may be left in the wine to add to the body. The entire package of a New World Chardonnay often presents a blockbuster white wine that seemingly has nothing in common with a Burgundy.

Despite the fame and respect the top Burgundies have achieved, the New World style has been more popular with **consumers** for decades—especially in the New World countries that produce these wines. Chardonnay is by far the most purchased **table wine** variety in the **United States**, with a 23 percent market share of all wines in 2006, according to *Adams Wine Handbook 2007*. Among **varietally labeled** white wines, it represents two-thirds of sales. White Burgundies also continue to have a strong following, but their variability between vintages and producers, their small volume by comparison, and of course the prices of the best Burgundian examples tend to keep the ranks of the Old World–style purchasers in check. This has prompted substantial investment in New World–style Chardonnays in sunnier European areas, especially Languedoc-Roussillon, which has about a quarter of French Chardonnay acreage. At the same time, many producers in the New World, especially in cooler areas such as **Oregon**, **Sonoma County**, and **New Zealand**, continue to seek what is often considered the "Holy Grail" of white winemaking: a truly Burgundian Chardonnay.

Chardonnay is planted on roughly 400,000 acres worldwide, with the largest amounts found in **France** (106,000 acres), the United States (100,000, of which California has 95,000), and Australia (77,000). It is well represented in all the New World countries, but has been slowly spreading in Europe, too. Long planted across the north of **Italy** and in Tuscany, Chardonnay has been a permissible variety in Cava since 1986, in **Germany** since 1991, and in white Rioja since 2007.

To many casual wine drinkers, "Chardonnay" and "white wine" are nearly interchangeable terms. This is unlikely to change anytime soon because no other pretender to the throne has the same versatility, power, and neutrality. The battle will be waged in breaking the monolithic front of this grape variety into stylistic variations—oak or no oak, medium alcohol or **high alcohol content**, crisp or soft, earthy or fruity—so consumers can begin to focus on which Chardonnays they really like and to recognize the usefulness in adding other grapes to their wine racks. *See also* Cult Wines; Ratings and Scores.

Further Reading
Broom, Dave. *Chardonnay: A Complete Guide to the Grape and the Wines It Produces.*
London: Mitchell Beazley, 2003.

CHILE

Chile is the 10th largest wine producer in the world, with 8.45 million hectoliters—the equivalent of 94 million cases (mc)—produced in 2006. Significantly, it is the fifth largest wine exporter. Chile began exporting wine only in the early 1980s and quickly became one of the world's most important suppliers of wines, known for great value and consistent quality. As the result of significant international investment of capital and expertise from some of the industry's most highly regarded producers, quality has improved dramatically.

In 2006, Chile exported just over half of its total production, 48 mc, valued at $960 million. Of this, a third was **bulk wine**; bottled exports totaled 31.9 mc, worth $860 million. Preliminary figures for 2007 show exports increasing by 28 percent in volume and 29 percent in value. Great Britain is Chile's largest trading partner, importing 9.0 mc of bottled wine in 2007. The **United States** was second at 6.6 mc, with **Canada**, **Germany**, and Brazil rounding out the top five.

Wine consumption in Chile in 2005 was estimated at 30.4 mc and per-capita consumption was 22.5 liters. This is nearly all domestic wine; imports are minimal.

History.   Wine grapes arrived in South America with the missionaries who accompanied the Spanish conquistadors and are thought to have been brought to Chile by ship about 1548. As elsewhere in the Americas, the first vines were undoubtedly the variety known in Chile as País and in **California** as Mission. Other, higher-quality vinifera varieties from **France** were imported for experimental purposes in the early 1800s. The test vineyards were a success, and commercial vineyards were soon planted with the French varieties in the Maipo Valley around Santiago.

For the next century and a half, Chile remained a quiet outpost of **grape growing** in the **New World**, supplying local demand and ships stopping on their way around Cape Horn. Through its relative isolation, Chile managed to avoid the **phylloxera** devastation that crippled almost every other winegrowing region in the world in the late nineteenth century. Grape growing spread north and south from Santiago.

Within the last quarter-century, Chile has been rediscovered by the wine industry. The combination of California-like climate and low land and labor costs made Chile a prime location for foreign investment. Many joint ventures were initiated, bringing winemaking expertise and capital for new plantings and modern **winery** facilities. The quality and low prices of Chilean wine were quickly noticed by buyers in wine-importing countries, and Chile rapidly moved from obscurity to its current status among the top exporting countries.

Grape Varieties.   Chile's acreage under vine was 472,000 acres as of 2005, 11th in the world (313,000 acres of wine grapes). The most widely planted varieties for wine production in Chile are **Cabernet Sauvignon**, **Merlot**, Carmenere, **Syrah**, **Sauvignon Blanc**, and **Chardonnay**. However with the emergence of several new cool-climate coastal areas, plantings of Sauvignon Blanc, **Pinot Noir**, and Syrah are increasing rapidly. País is still widely grown, primarily for **distillation** into *pisco* brandy.

While the typical international varieties have been the source of Chile's exporting success, Carmenere is considered by some to be the country's best chance to distinguish itself with a signature wine. Carmenere is a grape that was a substantial contributor to many of the top-rated **Bordeaux** wines in the mid-1800s, but it was a difficult variety to ripen in Bordeaux's climate and therefore was not replanted there after the phylloxera years. Long believed to be extinct, Carmenere was rediscovered in Chile in the mid-1990s, where it had been thought to be a late-ripening clone of Merlot. In Chile's more hospitable climate, Carmenere has great potential.

Regions.   From a wine standpoint, Chile's topography is reminiscent of California's North Coast. The Central Valley of Chile is like the **Napa Valley**—if the Napa Valley were 1,000 miles long. Running parallel to the coast, where the ocean is dominated by a cold current, the Central Valley has cooling breezes to keep temperatures manageable, but is protected from the coastal overcast and fogs by a range of low mountains. Numerous basins within the Central Valley provide slight variations on the climate, primarily based on their latitude. From north to south, the most important of these commercially are the Aconcagua, Maipo, Rapel (including Cachapoal and Colchagua), Maule, and Curicó valleys. Maipo has the longest history and most of the oldest properties, but as Santiago grows, winemaking is slowly being pushed out into other areas. The largest areas of production are in the southerly, and therefore cooler, Maule and Curicó valleys.

More recently, plantings have been greatly increased in areas where the coastal range is relatively low, giving more direct access to the cooling atmospheric conditions more like western **Sonoma** or Mendocino County in California. These areas, mostly notably the Casablanca and San Antonio valleys, are well suited for white varieties and Pinot Noir.

Outlook.   With continued foreign investment, Chile's wine regions are expanding in search of new **terroir**. Given the global **climate change** and a demand for more cool-climate vineyards, the coastal regions, which are still sparsely planted, as well as new southerly areas in the Itata and Bío-Bío valleys, will see new development. In Chile's benign growing conditions, more and more producers are farming **organically** and **biodynamically**. The quality of Chilean wine has increased considerably in the past decade and is expected to continue to be propelled upward. Exports, driven by the marketing organization Wines of Chile, will continue to increase and move into new markets.

Bruce Schneider

Further Reading

Hernandez, Alejandro M. *Chile Vitivinicola* [in Spanish]. Buin, Chile: Vitivinicola Los Reyes, 2006.

Richards, Peter. *The Wines of Chile*. London: Mitchell Beazley, 2006.

Tapia, Patricio. *Descorchados 2008: Guía de Vinos de Chile* [in Spanish]. Santiago, Chile: Planeta, 2007.

Waldin, Monty. *The Wines of South America*. London: Mitchell Beazley, 2003.
Wines of Chile. www.winesofchile.org.

CHINA. *See* Asia

CLIMATE CHANGE

Climate is a very complex, highly variable, and pervasive factor in our natural Earth and human-based systems. From controlling vegetation patterns and geological weathering characteristics to influencing water resources and agricultural productivity, climate is at the heart of the delicate equilibrium that exists on Earth. While it is clear from historical evidence that changing climates are a part of the Earth's natural adjustments to both internal and external forces (for example, volcanic eruptions and solar variability), more and more evidence is pointing to increasing human impacts on our climate. Processes such as desertification, deforestation, and urbanization, by which the global energy balance is disrupted, and changes in atmospheric composition that enhance the greenhouse effect beyond its natural equilibrium demonstrate that our role in climate change is increasing.

Evidence for contemporary climate change exists in many parts of the Earth system, including widespread reductions in sea ice and glacier extent, increased frequency of temperature and precipitation extremes, changes in drought severity, rising sea level, and numerous alterations in terrestrial and marine ecosystems. Although changes in these components have always occurred throughout Earth's history, the rate of warming today appears to be greater than anything experienced over the last 1,000 years, with the warming of the last 25 years nearly four times faster than over the last 150 years and the majority of the last 20 years being the warmest ever recorded.

In terms of agriculture, climate is a wide-ranging factor that influences where and how a crop is grown and also largely determines year-to-year yield and quality variability. The grapevine is one of the oldest cultivated plants, and along with the process of making wine, it has generated a rich geographical and cultural history. Our knowledge of this history has shown that wine-grape-growing regions developed when and where the climate was most conducive and that shifts in viable wine-producing regions have occurred due to climatic changes, making production easier (Medieval Optimum) or more difficult (Little Ice Age).

Observations and projections show that climate change impacts on viticulture and wine production are mostly evidenced through more rapid plant growth and out-of-balance ripening profiles. If a region experiences a maturation period (veraison to harvest) that allows sugars to accumulate to favorable levels, maintains acid structure, and produces the optimum flavor profile for that variety, then balanced wines result. In a warmer than ideal environment, however, the grapevine will go through its growth cycle more rapidly, resulting in earlier and likely higher sugar ripeness and greater loss of acidity through respiration as the grower or winemaker waits for the flavors to develop. This leads to unbalanced wines without greater after-harvest inputs or **must or wine adjustments** in the winery.

Given the warming trends, **higher alcohol content** levels over the last 30 years have been observed in many regions (for example, up 2.5 percent for white wines in Alsace, 1.6 percent for **red wines** in **Australia**, and 2.3 percent for **Cabernet Sauvignon** in the **Napa Valley**), while acid levels typically fell and pH climbed. While one could argue that this trend is due to the tendency for bigger, bolder wines driven by **wine writers**' preferences and the economics of vintage **rating** systems, other research has clearly found that climate change is responsible for much of the trend in alcohol levels either directly through warmer environments or indirectly by allowing "hang time" through longer growing seasons. Finally, harvests that occur earlier in the summer, in a warmer part of the growing season, result in fruit picked in hotter conditions, leading to a "dual warming impact" on fruit quality.

The growing-season warming over the last 50 years of 1.0–1.5°C (1.8–2.7°F) observed in the majority of the world's wine regions appears to have been largely beneficial for viticulture through longer and warmer growth periods with less risk of frost. The trends have been influential in cooler regions by providing more consistent ripening climates for existing varieties, making warmer-climate varieties more viable, or opening up once forgotten regions again. On the other extreme, already hot regions have experienced warmer and generally drier conditions that have produced challenges in ripening balanced fruit. Concomitant with the warming trends have come better technology, better plant material, and better vineyard management, and these adaptations have allowed growers to meet some of these challenges. However, projections for the future reveal climate changes that are likely to be more rapid and to a greater magnitude than our ability to adapt without increased understanding of the impacts and advances in plant breeding and genetics.

Given the knowledge of climate change today, some believe that society's role should shift from one of uncertainties, blame, or attribution to one of mitigation and adaptation. While the wine industry has some leeway to mitigate fossil fuel use and sequester carbon through more efficient processes both in the vineyard and the winery, the bulk of the response will likely be through adaptation. Because wine grapes can be grown across only a fairly narrow range of climates for optimum quality and production, a region's outlook all depends on where it is today in terms of climate and on the magnitude and rate of the future warming. The climatic tolerance for **quality wine** for most varieties appears to be just 2–3°C (3.5–5°F), so with projections of temperature increases around the world ranging as high as 7°C (12.5°F), there is the potential for large shifts in regional suitability of varieties and wine styles.

While most of the discussion regarding climate change has focused on temperature-related impacts, other potential issues affecting grape and wine quality include changes in vine growth due to a higher carbon dioxide concentration in the atmosphere, added moisture stresses in water-limited regions, and changes in the presence or intensity of pests and vine diseases. Even with the current state of knowledge, much uncertainty still exists in the exact spatial and temporal nature of changes in climate, and therefore the wine industry will need to be proactive in assessing the impacts, be ready to implement appropriate adaptation strategies, be willing to alter varieties and management practices or controls, or mitigate wine quality differences by developing new technologies. *See also* Temperature Control; Terroir.

Gregory V. Jones

Further Reading

Gladstones, J. *Viticulture and Environment*. Adelaide, Australia: Winetitles, 1992.

Intergovernmental Panel on Climate Change. *Climate Change 2007: The Physical Science Basis*. Cambridge: Cambridge University Press, 2007. www.ipcc.ch.

Jones, Gregory V. "Climate Change." Proceedings of the Australian Wine Industry Technical Conference, Adelaide, Australia, August 2007.

Jones, G., M. White, O. Cooper, and K. Storchmann, "Climate Change and Global Wine Quality." *Climatic Change* 73 (2005): 319-43.

Ladurie, Emmanuel Le Roy. *Times of Feast, Times of Famine*. Garden City, NY: Doubleday, 1971.

CLOSURES

Natural cork bark has been the default wine bottle closure for close to three centuries. Of the approximately 20 billion wine bottle closures produced every year, around 80 percent are either natural corks or so-called technical corks made principally from cork bark. However, increasing dissatisfaction with cork's performance has seen the rise of a number of alternatives, chief among them synthetic (or plastic) corks (currently 12.5 percent of the total market) and, growing fastest of all, screw caps (7.5 percent).

Corks.   The cork oak (*Quercus suber*) grows throughout the western Mediterranean, but commercial production of natural corks developed in three countries, **Portugal**, **Spain**, and Algeria. Today, Portugal dominates the cork industry, producing over half of the world's supply. The Portuguese cork industry association APCOR (Associação Portuguesa da Cortiça) boasts more than 170 members, a lot of them small, family-owned businesses. APCOR's biggest member (and the world's largest single producer of cork-based closures) is Corticeira Amorim, with an annual turnover approaching €500 million.

Natural cork's elasticity and impermeability are ideal properties for a bottle stopper, as is the fact that it is relatively inert and hence does not generally scalp aromas or flavors from the wine. However, natural cork may be affected by a series of different taints (chief among them 2,4,6-trichloroanisole, or TCA, the compound that spoils a wine said to be "corked"), and occasionally corks fail to protect the wine from oxidation. Corks range in price—depending on quality, length, and volume purchased—from around 6 to 50 cents each, averaging about 9 cents.

To maximize the use of lower-grade bark or cork granules and to reduce the incidence of **cork taint**, the industry has developed a series of technical corks, starting with the agglomerate cork over a century ago. APCOR's Twin Top is a popular and inexpensive brand, an agglomerate of glued cork particles to which has been added twin disks of natural cork at either end.

In 1995, Oeneo Bouchage (formerly Sabaté) launched the Altec cork, a mixture of treated cork dust and an inert polymer. However, rather than reducing TCA levels, it actually increased them. In response, the company went back to the drawing board and developed Diam. Made from cork flour treated with supercritical carbon dioxide, this latest technical cork is selling well in markets where the debate over cork taint has been vociferous. Technical corks cost about 4 to 12 cents each.

Synthetic Corks.   Synthetic or plastic corks have been in development for many years, but first began to be taken seriously in the early 1990s with the release of SupremeCorq in the **United States**. Along with the other pioneering synthetic cork, Integra, SupremeCorq was produced with a one-piece injection mold design. These early injection-molded synthetics proved difficult to extract from the bottle, as well as providing too much oxygen transfer and thus causing premature oxidation in the bottle.

Nowadays the better-performing synthetic corks, such as Neocork or Nomacork, both with lower oxygen transmission rates and ease of extraction, are generally those made via an extrusion process. Synthetic corks are cheaper than natural corks and the same price or less expensive than most technical corks. Synthetics have been most successful in the United States.

Screw Caps.   Roll-on metal screw caps were first invented over a century ago, although their application in the alcoholic beverage industry was largely restricted to spirits, **fortified wines**, cheap jug wine, and bottles for **airlines**. The French company Bouchage Mecanique first developed a screw cap for wine bottles in the 1960s. In the early 1970s, trials on this closure, dubbed Stelcap, began in both **Australia** and **Switzerland**, and in 1976, several Australian wineries began using it for a limited range of wines. But despite a glowing endorsement from the Australian trials, most stopped using it, and only in Switzerland during the 1980s did screw caps take off.

In 1998 legendary Australian winemaker (and one of the veterans of the original trials) John Vickery began bottling a wine under screw cap, and in 2000, a group of winemakers in South Australia's Clare Valley decided to bottle some of their **Riesling** production with screw caps, cooperating in order to import a shipment of suitable bottles. Inspired by this group, **New Zealand** winemakers established the New Zealand Screwcap Wine Seal Initiative in 2001, again to share the costs, but also to study and **promote** the changeover to screw caps. These winemakers were as concerned about random (or sporadic) oxidation—an area where screw caps have an inherent advantage over stoppers, natural or otherwise—as they were about cork taint. The initiative was very successful, and currently over 90 percent of all New Zealand wines are bottled under screw cap.

Until recently, most of the caps have used the same inner liner, a polyethylene wad coated with PVDC (polyvinylidene dichloride) with an impermeable tin liner. It is now alleged that this tin lining may contribute to the production of hydrogen sulfide (H_2S) and other off-odors in the bottle. This debate has raged for some time, and further research is needed.

Alcan Packaging's Stelvin is the market leader around the world, but there are other successful brands, such as GlobalCap (from **Italian** conglomerate Guala Closures) and Auscap. Screw caps cost around half as much as the lowest-grade natural cork, and there is an additional cost benefit in doing away with the enclosing foil or plastic capsule. However, in certain countries (most notably Italy), regulations prohibit the use of screw caps on wines marketed under **appellation** names.

Other Alternatives.   The Australian-designed and -made Zork is an all-in-one synthetic stopper and tamper-evident cap that provides the feeling (and sound) of a cork, with the convenience of not needing a corkscrew. Zork is slightly more expensive than a screw cap, but cheaper than high-grade cork, and has been seen on a small number of Australian brands and a few others internationally.

Vino-Lok is an elegant **German** product that fits snugly into the bottle: a glass stopper with an embedded plastic seal, protected by a tamper-proof capsule. The biggest drawback to Vino-Lok is that, like screw caps, it requires a specially molded bottle, which is produced by very few bottle manufacturers. Vino-Lok is currently several times more expensive than screw caps and is mostly seen on a few high-profile German wine brands.

The pressure inside **sparkling wine** bottles means they generally require a large, rigidly constructed technical cork. Yet most bottle-fermented sparklers spend some period under a crown seal, similar to the closures used on beer bottles. To eliminate cork taint, Australian producer Domaine Chandon has released several vintages of its ultrapremium zero-dosage sparkling wine under crown cap to widespread acclaim.

Issues.   Consumer and industry acceptability of alternative closures varies widely from country to country. The biggest unknown is how well wines develop and age under the different closures, and this will probably not be answered for some years. The understanding of how wine evolves in the bottle is incomplete, and the chemistry involved is very complex. What is evident is that wine under screw cap retains its fresh, fruity character longer than under stoppers.

There are a number of contentious environmental issues surrounding closures. The major cork companies in Portugal and Spain have suggested that a worldwide switch away from natural cork would lead to cork forests being felled, with the potential loss of rare animal species. However, as a number of these forests are in public hands, it is unclear whether they would be affected. More recent debate has centered on the carbon footprint of various closures, but if wine companies are truly serious about reducing their carbon dioxide emissions and helping to fight **climate change**, then weighty glass bottles are a much more serious problem than the relatively small and light closures that seal them. A more pressing environmental issue is that aluminum screw caps, along with their sleeves left behind on the bottle, are not being systematically recycled—but then neither are synthetic or natural corks. *See also* Alternative Packaging.

Paul Tudor

Further Reading
Goode, Jamie. *Wine Bottle Closures*. London: WinePress, 2006.
Taber, George. *To Cork or Not to Cork*. New York: Scribner, 2007.

COLONIAL ERA

The period during which Europeans colonized much of the non-European world (about 1500–1800), variously called "the Age of Discovery" and "the Age of Sail," saw important developments in the wine industry. From being concentrated in Europe, wine production was gradually extended throughout the Americas from the early 1500s to the late 1700s and beyond to **South Africa** in the mid-1600s, **Australia** in the late 1700s, and **New Zealand** in the mid-1800s. At the same time, new styles of wine and technologies of transportation were developed to allow for the more successful long-distance movement of wine.

Before this time, wine had been transported over extensive distances from vineyards to markets, sometimes overland, but generally by water. River and coastal shipping were less expensive than land and easier on barrels than carts with wooden or iron wheels traveling over unpaved roads. Wine traveled rivers from the Mediterranean to Russia, was shipped down the Rhine to the North Sea ports, and followed the coasts to the Baltic ports.

But there were constant problems of transportation, and the wine (which was frequently unstable and in any case was intended to last only a year) frequently reached its destination in poor condition. The most successful trading route was the substantial traffic in wine from **Bordeaux** to England and northern Europe that began in the thirteenth century. Sailing ships could make the voyage from Bordeaux to London in as short a time as a week, depending on weather conditions, but voyages much longer than that put wine at risk.

Various methods were used to slow the spoilage of wine. The **Dutch**, who were preeminent as shippers in the 1600s, burned sulfur in the barrels as a conservation measure. But a more common solution was to fortify wine with brandy and thus raise its alcohol level and extend its longevity. Brandy itself entered the commercial mainstream of Europe in the 1500s, thanks to the spread of information on **distilling** and the Dutch sponsorship of the brandy industry in the Charente region of western **France**.

Among the most important new **fortified wines** were Sherry from the Jerez region of southern **Spain** and Port from the valley of the Douro in **Portugal**, both initially developed for the English market. Other fortified wines were produced on the islands of Sicily, Cyprus, and Madeira. The keeping properties of fortified wine were so impressive that when wine industries were developed in South Africa, Australia, and New Zealand, much of the early wine was fortified in the style of Sherry and Port.

Far from all wine was fortified, however, and where it could be safely transported, it was left unfortified. The important trade between Bordeaux and England continued through this period, although there were interruptions at times when war hampered trade. The scale of the Bordeaux trade was immense. It peaked in 1687, when 15,500 tuns, or nearly 18 million liters (the equivalent of 2 million cases) of wine were **imported**, enough for three and a half liters for each man, woman, and child in England.

England and northern Europe imported wine because they were climatically unsuited to extensive viticulture, but that was not so in many of the lands colonized by the European powers from the 1500s. Viticulture spread to these regions in a variety of ways. When New Spain (Mexico) was settled in the 1520s, Spanish colonists who received grants of land and slaves were required to plant vines. Apart from some northern areas and Baja California, however, Mexico and the rest of Central America proved inhospitable to **grape growing**. But as the Spanish armies swept through South America, the Jesuit missionaries who accompanied them identified suitable sites, and they successfully established vineyards in the territories that later became Peru, **Chile**, and **Argentina**.

This new colonial industry was opposed by wine producers in Spain, who sensed that they were losing considerable export possibilities. However, it proved impractical to ship wine across the Atlantic, and the wine often arrived spoiled. By the 1600s, a large wine industry in Peru, Chile, and Argentina (and a brandy industry in Peru) was supplying the Spanish and indigenous populations of Latin America with the bulk of their wine needs.

In the second half of the eighteenth century, Franciscan missionaries (who replaced the Jesuits when they were expelled from Mexico) began to establish missions and vineyards in the northern reaches of **California**. It remained isolated and marginal until the population boom of the Gold Rush in the mid-1800s and the completion of the railroad to the West Coast of the **United States**.

The first vines in the Dutch Cape Colony (South Africa) were planted in 1655 in order to provide wine for ships making the long voyage from the Netherlands to the Dutch East Indies around the southern tip of Africa. This early South African wine was consumed by the sailors as one means of staving off scurvy, and it was also exported to Dutch settlers in the Indies. The first vineyard was planted in Australia in 1788, but it was not until the early nineteenth century that wine production took off. New Zealand followed in the mid-1800s.

North America's experience in developing a wine industry was more complicated. The British hoped to reduce their reliance on French wine by producing wine (and olives) in their American colonies just as the Spanish had done. However, attempts to cultivate European vines in the 1600s failed, probably due to a deadly combination of diseases, **phylloxera**, and harsh climate. Meanwhile, experiments with indigenous vines were largely unsuccessful because of their unpleasant (''foxy'') flavors. Despite official encouragement of viticulture in several colonies, it was not until the late eighteenth century that there were signs of consistent success. It might have helped that some of the first leaders of the United States, including George Washington, Benjamin Franklin, and Thomas Jefferson, were all enthusiastic about wine. Jefferson was keenly interested in viticulture and had vines planted on his estate at Monticello. Later, as American ambassador to **France**, he toured French vineyards and kept detailed records of his wine travels and purchases.

For the most part, Americans were supplied with wine from Europe during the colonial period, but wine was not a major part of the diet of Americans, who consumed more distilled spirits (whiskey and rum) than their European contemporaries. The Atlantic wine trade was buoyant, but one of the most important routes was between Madeira and the southern colonies. Indeed, thanks to being fortified, Madeira was shipped as far afield as the Portuguese and British colonies in India.

Rod Phillips

Further Reading
Francis, A.D. *The Wine Trade*. London: Adam & Charles Black, 1972.
Johnson, Hugh. *The Story of Wine*. London: Mitchell Beazley, 1989.
Phillips, Rod. *A Short History of Wine*. New York: HarperCollins, 2001.

CONSOLIDATION

Consolidation is part of the natural ebb and flow of many industries, but it has been a particularly important and disruptive aspect of the wine and spirits industries over the past several decades. Consolidation generally occurs through the merger of two companies or through the acquisition of one company by another. Most consolidation taking place in the wine industry today involves acquisitions, which differs from joint ventures in that the acquiring company assumes control and ownership over the other company. Consolidation affects every tier of the wine industry, including growers, producers, **importers**, **distributors**, and **retailers** worldwide, and it will continue to be an important market force shaping the industry in the coming years.

Causes.   One important force driving consolidation in the past two decades has been the continued decline in demand for spirits. Wine has historically been linked with and dependent upon the distribution of spirits; both require similar permits, licenses, and bonded warehouses, but spirits often offer greater **profit** margins than wine. The softening demand for spirits in the early 1980s set into motion a wave of consolidations at all levels of the industry. Many point to the amalgamation of Guinness and Grand Met in forming **Diageo** in the late 1990s as the start of the consolidation period in the wine and spirits industry.

Consolidation among large retailers such as Tesco, Sainsbury's Supermarkets Ltd., and Safeway in the United Kingdom and Costco Wholesale Corp. and Wal-Mart Stores, Inc., in the **United States** has added additional pressure for suppliers to become larger. Large retailers want to deal with fewer, larger suppliers that offer the technology, resources, and support services that will enable them to lower their costs of operation. It is estimated that Safeway, Costco, Wal-Mart, Sam's Club, and BJ's Wholesale Club now account for just under 10 percent of all U.S. retail sales.

At the producer level, consolidation has been driven by the need to become more competitive, increase sales, maximize shareholder value, and improve and strengthen distribution in the marketplace. Consolidation enables companies to realize economies of scale in the production, **promotion**, and sales of wine. Today, some 30 wine suppliers, including **Constellation Brands**, Inc., E.&J. **Gallo** Winery, **Foster's** Americas, Diageo, the **Wine Group**, and Brown-Forman Corp., make up more than 90 percent of the U.S. wine market. These companies have relied on recent acquisitions to augment their portfolios.

Constellation includes some half-dozen divisions comprising more than 180 wine and spirits companies.

Effects.   Consolidation at the supplier level enables companies to add existing **brands**, fill in portfolio gaps, and react to market demand more rapidly and efficiently than through the organic growth or development of new wine brands. One of the most costly aspects of the wine business is the development and branding of new wine labels, due to the challenges involved in securing broad market distribution and stimulating **consumer** demand. Buying an established wine brand or producer eliminates or bypasses much of this risk. Constellation has relied primarily on brand acquisitions such as Vincor, Robert Mondavi, and Franciscan to become the world's largest wine company. In recent years, even companies known for developing their own brands have begun to acquire existing ones, as in Gallo's acquisitions of Louis M. Martini, Barefoot, and Mirassou.

The **globalization** of wine has meant that consolidation impacts every region and country. Even prestigious, traditional wine regions such as **Burgundy**, **Bordeaux**, and **Champagne** have been affected. For example, consolidation has occurred among **négociants** in Burgundy, noted for its fragmented ownership of vineyards and domains: Jean-Claude Boisset has bought Bouchard Aîné & Fils, Jaffelin, Mommessin, and Ropiteau Frères and today is the largest négociant in the region. In the Champagne industry, LVMH (Louis Vuitton/Moët Hennessy) now owns Moët & Chandon, Dom Pérignon, Veuve Clicquot, Krug, Mercier, and Ruinart; it is estimated that LVMH, Pernod Ricard, Vranken-Pommery, Tattinger, and Nicolas Feuillatte control more than 95 percent of the Champagne sold in the United States.

Types of Consolidation.   Consolidation can occur either vertically or horizontally. *Vertical consolidation* involves the union of two wine companies from different segments or tiers of the industry. Companies gain a competitive advantage by having a presence in more than one tier. A producer may acquire or perform the role of importer, distributor, or retailer. In the **British market**, for example, large **supermarket** chains, such as Tesco and Sainsbury's, commonly source, produce, and directly import their own brands. The French producer Nicolas owns its own chain of retail stores both in **France** and Britain, guaranteeing that its wines will have immediate access to the consumer market. While helping to eliminate the middleman's markup and potentially lowering cost, vertical integration bypasses market forces and potential competition.

A distinguishing feature of the U.S. wine market is the noticeable lack of vertical integration. Laws created during the post-**Prohibition** era, stemming from the 21st Amendment, essentially prohibit vertical integration and have also indirectly made horizontal consolidation more difficult. These laws prevent a ''tied house''—vertical integration involving an on-premise seller—and mandate three distinct tiers of distribution for wine, beer, and spirits as a way of discouraging promotion of alcohol. However, the implementation differs greatly from state to state, especially between **control states** and licensee states. Control states effectively serve as governmental forms of consolidation. True vertical consolidation can be seen in control states such as Pennsylvania that control wholesale distribution and retail, or in a monopoly market, such as Sweden or the **Canadian** provinces.

Horizontal consolidation—mergers and acquisitions—is more typical of the forces at work in the U.S. distribution system. It can be seen at the supplier and retail levels, but is particularly evident in the wholesale distribution tier. Large wine suppliers have put pressure on distributors to consolidate by eliminating or buying out their competitors. While this allows suppliers to reduce their costs, it has had a tremendous impact on the selection, availability, and price of wine in the U.S. market.

Changes to the Industry.   In recent years, consolidation has completely reshaped the wholesale network and reduced the number of companies. Thirty years ago, several thousand licensed wholesalers distributed wines and spirits in the United States, but today there are less than a thousand. In the mid-1980s, states such as **California**, Florida, Texas, and Illinois had a dozen or more distributors each; today there are as few as two or three. Five national distributors with a multistate presence—Southern Wine & Spirits, Republic National Distributing Company (Republic and National merged several years ago, moving them into the second position), the Charmer Sunbelt Group, Glazer's, and Young's Market Company—currently account for more than half of the wine and spirits market, worth an estimated $20 billion in sales revenue.

Producers have been affected by consolidation at the wholesale level in several ways: it is more difficult to introduce new wines and brands into the market, they have less control over the type of distribution in the market and market penetration (on-premise versus retail, or chain versus independent or club), and it has become increasing difficult to command the attention of the distributor management and sales force. The shape of the wine industry is often compared to an hourglass, with producers attempting to get through the bottleneck posed by a shrinking number of distributors. Large wholesalers distribute thousands of different wines and cannot realistically focus on each one. In order to be successful, they must service the needs of their largest suppliers and wine companies, the 20 percent of their portfolios that makes up 80 percent of their revenues. Wholesalers are unable to spend time on traditional brand-building activities and have been forced to focus more on logistical activities, such as warehousing, shipping, and delivery of wine. Large suppliers have had to augment the efforts of the distributor with their own salespeople in the market.

Smaller producers without the resources to put their own sales force into the market must look to other ways to sell their wine and gain distribution. They must seek out cooperative marketing companies and brokers, rely on high **ratings** in the wine press to stimulate demand, or concentrate on cellar-door sales and direct sales through newsletters and **e-commerce** to survive. The market forces created by consolidation have created the most pressure on midsize producers; there is an increasing disparity between small and large producers as a result.

Outlook.   Consolidation will continue at all levels of the wine industry in the coming years, but due to the three-tier system and state control, this consolidation will occur primarily in a horizontal fashion. Large retailers will be unable to consolidate vertically, as seen by the recent court case between Costco and the Washington State Liquor Control Board. Suppliers will continue buy **wineries**, vineyards, and brands, which will provide liquidity for successful business owners looking to cash out of their businesses. There will, however, continue to be plenty of new investors willing to start wineries and vineyards and enter the market. For the consumer, consolidation may continue to affect the selection of wines available, but it will not compress pricing in the way vertical consolidation would.

Jay Youmans

Further Reading

Cook, Doug. "Review of the Industry: Consolidation in the Industry." *Wine Business Monthly,* February 15, 2008, www.winebusiness.com/ReferenceLibrary/webarticle .cfm?dataId=54416.

CONSTELLATION BRANDS

The largest wine company in the world, Constellation Brands, Inc., is a paradigm of **globalization** and **consolidation**, having grown to its current stature through dozens of acquisitions of small and large businesses in numerous countries. The company traces its roots to Canandaigua Industries, later Canandaigua Wine Company, in 1945, building its foundation on **bulk wine** and **fortified wines**, including Richards Wild Irish Rose, which is still the number-one selling **dessert wine** in the **United States**. Canandaigua grew steadily, acquiring **wineries** and **brands** and entering the beer and spirits industries with the purchase of Barton, Inc., in 1993. The company changed its name to Constellation Brands in 2000. It is based in Fairport, **New York**. The chairman and CEO is Richard Sands, son of the founder of Canandaigua.

The corporation's structure has undergone several reorganizations in recent years as it has tried to divide its wine portfolio into functional units. Constellation's fine wine division is Icon Estates, headquartered in St. Helena, California, which includes Franciscan Oakville, Robert Mondavi, Simi, and Kim Crawford wineries, among others. The mid-level tier of wines, including Clos du Bois, Hogue Cellars, Ravenswood, and Woodbridge, falls under the San Francisco–based VineOne unit. The Centerra Wine Company, located in Canandaigua, New York, manages the rest of Constellation's wine portfolio of about 50 brands, including Cook's, Arbor Mist, Mouton Cadet, Taylor Dessert Wines, Vendange, and Banrock Station. The Hardy Wine Company in **Australia** has been renamed Constellation Wines Australia, and Constellation also owns the Nobilo Wine Group in **New Zealand**. In addition, **Canada**'s largest wine company, Vincor Canada, was purchased by Constellation in 2006. The company's consolidation model allows its acquired brands considerable latitude to operate independently within the corporate structure.

Constellation sold 103.5 million cases (mc) of wine worldwide in 2006, accounting for 3.9 percent of the **global** wine market and tallying $5.22 billion in sales. In the United States, its volume totaled 50.7 mc, comprising 81 percent **table wine**, 4 percent **sparkling wine**, and 15 percent dessert and fortified wines. This total equated to 17.5 percent market share, placing it second after **Gallo** in volume; it was first in revenues, however, with retail sales reaching $3.35 billion.

Its leading brands in 2006 were Almaden (8.2 mc), Woodbridge (6.7 mc), Arbor Mist (4.0 mc), Inglenook (3.5 mc), and Vendange (3.4 mc).

As part of a move toward acquiring more premium wine brands, Constellation bought the Beam Wine Estates portfolio from primarily spirits-based Fortune Brands for $885 million in 2007. To help finance the purchase and realign the portfolio, in 2008 Constellation sold Almaden (the world's ninth largest brand) and Inglenook, along with the Paul Masson winery facility in Madera, to the **Wine Group** for $134 million. Without Almaden and Inglenook, Constellation moved to third place behind the Wine Group in U.S. sales. Later in 2008, Constellation sold eight brands, among them Geyser Peak, Gary Farrell, Atlas Peak, and Columbia Winery, to Ascentia Wine Estates, a group of investors and former Bean Wine Estates employees, for $209 million.

CONSUMERS

Although not technically part of the wine industry, the consumer segment is a crucial element that allows all the other segments of the industry to exist. If the only people who drank wine were the ones who made it, there would be far fewer **wineries** and no need for **distributors**, **importers**, or **retailers**. However, hundreds of millions of people around the world enjoy at least an occasional glass of wine, consuming more than 2½ billion cases of wine annually and supporting the millions of individuals who make and sell wine.

There are many reasons people consume wine. Historically, wine was often safer to drink than water in many places. For this reason, it became an important part of the diet in most regions where it was possible to produce or acquire wine, and it remained an aspect of these cultures long after it was needed for **health** purposes. Wine was integrated into **religious** ceremonies in Judeo-Christian tradition. And, of course, it is a great accompaniment for meals, celebrations, and social camaraderie.

In the **United States**, 64 percent of adults over the legal **drinking age** consume some type of alcohol, and of those, 34 percent consider themselves wine drinkers in preference to beer or spirits. In all, 37 percent of U.S. adults report that they sometimes drink wine. This is a low number relative to many other Western countries, especially in the Old World; for example, the comparable figure in the United Kingdom is more than 65 percent.

The demographics of American wine drinkers paint the picture of an affluent, well-educated, white, married woman in her late 50s as the quintessential wine consumer. Income and education are highly correlated with wine consumption; as they increase, consumption increases. According to data from *Adams Wine Handbook 2007*, people who make more than $75,000 a year are twice as likely to be wine drinkers as those who make less than $20,000, and the proportion of wine drinkers among individuals with a graduate degree is almost double that of high school graduates who did not attend college and three times that of nongraduates of high school (of course, income and education are themselves highly correlated).

Whites are more likely to drink wine than other racial or ethnic groups, although the differences are not quite as dramatic as those for income and education; Latinos have the lowest share of wine drinkers. Married people are slightly more likely to drink wine than never marrieds or those divorced or widowed, but the difference is not particularly significant.

More **women** than men drink wine; 58 percent of U.S. wine drinkers are women. However, men drink more than women, so the female edge is not clear-cut.

Age is also a factor in wine consumption, and the wine-drinking proportion increases with age. Only 32 percent of 21- to 24-year-olds drink wine, according to Adams, but perhaps with age comes wisdom, as wine drinking continues to increase through middle age, reaching a maximum of 40 percent of 55- to 64-year-olds. Of course, age also correlates to income, which is undoubtedly the most significant factor of all (apart, perhaps, from **religion**).

The American wine consumer currently has a slight preference for white **table wine** over all other categories. About 88 percent of wine drinkers report that they drink domestic table wines, but only 43 percent drink imports. Less than one-half drink **sparkling wine** and less than one-fifth say they drink **dessert** or **fortified wines**.

A great deal of hope has been invested in the Echo Boom generation (a subset of the ill-defined group known as the Millennials), who represent a population bulge formed by children of the Baby Boomers. The Echo Boomers, born between the mid-1980s and mid-1990s, have the potential to increase wine consumption by their numbers alone, and there is some early anecdotal information that indicates they may be more wine friendly than earlier generations, but since the crest of the wave has not yet reached legal drinking age, it is still too early to draw reliable conclusions. It is clear, however, that the next generation of wine drinkers will have a strong influence on several new issues in the wine industry— **alternative packaging** and **closures**, **sustainability**, **organic** production, **direct shipping**, **e-commerce**, and unpredictable changes in wine traditions caused by **climate change**—so, regardless of their per-capita consumption, the industry needs to ensure that they get a solid **wine education**. *See also* Fads and Fashions; French Paradox; Global Wine Industry; High Alcohol Content; Labels as Marketing; New World versus Old World; Promotion; Ratings and Scores; Red Wine versus White Wine.

CONTROL STATES

Each U.S. state has the autonomy to regulate the **distribution** and sale of alcohol as it sees fit within its borders, and 18 of them have chosen to exercise substantial direct control over spirits and, in some cases, beer and wine; these are known as *control states*. The other 31, known as *licensee states,* regulate alcohol primarily through the issuance of permits and licenses to private businesses. Control states vary regarding the degree and type of control they exert over the sale of wine. These states are an important segment of the wine market in the **United States**, as they are home to nearly 25 percent of the population.

One of the legacies of **Prohibition** and its repeal in 1933 by the 21st Amendment was the transfer of power over the regulation and sale of alcohol from the federal government to each state. This approach was modeled after practices already adopted in **Canada**. Prohibition in the United States had essentially failed, and it was believed that state governments were better positioned to limit consumption and promote temperance. This transfer of power to the state level would have a profound and lasting effect over the U.S. wine industry.

During the post-Prohibition years, views on alcohol differed greatly around the country, and it was hoped that state-level control would provide regulation better suited to the citizens of each state. Many feared that the **profit** motives of private business would lead to an increase in consumption and a return to widespread abuse, and this prompted some states to remain directly involved in the sale of all alcohol.

A common feature in all states, whether control or licensee, is the federally mandated partition of supply channels in the sale of alcohol. Commonly referred to as the "three-tier system," this law calls for three separate links in the chain of distribution: producer (**winery**), wholesaler (**importer** and/or **distributor**), and **retailer/restaurant**. Maintaining a division of ownership among the three was considered necessary to prevent any one from dominating the entire chain. This was seen as another critical measure in controlling consumption. (It is worth noting that the wine available after Prohibition tended to be sweet and highly **fortified**, often to 24 percent alcohol. Wine consumption during this time was driven by the desired effects of alcohol and rarely by its intrinsic taste and affinity for food.)

The 18 control states, plus two control counties in Maryland, can be divided into four categories based on the level of wine distribution oversight they maintain:

1. Control and management of all wholesale and retail: Pennsylvania
2. Control and management of wholesale, with a combination of government-owned retail stores and some licensed stores managed by private business: Utah and Montgomery and Worcester counties, Maryland
3. Control and management of wholesale, but all retail stores privately owned by licensees: Mississippi, New Hampshire, and Wyoming
4. Direct control over spirits only, with distributors and retailers licensed to sell wine: Alabama, Idaho, Iowa, Maine, Michigan, Montana, North Carolina, Ohio, **Oregon**, Vermont, Virginia, **Washington**, and West Virginia

Proponents of state liquor control boards emphasize their historic mission of promoting temperance, minimizing abuse, and providing education. The most common argument for state control today is the prevention of underage drinking. Perhaps the strongest motivation for maintaining state control, however, is the large amount of revenue generated from the sale of alcohol and the numerous government jobs created to oversee its regulation.

Statistical data suggest that consumption levels of wine in control states are lower. In 2006, the average apparent per-capita consumption of wine in all control states was around 30 percent less than that of licensee states (the true consumption levels are undoubtedly closer, though, as it is common practice for many residents of control states to do their wine shopping in neighboring states where the selection is better and prices are lower). Nevertheless, Pennsylvania, Washington, and Michigan are among the top 10 U.S. wine markets, with Virginia and North Carolina among the top 15.

Critics of control states argue that these systems are archaic. State control inhibits free trade, prevents competition, and is unfair to **consumers** who drink wine responsibly. Control state laws limit consumer choice and result in higher wine prices. Many wine producers, particularly smaller ones, find it more difficult and costly to enter these markets than licensee states. Those calling for reform would look to privatize these systems, maintaining that jobs and tax revenue would not be adversely affected. Still, it is unlikely that any of these systems will be privatized in the foreseeable future.

Control states continue to stress the equivalency of alcoholic drinks—spirits, beer, and wine—yet seemingly also acknowledge differences in consumption patterns for wine. As a result, some have become less restrictive in their approach to wine, while keeping a tight hold over **distilled** spirits. Many control states have begun to revise their laws, and some superficially have begun to resemble licensee states, introducing state-controlled wine shops with better selection than the typical state stores.

One indication of the changes occurring in control states can be seen in the laws affecting the **direct shipping** and **e-commerce** of wine. While some control states still prohibit direct shipment of wine, many have begun to allow it. Alabama, Maine, Mississippi, and Montana still prohibit direct shipments of wine— and Pennsylvania, Utah, and Montgomery County actually consider it a felony. However, Idaho, Michigan, New Hampshire, North Carolina, Ohio, Oregon, Vermont, Virginia, Washington, West Virginia, and Wyoming now permit direct shipments of wine under certain conditions. The most common restrictions concerning these shipments involve limits on the quantity of wine shipped, the mandatory permits and licenses required, and the procedures for paying applicable fees and taxes.

Jay Youmans

Further Reading
Free the Grapes. www.freethegrapes.org.
National Alcohol Beverage Control Association. www.nabca.org.
Wine Institute. www.wineinstitute.org/initiatives/stateshippinglaws.

CORK TAINT

On occasion, corks used as **closures** for wine develop a distinctive unpleasant aroma that infuses the wine, which is then—in an unfortunately confusing usage—considered to be "corked." The immediate cause of the disagreeable odor is a chemical compound known as TCA (because that is easier to remember than 2,4,6-trichloroanisole), although how the TCA gets into the cork is not well understood. It appears that, for problem corks, the TCA is typically present in the cork oak bark initially, although the processing of the bark can also induce or enhance the amount of TCA present. Perfectly sound corks, before or after insertion into the wine bottle, can also absorb TCA from the air if stored in close proximity to tainted corks or in a contaminated environment.

Individuals vary in their sensitivity to TCA's smell, but the threshold for most people is quite low, reportedly in the range of 3 to 6 parts per trillion. If a wine is very slightly corked, the TCA may simply mask or deaden other aromas, making the wine seem flat. At higher levels, TCA becomes offensive, like a dirty bar rag, and the wine will be undrinkable. The smell of TCA is unmistakable once a person learns to recognize it, but because not many people have the opportunity to have an expert point out the odor to them in the first place, most simply lump TCA in with other wine aromas they do not like and avoid that wine in the future.

This is a serious problem for the wine industry, because **consumers** usually mistakenly assume that the wine is the way it is supposed to be, but find it distasteful or subdued in fruit aromas, and they are not likely to buy the wine again. If the cork had visible damage, consumers or wine servers would realize that it was a random bad bottle and go for a replacement, but the damage is purely olfactory and is often misdiagnosed as bad winemaking. Thus, the losses to the industry from cork taint, estimated in the hundreds of millions of dollars, are far higher than the direct cost of wines that are returned because they were recognized as corked.

The frequency of TCA in corks is a subject of speculation, with anecdotal estimates ranging from less than 1 to 5 percent and possibly even higher. Cork taint is not uniformly random, but rather affects some batches heavily and others not at all. Sensory analysis does not necessarily produce the same results as more expensive gas chromatography studies in a laboratory when concentrations are near threshold levels. Another confusion factor is that it is possible to have TCA in a cork without it significantly tainting the wine in its bottle, if the wine is quite young.

Portugal produces a little over half of the world's cork, and the largest maker of wine corks is Corticeira Amorim in Portugal. Another major producer is Oeneo of **France**. Both have developed new procedures in recent years that they claim have reduced the incidence of cork taint by as much as 90 percent by careful selection of the raw material and processing techniques that avoid cross-contamination. Again, anecdotal evidence does seem to support the idea that the corks are getting better.

In the meantime, of course, cork taint has driven many **wineries** to adopt other closures that do not employ cork, notably screw caps, and even **alternative packaging** such as bag-in-box—as many as a quarter of the wines on the market use no cork. The widespread use of noncork closures, along with the recognition that these wines are almost guaranteed free of cork taint, has gone a long way toward eliminating the lowbrow stigma formerly associated with these closures. However, the opinion to date is that they are not suitable for wines that need to mature in the bottle over many years and that therefore require the slow air exchange that cork provides, so it is imperative that the cork and wine industries continue work to weed out problem corks in the future. *See also* Quality Control.

Further Reading
Taber, George M. *To Cork or Not to Cork*. New York: Scribner, 2007.

CRUISE LINES

From the traditional sail-away toast on deck to the final evening's gala dinner, cruise ship passengers represent a small but nontrivial slice of the wine market.

Wine is typically available in all the dining rooms and **restaurants**, bars, and lounges on board, as well as at special events and room service. Carnival Cruise Lines, one of the world's largest with 21 ships, reports selling about 150,000 cases of wine annually and giving away another 30,000–40,000 cases a year for complimentary receptions, welcoming gifts, and other promotional purposes. Royal Caribbean International, also with 21 ships, had a total wine consumption of almost 1.7 million cases for 2007.

In the main dining rooms, wine lists are provided and can be quite extensive. Newer ships and especially the very large cruise ships that have been coming into service in recent years have several themed restaurants aboard in addition to, or in place of, the large traditional dining room. These often have individualized wine lists, featuring mainly Italian wines in the Italian restaurant, for example. Upper-end ships usually have many **sommeliers** dedicated to wine service in the dining rooms and restaurants. A few also have specialty wine bars or dining areas designed especially for wine dinners. Wine classes, receptions, and tastings are frequently among the onboard activities, and some lines, such as Crystal Cruises, have special wine-themed cruises with winemakers and chefs aboard as celebrity guests.

Wine sales and procurement are usually handled by a Food and Beverage Department. The logistics of wine service aboard ship present some unique challenges beyond those experienced at shore-based bars and restaurants. Obviously, once out of port, there is little that can practically be done to replenish wine stocks, so a great deal of advance planning is needed to ensure that the ships can support their wine lists. This is less of a problem for a line based in Miami with ships doing out-and-back Caribbean cruises, because the line can keep its own warehouse at the port and resupply at the beginning of every trip. On the other hand, it can be a tremendous problem for a ship embarking on a round-the-world voyage, where wine must meet the ship at several ports along the way, without knowing very far in advance exactly which wines will need replenishment.

Aboard ship, wine is generally stored belowdecks in **temperature-controlled** spaces along with other supplies. Under normal circumstances, the ship will be stocked with about a 10-day supply of wine. An assortment of most of the wines is then transferred daily to a holding area near the dining room. In addition, the most popular wines will be stocked in small caches at the bars and lounges. When a diner or bar patron orders wine, the server or sommelier can then quickly retrieve the wine from the nearby storage area. Higher-priced reserve wines, of which there may be only a few bottles on board, are generally kept in a separate location where they will not be subject to the temperature fluctuations and handling of wines in the normal storage areas; thus, it may take a little longer to procure one of those wines.

Cruise ships see all the same trends that land-based venues do, although it may take a little longer to be adopted aboard ship due to the lead time required for provisioning. On the huge new vessels, there are enough passengers to support wine bars and wine-by-the-glass programs without excessive spoilage. Because a majority of cruises sail through warm waters and tropical climates, lighter wines tend to be somewhat more popular, and, of course, there is always plenty of cause for celebration, resulting in a higher-than-average consumption of **sparkling wine**.

CULT WINES

The most highly sought-after wines are sometimes called cult wines, originally a somewhat derogatory term meant to conjure up images of mindless adherents following a suspect idol or belief. These are wines that have gained a larger-than-life reputation, usually thanks to glowing endorsements and high **ratings** by respected **wine writers** and critics, such as **Robert Parker**, and that are made in such small quantities that demand for them far outstrips availability. This **supply and demand** situation makes the wines the object of competition among **consumers**, which can drive their prices to astronomical levels—and only fuels even greater desire for them. Cult wines are a type of **fad**, but they do not usually have the broad popular appeal of most fads because of their high prices. Oftentimes it is simply conspicuous consumption on the part of consumers that leads to the fury to own a cult wine.

Cult wines are typically made in quantities ranging from a few hundred to a few thousand cases, and it is this scarcity—or the perception thereof—through use of marketing initiatives, that pushes them into cult status. Prices can run from $200 per bottle to $2,500 or more and are sometimes driven more by prestige of ownership than by the actual merits of the wine. They are usually identified with the **New World**, especially **Napa Valley** and most especially Napa **Cabernet Sauvignons**, because such celebrity status is more in tune with the New World than the Old. Nevertheless, **Burgundy**'s Domaine de la Romanée-Conti or **Australia**'s Grange has enough devotees and small enough production to qualify as cult icons. **Bordeaux** first growths, on the other hand, are generally produced in large enough quantities that they would have to be considered merely great and expensive wines rather than cult wines. In **California**, Screaming Eagle, Harlan Estate, Caymus, and Shafer Hillside Select are just a few of the cult labels.

While the steep prices usually keep the numbers of would-be buyers at a manageable level, at the heights of cult-wine standing, the biggest problem is not paying the price, but simply finding a bottle for sale. Screaming Eagle, for example, sells its entire production to a select group of people on its mailing list, and anyone else is unable to buy the wine from the **winery** regardless of how much money they have in their pockets. Even at less lofty levels, wines must often be rationed, or *allocated,* among the potential markets. A **distributor** in a certain state, or a **retailer** or **restaurant** in a certain city, may be allotted only a few bottles for the year. Often, there is a waiting list of customers for these allocated wines.

The upside of cult wines is that they generate public interest in the industry, make wine alluring, and raise price levels for all well-made wines. On the downside, these wines can perpetuate an image of wine as elitist, push prices out of balance, and steal the spotlight from other excellent wines.

CUSTOM CRUSH FACILITIES

Custom crush is the practice of producing wine at an established **winery** or specialized custom crush facility under contract for a client. In this way, a new producer can make use of a facility with advanced equipment and some source of professional support without bearing the full financial cost necessary to run a similar private operation. Clients can decide what they want to produce, in any manner or style, and the production facility handles all labor and record keeping.

The world of commercial winemaking requires training, technology, and specialized equipment. With increasing prices for stainless steel, oak **barrels**, and automated processing systems, the practice of custom crush winemaking becomes very appealing to the aspiring winegrower.

Though distantly related to the idea of a cooperative, this practice is essentially a **New World** phenomenon. It has spread slowly from areas of **California** to nearby states and onward across the country. Any area that has started to see an abundance of wine grapes looks to creative means of using the extra fruit, and through custom crush, many small business owners, **retailers**, and **restaurants** have been given the means to produce their own wine with the contents, and label, of their choosing.

There is considerable overlap between custom crush facilities and **virtual wineries**, but they are not synonymous. Virtual wineries normally use custom crush facilities to produce their wines, but they have additional activities beforehand (for example, sourcing grapes) and afterward (marketing their wine, among other things) that are unrelated to the crush facility. Conversely, custom crush clients include not only virtual wineries but also vineyard owners, high-end **consumers**, and bonded wineries with insufficient production capacity.

Some **grape-growing** areas have developed such an extreme density of wineries that local officials have had to limit the number of winery licenses. This is rapidly becoming an issue in towns in the **Napa Valley**, for example. Custom crush facilities make it possible for one license to produce many different product lines of wine.

The custom crush facility benefits from these arrangements in a manner different from most of the wine industry. New wineries usually have multiple years of investment and maturation before they sell a single bottle. A custom crush winery, on the other hand, can begin generating revenue as soon as fruit arrives at the winery.

Areas of concern in the custom crush operation include sanitation, separation of product, and record keeping. An infection of spoilage yeast or bacteria can spread rapidly in any untidy winery, and with the greater traffic and turnover at a custom crush facility, such dangers are magnified. A well-practiced system of sanitation and **quality control** is essential. Furthermore, unlike at a standard winery, wines in one tank cannot be blended casually with other wines. The custom crush facility must be able to track every movement and addition to each client's wine. There is great responsibility in crafting a quality end product.

Custom crush facilities are a highly efficient use of equipment, technological, and personnel resources that can improve quality and lower overall cost at the same time. While they will never replace the traditional winery, they are an important component of the modern wine industry and can be expected to spread throughout the world's winemaking regions.

Chris Dowsett

Further Reading

Crowe, Alison. "How to Work with a Custom Crush Partner." *Wine Business Monthly,* October 14, 2006, www.winebusiness.com/ReferenceLibrary/webarticle.cfm ?dataId=45036.

Franson, Paul. "Custom Crush or Alternating Proprietorship?" *Wines & Vines,* March 4, 2008, www.winesandvines.com/template.cfm?section=news&content=53662.

D

DEALCOHOLIZED WINES

Nonalcoholic and alcohol-removed wines are currently a small category within the wine segment, but are still important because they offer alternative choices to those wishing to abstain from traditional wines, whether for philosophical, **religious**, **health**, lifestyle, or other reasons, such as the need to drive after drinking.

This wine category peaked at the turn of the millennium, when sales spiked as the demand for alcohol-free options increased. In 2007, an estimated 225,000 cases of dealcoholized wines were sold in the **United States**, which is the largest market for these beverages. Dealcoholized wines also became popular in the **British market**, particularly after a reduction in the legal blood alcohol levels for driving from 0.08 to 0.05 percent was proposed in 1998. They are distributed in at least 20 countries and are produced in **France** and **Germany**, as well as in the United States.

These "alcohol-removed" or "dealcoholized" products differ from simple grape juice in that they have gone through the fermentation process to become normal table wine, but, using a reverse-osmosis method or a spinning cone or even by adding water—the three procedures used to reduce alcohol percentages—winemakers reduce the alcohol content of the beverage. Thus, they still maintain typical wine flavors and aromas, minus the alcohol. In the United States, they are legally deemed "nonalcoholic" if they contain less than 0.5 percent alcohol by volume. The **European Union** does not use that term, and instead defines *alcohol-free* as less than 0.05 percent alcohol, *dealcoholized* as 0.05 to 0.5 percent, *low alcohol* as 0.5 to 1.2 percent, and *reduced alcohol* as 1.2 to 5.5 percent. Under the laws of most countries, however, these products are no longer technically "wine" and are best termed a "grape beverage."

In the United States, nonalcoholic and alcohol-removed products fall under the control of the Food and Drug Administration and are not subject to federal alcohol regulation (although five states—Alabama, Georgia, Kansas, Tennessee, and West Virginia—regulate them as an alcohol product). Typically, dealcoholized wines are sold by wine **retailers** or in the wine section of **supermarkets**, although they may also be sold with other nonalcoholic beverages in stores that do not have a liquor license. In most states, there is no age limitation on purchase or consumption, although the producers of dealcoholized wines generally market them as adult alternative beverages and discourage consumption by persons below the legal **drinking age**.

Nonalcoholic wines are bottled in wine bottles and marketed as a substitute for wine with food and as an aperitif. Popular **brands** in the category include St. Regis, Ariel, and Sutter Home's Fre; European producers include Pol Vignan and Carl Jung. While all of these wines are classified as alcohol removed, the processes by which they are made differ.

St. Regis and Ariel both use reverse osmosis to extract the alcohol. In this process, traditional, alcoholic wine is fed into a tank and then is pumped against a semipermeable membrane at high pressure. The small molecules of alcohol and water pass through the membrane, while the larger molecules of flavor and aroma compounds do not. Water is then added back to the concentrate to complete the process.

Fre is created using the spinning cone column. Traditional, alcoholic wine is fed into the top of a cylinder column while nitrogen gas is fed into the bottom. As wine descends over rotating metal cones, centrifugal force creates a thin film. The nitrogen gas extracts delicate aroma and flavor essences, after which the remaining liquid is passed again through the cones at a higher temperature to remove the alcohol. Afterward, the flavor and aroma essences are returned, along with unfermented varietal grape juice. *See also* High Alcohol Content; Must and Wine Adjustments.

Barry Wiss

DESSERT WINE

During the fermentation process that transforms grapes into wine, yeast consumes the natural sugars in ripe grapes and transforms them into alcohol and carbon dioxide. Hence, most wines are "dry" (meaning, no apparent sweetness or residual sugar) or almost dry. There are, however, many sweet wines made by various processes. These constitute the world of sweet or dessert wines.

Whereas to most people "dessert wines" are invariably sweet, the **Alcohol and Tobacco Tax and Trade Bureau (TTB)** of the U.S. Department of the Treasury defines the term solely on the basis of alcohol content, imposing a higher tax rate on the "dessert wine" category with more than 14 percent alcohol by volume (abv)—currently $1.57 per gallon (compared to $1.07 for **table wines** of 14 percent abv and below). Thus, to the U.S. government, a German Trockenbeerenauslese (TBA) is not a dessert wine, while all **fortified wines**, including dry fino Sherries, are.

Dessert wines are produced in almost every winegrowing region of the world. They generally fall into two categories: those that are made sweet by *concentrating the sugars* of the grape before fermentation, and those made sweet by *stopping the fermentation* before all of the natural grape sugar is converted. There are no globally accepted levels of sweetness, alcohol, or acidity that form a definition for sweet dessert wines, although some have legal requirements, such as Tokaji Essencia or German TBA, which by law meet minimum "must weights" for sugar content.

Sugar concentration in grapes may result from late harvesting (grapes remain on vine longer, becoming riper, with a higher sugar level); drying grapes after harvest (as for Vin Santo); or pressing frozen grapes to separate the sugar and water components (as for ice wine). Sometimes the methods are combined, naturally or by the producer. Sugar may also be concentrated after crushing by **must adjustment**.

Another important method of sugar concentration is exemplified by Sauternes in **France**, Beerenauslese and TBA in **Germany** and **Austria**, and Tokaji in Hungary. These and other similar wines depend on the beneficial fungus *Botrytis cinerea* or "noble rot" that strikes the vines under certain conditions of temperature and humidity. This fungus attacks ripe white grapes, which may already be at late-harvest sugar levels, perforating the skin with microscopic holes that allow the water in the grape to evaporate and thereby concentrate the sugars. The resulting wines are quite sweet—at least 6.0 percent residual sugar (600 grams per liter). Botrytized wines are also relatively high in acidity and have a distinctive honeyed or sometimes subtle but pleasant moldy aroma.

The other category of sweet wines is produced by intentionally stopping the ongoing fermentation while some of the natural sugars remain. One way to do this is by chilling the wine to inactivate the yeast and then filtering out the yeast to prevent refermentation. Some unfermented sweet grape juice (called *Süssreserve* in Germany, where this is common) may also be added. These wines are generally low in alcohol (7 to 11 percent abv) and mildly sweet (2 to 6 percent residual sugar). Another way to stop the fermentation is by *fortification*. In this process, a high alcohol spirit or liqueur is added during fermentation (in some cases, before fermentation has even begun), killing the yeast. These fortified wines, with more than 16 percent abv, include Ports, sweet Sherries and Madeiras, France's *vins doux naturels* and *vins de liqueur,* and **Australia**'s Liqueur Muscats and Tokays.

Most sweet dessert wines are packaged in smaller bottles. The most popular size is 375 milliliters (ml), but 500-ml and 750-ml bottles are also used. The serving size for dessert wines is about half that of dry wines, usually 2 to 3 ounces per pour. Dessert wines are often expensive, as many are labor-intensive to produce. Botrytis-affected grape harvests require multiple passes through the vineyard, often three or four times a day going on for a week or more, and the grapes must be harvested by hand. True ice wines are produced only in certain years, when the conditions are right. Late-harvest wines are also risky to produce, as leaving the sweet fruit on the vine can attract birds and the chances of weather damage increase.

Throughout history, sweetness in wine was important for preservation, and sweet wines were prized in ancient Rome and in the Middle Ages. The **Dutch** and **British** wine trade of the early eighteenth century promoted and marketed sweet wines. Sweet Madeira was the drink of choice in **Colonial** America. Today, however, sweet dessert wines have fallen out of favor and comprise a very small percentage of the overall wine trade.

The consumption of dessert wines in the **United States** has been dwindling in the last 15 years to a level of 3.4 percent of total wine consumption—9.6 million cases in 2006—down from 5.5 percent in 1995. This is perhaps because the predilection for sweet wine is seen as unsophisticated by the wine-drinking public. Only 18 percent of U.S. wine **consumers** report occasionally drinking dessert wines. The best-selling dessert wines in the United States today are Richards Wild Irish Rose and MD 20/20, low-priced large-production **brands** that together account for 40 percent of the category.

Nevertheless, there is growing interest in high-quality dessert wines. Sales of some of the greatest sweet dessert wines, particularly Sauternes, do not seem to be affected so much by changing consumer tastes as by the quality of the vintage, perhaps because they are favored by wine collectors. Many wine **retailers** feature a dessert-wine section, although these smaller bottles of sometimes very expensive wines must be merchandised carefully to prevent theft.

Nearly all fine-dining restaurants offer a range of dessert wines, the most popular of which are Ports. Tawny Ports and sweet Madeiras are useful in **restaurant** settings, as these wines do not lose quality once the bottle is opened. Late-harvest and botrytis-affected wines are offered in some forward-thinking restaurants as an aperitif or with a cheese course. Some have found it effective to offer a sweet wine as part of a feature with a particular food item, for instance, a serving of foie gras with a glass of Sauternes or a chocolate soufflé with a glass of Tawny Port, priced together as a single unit. *See also* Bordeaux; Canada; Eastern Europe; Greece; High Alcohol Content; Portugal; Spain.

Suzanne Haley

Further Reading

Brook, Stephen. *Liquid Gold: Dessert Wines of the World*. New York: Beech Tree Books, 1987.

DIAGEO

Diageo PLC was established in 1997 when the British conglomerate Grand Metropolitan PLC, which owned hotels, **restaurants**, and spirits companies, among other things, bought the London-based drinks giant Guinness, famous for Guinness beer and Baileys liqueur. Three years later, when the Seagram wine and spirits business was being sold by the newly created Vivendi Universal, whose core field was entertainment and was divesting its alcohol business, Diageo made a joint bid with **France**'s Pernod Ricard. The bid was accepted and, after a year of scrutiny, approved by U.S. antitrust regulators. Diageo and Pernod Ricard divided up the spoils, with Diageo taking the **winery** portfolio.

The Diageo Chateau & Estate Wines division consists of the venerable **Napa Valley** wineries Beaulieu (1.7 million cases [mc] sold in 2006) and Sterling (1.1 mc), along with the former Chalone Wine Group, including Canoe Ridge, Edna Valley, and Acacia, and the French Barton & Guestier (B&G). Diageo's top-selling **brand** is Blossom Hill, a **California** wine made for export, shipped in **bulk** and bottled in **Italy**; it is the second largest brand in the **British market**, selling 5.5 mc in 2005. Diageo Chateau & Estate Wines' total U.S. sales are estimated between 4.8 and 5.5 mc. The division is based in Napa, California, led by CEO Ray Chadwick.

DIRECT SHIPPING

At the most basic level, *direct shipping* is defined as the transportation of wine from a **winery** directly to a **consumer** without passing through a wholesaler or **distributor**. Although a fairly simple concept—selling wines directly to consumers has been a common sales practice by wineries around the world for hundreds of years—within the **United States**, where the sale of wine is complicated by an elaborate distribution system put into place after **Prohibition**, direct shipping is a significantly more complex issue. Central to the fight over the right of wineries to legally ship wine to consumers are such issues as states' rights, freedom of trade, underage access to alcohol, tax collection, and wine industry growth.

The crux of the direct shipping issue actually dates back to 1787, when Article I of the U.S. Constitution established the right of the federal government "To regulate Commerce. . . among the several States." This provision, referred to as the Commerce Clause, made it illegal for states to discriminate against interstate commerce; that is, one state cannot favor its own products or producers over those of another state.

Interstate commerce of alcohol, including wine, became a key political topic in the early 1900s, when many states went "dry" in an attempt to control alcohol consumption. In 1913, in a move that foreshadowed Prohibition, Congress passed the Webb-Kenyon Act, which prohibited the movement of alcoholic beverages from one state to another if the shipment violated the laws of the receiving state.

At the end of Prohibition in 1933, the backlash against the federal government for its role in enacting Prohibition and then failing to enforce it led to alcohol regulatory power being given solely to the states. However, this led to a complicated system of distribution, with **control states** and licensee states and many variations of each.

In the 1980s, in response to a growing level of interest in **California** wine, the state of California created the idea of *reciprocity*—essentially a free trade agreement with other states, such as Illinois and **Oregon**—and its wineries began to ship wine to consumers in cooperating states. Soon wholesalers and state alcohol boards began to take note of the wine that was being sold outside the three-tier system. While some took a "don't ask, don't tell" approach, others sought to clamp down on illegal shipping, and some, such as Kentucky and Tennessee, went so far as to pass laws that made it a felony to ship wine to their residents.

It is possible that the direct shipping issue might have continued to stay out of the national spotlight were it not for the changing face of the American wine industry and the dramatic expansion of **e-commerce**. While California has long been, and continues to be, the most important wine-producing state, the last 30 years have witnessed a winery explosion, the number of U.S. wineries increasing almost tenfold from 579 in 1975 to 5,425 in 2006. Licensed wholesalers, on the other hand, have experienced the opposite trend, as since the 1950s,

consolidation has reduced their numbers from several thousand to a few hundred. Rapid growth of consumer interest in wine, the expansion of **wine tourism** around the United States, and the availability of wine through **wine clubs** and winery Web sites helped to fuel the fire. Even though most states continued to bar interstate shipments of wine, *intrastate* wine shipments—that is, wine shipped to a consumer by a winery within the same state—started to expand.

Beginning in 1996, spurred on by increasingly restrictive shipping laws, consumers and wineries decided to take action, and litigation was filed in 11 states. Opposing rulings in different jurisdictions set the stage for a Supreme Court battle over interstate shipping. Opening arguments were presented in December 2004 on two cases: *Granholm v. Heald* (which also included the *Michigan Beer & Wine Wholesalers Association v. Heald* case) and *Swedenburg v. Kelly*. Both sides presented their positions, highlighting five main issues: states' rights versus the Commerce Clause, taxation concerns, underage access, the role of the three-tier system, and the growth and potential of the U.S. wine industry.

Wineries and consumers argued that the limitations on direct shipping were unconstitutional because the 21st Amendment barred discrimination against interstate commerce. They further argued that the ability to directly ship was crucial to the survival of small wineries that did not produce enough wine to find distribution through the traditional three-tier system and that consumers had a right to be able to buy these wines. Wholesalers and state authorities, on the other hand, pointed to the problems of ensuring that wine delivered to a consumer's home does not end up in the hands of minors under legal **drinking age**. The Wine & Spirits Wholesalers of America, one of the largest opponents of direct shipping, argued for the sanctity of the three-tier system that had been put in place after Prohibition and pointed out that direct shipping made it difficult to collect the proper taxes.

In May 2005, the Supreme Court handed down its ruling, referred to as the *Granholm* decision, declaring that the states in question (Michigan and New York) had violated the Commerce Clause. The justices found that there was little evidence that supported the argument that direct shipping made it easier for underage individuals to obtain alcohol or made it harder for states to collect taxes. The Court ruled that the 21st Amendment "does not allow States to regulate direct shipment of wine on terms that discriminate in favor of in-state producers."

While this was a victory for wineries and consumers, the complicated ruling stopped short of fully sanctioning direct shipping. While reaffirming the Commerce Clause, the Court also reaffirmed the rights of states to determine their own regulation systems, as long as they did not contradict the Clause: If any level of direct shipping by in-state wineries is permitted, then out-of-state wineries must be given the same rights; however, if *no* intrastate shipping of alcohol is permitted, then the state can legally outlaw direct interstate shipments as well.

Some states moved quickly to disallow all direct shipping so that there would be no violation of the Commerce Clause, while others removed some barriers to out-of-state direct shipping but changed the rules regarding how much could be shipped and the permits necessary for direct shipping. Currently, there are three main categories of shipping tolerance in the United States: states that still have reciprocity agreements in place, states that allow limited direct shipping, and states where direct shipment is not allowed in any form. Further muddying the waters, common carriers, such as UPS and FedEx, have not yet begun shipping to some of the states that have recently allowed direct shipping. Thus, a patchwork of different laws regarding direct shipping remains in place.

Overall, the *Granholm* decision has had numerous immediate implications for both the wine industry and state lawmakers, and more changes are sure to come. Since the ruling was announced, most states have modified their direct shipping statutes in some way or are in the process of debating and changing them. As the *Granholm* decision found that reciprocity agreements were not valid since they permitted shipments only from a limited number of states, those few states that still have those laws in place must change them, or it is likely that litigation will ensue.

In states where direct shipping is permitted, the focus has now turned to improving and fine-tuning the laws, as well as addressing the issue of compliance. Almost every state requires a different permit, and some states have quantity limitations on the amount of wine a consumer can receive.

The next question is whether the *Granholm* decision reaches beyond just wine and direct shipping from wineries. There have been several lawsuits filed by **retailers** arguing that the *Granholm* decision applies not just to wineries but to them as well. Contradictory decisions in some of these lawsuits may be setting the stage for a return to the Supreme Court. Although direct shipping is now permitted to more states than not, this chapter in America's long and complicated history of dealing with alcohol is far from being closed.

Sheri Sauter Morano

Further Reading

Coalition for Free Trade. www.coalitionforfreetrade.org.
Federal Trade Commission. *Possible Anticompetitive Barriers to E-Commerce: Wine* (July 2003). www.ftc.gov/os/2003/07/winereport2.pdf.
Free the Grapes! www.freethegrapes.org.
ShipCompliant. www.shipcompliant.com.

DISTILLATION

Although distilled spirits are beyond the scope of this volume, distilleries represent an important market for the **global wine industry**. Each year, they purchase a substantial amount of wine, as well as a small amount of grape pomace (the residue of skins, seeds, and stems left over from a wine press), providing a revenue source that keeps many grape growers and **wineries** in business. In the Cognac and Armagnac regions of **France**, this is the primary intention for winegrowing; in other areas, such as the Central Valley of **California** or the Riverglen area of **Australia**, some vineyards and wine production are dedicated solely to this purpose as well. At times, distillation of wine is a fallback or even punitive option for excess or subpar wine production.

Distilled wine is *brandy*. It is produced by heating the wine in a still to just above 173°F (78.4°C), the boiling point of ethanol, the primary alcohol in wine. The ethanol boils and is drawn off as a vapor, carrying with it some of the flavor components of the wine and leaving the water and solids behind. After cooling, the wine-flavored ethanol is mixed with water to achieve the desired proof level, typically 80 proof (40 percent alcohol by volume), and may be colored; high-quality brandy is then aged for years in **barrels**. Brandy is distilled in every wine-producing country (and a lot of non-wine-producing ones, as well, using imported **bulk wine**). Cognac and Armagnac are among the most highly regarded. Pisco is a South American brandy; most other distilled wines around the world use the word "brandy," as in Brandy de Jerez. The brandy may in turn be added to standard wine to produce **fortified wine**.

Wine is sometimes distilled for industrial purposes (that is, not for drinking), although it is more expensive than many other raw materials that can be distilled instead. Industrial ethanol is widely used in chemical processes, as a solvent, in medicines, and as a gasoline additive. Usually when wine is distilled into industrial ethanol rather than brandy, it is an extraordinary measure due to some sort of problem. One such problem is overproduction. The **European Union** has on numerous occasions over the past quarter-century approved a "crisis distillation," buying the equivalent of as much as 7.5 million nine-liter cases (mc) of unsalable wine from producers as a way of propping up prices on the oversaturated wine market. In addition, producers may have no choice but to sell the wine for industrial distillation if it has a serious flaw that cannot be remedied, and, in the Old World at least, forced distillation may be a punishment meted out for transgressing **appellation** rules or national wine laws.

Every year, 33 million hectoliters, the equivalent of about 365 mc of wine, is used worldwide for nonwine purposes, almost all of which goes for brandy or industrial distillation, with a minuscule proportion being used for wine vinegar. In 2006, 42 mc of wine in the **United States**—14 percent of production—went for distillation.

Another category of grape-based spirits is distilled from grape pomace—in this case, from a wine that has gone through a period of maceration with the skins after fermentation and therefore has ethanol permeating the pomace. The sale of pomace after pressing is extra revenue for the winery, as it does not affect the separate sale of the wine. The distilled pomace produces an eau-de-vie that is known as *grappa* in **Italy** and *marc* in France, the two main places where this type of spirits is made.

DISTRIBUTORS

The traditional structure of the U.S. wine industry is an outgrowth of the repeal of **Prohibition** by the 21st Amendment to the U.S. Constitution, which gave to each state the authority to regulate alcoholic beverages within its borders. Under the "three-tier" structure that developed, alcoholic beverage producers, licensed at both the state and federal levels, sell their products to distributors, themselves also licensed at the federal and state levels. The distributors then sell the product to licensed **retailers** (off-premise) and **restaurant**/bar/hotel (on-premise) venues, which sell the product to the **consumer**. Thus, producers traditionally have limited contact with the final consumer, or even the retail outlet selling their products, and are dependent on their distributor in each state to move their output. Distributors are generally free to choose which wines to carry in their portfolios and how to market them.

"Tied-house laws," which grew out of the Prohibition-era conviction that producers and distributors were encouraging drunkenness by their control of the sales chain, restrain the combination of tiers within the three-tier system. Thus, distributors cannot own retailers or restaurants without obtaining special exemptions from state and federal authorities. Likewise, producers technically cannot own distributors, although a number of producers have created distributorships under separate legal structures.

Furthermore, in a few **control states** (Mississippi, New Hampshire, Pennsylvania, Utah, Wyoming, and two counties in Maryland), the state government acts as the sole distributor for wine in another holdover from Prohibition. The other states can be divided into franchise and nonfranchise states, which refers to the conditions under which a supplier can change distributors; in franchise states, such as New Jersey, Connecticut, and Massachusetts, wineries and importers cannot switch distributors at will, which stifles competition and privileges the existing wholesalers over entrepreneurial start-ups.

Distribution Companies.   The **Alcohol and Tobacco Tax and Trade Bureau (TTB)** lists nearly 16,000 licensed distributors/wholesalers (it is the same license), but this greatly overstates the number of actual distribution companies. Many wine producers, especially those using **custom crush facilities** or pursuing **négociant** strategies, seek wholesale licenses, which allow them to sell wine, rather than the more-difficult-to-acquire **winery** licenses. Retailers often find it convenient to also have wholesale licenses—and some states may require each location in a chain within the state to be separately licensed. Thus, one large drugstore chain has some 82 licenses in just two states. All types of entities are required to have a separate license for each state in which they operate. The largest distributor has 78 licenses in its own name in 16 states, while also operating through subsidiaries and joint ventures in other states.

Most of the major distributors are spirits focused but also sell wine, including many of the largest **brands**. Several smaller distributors specialize in wine; the largest of these is Wine Warehouse, and others include the Henry Wine Group, Atlanta Wholesale Wine, Martin Scott Wines, and Epic Wines. Traditionally beer wholesalers have specialized in beer and other products from beer producers, but lately they have been diversifying into other alcoholic beverages as growth in the beer market has slowed.

The number of wine and spirits distributors in the United States declined from more than 5,000 in 1995 to between 500 and 700 in 2007, employing more than 64,000 people. Through **consolidation**, a few distributors have grown to dominate the distribution segment, with operations across the country, although no distributor is yet national in scope. The largest U.S. distribution company is Southern Wine & Spirits, which operates in 30 states and had an estimated 18.2 percent market share in 2007 with total sales of $7.6 billion. The other major distributors that operate in more than five states are Republic National Distributing Company, the Charmer Sunbelt Group, Glazer's, and Young's Market Company. These top five distributors now control more than half of the $42 billion (in 2007) U.S. market for distilled spirits and wine, and their share is expected to rise. The market in many states is dominated by just two of the largest distributors.

Challenges of Wine Distribution.   The Nielsen Company estimates that there are nearly 450,000 locations in the United States that can sell wine, of which 298,000 are "on-premise"—venues where wine can be served rather than just sold in packages. The vast majority of these locations are single-site operations. Thus, simply accessing potential sales outlets for wine across the country is a complex logistical challenge. This challenge is further complicated by the vast number of wine brands, totaling at least 14,000 just in the grocery and **supermarket** channel and possibly reaching 80,000 in all types and channels. Moreover, wine generally needs to be "hand sold"—faced with so many choices, restaurant and retail wine buyers need extra attention in shaping their purchasing decisions.

Professional distributors, with their large sales forces and extensive networks of warehouses, transport, and administration, thus perform an essential function in the wine market. In addition, most states expect distributors to function as their agents in collecting taxes and reporting on beverage alcohol movement.

Distributors usually handle all logistics of distribution and are required by law to purchase and take title to the product. In many states, immediate payment in cash by both distributor and retailer or restaurant is also required. Wine also tends to move in relatively small volumes, case by case, as compared with spirits, which move in pallet sizes and are usually handled by the same distributors. Wine is one of the slowest-moving product categories, averaging inventory turns of about three months, compared to one day for beer and one month for spirits. Thus, both distributors and retailers face heavy inventory costs for wine products.

Consolidation.   Distributor consolidation is partly driven by the search for increasing economies of scale in the highly capital-intensive logistics industry, and also by the rapid consolidation of the spirits industry. Large spirits (and wine) producers have made growing demands on distributors for special services, dedicated sales forces, and very low-margin terms. The retail market has also consolidated, with so-called big-box discounters claiming growing shares of the market, adding to the pressure on distributors to increase their own scale. Efforts by some of these big-box retailers, whose large-scale purchases are important **profit** centers for the distributors, to escape the three-tier system by sourcing directly from wineries, as suggested by Costco's legal actions, are seen as a major threat to their survival by many in the distribution industry.

As distributors have consolidated, they have streamlined their wine portfolios, making it increasingly difficult for smaller wineries to access the market and even for larger wineries to get their smaller products out. Wineries complain of limited sales support and slow payment by distributors. They also traditionally have had difficulty obtaining information on what distributors are selling and where they sell it—known as "depletion data," relating to the drawdown of inventory—and the terms on which the product is sold. Each distributor has a different system for identifying product and retail or restaurant accounts, requiring the suppliers to pay third-party processors to make sense of their own data. Some distributors have begun limiting the data they are willing to share even on these terms. These frustrations have driven the winery **direct shipping** trend, as well as the growth of specialized sales and marketing companies to supplement winery and distributor sales services.

Distributors in Other Countries.   Outside the few other three-tier systems, such as Japan and Russia, distributors are more a convenience than a necessity, but they provide greater access to markets than a supplier can usually manage on its own, and for **imports**, they provide a familiarity with local customs and language that the producer may not have. Within the **European Union**, distributors typically act as brokers, facilitating a transaction without taking physical possession of the wine; once the deal is set, it is the responsibility of the producer to deliver the wine to the purchaser (and to collect payment). In **Canada** (except Alberta), the provincial governments are the sole distributors of wine.

Barbara Insel

Further Reading
Wine & Spirits Wholesalers of America. www.wswa.org.

DRINKING AGE

The most significant issue regarding the minimum legal drinking age (MLDA) for the wine trade is an economic one: How do employees who are under 21 years of age—20 percent of restaurant waitstaff at full-service establishments—sell a product about which they have very little understanding or training because they are unable legally to taste the product they are supposed to suggest to their customers? Thirty-seven U.S. states and the District of Columbia allow servers under the MLDA to serve alcoholic beverages in on-premise **restaurants**.

At the close of **Prohibition**, most states established an MLDA of 21 years. Decades later, in response to criticism of the perceived hypocrisy of having 18-year-old draftees who were not yet legally adults dying in the service of their country in Vietnam, with the concomitant lowering of the voting age to 18 in 1971, many states experimented with lowering their MLDA to 18, 19, or 20 years of age. However, due to the rise in automobile accidents and fatalities for this age group and increases in reported underage drinking, the federal government succumbed to the pressures of various citizen groups that lobbied for a return to a national MLDA of 21.

The Uniform Drinking Age Act, enacted in 1984, provided for the withholding of federal highway funds from any state that did not require a minimum age of 21 for the purchase of beverage alcohol. The Uniform Drinking Act is poorly understood, as it does not prohibit underage consumption but rather possession, and many states have exceptions to the MLDA, such as when

- a parent or guardian gives consent or is present,
- the underage drinker is married to a legal-age spouse,
- the underage drinking occurs on specified private property,
- the underage drinking is for religious or medical reasons, or
- the underage drinking is for educational purposes, including restaurant server training.

There has been added pressure on state legislatures to enact tougher standards and penalties of alcohol licensees. One area of note is in the field of beverage service training programs, such as ServSafe (www.servsafe.com) and TIPS (www.gettips.com). There are currently 17 states with mandatory and volunteer beverage service training program laws and a further 15 with volunteer program laws only. Several states, including Rhode Island, Florida, and Colorado, allow underage students in **hospitality** and culinary programs to receive responsible and supervised training in sensory analysis of wine to provide these students with the skills to understand food and wine pairing.

The MLDA for **European Union** countries in general is between 16 and 18 years of age, depending on the type of alcohol—lower for beer and wine than for spirits.

A recent national survey shows that 84 percent of the U.S. population age 18 and over opposes lowering the age from 21 to 19. More than 50 studies based on scientific research reported in medical journals have concluded that there is a significant correlation between the MLDA being increased and the lowering of traffic injuries and fatalities. Studies also demonstrate that a higher MLDA results in fewer underage youths drinking and impacts both their current and future age-eligible drinking habits. Furthermore, there is scientific evidence to suggest that alcohol consumption impacts brain development more significantly among teens than adults.

Advocates for lowering the MLDA include Choose Responsibility, which promotes some form of licensing of 18-year-olds to drink beverage alcohol. More than 100 college presidents have signed the "Amethyst Initiative" petition, calling for a reevaluation of the MLDA as a way of combatting secretive binge drinking. The goal would be to teach responsible consumption in environments where adults are present. Research indicates that underage alcohol consumption by students at colleges and universities is significantly higher than among their peers in the workforce. Industry-supported advocates and some independent researchers cite research supporting the "forbidden fruit argument"—the idea that drinking attracts so many young people precisely because it is forbidden, making it a "badge of rebellion" and a symbol of adulthood rather than an attraction for its own sake. If the MLDA were lowered, they argue, drinking would lose much of its attraction. They also suggest that the decrease in auto fatalities and binge drinking in recent years has not been due to raising the MLDA, but instead is more a reflection of changes in age demographics, increased awareness of DUI enforcement, and improved vehicular safety measures. *See also* Direct Shipping; Health; Wine Education.

Edward M. Korry

Further Reading

Anderson, Peter. "Reducing Drinking and Driving in Europe." Institute of Alcohol Studies, London, July 2007. www.ias.org.uk/resources/papers/europe/phproject/drink-driving.pdf.

Center on Alcohol Marketing and Youth, Georgetown University. "Underage Drinking in the United States." February 2005. http://camy.org/research/underage2004/report.pdf.

Wagenaar, Alexander C., and Traci L. Toomey. "Effects of Minimum Drinking Age Laws." *Journal of Studies on Alcohol* suppl. 14 (March 2002): 206–25.

DUTCH MARKET

The Netherlands has historically been a major importer of wine, especially for **distillation** into brandy. Because of its northerly latitude, its climate is too cold for significant wine production (though there are more than a hundred small estate vineyards), and beer has been the traditional favorite, but there has always been a good Dutch market for wine. Since World War II, wine consumption has grown steadily, from a historical low of 0.6 liters per capita to 21.6 in 2007. As of 2006, the Netherlands was sixth among wine-importing countries of the world, with imports of 45.8 million nine-liter cases (mc) worth €881 million. Its primary trading partner is **France**, source of fully a third of the wine imports. Not surprisingly, there are also strong imports (around 5 mc each) from the other major **European Union** producers **Germany**, **Spain**, and **Italy**. Its major **New World** partner is **South Africa**, a country with which the Netherlands has a very long history.

The Netherlands was one of the world's great merchant countries during the Age of Discovery and the **colonial era**, sending ships to the far reaches of the globe in search of trade goods, as well as throughout Europe to export brandy and import wine, among other products. A supply colony for the Dutch East India Company was established around Cape Town, South Africa, in 1652, and the winegrowing regions of South Africa were under Dutch control for most of the next 160 years. A series of wars with Great Britain reduced Dutch global influence, but the Netherlands has continued to have a strong mercantile philosophy.

The Dutch have had a connection with the Port and Sherry trade for centuries, and **fortified wine** remains exceptionally popular, accounting for more than 8 percent of consumption, compared to 2 percent average worldwide. Conversely, **sparkling wine** is not particularly popular, with less than 2 percent of the market, versus 6.5 percent globally. In **table wines**, the Dutch drink almost 50 percent **red wine**, 38 percent white, and around 13 percent **rosé**, a category that has nearly doubled in sales in three years.

The Netherlands' neighbor Belgium is the world's seventh largest wine importer, tied with **Canada**, bringing in around 32 mc per year. The small grand duchy of Luxembourg, located immediately west of Germany's Mosel Valley, produces a respectable 1.5 mc of wine annually on average. The nation also has one of the largest per-capita consumption rates in the world, occasionally outpacing France.

E

EASTERN EUROPE

Eastern Europe is a crucial part of the wine world, yet it is often left off the wine maps or shown as a big void. This is changing, however, as the **European Union** (EU) has now expanded to encompass several wine-producing Eastern European countries and as more and more wine from the region makes its way to Western markets. The region's combined production is roughly on a par with that of the **United States**, in the range of 20 to 25 million hectoliters (the equivalent of 225 to 275 million nine-liter cases [mc]). Its long history and some of the world's oldest grape-growing traditions alone justify a serious fresh look at this region, especially in the new political climate.

There are different definitions of "Eastern Europe," but it is generally considered to encompass the 1955 Soviet occupational borders—the Iron Curtain—including Russia as far east as the Ural Mountains. The main rivers affecting grapevine cultivation are the Volga, Don, Dnieper, and Danube, and the Black and Adriatic seas to the south add to the variety of macroclimates. The region's viticulture has been influenced by the **Greek**, Roman, and Ottoman empires, as well as the Napoleonic occupation, but is marked by an adamant insistence on preserving most indigenous grape varieties. The Communist collapse redefined the state-run wine industry and began a desperate search for Western markets. The influx of significant investment from the West and imported know-how rejuvenated the industry through modernization and the introduction of international grape varieties.

Many problems hamper the industry's growth. Laws and regulations are often disregarded. Homemade wine production escapes taxation and is a substantial underground economy; official production statistics do not account for this output. Wine faults are common. Hygiene and sterile winemaking are found only in the most modern **wineries** and bottling plants. A Russian blockade of container wine imports dramatically increased Bulgaria's exports, but in Moldova and Georgia created a terrible 750-milliliter bottle shortage, crippling the rejuvenating wine industry there. Fraudulent and artificial wine production is a problem in Moldova, Georgia, and Bulgaria, where hopeless producers add water and sugar to the pressed grape skins to produce more "wine." Most wines produced here are **organic**, as the growers cannot afford chemicals.

Nevertheless, this region has the opportunity to become the "new **Chile**," as it is already turning out excellent **quality wines** from some countries, with bargain pricing. To overcome consumer confusion, **varietal labeling** has been adopted by many wineries. Eastern European wines are visible in the **British** and **Scandinavian markets** and in **Germany**, but are scarce and little known in the United States. In **restaurants**, Eastern European wines are generally found only on ethnic wine lists and a few unique wine bars. Overall, marketing efforts are lacking from the region. Yet these wines have a promising future as **consumers** continue to look for undiscovered and value-priced labels.

Romania.   Romania is the leading wine-producing country in Eastern Europe, with production of around 55 mc in 2006. Romania joined the EU in 2007 and has reduced its production somewhat due to EU limitations. Yield is generally very low in Western terms. The world mainly knows this intricate wine country for its sweet Cotnari, which used to be referred to as one of the world's three best wines (along with Constantia and Tokaji Aszú). A suitable **appellation** system is being enforced, featuring DOC (*denumire de origine controlata*—controlled appellation of origin) wines. The best wine regions include Cotnari, Murfatlar, Dealul Mare, and Tîrnave.

Russia.   The Soviet Union was once the fourth largest wine producer on Earth, but the majority of the Soviet vineyards were in the independent republics. Russian production has been less than Romania's, but has been rising quickly; in 2006, Russia produced 50 mc, most of it in its European areas. Russia was long known for **sparkling wine** made in the Crimea region, produced for the aristocracy using the classical method by masters trained in **France**, but during the Soviet era, the wine was often diluted, resulting in unacceptable quality. Today, classic sparkling wine production has returned with promising quality improvements. However, local production does not satisfy demands, and it is not likely that Russian labels will be seen in the West in the near future. Russia has become a major importer of primarily inexpensive wines from other Eastern European countries and the West: It was the fourth largest wine-importing country in the world in 2006, bringing in about 80 mc.

Hungary.   The sweet, unctuous Tokaji—dubbed the "king of wines, wine of kings" by Louis XIV—is one of the world's great **dessert wines** and the most famous of today's Eastern European wines. The village of Tokaj is the birthplace of the first known appellation law, drawn up in 1641, citing vineyard restrictions for making the sought-after Tokaji Aszú.

U.S. and British consumers in the 1970s became familiar with Egri Bikavér (Bull's Blood). The quality of this mass-produced wine from the towns of Eger and Szekszárd (where it is Szekszárdi Bikavér) has dramatically improved; in addition to the original Kékoportó and Kadarka grapes, today Cabernet Franc and **Merlot** are also permitted in the blend. Other noteworthy wine areas are found on the northern shores of Lake Balaton. Hungary also bottles some exceptional quality **Cabernet Sauvignon**, **Sauvignon Blanc**, and **Pinot Grigio** wines.

In 1977, new wine laws were instituted echoing those of Western Europe. After the fall of the Iron Curtain, Hungary became the most aggressive wine producer in the region, with quality improvements and the reinstatement of prior regulations, attracting substantial investment from the West. Hungary joined the EU in 2004, and its production today is about 35 mc.

Other Countries.   Most other Eastern European nations are also wine producers. Bulgaria, Moldova, Croatia, and Ukraine, in particular, each produce around 20 mc annually. In general, very little of the production of these countries is exported, with the exception of Bulgaria, which used to produce the highest-quality wines in the Soviet Bloc and became the most accepted country from Eastern Europe for wine exports to the West, especially to Britain, Sweden, and Germany. Its best-known wine was Gamza red, made from Kadarka. A large project of the Communist government replanted three-quarters of all Bulgaria's vineyards with nonnative grapes. Bulgarian wines are likely to become more prominent now that it has joined the EU.

Thomas Belelieu

Further Reading
Bulgaria. www.bulgarianwine.com.
Croatia. www.bluedanubewine.com/regions/croatia.
Czech Republic. www.wineofczechrepublic.cz/en.html.
Georgia. www.gws.ge.
Hungary. www.winesofhungary.com.
Moldova. www.turism.md/eng/wine.
Romania. www.aromawine.com/wines.htm.
Russia. www.russiawines.com.
Slovenia. www.matkurja.com/projects/wine.

E-COMMERCE

Electronic commerce, or *e-commerce,* refers to the use of the Internet—e-mail and the World Wide Web—to conduct business, and companies in almost all fields have ventured into this medium. The wine industry is certainly no exception. The first thing that comes to mind regarding wine e-commerce is businesses (**wineries**, **retailers**, and so forth) selling wine to **consumers**—that is, business-to-consumer (B2C) trade—using electronic communications, but it also includes many business-to-business (B2B) transactions. As today's business world has been systematically transformed by the Information Age, the Internet and other Web-based technologies have allowed the wine industry to tap into smaller niche segments and to offer customized and even personalized products and services to a wider audience of consumers.

Almost all transactions in the wine trade can be conducted electronically, apart from the actual physical delivery of a product. Some, such as visually selecting plant material at a **nursery** or buying blending wines from a **bulk wine** broker, do not lend themselves especially well to e-commerce due to the sensory nature of the selection process. Nevertheless, everything from vineyard land to wine labels is being purchased over the Internet. Wineries and wine industry companies are also engaging in e-marketing to **promote** themselves and communicate various messages to potential buyers.

The use of the Internet to buy wine is well established at this point, and growth has continued at a steady rate, although it has not eclipsed other forms of sales as some in the 1990s predicted it would. At its simplest, B2C e-commerce consists of a buyer placing an order for wine over the Internet to a winery, retailer, or e-commerce-only establishment, which then fills the request using a delivery service or specialized fulfillment company (or possibly by merely preparing the wine for pickup by the customer) and processes the payment, in most cases, by credit card. A slightly more complicated, but more common, scenario involves the purchaser making his or her order via a form on the company's Web site.

The retailer engaged in this transaction may be a physical ("brick-and-mortar") business, such as a wine shop or a **supermarket**, but in the ephemeral world of e-commerce, it may also be a "virtual" store or "click-only" enterprise—that is, one that only fully exists on the Internet. Wine.com, one example of this business model, started in the 1990s and did business solely over the Internet as part of the initial frenzy of dot-com start-ups.

Even virtual businesses have *some* physical location, but such an e-commerce trader does not normally have a storefront where the general public can visit and browse wines on a shelf. Instead, it typically consists of a Web site that offers wine shopping lists, periodic wine specials, expert advice, wine and food pairing suggestions, vintage information, and the like. Computer systems collect orders electronically and relay them to the people who fulfill the orders. This can be a warehouse where wine is kept ready for delivery, but it is also possible for the e-commerce portal simply to be a conduit that (for a fee) passes the order along to a winery or a brick-and-mortar retailer for fulfillment. **Auction houses** have also taken advantage of e-commerce to enhance buying and selling of wine collections worldwide.

The advantages of e-commerce are readily apparent: From the Internet-only business's point of view, there is less overhead, probably fewer required staff, and perhaps not even any inventory to stock and maintain. Their offerings can be more diverse because shelf space is not a concern, and they may not need to actually invest in a specific wine until they have an order for it. In addition, they can access a segment of the market that, because of distance, transportation, parking, or other issues, would not visit them at a physical location. For the consumer, there are the attractions of easy comparison shopping, almost unlimited choice, access to detailed information about each wine, and the ability to shop from home.

The disadvantages can be substantial, however, and for some people—a large majority of people, based on the market share of e-commerce—they outweigh the considerable advantages. Some of these problems are common to most forms of e-commerce, but others are generated by the additional complications of selling an alcoholic product.

In general, the brick-and-mortar retailer's challenges have their electronic counterparts for the virtual retailer. While e-commerce does not necessarily require sales staff, it does require programmers and people who know how to use the appropriate software. It may not be necessary to decorate a wine showroom, but it is necessary to design a Web site that is reliable and easy to navigate—not to mention eye-catching; if the process of shopping, ordering, and paying is not easy and seamless, potential buyers are likely to get frustrated and "walk out" of the virtual store.

One factor that will prevent e-commerce from ever overshadowing physical retailers is the speed of delivery. It is often cited that a significant proportion of off-premise wine is consumed within hours of its purchase, say, when someone stops by the wine shop to pick up a bottle for dinner that night; e-commerce cannot compete for this segment of the market. Furthermore, the convenience of shopping from home does not satisfy those customers who like to be able to hold a bottle in their hand before buying it, and surfing the Web for wine is not always as fast as simply scanning down a wine shelf at a store. A winery or retailer that can offer actual tastes of some of the wines for sale clearly has a leg up on the e-retailer who can offer only written descriptions. Also, visits to some prime Internet retail sites often yield "out of stock" notices after the purchaser has started to complete the transaction. The most successful Internet businesses are those that offer a product or service that is not offered somewhere else by another seller, but this has been difficult for Internet merchandisers competing with real wine merchants.

The major U.S. player in this genre is Wine.com, which was the first to market with an all-Internet business and later absorbed WineShopper.com. Others include Wine-Searcher.com and WineBid.com. Gary Vaynerchuk's WineLibrary .com is unusual in that it is very successful as both a B2C virtual store and a brick-and-mortar wine shop in Springfield, New Jersey. Another company with applications to both the B2C and B2B arenas is LocalWineEvents.com. While this site started off slowly, it is now one of the most robust in offering a comprehensive calendar of wine events—both for the trade and consumers—taking place around the world; businesses can post events themselves, and tickets for events are also sold through this medium. The **United States** and the United Kingdom seem to be the biggest players thus far in wine e-commerce, but **Australia** is getting into the act with its own Wineshopper.com debuting in 2008. Internet sales typically trend like traditional retail sales, with numbers being highest at Thanksgiving and Christmas.

The B2B side of e-commerce has had a much larger impact on the wine industry—as it has in many other fields—than B2C. The supply chain has benefited enormously from being able to share data and process transactions. The Internet has also been used by many wineries for advertising and cross-promotion on wine publication Web sites as well e-commerce-only sites.

In the United States, in particular, the shipping of wine invokes a complex set of federal, state, and local laws that quickly become a minefield for a retailer. Sending a delivery truck across town to drop off some wine purchased over the Internet may not be a big deal, but the complications multiply rapidly if the wine crosses into another jurisdiction, especially a different state (let alone a different country). This has been the major hurdle that has tripped up many entrepreneurs who tried to conduct e-commerce on a large scale in the 1990s. Shipping between some states is relatively straightforward, but in many instances, the wine is required to pass through a state-licensed **distributor** or retailer. In a number of states, shipping of wine is simply illegal, and the customer is required to go to a physical retailer to collect the electronically ordered wine shipment (largely defeating the whole purpose of e-commerce). Third-party delivery services, such as UPS, FedEx, and others (but not the U.S. Postal Service, because mailing alcohol is illegal), generally have additional procedures involved in wine shipments, in large measure to avoid delivering alcohol to someone under the legal **drinking age**.

Building a **brand** for a tangible good over the Internet is inherently challenging for a new entrant into the B2C end of the business. Services are much easier to market and sell over the Internet than products, and trust is an important aspect of doing business successfully over the Internet in any arena. Unless a trusted wine merchant—be it real or virtual—plays a role in the transaction, sales will be difficult. Despite what appears to be positive growth in this segment, **profitability** continues to be a challenge for many Internet wine retailers. Still, wine e-commerce vendors that do not misrepresent product, are able to avoid out-of-stocks, provide great customer service, serve a targeted segment of the market, and offer interactivity at their Web sites will be the most successful in this aspect of the industry. *See also* Direct Shipping; Information Technology.

EUROPEAN UNION

With its 2007 expansion, the European Union (EU) now comprises 27 European countries. The borders of the EU stretch from **Portugal** in the west to Latvia and Lithuania in the east and from Finland in the north to Malta in the south. Due to its vast size and consolidated governing body, the EU will begin to take a more powerful role in determining standards and creating the rules to be followed by other players on the **global** wine scene and may someday replace the **United States** as the important single market.

The European Union currently accounts for 45 percent of the world's wine-growing area, 65 percent of production, 57 percent of consumption, and 70 percent of exports (including internal cross-border trade). It has more than 2.4 million holdings producing wine, covering almost 9 million acres, or 2 percent of the EU's agricultural area. Wine represented 5 percent of the value of EU agricultural output in 2006. EU wine consumption is falling steadily, although sales of **quality wines** are increasing. Over the last 10 years, imports have grown by 10 percent per annum, while exports are increasing only slowly. According to current trends, excess wine production will reach 15 percent of annual production by 2010–2011.

Following World War II, much of Europe's farmland was in ruin. Farmers had been displaced and their resources depleted. Europeans realized that the only way to become an important force in the global market again was by consolidating and creating a unified agricultural plan, one that would more effectively manage the entire area's resources and institute regulations to control production. Accordingly, the CAP (Common Agricultural Policy) was established in 1962.

The policies regarding wine production have changed considerably since those early days, as the bureaucrats in the European capital Brussels slowly came to realize that grapes for wine production could not be treated in exactly the same way as, say, apples or livestock. Initially the CAP put no curb on plantings and virtually guaranteed compensation for all production. This set the stage for the development of the infamous European ''wine lake,'' with growers producing grapes and making wine with the sole intention of obtaining government payouts, not selling to **consumers**. This shocking state of affairs led to a decade, starting in 1978, of fierce control and intervention from the EU governing bodies. The CAP was radically reformed between 1995 and 2000 to rectify the policies that had encouraged overproduction. However, undoing the damage has proved to be a slow, arduous, and complicated operation.

In late 2007, the European Commission reformed the Common Market Organization for wine, with the intention of making EU producers more competitive. The stated goals included winning back markets, balancing **supply and demand**, and simplifying rules governing wine labeling and production, while at the same time preserving the best traditional production methods and respecting the environment. From 2008 on, a much larger slice of the EU budget is being devoted to **promoting** wine outside the EU and creating informational campaigns within the EU that focus on explaining the new labeling regulations and on responsible/ moderate wine consumption. Plans call for national **appellation** systems to be replaced with a Europe-wide system of Protected Designations of Origin (PDOs) and Protected Geographic Indications (PGIs) by 2009.

For a five-year transitional period, planting restrictions are being kept in place and uncompetitive producers are receiving financial incentives to encourage them to leave the sector. To avoid social or environmental problems, states are allowed to limit the removal of vineyard areas in environmentally sensitive regions and to stop the process completely if the total reaches 10 percent of the country's area under vines. It is projected that a total of around 200,000 hectares (500,000 acres) will be grubbed up during this period.

After 2013, planting restrictions will be lifted, allowing producers to increase their vineyard holdings. Certain winemaking practices accepted by all producer countries in the International Organization of Vine and Wine (OIV) will be adopted by the EU, and quality policy will be based on geographical origin. Wines without geographical indications will be allowed to indicate the variety and vintage on their labels. States will receive a budget and a list of suggested measures from which they may choose those best suited to their local situation. The amount of money available for each country will be calculated according to vine area, production, and historical expenditure. Possible measures include promotion in foreign markets, vineyard restructuring/conversion, support for green harvesting, insurance against natural disasters, and the administrative costs of setting up a sector-specific mutual fund. Also, more money will be made available for the Rural Development scheme, a part of which is used for vocational training and to help young wine producers. *See also* Austria; British Market; Dutch Market; Eastern Europe; France; Germany; Greece; Italy; Scandinavian Market; Spain.

Patricia Guy

Further Reading
European Union Agriculture and Rural Development. http://ec.europa.eu/agriculture.
Ginsberg, Roy H. *Demystifying the European Union*. Lanham, MD: Rowman & Littlefield, 2007.

McCormick, John. *Understanding the European Union*. 3rd ed. London: Palgrave Macmillan, 2005.

Reid, T.R. *The United States of Europe*. New York: Penguin, 2004.

EXCHANGE RATES

The issue of currency exchange is both a complex and a critical one for the **global wine industry**, as it is for any type of international trade. Rapid changes in the values of different currencies impact the sourcing, the pricing, and potentially the **distribution** of wine. A wine **importer** must consider the currency risk of committing to a contract fixed in a foreign currency when planning purchases of wine from other countries and preparing pricing strategies for its domestic market.

If the foreign currency appreciates between the signing of the contract and the actual payment to the supplier—that is, if the foreign currency's value compared to the domestic currency goes up—the price paid in domestic currency terms will be higher. The result (assuming there is no contingency for this in the contract and it is not possible to renegotiate a higher price with the supplier) will be either a higher selling price at market, which could hurt sales volume, or a reduction in the importer's **profit** margin. In reality, the first option may not be feasible in the short term because many states require price postings 30, 60, or even 90 days in advance and retailers publish catalogues and restaurants—especially restaurant chains—publish wine lists that have a long lead time and will not accept price fluctuations. Of course, the currency exchange rate fluctuation could also work to the importer's advantage should the foreign currency devalue before delivery of payment is made; the foreign currency will then be purchased at the lower market price.

Savvy importers will commit to a purchase of the transaction currency from a bank at the moment that their purchase contract is signed with the supplier. By locking in an exchange rate, they are able to eliminate the currency risk and guarantee the cost of goods in terms of their own domestic currency. The most common type of contract for purchasing currencies in advance is called a *forward contract*. The exchange rate at which the foreign currency will be purchased on a future date is determined by taking the current "spot rate" observed in the market and adjusting it to the "forward" date, the date on which the importer will need the foreign currency to complete the transaction. The adjustment is determined by the interest rate differential between the two currencies being exchanged.

An alternative to the forward contract is the *currency option*. This contract, which is purchased for a premium, much like an insurance policy, serves to guarantee a maximum exchange rate for the purchase of the needed currency. The advantages of the currency option are twofold. First, the contract is a *right,* but not an *obligation,* to exchange currencies on a given date. As an example, should an importer anticipate the purchase of a quantity of foreign wine, he may contract an option before signing the contract with a supplier as a hedge against the currency risk. If the contract is not concluded, then the importer holds a financial instrument that does not require an actual exchange of currency—hence the "option." The second advantage of a currency option is that it sets a ceiling on the purchase price of the needed currency. Should the currency that is being bought end up trading in the market at a more favorable rate than the option rate or "strike price," the owner of the option is not obliged to buy the currency at the guaranteed rate and is free to purchase it in the open market at the better rate.

Foreign exchange risk is an issue not only for importers but also for suppliers, who may see diminished demand for their products in markets where the purchasing power of the domestic currency is affected by poor exchange rates, as well as for **consumers** of imported wines, who ultimately must choose between paying the higher price or switching to a different wine. A weakened currency, on the other hand, may be a boon for a wine-exporting country as its products become more price competitive in foreign markets.

The most significant recent exchange rate trend has been the weakening of the U.S. dollar. Between January 2006 and March 2008, the dollar declined precipitously against other major currencies, from being worth, for example, 0.83 euros (€) or 1.33 Australian dollars (A$) to just €0.63 or A$1.09. Thus, everything else remaining the same, wine from France cost 30 percent more in the United States in 2008 than in 2006—pain that was shared by the French suppliers, their U.S. importer, and especially the dollar-paying consumer. This was all great news for American wineries, however, because not only did their wines become much more reasonably priced and attractive compared to imports on the U.S. market, but they also became 24 percent cheaper for Europeans to buy, at the same wholesale price in dollars.

The foreign exchange market that deals in the purchases and sales of currencies and related products is a 24-hour-a-day operation. It is the largest financial market by volume, with a daily turnover estimated at $3.2 trillion.

Philippe Newlin

F

FADS AND FASHIONS

As with any **consumer** good, the wine market can be driven by fads and fashions. There are many types of fads, and they can have many causes. In addition to increased sales, fads can have short-term and long-term effects on the industry. Wine producers and traders have always paid heed to fashions in the wine world, as wine was one of the first forms of global currency. Of course, observing trends is much simpler than predicting them or determining how long they will last.

The difference between a fad and a trend is indistinct, but a true fad is something that is suddenly embraced with inexplicable fervor by the public. Demand for it grows sharply for a while, out of all proportion to other seemingly similar items, after which it may just as suddenly disappear, or it may gradually fall back to a more sustainable level to become a long-term trend.

Wine fads can come from many sources. Successful marketing by producers may provide the seed, and scientific findings and global politics can also ignite a new fad. Certainly pop culture has always been a factor in fads and fashions for any consumer industry, and food trends, such as the Atkins diet and popular shows on the Food Network, sometimes have an immediate and remarkable effect on the wine market. However, reaching fad status requires the unpredictable development of a self-perpetuating feedback loop among consumers, who spread interest in the product to people who have never been exposed to whatever started the ball rolling.

Types of Fads.   *Style fads* encompass an entire wine style or category. For example, post–World War II consumers preferred lighter and sweeter styles of wine, spawning demand for such wines as Liebfraumilch and Canei. Later the trend switched to semisweet and slightly effervescent wines, prompting the rise in popularity of Riunite, Mateus, and Lancers. The popularity of these wine **brands** declined, however, when their key customers switched over to **wine coolers** in the late 1970s and 1980s. Once these coolers became a malt-based product, many of their consumers never returned to wine, but instead embraced the flavored malt beverage and beer categories.

Broad changes in the market can also happen almost overnight, as in the case of the November 1991 episode of *60 Minutes* that discussed the phenomenon known as the "**French paradox**," citing the **healthful** effects of **red wine**. Red wine sales in the **United States** increased by 44 percent within the next six months.

Micro fads may be so narrow as to focus entirely on one wine from one producer. The appeal of these products develops a momentum of its own, independent of **promotion** by the producer. So-called **cult wines**, such as Harlan Estate or Screaming Eagle, could fall into this category. Another example would be the recent popularity of Cristal **Champagne** by Louis Roederer. First mentioned in song lyrics by rapper Jay-Z in 1996, and then by other artists in their own songs, Cristal's retail price more than doubled over the next decade, and it became synonymous with luxury for a whole generation.

Varietal fads—market trends focused on a single grape variety—tend to be more cyclical in nature, although they can have lasting effects. Oak-aged **Chardonnay** became popular in the late 1970s, with consumers first embracing the richer tastes of Pouilly-Fuissé and riper white **Burgundies**, then shifting to bold, creamy, buttery Chardonnays from **California**, which replaced the then-popular **Sauvignon Blanc**. As consumers gravitated toward lighter foods and styles, these ubiquitous oaky Chardonnays became less popular, sparking the ABC (Anything But Chardonnay) reaction and creating the right environment for the rise of **Pinot Grigio** in the 1980s.

Pinot Grigio's popularity was mainly due to focused marketing by northern **Italian** cooperatives, but it has had a lasting effect, and Pinot Grigio now appears on almost all **restaurant** wine lists as a by-the-glass pour. Its simple, crisp fruit flavors actually converted many white **Zinfandel** drinkers back to white wine, which they had abandoned because they did not care for oak tannin. Eventually, however, so many mediocre-quality Pinot Grigios were released during the height of its popularity that many wine enthusiasts' opinions of the variety turned lukewarm, triggering an ABPG (Anything But Pinot Grigio) backlash. Now, with the popularity of **New Zealand** Sauvignon Blanc, that variety is back on the rise around the world, and the trend has come around full circle.

There are numerous examples for red varieties, as well. The ascendance of **Merlot** in the United States to replace **Cabernet Sauvignon** continues today. Other varietal fads, such as the rise of **Syrah/Shiraz**, Petite Sirah, or Old Vine Zinfandel, have come and faded, but have had the effect of diversifying the market. Meanwhile, the "*Sideways* effect" of 2005 prompted a sudden rise in sales of **Pinot Noir** after that grape was championed by the main character of a popular movie. Nielsen data show a 34 percent increase in California Pinot Noir sales within the first 12 weeks after the movie's release. To date, sales of this variety have held steady.

Regional fads boost the sales of the wines of a particular region or country. **Australian** wines became popular in the late 1990s coinciding with the Summer Olympics held in Sydney in 2000, and through successful cooperative marketing by the Australian wine industry through Strategy 2025. The wines of many other regions or countries have had their spurts of trendiness as well, from the spike in popularity of **German** wines in the **British market** due to their favor by Queen Victoria to the **Greek** wines that are showing up everywhere today.

Effects on the Industry.   Fads can have many effects on the **global wine industry** besides sales. For instance, varietal fads may encourage field grafting of new, chic varieties in established vineyards. This has a financial impact because the new vines will not produce a crop for a few years, and it can result in the loss of many old vines and traditional varieties. **Grape-growing** techniques and harvesting decisions can also be affected by changes in wine style preferences, such as changing from a crisp, neutral Pinot Grigio to a richer Pinot Gris without the need to regraft.

The trend toward riper and riper styles to appeal to **wine writers** and critics—and the tendency of many consumers to follow their **ratings and scores**—has also changed the way grapes are grown and wines are made around the world, perhaps using **must adjustments** to create wines that appeal to these critics. This has caused a great deal of controversy within the industry, as some claim that the wines are becoming too homogenous in order to satisfy a singular taste, while others argue that technology is simply producing a better, cleaner, and more correct wine.

The pace of "fashionableness" continues to accelerate. Hundreds of years ago, wine fads were usually generated in royal courts and took decades to filter down to more common folk. By the middle of the twentieth century, focused wine marketing efforts could create demand for niche wines among specific demographic groups, which then sometimes erupted into a full-blown fad. As populations age and times change, however, that which was new and exciting naturally loses its luster and is eclipsed by something newer and more exciting. Brand names and wine styles diminish and sometimes disappear entirely. **Globalization and the Internet** have changed the way and the speed with which consumers receive information. In the future, this will no doubt mean that fads and fashions in the wine world will be more abrupt and less predictable. *See also* Varietal Labeling.

Jennifer D. Pereira

FESTIVALS, TRADE SHOWS, AND COMPETITIONS

Wine festivals are sponsored events that bring together wine-interested **consumers** and corresponding components of food, **restaurants**, and **wine tourism**. *Wine trade shows* are tasting and evaluation events that focus on and attract industry professionals in the wine, food, and **hospitality** trades; the setting is a business-to-business opportunity for professionals in the field to buy, sell, and learn about wines from specific regions or around the world. *Wine competitions* are invitational events where producers are invited to submit wine entries, for a fee, to be judged by a select group of wine professionals and/or consumers in a blind-tasting format.

Many European countries have a long tradition of celebrating the annual harvest with a festival, in which wine was a fundamental component. While such festivals have been going on for hundreds of years, wine trade shows and competitions are more recent phenomena that are increasing along with the **globalization** of the wine industry.

Wine Festivals.   Hundreds of wine festivals are held throughout the world today. Many festivals in the **United States** and the **European Union** are tied historically or actually to a real harvest; however, a growing number of food and wine festivals are sponsored by wine marketing associations, the wine industry press, or charitable organizations within a community. Some festivals now run for several days and attract national and even international supporters and participants. Wine festivals afford **wineries** and wine regions the opportunity to **promote** their products to participants. These festivals are fee-paid public events offering consumers general wine knowledge through wine tastings and seminars that may include food tastings, chef demonstrations, special dinners, and auctions of wine, restaurant meals, and travel. Some of the better known wine festivals in the United States include the Food & Wine Classic in Aspen, Colorado; the Boston Wine Expo; the South Beach Wine & Food Festival in Miami; and the Wine Experience in New York and other selected cities.

Trade Shows.   Trade shows target industry professionals to develop business-to-business relationships. Wine producers drive wine trade shows by renting booths to display and present their wines to attract key participants, including **importers**, **distributors**, **retailers**, restaurateurs, **wine educators**, and, in some cases, consumers. At some large international events, the producers serve foods to go with their wines and may even bring in a star chef to serve full meals to special guests. The two largest wine trade shows are Vinexpo, which alternates annually between **Bordeaux** and other international locations—Hong Kong in 2008—and Vinitaly, held annually in Verona, **Italy**. Trade shows may be international, national, or regional in focus. In the United States, most wine trade shows are regional or local.

The burgeoning number of festivals and trade shows has caused significant competition for obtaining the best **brands** and participants. Producers exhibiting their product make a significant investment for booth rental and product display. The additional cost of having several key executives and members of the sales and marketing team at the show makes it imperative that attendance choices be tied to a strategic sales and promotion plan.

Wine Competitions.   Wine competitions are closed professional events that provide producers with a professional review of their wines judged against other competitive wines. For successful wines, they supply a marketing tool that helps sell the award-winning wine to retailers and consumers. Wine competitions were initially established to meet a local or regional need because most wine sold was local or regional. Today, many competitions judge wines from all over the world as international wines are available in every market.

The reputations of the judges are an important component of the competitions because the quality of the competition is determined by the perceived expertise of those judging the wine. Competitions vary on the judge selection process: Some feature only wine critics and others only winemakers, but most competitions look for a variety of wine professionals, including Masters of Wine, Master **Sommeliers**, **wine writers**, winemakers, wine retailers, wine educators, restaurateurs, and other key professionals in the wine industry. Some may also include knowledgeable consumers.

Wines are judged by varietal or style in a blind tasting: **Chardonnay** against Chardonnay or Rhône blend against Rhône blend, for example. Some specialize in one varietal or niche, for instance, wines made by **women**. Wine competitions continue to grow in number in the United States, Europe, **Australia**, and other wine-producing countries. Large consumer markets outside of wine-producing regions, such as Tokyo or Florida, also hold competitions.

Typically, gold, silver, and bronze medals are awarded by judging panels. A gold medal at a noted competition means increased sales. The largest wine competition is the International Wine and Spirit Competition held in London, followed by the Los Angeles International Wine & Spirits Competition and the San Francisco International Wine Competition.

Competition results are considered important third-party endorsements, similar to **ratings and scores** from wine critics. Medals and awards are heavily promoted by wineries to market their wines, particularly in winery tasting rooms and through **wine clubs**, or to attract a distributor in a region where the wine is not currently represented. For larger wineries, it is a good way to measure consistency. Evaluation from a wine competition, based on a blind tasting by several judges, may have the perception of being less biased than a score from a critic who knows the varietal, **appellation**, and producer of the wine that is being rated.

Trends.   Festivals, trade shows, and competitions increasingly overlap in their target markets. Many festivals try to attract wine industry professionals, and most trade shows now allow consumers in for at least a portion of the event schedule. Competitions sometimes sponsor festivals or special events to showcase award-winning wines. The *San Francisco Chronicle* hosts a tasting of its award-winning wines that attracts hundreds of consumers. The *Dallas Morning News* Wine Competition holds a festival that identifies the best new restaurants of Dallas as well as the best wines from the competition. The Los Angeles International Wine & Spirits Competition showcases and makes available for tasting all gold medal wines, usually 300 in number, and offers 60 classes by competition judges during the monthlong Los Angeles County Fair.

Specialized festivals, shows, and competitions that focus on a particular segment of the business are becoming more common. Some focus on only one varietal or on wines of a particular region; others promote wines that pair with a particular food or market segment. **Zinfandel** Advocates & Producers (ZAP), which hosts a festival and trade show, exhibits only Zinfandel wines, and the Pinot Shootout competition, only **Pinot Noir**. The Pacific Coast Oyster Wine Competition seeks to find wines that pair with oysters on the half shell.

Education is becoming an ever-increasing component of festivals, shows, and competitions. Every event is likely to have several educational classes with different topics of interest to the trade and/or consumers.

Mary Ellen Cole, Margie Ferree Jones, and Robert Small

Further Reading
Berger, Dan. "Competition vs. Scores." *Wine Press Northwest* (June 15, 2006).
Block, Corliss, and Gail Bradney. *Best Wines! Gold Medal Winners from the Leading Competitions Worldwide*. Bearsville, NY: Print Project, 1996.

Caputo, Tina. "Wine Competitions That Help You Sell." *Wines & Vines* (October 2007): 60–63.

Hall, Lisa Shara. "Understanding Wine Competitions." *Wine Business Monthly* (November 2006): 53–61.

Steinberger, Mike. "Judgment of Paris." *Slate* (May 24, 2006). www.slate.com/id/2142365.

FLYING WINEMAKERS

A "flying winemaker" is a winemaker who manages multiple **wineries** separated by great distance—and hence is often on a plane, jetting from one harvest to the next. The phenomenon began in the late 1980s when winemakers from **Australia** and **New Zealand**, armed with the latest winemaking technology and science, took advantage of the off-season in the Southern Hemisphere to consult to wineries in Europe and North America. Today, winemakers from **France**, **Italy**, the **United States**, and other nations have joined the ranks of flying winemakers, and their imprimatur can be found on some of the world's most successful labels. Their wines typically are characteristic of the **New World** style, with ripe fruit, liberal use of oak, and smooth tannins.

The best-known flying winemaker is Michel Rolland, an enologist from **Bordeaux** who directs winemaking for more than 100 clients in over a dozen countries as far afield as India and Uruguay. His clients have included Harlan Estate, Staglin, and Robert Mondavi in **California**; Tenuta dell'Ornellaia in Italy; dozens of châteaux in his native Bordeaux; and Clos de los Siete in **Argentina**. Rolland was memorably featured in *Mondovino,* Jonathan Nossiter's 2004 documentary deploring the **globalization** of the wine industry.

Other notable flying winemakers include American Paul Hobbs, Australians Kym Milne and John Worontschak, and Hugh Ryman, the English winemaker portrayed by Russell Crowe in the 2006 film *A Good Year.*

For their expertise, flying winemakers charge hefty fees. Although they sometimes merely consult, they generally control the winemaking process for their clients. Increasingly, they have an ownership stake in the operations as well.

These globe-trotting wine mavens are a product of the modern world and are not without controversy. Critics charge that they apply the same techniques to vineyards around the world and contribute to the homogenization of wine by pursuing an international style that emphasizes market preferences over **terroir**. In *Mondovino,* Rolland is shown in an unflattering light, dispensing the same advice ("micro-oxygenation") to far-flung clients. Flying winemakers and their advocates counter that they have improved the quality of wine in many regions by bringing better hygiene and modern winemaking and viticultural techniques to their operations.

In either case, flying winemakers have had a profound impact on the business of wine and will continue to do so, especially as aspiring winemaking regions emerge around the globe. For wineries, these celebrated winemakers can bring expertise, market savvy, and an elevated profile. The downside includes higher costs and less than full-time attention.

Amy Cortese

FORTIFIED WINE

A fortified wine is a wine to which brandy has been added during or after fermentation. The addition of brandy raises the alcohol level high enough to kill the yeast, thus arresting the fermentation. Fortified wines vary in alcoholic strength and range from dry to sweet according to how much sugar in the must had been converted to alcohol before fortification.

Many wine-producing countries make fortified wines. The "classics" are Port, Sherry, and Madeira. However, this is not intended to dismiss the significance of some of the other great and historic fortified wines. There are the less revered, a good example being **vermouth**, which is a fortified wine flavored with herbs and spices and is not often given its due respect. There is also the important category of *vin doux naturel*, French for "fortified wine," which was pioneered in 1299 by Arnaldus de Villanova, a Catalan alchemist, working in Montpellier. Indeed, **France** produces some delicious fortified wines, most prolifically in the Rhône Valley, including Muscat de Beaumes-de-Venise and Banyuls.

Muscat is one of the most common grapes grown for the production of fortified wines, and sadly some of the best producing areas are disappearing. Setubal, a peninsula close to Lisbon in **Portugal** that is being gobbled up by property developers as the city expands, is one of the greatest losses to the world wine community. Wines of the few remaining producers, most notably José Maria da Fonseca, rival the world's greatest and, with stocks in cask dating back to the 1880s, are some of the longest lived.

Spain's Málaga is another disappearing region. It once produced about 2.4 million nine-liter cases (mc) a year, but fell victim to **phylloxera**, forcing hundreds of producers to abandon their businesses. Today, there are just a couple left, making under 80,000 cases. Sicily's Marsala, also in decline, formerly reached close to 7 mc in sales and has now dropped down to around a million, most of which is cooking wine.

The **United States** makes fortified wines—officially classed as "**dessert wines**" in government terminology—and because the General Agreement on Tariffs and Trade protocol to protect European place names was never signed, some U.S. producers use names that are recognized by the rest of the world as coming only from specific regions in Europe. Such wines cannot be exported. The same applies to some wines made in **South Africa** and **Australia**, although they have since signed the agreement and these wines will soon be marketed under **brand** names, such as Galway Pipe, without mentioning the word "Port."

Many other fine fortified wines are made in Australia, including Muscat and Tokay in Rutherglen by such noteworthy producers as Bailey's and Morris Wines. South Africa's Cape also excels in fortified wines, but none of them shares the success of Port and Madeira from Portugal or Sherry from Spain.

Port.   Port, the king of fortified wine, comes from the Douro, a strictly demarcated region in Portugal, and the entire production is rigorously controlled by **appellation** regulations. Port's name is derived from the town of Oporto at the mouth of the Douro River, but the Douro, the world's second oldest demarcated region (after Hungary's Tokaji), predates Port. Judging by its Roman ruins, wine production in this part of Portugal has an ancient history. Initially a dry **table** wine–producing region, its fortified wine developed when **British** traders shipped wine back to England late in the seventeenth century and the long sea journey required fortification of the wine for it to survive the primitive shipping conditions. Today, Port is produced by adding brandy to the must within 24 to 48 hours of the beginning of fermentation, at which point the wine is usually around 7 percent alcohol by volume (abv) and is raised to 20 percent abv. This kills the yeast and fermentation stops, leaving a wine with significant residual sugar.

Most Port is **red**, but there are also white Ports, and in 2008 production of the first **rosé** Port was announced. Among the reds, the majority is bottled after three years of aging in stainless steel tanks or oak casks. Those sold for immediate consumption are called *ruby* or *tawny,* depending on the depth of color. Some Ports are deemed of sufficient quality and structure to warrant special aging in bottle or **barrel**. High-quality tawnies may be age-worthy enough to warrant 20 years or more in barrel. *Vintage* Port is top-quality Port that generally has the potential to age 50 years or more in the bottle; the earliest known vintage Port still available, the 1815 Ferreira, continues to make thought-provoking drinking. Other styles of Port include *late-bottled vintage* (LBV), which is bottled between four and six years of age; *reserve* Port; *colheita,* a tawny from a single year; and *crusted.* There are more than a hundred indigenous grape varieties used for Port production, the best-known being Touriga Nacional, Touriga Francesa, Tinta Roriz, Tinta Amarela, Tinta Cão, and Tinta Barroca.

Port exports in 2006 totaled 8.7 mc, with a total value of €330 million. Almost a third of this went to France. Other important destinations included the **Dutch market**, Belgium, Britain, and **Germany**. The United States imported about 470,000 cases of Port, which represented 51 percent of all fortified wine brought into the country; the largest imported brands were Warre's and Sandeman.

Sherry.   Sherry (or Jerez), from Andalucia in southwestern Spain, is the second of the three classic fortified wines. Though Port has fully recovered from its depression years (the 1960s), Sherry is still struggling to find its footing in today's market. Exports were down to 4.6 mc in 2007, a 20 percent decline from four years earlier. Sherry is where **Riesling** was 15 years ago and, like Riesling, is the darling of many top **wine writers**, such as Jancis Robinson, Hugh Johnson, and Michael Broadbent.

Sherry is quite different from other fortified wines. In the first place, fortification takes place after fermentation rather than during it; thus, the wines are initially fully dry. Sherry's two most unique features, however, are *flor* and the *solera.* Flor, an unattractive-looking but beneficial yeast that develops in the barrels of *fino* Sherry, protects the wine and gives it a distinctive tang. Those Sherries that do not develop flor become *palo cortado* or *oloroso;* those that lose their flor become *amontillado.* Flor resembles yellowy cottage cheese and floats on top of the wine. It is rather volatile and needs to be kept alive by feeding on nutrients in the Sherry. For this reason, Sherry undergoes a solera method of aging, in which young wine is added to older wine barrels to replenish these nutrients. The solera system conceptually acts like a waterfall in that the final barrels are a mix of very old wine, and every vintage of wine eventually reaches the blend.

Three grape varieties are grown in Sherry's 26,000 acres of vineyards. The primary grape, Palomino, is used for most styles. Pedro Ximénez and Moscatel (Muscat of Alexandria) are used as sweetening agents for some blends and by themselves for very sweet dessert wines. Finos tend to be about 15.5 percent abv, whereas oloroso is around 18 percent and can go higher.

Sherry production in 2006 was 5.4 mc, down from an average of 7.8 mc in the previous four years. Exports in 2006 were valued at €76.3 million. The United States imported 278,000 cases of Sherry in 2006, roughly a third of the total imports of fortified wine. The largest-selling Sherry brand in the United States was Harveys Bristol Cream, which alone accounted for about 100,000 cases.

Madeira.   The third classic fortified wine is from the Portuguese island of Madeira, 400 miles off the coast of Morocco, directly in the trade winds between Europe and North America. In the **colonial era**, all passing ships used to stop in Madeira to stock up on provisions and would use casks of Madeira wine as ballast in the bottom of the boats. It was discovered that the wine in the holds was heated and improved during the transit to the West Indies and America from Madeira, and for a while it was required that the best Madeiras be treated by being sailed around the world twice. It became the largest selling wine in North America, where the illustrious following included the likes of Thomas Jefferson and George Washington (who drank a pint of Madeira daily for dinner), and such historical events as the signing of the Constitution and the Declaration of Independence were toasted with Madeira.

America remained the largest market for Madeira until **Prohibition**, at which time, with the collapse of sales, most producers had to uproot the vines and plant other crops. In 1988, Madeira experienced a revival when the Port trade's Symington family invested in the ailing Madeira Wine Company and relaunched it in the United States.

The unique difference in the method of production of Madeira is that the wine is heated after fortification for a minimum of three months to simulate the voyage through the tropics, at a temperature of 115°F to 120°F (about 45°C). The result of this *maderization* is a wine that is indestructible—it does not go off even after a bottle has been opened. The grapes used for Madeira include four white varieties, which are also synonymous with styles of wine: Sercial, Verdelho, Bual (or Boal), and Malmsey (Malvasia), from driest to sweetest. The red variety Negra Mole today is also considered a "classic" variety.

Total production of Madeira for drinking in 2005—not counting a large volume that is salted and sold for cooking purposes, much of it to France—was a little more than 100,000 cases. Major markets are Britain, Germany, Japan, and the United States, which imported 18,500 cases in 2006. *See also* Eastern Europe; Greece; Italy; Must and Wine Adjustments.

Bartholomew Broadbent

Further Reading

For the Love of Port. www.fortheloveofport.com.
Jeffs, Julian. *Sherry*. London: Mitchell Beazley, 2004.
Madeira Wine Guide. www.madeirawineguide.com.

FOSTER'S GROUP

The parent company of Foster's beer in **Australia** dove into the wine industry in a big way by purchasing major premium Australian wine companies Mildara Blass (1996), Rothbury Estate (1996), and Southcorp Ltd. (2005), as well as Beringer Wine Estates in the **Napa Valley** (2000). With global sales of 39.7 million cases (mc) in 2006, Foster's is the fourth largest wine seller in the world. The Beringer **brand** is the seventh largest brand globally (8.9 mc in 2006). Other well-known names in the Foster's portfolio include Black Opal, Chateau St. Jean, Lindemans, Meridian, Penfolds, Rosemount Estate, Stone Cellars, and Wolf Blass.

The U.S. subsidiary of Foster's is known, since 2007, as Foster's Americas. It is located in Napa, California. Foster's was fifth among wine companies in the **United States** in 2006, according to *Impact,* with sales of 19.0 mc and a 6.5 percent market share. By value, it was third, tallying retail sales of $1.77 billion. Again Beringer was the principal brand, accounting for 7.2 mc. Foster's Americas is the third largest U.S. **importer**.

FRANCE

France, whose history of winegrowing dates back more than two millennia, plays a principal role in the contemporary **global wine industry**, accounting for around two-fifths of international trade by value (€6.2 billion in 2006). France was the perennial world leader in production (with 52.3 million hectoliters or about 581 million nine-liter cases [mc] in 2006) until overtaken by **Italy** in 2006, although it is still well ahead of third-place **Spain**. It remains the largest consumer country in the world (367 mc).

France's latitude and position on the European land mass, benefiting from Mediterranean, Atlantic, and continental influences, enables cultivation of a myriad of grape varieties and an extensive portfolio of wine styles, including **sparkling wines** produced by multiple methods; **red, rosé**, and white **table wines**; late-harvest wines; and sweet **fortified wines**. Grape varieties of French origin, notably **Cabernet Sauvignon, Merlot, Syrah, Pinot Noir, Chardonnay**, and **Sauvignon Blanc**, have been propagated around the globe. With varying degrees of success, wines made from these and other varieties originating in France pose a commercial challenge to their French counterparts on the world market.

Viticulture contributes nearly €10 billion or 17 percent of France's agricultural output in monetary terms. France's planted surface dedicated to wine production (excluding wine destined for **distilled** spirits such as Cognac) totals 2.1 million acres, placing France second after Spain among wine-grape producers.

History.   The earliest origins of a wine culture in France can be traced to the Phocaeans, who settled on the **ancient Mediterranean** coast and founded Massalia, today's Marseille, around 600 BC. The development of organized viticulture can be credited to the Romans, who conquered Narbonne in the Languedoc-Roussillon in 120 BC. Vineyards were planted near settlements, often along or close to navigable rivers, such as the Garonne, Rhône, Saône, and Loire, facilitating access to market. By the fourth century AD, viticulture had reached Alsace, **Champagne**, and the environs of Paris. With the arrival of Christianity, wine assumed a sacramental function, and the Catholic Church played an active part in winegrowing. Starting in the twelfth century, **monastic** orders—such as the Benedictines and Cistercians in **Burgundy**, Champagne, and other regions—acquired substantial vineyard holdings. The French Revolution (in 1789) served to break up large estates owned by the Church and the aristocracy. In the second half of the 1800s, successive crises disrupted French vineyards. Oidium (powdery mildew) arrived in 1851. **Phylloxera**, an aphid and root louse, was introduced in the 1860s, spread throughout France, and caused devastation over more than four decades. Downy mildew followed in 1878. These crises brought about a fundamental restructuring of French viticulture.

Organization.   Overproduction and fraud created an impetus to delimit controlled **appellations** of origin. Introduced in 1935, *appellation d'origine contrôlée* (AOC) legislation became a model that was later replicated in varying forms by other countries. The concept of **terroir** underlies the AOC system, which is managed by the Institut National de l'Origine et de la Qualité (INAO).

At the top of the **quality wine** hierarchy are areas classified as AOC, numbering more than 470. AOC wines must meet strict criteria for each appellation, including delimited area of production, authorized grape varieties, maximum yield, minimum alcoholic content, and viticultural practices. France's yields for quality wines range from less than 40 hectoliters per hectare (about 2.3 tons per acre) in Languedoc-Roussillon to more than double that in Champagne. Quality wines also include a subgrouping, *vins délimités de qualité supérieure* (VDQS), which is of lesser commercial significance. Below the quality wines are country wines (*vins de pays*) and basic table wines (*vins de table*). Vins de pays come from one of roughly 150 geographic zones and are often marketed with a varietal name on the label. Vins de table are sold without stated variety or origin.

Quality wines account for 57 percent of vineyard land. A further one-third yields vins de table and vins de pays; the balance yields wines for distilled wines, *eaux de vie*. An estimated 240,000 people are employed full-time in **grape growing** or winemaking. In all, there are 117,000 enterprises that ferment grapes into wine, and an estimated 1,000 shippers or **négociants** who perform various functions, such as vinification, maturation, bottling, and marketing.

Regions.   The commercially important appellations are too numerous for inclusion here, but the major regions are the following, in descending order by size:

Languedoc-Roussillon, along the Mediterranean coast, has the largest total vineyard surface in France, with more than 660,000 acres. AOC wines produced from red grapes such as Carignan, Grenache, and Syrah constitute less than 30 percent of production, while the share of vins de pays is above the national average.

Bordeaux has 300,000 acres under vine situated along, or close to, the Garonne and Dordogne rivers and the Gironde estuary that joins them to the Atlantic Ocean. Roughly half the plantings are Merlot, followed by Cabernet Sauvignon and Cabernet Franc. Sauvignon Blanc and Sémillon are cultivated for dry and sweet white wines, such as Sauternes. The Merlot-dominated Bordeaux and Bordeaux Supérieur, with 75 mc produced annually, are France's largest-volume AOCs.

The *Rhône Valley* has nearly 200,000 acres of AOC vineyards. Grenache is the main variety in the Southern Rhône, and this grape is the primary component of Châteauneuf-du-Pape, in combination with Syrah, Mourvèdre, Cinsault, and other varieties. The Rhône's leading product is regional Côtes du Rhône, a Grenache-based red wine with a yearly output of nearly 20 mc. Northern Rhône AOCs such as Hermitage, Côte Rôtie, and Cornas are principally red wines based on Syrah.

The *Loire Valley* (128,000 acres, 32 mc) produces a diversity of sparkling and still wines from vineyards along the Loire River and its tributaries. Primary varieties are Cabernet Franc for red AOC wines such as Chinon and Saumur-Champigny, and Melon, Chenin Blanc, and Sauvignon Blanc for whites such as Muscadet, Vouvray, and Sancerre.

Champagne (80,000 acres, 29 mc) is France's and the world's preeminent sparkling wine region, relying on Pinot Noir, Pinot Meunier, and Chardonnay. The process created in Champagne, the *méthode champenoise,* based on a secondary fermentation in the bottle, is employed internationally to produce the highest-quality sparkling wines.

Burgundy (64,000 acres, 17 mc) is essentially monovarietal, either Chardonnay or Pinot Noir, and encompasses subregions such as Chablis, the Côte d'Or, and the Mâconnais with fragmented vineyards and holdings. The most famous Burgundies are among the world's most expensive and collectible wines, while the largest-volume products are regional Bourgogne (red and white), Chablis, and Mâcon-Villages.

Beaujolais (55,000 acres, 14.5 mc) depends on Gamay to produce a light and fruity red wine, of which a third is sold as Nouveau or the "new wine" of the vintage.

Alsace (38,000 acres, 13 mc), which borders **Germany** and the Rhine River, is essentially a white wine region with a balanced mix of cultivars such as **Riesling**, Gewurztraminer, Pinot Blanc, and **Pinot Gris**. Unlike almost all other AOC wines, those of Alsace are **varietally labeled** with the grape name and are bottled in a tall, slender bottle. Alsace has a *grand cru* system applying to 50 vineyard sites composing less than 5 percent of the planted area.

Wine Trade.   With shipments of more than 160 mc, France is tied with Spain as the world's second largest exporter, behind Italy. Other **European Union** (EU) members are France's primary trading partners. EU countries are the destination for 70 percent of French wine exports by volume. The top five exporting regions by volume are, in descending order, Bordeaux, Champagne, Languedoc-Roussillon, the Rhône Valley, and Burgundy. The country ranks fifth in the world as an importer; Spain and Italy are its largest suppliers.

Even though France remains a leading exporter, total shipments have been largely static in the 2000–2006 period, declining 5 percent in volume while aggregate nominal value has increased by a similar amount. Volumes peaked in 1997–1999, when exports averaged 184 mc. Quality wines have suffered the largest losses since 2000, a drop of 17 percent, while table wine shipments have not changed significantly. Champagne has been the most dynamic region, with 2006 shipments reaching 11.7 mc, a 30 percent gain over the 1995–1999 average. Bordeaux exports of around 20 mc are by far the largest of all AOC types.

France's international market share has been undermined by **New World** producers such as **Chile**, **South Africa**, and **Australia**. These difficulties have been compounded by a decline of consumption at home. Per-capita intake in France has dropped from more than 150 liters in the 1960s to 59 liters today—though still the highest in the world among large countries—and total domestic consumption has fallen from 511 mc to 368 mc as a result. Consumption habits have also evolved: AOC wines now comprise half of all wines consumed as opposed to one-tenth 40 years ago.

The lagging demand has led to economic dislocation in the wine sector. A number of official and private initiatives to enhance France's global competitiveness have been advanced, recommending ways to adapt and simplify France's product offerings and improve its export strategy and **promotion**. Such actions are inherently difficult, however, given France's complex product mix, its labeling relying on place names rather than varietals, and the fragmentation of the wine industry.

In addition to the commercial tensions within the contemporary French wine industry, **climate change** poses further challenges. Higher temperatures bring about a shorter vegetative cycle that could affect the suitability of cultivars currently associated with many of France's most celebrated appellations. Warming may dictate modifications of rootstocks and training systems. Endemic drought in southern France may make regular irrigation a necessity, while rising sea levels could inundate low-lying Bordeaux vineyards. Pinot Noir and Sauvignon Blanc may no longer fall within the range of optimal maturity in Burgundy and Bordeaux, respectively. As a warming trend moves northward, Syrah could become a more suitable cultivar for Burgundy, Pinot Noir may be able to ripen fully in the eastern Loire and other northern regions, and Champagne may no longer possess the marginal climate to yield base wines of high natural acidity. Climate change could therefore force profound changes in appellation laws and alter France's competitive profile in unpredictable ways. *See also* French Paradox; Futures.

Roger C. Bohmrich

Further Reading

INAO. www.inao.gouv.fr.

Office National Interprofessionel des Vins. www.onivins.fr.

Pomel, Bernard. "Réussir l'avenir de la viticulture française." www.agriculture.gouv.fr/spip/IMG/pdf/rapport_pomel_mars2006.pdf.

Ribéreau-Gayon, Pascal, ed. *The Wines and Vineyards of France*. New York: Penguin, 1990.

FRENCH PARADOX

The "French paradox" refers to medical studies demonstrating that, despite a diet rich in saturated fat, a sedentary lifestyle, and substantial tobacco usage, the French have lower rates of coronary artery disease (CAD)—the leading cause of death among Americans—than most Western nations. When this fact became widely known in the **United States** following an episode airing this topic on the television program *60 Minutes* in 1991, rebroadcast in 1992, wine sales, especially **red wine** sales, increased more than 40 percent. *60 Minutes* did a follow-up segment in 1995 that added information from the Copenhagen City Heart Study demonstrating a similar lowering of CAD with moderate wine consumption for people in Denmark. As expected, sales of red wine increased again in the United States following this broadcast.

Although the term was first coined in the late 1980s to describe findings from epidemiological studies, the French paradox had been discovered much earlier. Samuel Black, an Irish physician, noted the relative lack of CAD among the French in 1819. Between 1979 and 2000, many epidemiological studies on this subject were published in the medical literature. Some demonstrated that moderate consumption of alcohol decreased the risk of CAD, and a host of studies from a broad range of nations confirmed that moderate red wine consumption (defined as up to one or two glasses per day for women, one to four daily glasses for men) seemed to provide further protection from CAD and deaths from heart attacks. The magnitude of such protection suggested by the published investigations varied, but was up to a 50 percent reduction of deaths from CAD.

This research remains controversial because of concerns about the concomitant **health** risks associated with alcohol consumption in general. The decreased likelihood of heart disease due to alcohol consumption comes with social risks, as well as an increased risk of a range of cancers. In addition, studies show that fruit and vegetable consumption also protects from heart disease and that wine drinkers in **France** and other parts of the world are more likely to eat fruits and vegetables. Such confounding variables cloud the findings somewhat.

Thousands of medical studies have been published in an attempt to discover the mechanism by which red wine protects from CAD. Polyphenols found in wine as a result of skin and seed contact have medical effects that may explain some of the benefits of red wine. These include antioxidant, anti-clotting, and anti-inflammatory activities, as well as a tendency to open up blood vessels.

Patrick Farrell

FUTURES

Wine futures, also known as selling *en primeur,* is a mechanism by which wine is sold in advance of its actual release by producers, with the purchaser contracting to take delivery on an agreed-upon future date. It is generally used to describe the sales of relatively high-end, long-lived wines that require significant maturation time between harvest and bottling, as opposed to the **bulk wine** market.

Selling wine as futures evolved as a way for growers to spread some of the risks inherent in the capital-intensive nature of the wine business. These include the unpredictability of producing an agricultural product whose quality and quantity are largely subject to the vagaries of weather conditions during the growing season, the length of time required to bring the finished wine to market, and the related economic and political factors that can dramatically affect the value and demand for the wine during that time.

By selling all or part of their wine as futures, producers have options that enable them to hedge against these risks, generate cash flow, and outsource certain aspects of wine production, **promotion**, and sales. This has resulted in the creation of a large speculative market that involves a host of **wineries**, brokers, **importers**, merchants, **retailers**, critics, and **consumers**.

Bordeaux, by virtue of its long history and highly organized trade, is the region most strongly associated with the sale of wine futures. For more than 300 years, Bordeaux wines have been sold through a three-tier system known as the Place de Bordeaux. This structure has allowed proprietors to shift risk and recoup capital tied up in inventory by selling futures to merchants (also known as shippers or **négociants**), who handle marketing and sales. The third tier consists of brokers or *courtiers*—middlemen who negotiate and facilitate the transaction on commission (*courtage*). About 5 percent of Bordeaux's total annual wine sales of 60 to 70 million cases is in futures; the actual volume of wine sold as futures varies each year in relationship to vintage quality, supply, and demand.

Historically, the futures market was conducted almost exclusively among the three tiers of the trade. In the 1980s, however, the increasing influence of the wine press, combined with greater consumer interest in wine, resulted in substantial consumer participation in the futures market, a trend that has continued to the present. The power of the press plays a large role in the futures market, fueling demand for wines and vintages that receive high praise—and creating difficulties selling vintages and wines that do not—often causing large swings in price and demand.

In Bordeaux, the futures campaign takes place in the spring following the vintage with a series of tastings of the wines, which at this point are still unfinished and in **barrel**. Shortly thereafter, the proprietors set prices based on the quality of the vintage, estimated demand, and the stature of the château, its classification, and its reputation. The wines are then offered in series of releases known as *tranches,* with each successive offer issued at higher prices (depending on demand) until all of the wines allocated for futures are sold. The entire campaign is completed over a period of several months. Delivery of the wines generally takes place two to three years after the vintage.

Many other regions and producers engage in some sort of futures sales, albeit without the same organized structure and scale as Bordeaux. These are sometimes held in conjunction with charitable organizations or local trade groups. The presales, auctions, and tastings (such as the annual Auction **Napa Valley**) can help to generate interest in the specific region, build goodwill through charitable donations, and strengthen winery **brand** image, as well as providing a way to recoup some of the capital tied up in inventory. Many wineries also independently offer their preferred clients opportunities to purchase limited, allocated wines in advance of release or bottling as a reward for customer loyalty.

Reasons for buying futures range from the pure pleasure of collecting and eventually enjoying the wines to acquiring wines as an investment to be resold at a later date. The risks are similar to many other investments and include changes in **exchange rates** and market conditions that can cause prices to fall, as well as fraud or bankruptcy of disreputable sellers. At the consumer level, and even at the merchant level, a considerable amount of futures wine is purchased without having been personally tasted. Trust is thus placed in the hands of the press or the seller, who has at best tasted only unfinished wines. The cost of money required to hold expensive wine to delivery and beyond to maturity has to be considered, as do other expenses such as shipping and storage. The benefits to buyers, of course, include the opportunity to buy at reduced prices and the ability to secure wines that may be very difficult to attain at a later date. *See also* Auction Houses; Cult Wines; Ratings and Scores.

Christopher Cree

G

GALLO

The E.&J. Gallo Winery was founded by brothers Ernest (1909–2007) and Julio (1910–1993) Gallo in 1933 after the end of **Prohibition** and became the largest winery in the **United States** in 1966. The company built its empire and reputation on value wines produced in high volume at low prices. These were classic **table wines**, simple, straightforward, and generically labeled: white, **red**, **rosé**, burgundy, chablis, and so on; the company did not begin selling **varietally labeled** wines until 1974 and vintage-dated wines until 1983. The company was also well known for producing **fortified wines**, such as Thunderbird and Night Train. The brothers Gallo deserve credit for helping to establish **California**, and by extension the United States, as a major force in the **global wine industry**.

The Gallos' winery began in Modesto, California, and is still there, albeit moved to a much larger property nearby. From 75,000 cases in 1933, the winery now produces around 60 million cases (mc) annually. The company also imports wine from **Italy**, **Argentina**, **Australia**, and elsewhere. Gallo's worldwide sales of 72.4 mc in 2006 gave it a 2.7 percent global market share, according to *Impact* data, second only to **Constellation Brands**, Inc. The recently renamed Gallo Family Vineyards is the world's second largest **brand** (after the **Wine Group**'s Franzia), with a volume of 23.7 mc in 2006, and Gallo's Carlo Rossi brand is fourth globally at 12.6 mc.

In the United States, Gallo is number one in volume, selling 60.5 mc in 2006 and capturing 20.9 percent of the market. Its sales broke down as 84 percent table wine, 5 percent **sparkling wine**, and 11 percent **dessert wines** and other products, such as **wine coolers**. Given the low average price point, however, Gallo was slightly behind Constellation in sales revenues at $3.31 billion.

As a means of market penetration and product positioning, Gallo has long sold wine under an assortment of labels and brand names, many of which do not carry the Gallo name. The company's top brands in the United States, according to *Impact,* are Carlo Rossi (the nation's second largest brand with sales of 10.3 mc in 2006), Gallo Livingston Cellars (7.8 mc), Gallo Family Vineyards Twin Valley

(6.5 mc), Peter Vella (5.5 mc), and Turning Leaf Vineyards (3.4 mc). Other familiar brands include Andre, Barefoot, Bella Sera, Black Swan, Boone's Farm, Cop-
peridge, Ecco Domani, Mirassou, Redwood Creek, and Wild Vines.

In a bid to shed its low-end image and move into the premium wine market, the
company began buying a considerable amount of acreage in **Sonoma County** as
early as 1971, becoming one of the largest vineyard owners in the county, and
introduced the Gallo of Sonoma brand in 1994. The winemaking facility there
has a capacity of 4.9 mc. In 2006, the company announced a rebranding of many
of its products in the United States, including Gallo of Sonoma, and almost the
entire line overseas to Gallo Family Vineyards, featuring a new logo with twin
rooster heads. The company's copresidents are James Coleman, Joseph Gallo,
and Robert Gallo, and 15 family members are active in the organization.

GERMANY

Germany is the home of **Riesling**, death-defyingly steep vineyards, and some
classic **dessert wines**. One of the most northerly wine regions in the world, it
was the ninth largest wine-producing country in 2006 at 8.9 million hectoliters,
the equivalent of 99 million nine-liter cases (mc). With 252,000 acres of vineyards, Germany's growing area is about the same size as that of **Bordeaux**.

Riesling is Germany's most widely planted grape variety and the one that shapes
Germany's wine image worldwide. Its 52,000 acres represent nearly two-thirds of
the world's Riesling vineyards. German Rieslings thrive in various soil types,
which helps account for the fascinating diversity they offer in terms of bouquet
and flavor. The other principal white varieties grown in Germany are Silvaner,
Müller-Thurgau, Kerner, Weissburgunder (Pinot Blanc), and Grauburgunder
(**Pinot Gris**). Spätburgunder (**Pinot Noir**) is Germany's most important red variety
with 28,400 acres planted, followed by Dornfelder.

Germany exported 35 mc in 2006. Its primary trade partner for wine exports is
the United Kingdom, with the **British market** representing almost 30 percent by
value and 40 percent by volume. The **United States** and the **Dutch** and **Scandinavian markets** were also major importers of German wine, and exports to the
United States have tripled in the past five years.

Germany is the world's fourth largest wine-consuming country, at about 222 mc.
Wine consumption in Germany has increased in recent years, while production has
remained relatively steady, and therefore Germany has become the world's largest
wine-importing country, bringing in about 145 mc in 2006. **Italy** was Germany's
main source of imports (45 percent share), a large portion coming in as **bulk wine**.
Italy, **France**, and **Spain** combine to supply more than 90 percent of Germany's
imported wine—therefore about half of all wine consumed in Germany.

History.   **Grape growing** reached the area that is currently Germany around
2,000 years ago, following the conquest of the Germanic lands by the Romans,
who had learned viticulture from other **ancient Mediterranean** cultures. After the
fall of the Roman Empire, Charlemagne reinstated the cultivation of vines in the
eighth century.

In the Middle Ages, monks came, particularly from **Burgundy**, and extended
winegrowing from many newly founded **monasteries**. Wine cultivation continued

to be a privilege of the clergy, and today many vineyards still carry names going back to this time, such as Abtsberg (Abbot's Mountain). Napoleon's conquest brought this to an end, secularizing the Catholic Church's possessions. The German nobility and many rich merchant families acquired the vineyards, and they largely remain in the possession of these families today.

German wine became very popular in Britain in the 1800s, when it was a favorite of Queen Victoria. As the nineteenth century ended, however, the **phylloxera** catastrophe almost brought German viticulture to a standstill. Then the two world wars and the intervening depression continued the hard times in Germany.

In the 1950s, German wines again became quite fashionable in other countries. The semisweet blended wine Liebfraumilch took western Europe and the United States by storm in the 1970s and 1980s. However, tastes then began to turn toward drier styles of wine, especially in the **New World**, and German exports have remained stagnant at 25 to 30 mc for most of the past two decades. The latest figures indicate that exports may today be entering a new growth phase.

Regions.   German vintners primarily have the warm North Atlantic Drift, an extension of the Gulf Stream, to thank for viticulture being possible at the country's latitude. Almost all of Germany's winegrowing is concentrated in the southwest. The vines are planted on the southern slopes for greatest exposure to the sun, usually in the river valleys where the chains of hills that lie around them afford protection from cold winds.

The most commercially important wine regions of Germany are the Mosel, Rheingau, Pfalz, Rheinhessen, and Baden. The Mosel and Rheingau are home to most of the best sites for top-quality Rieslings. The Pfalz and Rheinhessen are the two largest regions, producing nearly half of Germany's wines between them. Baden is the warmest and most southern region, known for being a high-quality producer of Pinot Noir, Pinot Gris, and Pinot Blanc.

Quality Levels.   The lowest quality of German wine is *Tafelwein* (**table wine**), but few wines bear this designation. A marginally higher category is *Landwein* (country wine), which establishes a broad geographical identity for the wine. The two **quality wine** levels are *Qualitätswein bestimmer Anbaugebeite* (QbA) and *Qualitätswein mit Prädikat* (QmP), which are made from riper grapes that are subject to higher standards. QbA represents basic quality wines; more than two-thirds of German wines are at this level. Germany's premium quality wines, QmP, are made from fully ripe grapes and are elegant, noble, and long lived. About a quarter of German production qualifies as QmP.

The following *Prädikate* (special attributes) denote six ascending levels of ripeness within the broad designation of QmP: *Kabinett* (fully ripened grapes), *Spätlese* (late-harvest, fuller-bodied wines), *Auslese* (selected fully ripened grapes), *Beerenauslese* (BA; overripe, individually selected grapes), *Eiswein* (ice wine, made from grapes that are harvested and pressed while frozen), and *Trockenbeerenauslese* (TBA; highly raisinated, botrytis-affected grapes).

Trends.   The **climate change** over the last few years has produced a nearly unbroken string of good vintages since the early 1990s. With the expectation of continued warming, ''southern'' grape varieties, such as **Chardonnay**, have increasingly been introduced, and plantings of red varieties have increased.

Germans have recently begun drinking more **red wine** than white for the first time, and more than a third of German winegrowing areas have already been planted with red varieties.

As wine has become more popular as an accompaniment to German meals, the preference nowadays is for dry wines. The association of Germany with sweet white wine is so deeply fixed abroad that it has been possible only in the last few years to export modern dry German wines to other countries, along with red wines, but the recent upsurge in exports may be an indication that this is changing. In the United States, Riesling is currently experiencing a remarkable renaissance, becoming more and more popular in **restaurants** in particular, although dry wines remain underrepresented. This new appreciation for Riesling is also spreading to other countries and promises a magnificent future for German wine.

Bruce Schneider

Further Reading

Diel Armin, and Joel Payne. *Gault Millau, the Guide to German Wines*. Munich: Johannes
    Heyne Verlag, 2005.
Brook, Stephen. *The Wines of Germany*. London: Mitchell Beazley, 2003.
Price, Freddy. *Riesling Renaissance*. London: Mitchell Beazley, 2004.
Wines of Germany. www.germanwineusa.com.

GLOBALIZATION

Globalization refers to the growing interconnections among individuals, businesses, and governments that transcend national boundaries and threaten—or promise, depending on one's point of view—to make the concept of countries obsolete. It is usually focused on multinational corporations that have ownership, production facilities, and business interests spread among numerous countries or on supranational official organizations, such as agencies of the United Nations or the **European Union** that have the power to override the preferences of specific governments in the interests of the collective group. Globalization is often tied in with **information technology**, because the Internet and related technologies have made it feasible to conduct business or governmental affairs worldwide as easily as across the street.

For the wine industry, globalization takes on a somewhat different meaning, because there are far fewer opportunities for the globalization of wine than of most other products. In the first place, wine is an alcoholic product and is therefore subject to much closer scrutiny when crossing national borders than, say, soft drinks, electronic components, or textiles. Second, wine is perishable, as well as bulky and heavy, so there are few economies available in transporting it other than in a more or less straight line from producer to consumer. In a wine discussion, the term *globalization* is more likely to refer to the ever-increasing availability of wines from other countries in local markets or to a trend toward greater uniformity among wine styles from all countries.

There are multiple ways of "going global." The most basic is becoming an *exporter*. Selling products abroad allows a company to spread risk or capitalize on opportunities in multiple markets and hopefully avoid the wild ups and downs that are possible in a single market. Many wine companies, and indeed entire wine-producing countries such as **Australia**, seek at least this level of globalization. Some wines, such as **Diageo**'s Blossom Hill and initially **Yellow Tail**, are made solely for export.

The next step might be to establish a physical presence in another country, either by *direct investment* in a foreign company or through a *joint venture*— setting up a new company in association with foreign partners. Both of these models exist in the wine industry, although the logistics and capital involved in transnational ownership generally limit these enterprises to the largest wine companies. Ownership in a foreign market may help avoid some of the **trade barriers** and other problems that exporting firms have by in effect becoming a domestic company in that overseas market. Despite the transnational ownership, however, all firms are typically required to function as national companies in the country where they are physically located in order to qualify for the necessary government licensing, and therefore the wines of the overseas parent company are still considered imports.

Joint ventures are well known in the world of wine, perhaps the best-known being Opus One Winery, a joint venture between **Robert Mondavi** and Baron Philippe de Rothschild in the **Napa Valley**. Mondavi also had joint ventures in **Italy** with the Frescobaldi family and in Australia and **Chile**. Casa Lapostolle in Chile is another example of a joint venture, between the Chilean Rabat family and the Lapostolle family of **France**.

The most advanced form of globalization involves multinational conglomerates that have offices and facilities in many countries to reduce costs by taking advantage of differentials in labor and raw materials prices, skilled or unskilled labor pools, tax structures, and ancillary support activities between countries. These financial gains are often augmented by the marketing advantages of being able to portray the company as a domestic entity. In many industries, the basic model is to break production down into discrete units or functions and then to locate those divisions in whatever country provides the most advantageous conditions. However, the wine industry (and agriculture in general) cannot take advantage of these economies because the major functions of **grape growing** and winemaking cannot be broken down into smaller isolatable parts, and it is usually not cost-effective to separate them geographically by a great distance. While there are good reasons a **winery** might buy **bulk wine** from another country through a local broker, if it actually owns the vineyards in another country, it usually makes sense to make the wine there, as well. Most segments of the industry outside of production—**importing**, **distribution**, **promotion**, and so forth—are similarly tied to a single country due to both legal restrictions and the practicalities of dealing with a specific market.

Thus, the wine industry sees little of the diversification of business functions around the globe ("offshoring") that characterizes other industries' globalization, and the primary effect of globalization on wine companies' business model is transnational ownership. Still, compared with most other industries, there are very few large multinational corporations in the wine industry, as there are very few publicly traded wine companies, which are most conducive to multiple partial ownership. The primary example is **Constellation Brands**, Inc., which over the past decade has snowballed in size by acquiring wineries first in the **United States**, but recently abroad as well, including Vincor **Canada** and the Hardy Wine Company (now Constellation Brands Australia). Another example is LVMH (Moët Hennessy Louis Vuitton), which owns not only wine companies in more than one country, but also firms in several other industries as well.

With regard to the supranational governance, the poster child for globalization has been the World Trade Organization (WTO), a transnational authority that takes the reins out of the hands of national governments with regard to many aspects of international trade. The WTO has had little direct effect on the **global wine industry** so far, but it has forced some countries to remove excessive trade barriers that have affected wine. For example, WTO threats resulted in India reducing its 550 percent tariff on imported wine to the maximum permissible rate under WTO rules, 150 percent. Another instance of this sort of globalization has been in the movement to protect place names and **appellations**. Pushed largely by the European Union, bilateral international treaties have been negotiated to change national laws on the use of designated appellations on wines from other places.

The final facet of globalization is conceptual and affects more the intellectual aspects of the business: the shift from wine as a local industry to wine as a global commodity. As with all aspects of globalization, this change in mind-set results in winners and losers, but in theory will in the end provide more advantages than disadvantages. For decades, wine businesses in wine-producing countries have watched their formerly captive **consumer** base being lured away from domestic wines by the greater and greater accessibility of wines from around the world, offering interesting new styles and sometimes better prices. On the other hand, some wine-producing countries have seen great opportunities in exporting wines to new markets abroad. As well, the Internet, **flying winemakers**, and consultants have all contributed to the move toward globalization.

In principle, the consumer should be well served by the greater competition and range of choices brought about by globalization, but some critics believe that the opposite is true—that producers' desire to appeal to the largest possible group of consumers is causing wineries to abandon traditional winemaking practices, **terroir**-driven wines, and obscure indigenous grape varieties in favor of standardized, **branded** wines made with international varieties. The reality is undoubtedly somewhere in the middle. Consumers will have more choices, but many of these options will be essentially interchangeable. Those who desire something different, or simply a change of pace, will have to dig deeper through the range of labels available, and the role of the **retailer** and the **wine educator** will continue to grow in importance in helping the consumer make sense of the overwhelming choices available.

GLOBAL WARMING. *See* Climate Change

GLOBAL WINE INDUSTRY

Millions of people worldwide make their living making or selling wine, and hundreds of millions enjoy drinking it. Wine, whether domestic or imported, is a significant economic good in dozens of countries, and wine sales worldwide are estimated at around $115 billion.

History.   Grapes have been traced back to origins in the Caucasus Mountains area of modern Georgia and southern Russia. From there, undoubtedly because their ability to become wine had been discovered long before, vines were carried by traders or migrants to the developing centers of Western civilization, spreading to Phoenicia, Egypt, **Greece**, the Roman Empire, and the **ancient Mediterranean**. Wine was part of a thriving and far-reaching trade 2,000 years ago.

Winegrowing became well entrenched throughout Europe, nurtured after the fall of the Romans in particular by **monasteries** and other Catholic Church properties. During the Age of Discovery and the **colonial era** as European explorers and settlers ventured out to new lands, they took grapevines with them and planted them wherever they would grow. Wine was needed for **religious** purposes, for **health** reasons—often being safer to drink than water—and for simple enjoyment. Thus, as more and more people lived in places where it was not possible to make one's own wine or get it from a neighbor, it became a commodity that is now traded the world over.

Viticulture.   Grapes are an agricultural product in almost all countries that lie within the temperate latitudes where viticulture—that is, **grape growing**—is feasible. Tropical areas do not have a winter season that signals the vines to stop spreading and start producing grapes, while polar regions are too cold for vine survival through the winter. Thus, the temperate band, roughly between the 30th and 50th parallels in both hemispheres, is the home of viticulture—although local conditions such as ocean currents and mountain ranges prevail over this rule of thumb in a number of places, most notably Europe, where the warm North Atlantic Drift allows grape growing at higher latitudes, and South America, where the cold Southern Ocean does the opposite.

Vineyard area worldwide is almost 20 million acres (8 million hectares). For historical and cultural reasons, nearly 60 percent of this acreage total (11.5 million acres) is in Europe, mostly for wine production. Another 22 percent is in **Asia**, although the majority here is intended for raisins and table grapes. The remaining vineyards are in South America (7 percent), North America (5 percent), Africa (5 percent), and Oceania (2 percent).

The worldwide area under vines declined by more than 2.5 million acres during the 1990s, but has grown by half a million acres since then. Almost all of the vineyard area removed has been in Europe, where some 3.2 million acres have been grubbed up since 1990. The European shrinkage has been offset by growth in the **New World** and especially in Asia; outside of Europe, new plantings in the twenty-first century have added around 1.25 million acres, about half of that coming in Asia.

Wine Production.   In 2006, world wine production amounted to 287 million hectoliters, or the equivalent of 3.18 billion nine-liter cases; 2007 was predicted to be about 7 percent less. Europe—the "Old World" in wine parlance—was

Top 10 Wine-Producing Countries, 2006

Rank	Country	Production Hectoliters (millions)	Cases (millions)
1	Italy	53.5	594
2	France	52.3	581
3	Spain	38.2	425
4	United States	20.7	230
5	Argentina	15.4	171
6	Australia	14.3	159
7	China	11.0	122
8	South Africa	9.41	104
9	Germany	8.92	99
10	Chile	8.45	94

Note: Statistics based on provisional estimates for 2006 and subject to revision.

Source: Organisation Internationale de la Vigne et du Vin (International Organization of Vine and Wine) estimates and national sources.

the source of 63 percent of this wine. The **United States** was the largest producer in the New World, with a bit less than 7 percent of the total. South America added 9 percent, **Australia** and **New Zealand** 5 percent, Asia 12 percent, and Africa 4 percent.

The largest wine-producing country is **Italy**, which alone accounted for 594 million cases (mc) in 2006, or 19 percent of the world's wine. **France**, long the world leader, was a close second at 581 mc, followed by **Spain** at 425 mc. These three represented half of global production. After the United States, the top 10 producers were rounded out by **Argentina**, Australia, China, **South Africa**, **Germany**, and **Chile**; the top 10 accounted for 81 percent of production.

Wine Consumption.   Global wine consumption in 2006 was 2.68 billion cases (241 million hectoliters), and this was expected to remain steady for 2007. The difference between wine production and consumption, 450 mc in 2006, is largely taken up by industrial requirements. About 400 mc is used annually for **vermouth**, vinegar, **distillation** into brandy, and other ethanol needs.

Not surprisingly, two-thirds of the total world wine consumption (1.8 billion cases) takes place in Europe, where most of it is made. France is the largest portion of this, accounting for 367 mc in 2006, 13.7 percent of global consumption. However, this is less than in years past, down from 440 mc as recently as 2000. Per-capita consumption in France is the highest of any large nation, at about 59 liters (6.5 cases) per adult. Italy ranks second among consuming countries (304 mc).

The third largest wine-consuming country, and the market with the largest volume growth, is the United States. Americans consumed nearly 290 mc in 2006, up almost 25 percent from the 233 mc of 2000 (2007 consumption was up almost 9 percent to 313 mc, likely moving the United States ahead of Italy). The top five countries, including Germany (222 mc) and Spain (150 mc), account for 50 percent of world consumption. China was close behind Spain, and the others in the top 10 were the United Kingdom, Argentina, Russia, and Romania.

Top 10 Wine-Consuming Countries, 2006

Rank	Country	Consumption Hectoliters (millions)	Consumption Cases (millions)
1	France	33.0	367
2	Italy	27.3	304
3	United States	25.9	288
4	Germany	19.9	222
5	China	13.5	150
5	Spain	13.5	150
7	United Kingdom	11.7	130
8	Argentina	11.1	123
9	Romania	5.55	62
10	Portugal	4.70	52

Note: Statistics based on provisional estimates for 2006 and subject to revision.

Source: Organisation Internationale de la Vigne et du Vin (International Organization of Vine and Wine) estimates and national sources.

Wine Trade.   International exports and imports of wine in 2005 reached 875 mc, representing 28 percent of all production. France and Italy have long dominated the export trade, followed by Spain; in 2006, those three countries accounted for 57 percent of all exports. Europe as a whole made up about 71 percent. Most of the European countries' exports stay within Europe, the cross-border trade mostly moving from the southern half of the continent to the northern half.

The Southern Hemisphere is also a major source of exports, providing almost a quarter of global exports primarily to thirsty Northern Hemisphere countries. Australia is the heavyweight here, the fourth largest exporter in the world with about 90 mc in 2006. Chile is fifth at 48 mc.

Top 10 Wine-Exporting Countries, 2006

Rank	Country	Exports Hectoliters (millions)	Exports Cases (millions)
1	Italy	18.0	200
2	France	14.4	160
3	Spain	14.3	159
4	Australia	8.1	90
5	Chile	4.3	48
6	United States	3.9	44
7	Germany	3.1	35
8	Argentina	2.9	32
8	Portugal	2.9	32
10	South Africa	2.7	30

Note: Statistics based on provisional estimates for 2006 and subject to revision.

Source: Organisation Internationale de la Vigne et du Vin (International Organization of Vine and Wine) estimates and national sources.

Top 10 Wine-Importing Countries, 2006

Rank	Country	Imports Hectoliters (millions)	Cases (millions)
1	Germany	13.2	147
2	United Kingdom	12.7	141
3	United States	7.8	87
4	Russia	7.2	80
5	France	5.2	58
6	Netherlands	4.1	46
7	Belgium	2.9	32
7	Canada	2.9	32
9	Denmark	1.9	21
10	Switzerland	1.8	20

Note: Statistics based on provisional estimates for 2006 and subject to revision.

Source: Organisation Internationale de la Vigne et du Vin (International Organization of Vine and Wine) estimates and national sources.

The sixth largest exporter is the United States, one of the few countries (along with France) that actually produces enough wine for domestic demand and yet engages in a lively import/export trade. U.S. **wineries** export 44 mc, placing the country sixth overall, while U.S. **importers** bring in 87 mc, third most in the world.

Germany is another interesting case: despite a shortfall of 123 mc in production compared to demand, it nevertheless exports another 35 mc, making it the seventh largest exporter. This combination necessitates Germany's position as the world's largest importer of wine, 147 mc in 2006, much of it red given the country's white-wine-heavy production portfolio.

The **British market**, at 130 mc, is second only to Germany in imports. Other significant importers are Russia, France, the **Dutch market**, and **Canada**.

Market Structures.   There are several different models for the structure of nations' wine trade. The openness of the country to trade is usually directly related to the importance of wine production within the country itself. Most places where winegrowing is a significant agricultural sector take a fairly liberal stance on the wine trade, whereas places that do not make much wine view it with a certain skepticism and may be more likely to erect **trade barriers**. Other factors, such as history and **religion**, also play a role. In some cases, wine may be handled differently than other alcoholic beverages.

Most countries' wine markets can be categorized as monopoly, direct trade, or three-tier systems. In Sweden's monopoly, for example, the government's Systembolaget brings in wine and sells it to consumers as the sole **retailer**. Similar systems are found in Canada and some **control states** in the United States. These organizations are found in places where the government has a strong social engineering platform, and they typically exist in limbo between discouraging alcoholic consumption and **promoting** sales of alcoholic products.

Direct trade systems are the norm in regions that produce wine. Within member states of the **European Union**, for example, wineries are able to sell directly to independent retailers. They may elect to use brokers, agents, or wholesalers, but this is not a requirement. The government takes its share of taxes from the winery, retailer, or both, but does not get involved in the transaction. These systems theoretically provide the consumer with the greatest range of products.

Three-tier systems add a mandatory wholesale level to the equation. The primary reason for this tier is to provide a local bottleneck where government authorities can monitor sales and collect taxes. The United States has such a system, as do many countries in Asia, including Japan and China. In the United States, wineries are generally required to sell their products to **distributors**, who then sell them on to retailers and **restaurants** (the main exceptions being that wineries can usually sell direct to the public and sometimes retailers within their own states). For foreign wines, the middle tier also includes a mandatory importer between the producer and the distributor. The three-tier system in principle makes a winery's products available on a much wider basis than would be possible if the winery were responsible for all its own sales, but at the cost of another markup in price.

Outlook.   The volume and revenues of the global wine industry will continue to grow as more and more consumers become at least occasional wine drinkers. The youngest generation of legal **drinking age**—the so-called Millennials—has demonstrated an interest not only in wine but also in **quality wine**, ensuring ongoing strong growth in the sector. At the same time, wine is continuing to increase its market share in the United States and has begun to gain a foothold, albeit small, in the huge maturing economies of China and India, where the greatest potential for industry expansion exists. Europe will continue its declining consumption as the major markets in France, Italy, and Spain move toward per-capita levels closer to other developed nations, but growth in northern Europe's wine markets will offset much of the decrease.

Climate change in the future may cause instability in some wine-producing regions, but overall the trend will be toward expanding winegrowing possibilities, especially in the Northern Hemisphere. Warmer average temperatures may tilt consumer preferences somewhat toward lighter styles and more interest in white and **rosé** wines. *See also* Eastern Europe; Scandinavian Market.

Further Reading
Organisation Internationale de la Vigne et du Vin. www.oiv.int.

GRAPE GROWING

Wine is an agricultural product that has its foundation in the combination of air, water, sunlight, soil, and grapevines. Hundreds of thousands of people worldwide make their livelihood from tending to this miraculous process—overseeing nature's progress, helping out when possible, worrying about intemperate weather, and breathing a sigh of relief after finally bringing in the year's harvest, before starting the process over again for the new vintage.

Although the conversion to wine does not technically start until after the grape grower's job is essentially finished, the production of high-quality wine cannot begin at all unless the grape grower has done his or her job well. It is the grape grower's task to see that nature packs as much distinction into the grapes as possible during the growing season; the winemaker then needs only to release the grapes' potential in order to produce an excellent wine. Conceptually, at least, great wines are made in the vineyard.

Vineyards range from small patches with a few vines tended by a single person up to vast rolling tracts of hundreds of acres that require a small army of workers to care for and harvest their grapes. There were about 24,000 vineyards in the **United States** in 2002, covering just about a million acres. Roughly half are five acres or less, but the majority of vineyard land is owned by large holdings of more than 250 acres. By contrast, European vineyards tend to be smaller, with holdings of one or two acres quite common. The number of vineyard employees in the United States is 35,170 full-time equivalents, with estimated annual wages of $698 million, although the actual number of workers is far higher given the seasonal nature of the majority of jobs, as well as the unpaid labor of owners and their families. Vineyard contracted services add another 15,860 full-time-equivalent employees.

The work of grape growing follows the annual agricultural cycle. During the winter, vineyard workers prune the vines in preparation for the new year. Once new growth develops in the spring, tasks include training the shoots into the desired trellis system, weed and pest control, cover crop maintenance, green harvesting, and, where allowed and needed, irrigation, fertilization, and soil treatments. After veraison as the grapes begin to ripen, disease control, installation of bird netting, shoot trimming, leaf pulling, and crop thinning may be necessary. Harvest is always a particularly labor-intensive time, as there is often a fairly narrow window during which the grapes must be brought in while they are at their optimum ripeness.

In an average vineyard plot, these tasks are usually overseen by the vineyard owner or manager, with perhaps two full-time assistants. Of course, at a family-owned vineyard, the workers may all be family members. As required, these individuals will be augmented by any number of seasonal, often migrant, laborers who are hired for a few days or weeks to carry out some of the routine tasks, especially harvest. Sometimes volunteers—or even paying guests—will help out, as well. The number of workers needed depends on many factors, including the level of **mechanization** of the vineyard. For example, a vineyard that uses mechanical harvesting will require far fewer laborers than one where hand-picking is done.

In addition to regular vineyard maintenance, workers may be called upon to grub up old or nonproductive vines or to plant a whole new vineyard with cuttings from existing plants or, more often nowadays, with fresh plant material from **nurseries**. Establishing a brand-new vineyard on land not used for that purpose before can entail regrading the land, soil analysis and preparation, and installation of irrigation, frost control, or trellis hardware.

The grape-growing industry includes grapes that are destined for wine, table grapes, grape juice, and raisins. Small- and medium-size vineyards usually focus on one category or another, but large properties may grow more than one type as a hedge against a decline in prices in one sector. Wine grapes and raisins are, for the most part, *Vitis vinifera,* whereas grape juice is typically made from

Concord or Niagara grapes, which are *Vitis labrusca.* Table grapes are usually Concord or Thompson Seedless, a vinifera variety.

Worldwide, there are 19.6 million acres under vines. Of this total, more than 59 percent are in Europe and 22 percent in **Asia**. The United States has 5 percent of the world's grapevines, and half of the grapes grown end up as wine. The other half is used for raisins (30 percent), table grapes (11 percent), or juice (9 percent). The total wine-grape crush in the United States in 2006 was 3.38 million tons, bringing growers $2.1 billion, an average of $619 per ton.

The price for grapes varies significantly, depending on such factors as grape variety, vineyard location and reputation, overall quality, degree of ripeness, and specifics of a grower's contract with the buyer. Average **California** prices for different varieties range from around $200 per ton for French Colombard, used primarily for blending and generic white wines, to more than $2,000 for the greatly in-demand **Pinot Noir**. Grapes from great **terroirs** command higher prices than those from lesser areas. Quality and ripeness are often significant in the price equation, as well, most obviously in **Germany** and at many cooperatives, where growers are paid upon delivery based almost entirely on the must weight or sugar content of their grapes. The price of the grapes represents about one-eighth of the retail price of a bottle of wine.

The grower's **profit**, of course, depends to a great degree on the cost of growing the grapes and does not necessarily correlate with the selling price, except insofar as the cost relates to the grapes' quality. Hand harvesting and extra care lavished on the vines during the growing season may result in a better price per ton due to higher quality of the grapes, but higher labor costs, debt servicing, hail damage, and other factors that do not improve quality serve only to lower profits. Growers in areas with higher humidity are likely to have a smaller margin due to the need to treat the vines more frequently to avoid disease problems; those who must install bird netting or deer fences have higher costs than those who do not.

Yield is a wild card. The tonnage per acre (or number of hectoliters [hl] per hectare [ha] in metric countries) can vary considerably depending on the grower's strategy and desires, as well as on weather conditions for a given year. Yields can range from 1 ton per acre or even less with very old vines up to 10 tons per acre in a very fertile vineyard with vigorous vines left unchecked (15 to 150 hl/ha). In **appellations** where laws govern the maximum yield, the grower's choices are circumscribed, but in places where there are no such restrictions, the grower must inevitably choose between the paths of high yields of relatively low quality (and low price per ton) and low yields of superior quality. The optimum position, of course, is somewhere in the middle, with as high a yield as is possible without significantly sacrificing quality. And as esteemed grape-growing consultant Richard Smart has demonstrated, that optimum yield can be pushed up quite high if the grower has "balanced vines," using appropriate trellising and canopy management techniques to match the vines' vigor.

Another big decision for some growers is what to grow. Again, in some appellations, there may be few choices of variety, and tradition and the market may leave no choices at all. The terroir of a given vineyard may limit the options, as well. However, in many, especially **New World**, vineyards, the possibilities are almost endless as to which grapes to grow. Whether planting a new vineyard or considering what to do with a relatively unprofitable one, a grower must try to envision the market several years in the future, because a newly planted or replanted vineyard will not produce a saleable crop for two or three years and thereafter will be expected to stay in service for at least 25 or 30 years. Will the variety that is hot today remain in demand, or is it just a **fad** that will be considered trite a decade from now? *See also* Consolidation; Organic Grapes and Wine; Phylloxera.

GREECE

Since antiquity, the vine and wine have played a role in Greece's culture and history. In virtually every part of Greece, some form of archaeological evidence of winemaking has been found. While acknowledging the country's rich and complex relationship to wine over the centuries, modern-day Greece is at an important crossroads in terms of its wine industry and where it fits into the **global wine industry**.

A series of wars in the first half of the twentieth century left Greece's infrastructure in ruins, and the country was forced to rebuild itself. The foundation for modern Greece's wine industry thus began only in the 1950s. Vineyards were replanted and the first **wineries** were built. Initially, the industry was dominated by large producers and cooperatives making cheap, low-quality **bulk wine**. Some large producers, such as Boutari Wines, Cambas Winemakers, Achaia Clauss Wine Co., Tsantali Vineyards, Wineries & Distilleries, and Kourtaki Wines, successfully managed to create **brands** and an export market.

During this time, the first Greek wine laws were established to give a framework to the industry. Greece's **appellation** system highlights indigenous grape varieties in areas where they are thought to be at their best. In typical European fashion, the **quality wine** (known by the Greek acronyms OPE and OPAP) appellations in Greece have numerous restrictions, including style and specified grapes. Any nontraditional blending or grape varieties are classified as regional wine (TO) or **table wine** (EO).

Modernization took place rapidly. The first boutique wineries, including Porto Carras Wines, Hatzimichalis, and Katsaros, opened in the 1970s and paved the way for future generations. In the 1980s, foreign-trained Greek winemakers began returning to their homeland and implementing their skills on every level, from the vineyard—with innovations in canopy management, lower yields and different planting densities to increase quality, and the introduction of international varieties, such as **Cabernet Sauvignon**, **Chardonnay**, and **Merlot**—to how to market the wine. The 1990s was a time of excitement and growth in Greece as these new wines reached the market, and many smaller wineries established themselves and began producing wines from both international and indigenous grapes. The Greek wine renaissance was born. Today, these wineries are working with modern interpretations of native grapes, as well as pushing the envelope by planting international grapes, such as Tempranillo in northern Greece. The results are promising and the quality is excellent.

Greece produces only 2.2 percent of the **European Union**'s wine, about 44 million cases (mc) in 2006. Legislation and its topography prohibit Greece from becoming a major player in the global wine trade. Due to strict legislation, it is cost-prohibitive and can take years to establish new vineyard land. Existing vineyard land is typically passed down from one generation to the next. With mountainous terrain, virtually all vineyard work is done by hand, and **mechanization** is not a viable option.

Greece is the largest consumer of its own wines; total consumption in 2006 was estimated at 36 mc. Traditionally, there has been a small but steady export market and few imports. In the past five years, however, that has begun to change. **Chilean**, **Australian**, and American wines have appeared in the Greek market—with the strong euro, it is becoming cheaper to buy wines from these countries than to drink the domestic product. As a result, more wine has become available for export. Greece's top export markets are the **United States** (240,000 cases in 2007), **Canada**, the **British market**, and other EU nations. In the past few years, interest from **Asia** has increased as well. In the United States, top sommeliers at non-Greek restaurants in large metropolitan areas have embraced Greek wine, and at least for the short term, the United States appears to be a viable growing market for Greek wines.

Given Greece's progress, there are still many problems plaguing the industry as a whole. Due to the complexities of the Greek language, many outside the country have a difficult time pronouncing grape and region names. Many labels are outdated and contain limited amounts of English, although this has begun to change and more producers are switching to English-only labels. Another significant problem is the lack of a wine bureau that can act as a clearinghouse for information about Greek wines, although the Greek government is in the process of establishing a strategic marketing plan for the domestic and export markets. Only within the past decade has there been a concerted effort to create the "Wine Roads of Greece" to promote **wine tourism**.

Nevertheless, **consumers** worldwide are beginning to tire of drinking the same international grapes all the time and are looking for interesting alternatives to expand their palate and knowledge. Greece has more than 200 indigenous grape varieties, as well as dozens of distinct appellations for dry and **dessert wines**, although less than a dozen varieties have shown an ability to produce quality wines that appeal to many different consumers. Examples of the most well-known Greek grape varieties are Assyrtiko, Moschofilero, and Malagousia for white wines and Agiorgitiko and Xinomavro for reds. These grapes make wines that cannot be associated or compared with any other region in the world, and that will be a great strength for Greece in the future.

Andrea Englisis

Further Reading

Lambert-Gócs, Miles. *The Wines of Greece*. London: Faber & Faber, 2002.
Lazarakis, Konstantinos. *The Wines of Greece*. London: Mitchell Beazley, 2005.

H

HEALTH

Health issues can have a significant impact on the business of wine, both negatively and positively. Wine has a long history as a health-promoting beverage and medication. In the twentieth century, medical studies correlated moderate consumption of wine with fewer heart attacks (myocardial infarctions) and lower death rates from coronary artery disease (CAD). As an alcoholic beverage, wine can also be associated with negative health consequences, particularly when immoderate drinking takes place. Members of the wine trade need to be aware of such perils as alcohol addiction, cirrhosis of the liver, alcohol withdrawal, and alcohol-related cancers.

Historical Overview. Wine has long been used as a therapeutic agent. Ancient Greek and Roman physicians prescribed wine—white and red, dry and sweet, as well as herb-infused—to treat a range of diseases and illnesses. They successfully used wine to relieve pain, reduce anxiety, and induce sleep. Being a solution of alcohol and water, wine is an excellent vehicle for delivering therapeutic herbs, medications, and supplements such as iron. Wine kills off such disease-causing bacteria as *E. coli, Salmonella, Shigella,* and *Staphylococcus.* It was successfully used as a wound dressing until the invention of antiseptics in the nineteenth century. Europeans used wine to sanitize water from the time of Hippocrates, the father of Western medicine, until the mid-twentieth century. Wine and alcohol were standard therapy for diabetes prior to the discovery of insulin. They were also successfully used to treat chest pain caused by CAD (angina pectoris) prior to the usage of nitroglycerin tablets.

Advances in pharmacology and chemistry during the nineteenth century decreased wine's role in medicine. At the dawn of the twentieth century, temperance movements gained strength, leading to the institution of **Prohibition.** Wine, once considered a health-promoting beverage, came to be considered just another intoxicating beverage and another form of "booze." Wine's rich history as a healing tool disappeared from medical education, which thereafter focused on alcohol abuse, alcoholism, and alcohol-related diseases—all of which remain problematic in society today.

During the 1980s, a number of medical studies demonstrated that moderate wine consumption was associated with less CAD. These studies confirmed a study that predated Prohibition, which found that the French, despite their reputation for fine dining, had low rates of CAD, a phenomenon dubbed the "**French paradox**." This led to marked increases in **red wine** sales, particularly in the **United States**. Thousands of medical studies have since been published looking at both the health benefits and the risks of wine and alcohol consumption.

Health Risks from Alcohol.   Although Hippocrates and his followers used wine both to prevent and to treat disease, they did preach against overindulgence. Moderation was their watchword, something that is essential when considering any health benefit from wine. Modern medicine has recognized alcohol abuse as a disease and alcohol as an addicting chemical.

Alcohol abuse may be sporadic—also known as "binge drinking"—or chronic. Alcohol intoxication takes a toll by altering judgment, slowing motor reflexes, and causing a depression of the central nervous system. This can cause social and health problems ranging from marital discord, child abuse, and automobile accidents to suicide, violence, and even death from an alcohol-caused coma. The lining of the stomach can be damaged during such acute abuse, causing bleeding. Drunken vomiting can tear the esophagus. High levels of alcohol cause damage to numerous organs, especially the liver, pancreas, brain, and heart.

Alcohol intake can also cause the reflux of acid from the stomach into the esophagus. Drinking, especially to excess, can cause snoring and sleep apnea (when someone stops breathing and resumes with a loud snort), which in turn causes high blood pressure, heart disease, and memory problems. High levels of alcohol consumption may also cause hypertension or high blood pressure.

Chronic alcohol abuse can lead to addiction and alcoholism. Alcoholism is a disease, and certain individuals are at increased genetic risk. Easy access increases alcohol risks for members of the trade. Alcohol addiction leads to daily immoderate consumption. Such chronic abuse increases the risk of inflammation of the liver (hepatitis), scarring of the liver (cirrhosis), inflammation of the pancreas (pancreatitis), heart damage (cardiomyopathy and arrhythmias), and damage to the brain and the central nervous system.

When an alcoholic stops drinking suddenly, this leads to alcohol withdrawal, whose symptoms can range from anxiety, sweating, and rapid heart rate to severe agitation, hallucinations, seizures, coma, and death. Alcohol withdrawal can be life-threatening and must be managed by a physician.

Alcohol and Cancer.   Alcohol intake is associated with increased risks of a variety of cancers. Usually, this increased risk is in proportion to intake. One problem facing the wine business is that of breast cancer. Alcohol increases the risk of breast cancer among postmenopausal **women**. This increased risk seems to begin with consumption of more than one glass of wine per day. The second daily glass may increase a woman's risk 10 to 20 percent. In addition, certain conditions, such as a family history of breast cancer or fibrocystic breast disease, may cause alcohol to have an even greater effect in increasing the risk of breast cancer. All forms of alcohol, including wine, have this increased risk of breast cancer.

That said, some women are at higher health risks from CAD, the number-one killer in the Western world, and may obtain a net health benefit from that second glass. Studies on premenopausal breast cancer and alcohol are not as consistent, with some showing an increased risk and others no such increase.

Alcohol increases the risks of a host of other cancers, especially at high consumption levels. These alcohol-related cancers, besides postmenopausal breast cancer, include cancers of the mouth, pharynx, esophagus, larynx, stomach, liver, colon, rectum, and ovaries. On the other hand, there is some evidence that wine may protect against some skin cancers, non-Hodgkin's lymphoma, and lung cancer.

Wine and Teeth. All wines are acidic, some more so than others. Prolonged contact of teeth and wine results in a demineralization of the protective enamel. This softened enamel is easily lost and not replaced. Members of the wine trade are at increased risk of losing enamel, which causes pain and increased risk of cavities and tooth loss. Rinsing with water or protective dental rinses may slow this process. Dentists offer protective varnishes and coatings that can also help prevent the loss of enamel. When attending a wine tasting, the worst thing that one can do is to brush one's teeth afterward, as the toothbrush will remove softened enamel.

Moderation Defined. The genetic makeup of humans may predispose individuals to some diseases while protecting them from others. A woman with a family history of postmenopausal breast cancer may need to define moderation as the occasional glass of wine, or certainly no more than one glass per day. Women concerned about breast cancer, especially when over the age of 45, should define moderation as one glass of wine per day, maximum. At a given level of alcohol consumption, women are at higher risk of alcoholism and should never consider moderation as anything more than two four- to six-ounce glasses of wine per day.

Men may define moderation along similar lines, although they can extend the safe level of consumption up to four glasses per day. Obviously, as one increases consumption, the risk of alcohol addiction and alcohol-related illnesses increases.

Health Benefits of Light-to-Moderate Wine Consumption. Thousands of medical studies regarding wine have been published over the past 25 years. As an anti-infectious agent, wine decreases the risk of *Helicobacter pylori* infection of the stomach (less peptic ulcer disease) and may also decrease one's risk of viral infections, such as the common cold. While moderate alcohol consumption decreases the risk of CAD, *wine* consumption (especially red wine) adds additional protection from CAD. This also seems to be the case with other vascular diseases that involve the brain (fewer strokes) or peripheral circulation. Wine consumption decreases the risk of dementia and Alzheimer's disease. It also seems to decrease the risk of macular degeneration. Moderate wine consumption lowers blood pressure, while excessive wine consumption raises it.

Overall, moderate wine consumption decreases one's risk of dying at any given age. When a population is followed over a number of years, moderate wine drinkers are less likely to die during the study period than those who do not drink or those who drink heavily.

The Health Effects of Wine. Tannins and pigments from the skins and seeds of grapes contain health-promoting compounds called *polyphenols*. Red wines are fermented on the skins and have lots of polyphenols. White wines with skin contact also have some polyphenols, as do all **rosé** wines.

Thousands of scientific studies of polyphenols have been published in the medical literature. These compounds are strong antioxidant, antibacterial, anti-blood clotting, and anti-inflammatory agents. They also cause blood vessels to dilate (relax) and inhibit some forms of abnormal cell growth associated with plaque formation in arteries.

Good evidence exists that fats in meals cause oxidative and inflammatory stress while promoting blood clot formation and damage to blood vessels and organs. Wine consumed with a meal seems to decrease these stresses to bodies. Again, wine seems to be healthful when consumed in moderation. *See also* Dealcoholized Wines; Drinking Age; High Alcohol Content; Organic Grapes and Wine; Quality Control; Sulfites.

Patrick Farrell

Further Reading

Australian Wine Research Institute. ''Wine and Health Published Papers.'' www.awri.com.au/industry_development/wine_and_health/papers/.

Das, Dipak K., and Fulvio Ursini. *Alcohol and Wine in Health and Disease.* New York: New York Academy of Sciences, 2003.

HIGH ALCOHOL CONTENT

One of the most significant trends in winemaking in recent years has been the movement toward riper fruit, which usually means higher levels of alcohol in the finished wine. In the 1970s, grapes were typically picked based solely on the sugar content of the fruit, without giving too much importance to the flavor development or the skins' and seeds' tannins. The fruit was basically considered ready to be picked as soon as the sugar reached 22° to 23° Brix (that is, 22 to 23 grams of sugar per 100 grams of juice), and the result in terms of wine quality was not terribly exciting: the 1970s and part of the 1980s were years of greenness and vegetative character, a lot of underripe flavors, and, in red wines, underpolymerized tannins that gave a high degree of astringency and a dry finish in the mouth. On the other hand, the vinification was a lot easier than today with very few stuck fermentations.

As a reaction to this wine style, a completely different approach to the maturation issue and wine style developed in the 1990s. Producers started looking seriously into flavor development and the maturation of polyphenols, ideas that 20 years earlier were not even part of a winemaker's conversation. This was a big step forward for the concept of fruit and wine quality. Winemakers began to realize that wine flavor is the result of the fruit flavor and that, to avoid the underripe and dry tannins of the earlier style, it was necessary to take a different approach to the grapes' maturation.

Under the new strategy, the numbers that had formerly been relied upon to determine harvest timing—sugar and total acidity—were not the only important factors anymore. The focus was on the flavor and how the berries, skins, and seeds tasted. To get rid of the astringency and greenness, it was necessary to pick the grapes later, when the skin was soft and sweet, the seeds were brown and lignified, and the overall flavor was riper. However, using these new concepts and following the flavor development meant picking the fruit not at 21° to 23° Brix, but more often at 25° to 27°, which, when fermented dry, produced a wine with an alcohol content of 15 percent or more. At these levels, winemakers experienced a lot more difficulties with stuck fermentations, but the finished wines had a much better, more intense flavor with a riper fruit profile and greater density, depth, and complexity; the wines were more interesting and sexier without the astringency and green acidity of years before. The market and the **consumer** received this new style with a lot of excitement, and most of the wine writers and critics joined in the praise of this new style of wines, rewarding them with high **ratings and scores**.

As is often the case with such a radical change of philosophy, it was eventually taken too far. After the initial excitement, in the early 2000s, people began to notice that the high alcohol was affecting the elegance and complexity of the wine. It was essentially burning off the finer aromas. Also, because alcohol is a very strong extractor, during extended maceration it extracts too many polyphenols from the skins, making the wine heavier and less refreshing; furthermore, during barrel-aging, it overextracts tannins and flavors from the oak and consequently overpowers the wine flavor. Too often, the wines are not well balanced, with a lot of black, overripe fruit, very low acidity, and a jammy flavor that detract from the elegance and finesse of a great wine. In addition, the excess of maturation in the grapes affects the varietal character of a wine negatively, and wines made with different varieties taste too much alike.

In the last few years, winemakers have started to reconsider their strategy to obtain wines with better balance: still avoiding the greenness and the underripe flavors, but at the same time also avoiding the overripeness and low acidity associated with high alcohol. The challenge is how to achieve the ideal wine with ripe tannins, good flavor, and nice freshness while keeping a moderate alcohol content.

The climate is a very important factor, because in a moderate, slightly cool climate, it is easier to get good flavor development and maturity at a reasonable sugar content; the problem is much more challenging in warm to hot environments, because in such situations, the sugar accumulates in the grapes at a much faster rate than the flavor, and ideal flavor development and phenolic maturity in the grapes are usually associated with very high sugar, and thus alcohol, content.

Grape growers have a number of tools available to achieve a better sugar/flavor balance, including irrigation, canopy management, use of new clones, and so on. With properly balanced vines, the grapes can be closer to the ideal of being ripe and fresh at the same time without an excess of sugar. In the winery, various **must and wine adjustments** can be used to avoid an excess of alcohol in the finished wine. For example, an open-top fermentor can be used, which will allow a little of the alcohol to evaporate, or a specific industrial yeast that has a lower sugar-to-alcohol conversion rate can be selected. With less alcohol, there will be a lot more fruit and freshness in the wine, improving its elegance and finesse, without the unpleasant burning feeling of very high alcohol wines.

One approach that winemakers have tried in recent years is using high-tech equipment to remove a portion of the alcohol after fermentation. The **dealcoholization** technology available includes reverse-osmosis machines and spinning cone columns. Some wineries with large-scale production volumes have purchased their own equipment for this purpose, which can run $70,000 to $100,000. Others, especially smaller producers, pay a fee to have another facility remove alcohol from a batch of wines. While flavor profile and style are the ultimate motivators for pursuing this option, significant savings in taxes can potentially be realized for lower alcohol wines, at least in the **United States**, where the **Alcohol and Tobacco Tax and Trade Bureau (TTB)** imposes an extra 50-cent-per-gallon tax on "**dessert**" **wines** that exceed 14 percent alcohol by volume (abv). Going rates to remove one percentage point of alcohol are roughly 10 cents per gallon. Thus, reducing the alcohol in a 15 percent abv wine down to 13.9 percent results in a net savings of almost 40 cents per gallon or 95 cents per case. Fierce detractors claim that the wine's flavor suffers from this process; others disagree.

A high alcohol wine (over 15 percent) does not necessarily mean a bad wine. The quality is not determined by a single parameter but rather by the whole experience, which can give the consumer a good or bad feeling. There are certainly high alcohol wines that have their own charm and personality. In general, however, wines with lower-alcohol content (14.5 percent maximum) tend to show more elegance, freshness, and vibrancy and are also perhaps **healthier** for the consumer.

Alberto Antonini

Further Reading

Boyd, Gerald D. "High Alcohol Wines: Boon or Bane?" *Wine Review Online,* November 6, 2007, www.winereviewonline.com/gerald_boyd_high_alcohol_wine_feature.cfm.

Franson, Paul. "Wine Alcohol Reduction and the TTB." *Wine Business Monthly,* April 15, 2007, www.winebusiness.com/ReferenceLibrary/webarticle.cfm?dataId=47186.

HOSPITALITY INDUSTRY

The hospitality industry is made up of many interrelated businesses, including lodging establishments, which can be segmented into hotels, motels, resorts, spas, inns, and bed and breakfasts; eating and drinking establishments, comprising quick-service **restaurants**, casual-service restaurants, full-service restaurants, catering operations, clubs, wine bars, and full-service bars and lounges; **cruise lines**; casinos; convention centers; and **wineries** that have hospitality-related facilities. This segment is sometimes referred to as HORECA, short for hotel/restaurant/catering.

The size, scope, and economic significance of the hospitality industry in the **United States** are evident when one examines the key statistics of employment, sales, and number of units in operation. In 2007, the food service industry employed 13.1 million people and the lodging industry another 1.8 million. As of 2006, there were 47,135 hotels of 15 rooms or more, totaling 4.4 million guest rooms and producing $133 billion in revenues. This was dwarfed by the food service industry's 945,000 eating and drinking establishments and $534 billion in sales in 2007.

The top 10 hotel companies (ranked by total number of rooms) are Inter-Continental Hotels Group, Cendant Corp., Marriott International, Choice Hotels International, Hilton Hotels, Best Western International Hotels, Starwood Hotels & Resorts Worldwide, Accor International, Carlson Hospitality Worldwide, and Accor North America. When combined, these companies control 20,778 hotels in the United States and many more worldwide. All of them operate multiple brands (as many as 15) to capture different market segments of consumers. Some of these brands have limited food and beverage facilities, but others feature multiple restaurants, lounges, bars, spas, and clubs, in addition to banquets and catering, room service, and in-room minibars—all of which add up to a huge volume of wine sales.

Casino resort hotels, especially the megasize examples in Las Vegas, such as the Wynn Las Vegas Resort and Country Club, the Venetian Las Vegas, Bellagio, and Mandalay Bay, are a particularly lucrative outlet for wine sales. The largest are like miniature cities, with dozens of bars, nightclubs, shopping malls, and up to 20 restaurants all in one complex. Many of them have restaurants operated by well-known chefs and restaurateurs from around the world; others are brands owned by chain restaurant companies. Each of these restaurants may generate revenues of more than $10 million a year, and wine is a significant part of their revenues and **profits**.

Hospitality operations have always been important to the wine industry, as they offer multiple venues for **promoting** and selling wine to diverse **consumer** segments. Since successful food and beverage operators tailor their concept, service, and food and beverage offerings for specific target markets, there is an opportunity for wines of many different styles and price points to be featured in various restaurants. Family-oriented food service operations offer a different selection of wines than restaurants that cater to a business clientele, for example.

In the early days of his winery during the late 1960s and 1970s, **Robert Mondavi** would travel around the country to promote his wines. He would invite **retail** wine shop owners and restaurant wine buyers to join him for dinner at a local restaurant and would place his wine on the table to be served with several of the prestigious classified growths of **Bordeaux**. He understood the value of being on the wine list and of promoting wine with food.

There is certainly a prestige factor associated with having one's wine on the list of a well-known celebrity chef's restaurant or of a restaurant that has been selected as a Grand Award Wine List winner by the *Wine Spectator*. Today, wine-makers and winery owners allocate wines to high-profile restaurants and participate in winemaker dinners in restaurants, at resorts, and on cruise ships. Wine-by-the-glass programs in high-volume restaurants and clubs give wine **brands** unique exposure and can move large volumes of wine. This exposure requires deep discounts, however, which are negotiated by the wine buyer through the **distributor**. Many of these high-volume operations price a single glass at the wholesale cost of the bottle, which makes this very profitable and helps the restaurant lower its overall wine cost.

On-premise (restaurant and hotel) wine consumption generated $12.9 billion in wine sales and accounted for 49.8 percent of retail sales of wine (by value) in the United States in 2006. These sales are certainly an important outlet for wine producers, but they are also critical to generate reasonable returns in food and beverage operations. Wine sales in restaurants that sell wine range from a low of 3 percent to as much as 40 percent of total sales. These revenues contribute a great deal to profitability, as markups on wine in most operations start at two times wholesale cost and may rise to four times cost or even higher in some restaurants. It is not simply about profit, though, as wine adds pleasure to the whole dining experience. Wine can often differentiate a restaurant. A thoughtfully selected, well-written, and appropriately priced wine list makes a statement about a restaurant. Those with good wine programs build customer loyalty not only because of their food, but also because of their wine.

Stephen A. Mutkoski

Further Reading

Cornell Hospitality Quarterly. www.hotelschool.cornell.edu/research/chr/pubs/quarterly.

Hotels. www.hotelsmag.com.

Lodging. www.lodgingmagazine.com.

I

IMPORTERS

Despite **globalization**, the transfer of merchandise across national boundaries is still much more complicated than local transactions, all the more so when it comes to alcoholic products. While not all countries use a three-tier system for domestic sales, almost all do for wine (and spirits) that originate in another country. The 27 nations of the **European Union** are an exception when trading with each other, but not when it comes to wine from outside the bloc (for the purposes of this entry, the European Union is considered a single country).

In general, wine from a supplier in another country (the first tier) must always go through a licensed importer (the second tier) before being made available to **retailers** or **restaurants** (the third tier). The fairly small number of importers (compared to the numbers of suppliers and retail licensees) creates a bottleneck that allows the national regulatory authorities to more efficiently monitor the volume of trade and collect taxes, tariffs, and duties. It also makes a person or company within the country—and therefore within reach of national law enforcement—responsible for the wine so that the authorities can better enforce national statutes regarding labeling and consumer product safety.

Importers provide an important service to **wineries** by helping them navigate the paperwork and procedures necessary to sell their wine in a foreign country. Few wineries are large enough to have the personnel and expertise that would be required to do this in one foreign country, much less all the countries to which they would like to export. The importers also usually represent the winery in the country, helping to **promote** the wines to potential customers nationwide—again, a task few wineries would be willing or able to do for themselves.

The contract between a supplier and the importer will specify, among other things, the amount of wine the importer will receive, the time and place for the delivery, and the price for the wine. The currency to be used must be specified because **exchange rate** changes may significantly affect the relative cost.

Usually the importer will work with the winery to arrange to take delivery at a port or central warehouse in the country of origin and is responsible for the transportation to the destination. More often than not, the transportation will be by ship, as the major markets and suppliers (not counting intra-European trade) are on different continents. It is primarily the importer's responsibility to ensure that the wine is not damaged by overheating, either on the dock or aboard ship, especially if being shipped between hemispheres. **Temperature control** is crucial during this phase.

Most often, the wine is shipped to the port of entry nearest the importer's headquarters and main warehouse, although if a large enough quantity of wine is headed for a specific market or purchaser, the shipment may be sent to a different port closer to the ultimate destination. The wine will be cleared by customs authorities and then put into temporary storage at the warehouse awaiting orders.

In the **United States**, importers typically work with **distributors** to move the product through the chain, since the distributors already have networks of sales representatives calling on off- and on-premise licensees. The importer therefore usually requires a smaller group of sales personnel, who provide expert assistance to the distributor sales reps, although some national importers who have distribution of their products in all 50 states can have national sales teams of 100 or more people. Some importers own their own distributorships, but this is not usually the case, and no importer has its own nationwide distribution. The United States has a highly fragmented and diversified distribution chain.

The distributor buys a quantity of the imported wine, based on projected sales, and then takes product from the importer's warehouse to its own. It is then up to the distributor to find retailers to take the wine, and the importer's job is technically finished. If the wine does not sell, it is the distributor that takes the loss. However, in practical terms, the importer still has a stake, because if the wine is not selling, there will be fewer reorders, causing a backlog at the importer's end. This is the reason that importers keep their own representatives active in the various markets: to make sure that the distributors are successfully getting the wine into stores and restaurants.

The largest importer in the United States is W.J. Deutsch & Sons, primarily on the strength of the **Yellow Tail brand**. Deutsch brought in 9.4 million cases (mc) in 2006, including 8.1 mc of Yellow Tail. The next tier of importers consists of **Banfi Vintners** (6.85 mc), **Foster's** Americas (6.81 mc), and E.&J. **Gallo** Winery (6.01 mc). Palm Bay International imported 4.3 mc in 2006, primarily from **Italy**, and the various subgroups of **Constellation Brands**, Inc., did about the same volume. Other importers bring in 1.5 mc or less.

The largest import firm in the **British market** is WaverleyTBS, which brings about 6.0 mc a year into the United Kingdom, worth around £500 million, followed by Matthew Clark, Bottle Green, and Bibendum Wine Co., each of which imports 3.5 to 4.5 mc valued at £100–180 million.

In some cases, importers act simply as agents or brokers, doing little more than processing the paperwork for a fee to allow the winery to have its wines available in the country. This is usually done as part of a *direct import* arrangement between a supplier and an on- or off-premise retailer. For example, a U.S. wine shop or restaurant chain might purchase the entire output of a small producer in **South Africa** or have a specially labeled wine created by a cooperative in **France**, thereby acquiring a wine that no one else sells. Since the sale has already been agreed upon, an importer—which may be a major import company or a small import business created specifically for this purpose—is needed only as a formality, passing the wine through its office (or simply passing the paperwork across its desk) to preserve the three-tier requirement. *See also* Bulk Wine/Juice Trade; Consolidation; Global Wine Industry; Trade Barriers.

INFORMATION TECHNOLOGY

Despite winemaking's status as an agricultural product, one of the most dramatic innovations in the wine industry of the past few decades has been the revolution in information technology (IT). The development of computers and electronics has changed almost every facet of the industry in one way or another, from vineyard design to home wine cellar management software. The basics of winemaking remain the same, and it is certainly possible to make and sell wine without a single electronic device, but IT has made each segment of the industry easier and/or more powerful than could ever have been imagined half a century ago. Regardless of segment, the biggest benefit of IT is to provide reliable information that helps personnel make accurate and informed decisions, while at the same time reducing costs and improving the quality of the specific product or process within that sector.

In the Vineyard. Although nature does most of the work in creating grapes, computers have an impact even in this phase of winemaking. High-tech devices can now monitor almost all the vital conditions and activities in the vineyard for both soil and plants. Growers can map soils, track weather activity, or assess plant growth, nutrition, and water levels throughout the year by computer. At harvest, electronic equipment can be used to measure wine chemistry and forecast yield and quality.

While most farmers by nature are slow to adopt technology, many of the world's modern vineyards, particularly in the **New World**, use at least some of this technology. Initial investment can be high, however, so backfitting of sensors and installation of IT solutions is often limited to very large or high-quality vineyards. Additional advancements are afoot with new real-time software and the use of wireless as well as GPS technology. With **climate change** a potential threat worldwide, more accurate understandings of climate and weather could help growers better prepare and adapt.

In the Winery. **Temperature control** of tanks and **winery** buildings is an essential part of modern winemaking, and any medium-size or larger winery with numerous tanks and multiple simultaneous fermentations is likely to use some form of computerized temperature control system. Some facilities have control rooms where the cellar master or winemaker can monitor data on all the tanks, initiate automated pump overs or micro-oxygenation, or move wine from one place to another without leaving the room. Computerization has made the collection and analysis of must and wine chemistries in the laboratory much more detailed and accurate, as well (although, of course, nothing will ever substitute for the nose and palate of the winemaker when it comes to fine-tuning the style and character of the wine or blend). Buy-in costs for the more sophisticated equipment can be steep and therefore must be justified against sales volumes and amortized over time.

Distribution, Sales, and Administration.   For supply chain management, software options have been added since the late 1990s that allow suppliers and **distributors** to manage inventory status, orders, shipping logistics, and customer service functions. With computer systems, perhaps using the Internet, they can track the product throughout its movement, eliminating errors and allowing for inventories to remain fresh. Sales reps now use handheld electronic devices and notebook computers that provide them with product availability data in real time and allow them to place orders for 24-hour turnaround. In on- and off-premise retailers, point-of-sale software allows buyers and managers to closely track inventory and sales.

The Internet has had its most obvious effect in the area of **e-commerce**, including online retail, **direct shipping**, online auctions, and more. In addition to sales, the Internet is being used for marketing by wineries, retailers, and **restaurants**, and special providers offer software that gives marketers the ability to create and print brochures, shelf talkers, wine lists, fact sheets, labels, and the like on demand. Scanner data in **supermarkets** allow direct communication back to the buyer, and cost savings are realized on both ends. Wine education is in the game as well with a multitude of education-oriented Web sites, online courses, and wine discussion groups that make full use of Web technology.

The IT revolution has made its mark on the **global wine industry**, making the world of wine much more interconnected, with flows of information—from general wine knowledge to detailed product data—available worldwide on a moment's notice. As with all technology, it makes many things more efficient, but also introduces its own set of new challenges. IT makes more and better wines available to more people and is irreversibly part of the modern business of wine. *See also* Globalization; Mechanization.

ITALY

No country on Earth can claim a longer continuous heritage in the wine trade than Italy. Countries to its east, sources for Italy's vines in antiquity, had wine earlier, but their wine industries were disrupted by **religion** and war. Countries to Italy's west obtained their vines later—and in many cases, from the Romans themselves. But in Italy, wine has been part of the culture and has been a valuable trading item from the establishment of ancient **Greek** colonies in the south through to the present, thanks to the outstanding growing conditions, the Catholic Church, and the Italians' love of food and wine. Wines that were made 2,000 years ago, such as Recioto, as well as ancient varieties like Falanghina and Greco, are still going strong.

Italy is the world's largest wine-producing country, producing the equivalent of 594 million nine-liter cases (mc) of wine in 2006, the first year Italy outproduced **France**. Despite one of the highest per-capita consumption rates, 57 liters per adult in 2006, the national consumption—around 304 mc—is only a little over half of this volume, and thus wine represents a major export commodity for Italy. In fact, Italy is the global leader in wine exports, sending abroad an estimated 200 mc in 2006. This represents 30 percent of production (the remainder beyond domestic and export consumption going into **distillation** and other products), and 19 percent of the international wine market.

Wine and Italian Culture.   With such a long history of wine production and consumption, wine has become part of the Italian culture, part of the lifestyle. Italians agree on their love of wine, if not necessarily on which Italian wines are the best. Politically, Italy has been a nation of separate, competing regions, city-states, kingdoms, duchies, papal territories, and villages since the fall of the Roman Empire, and even a century and a half after unification, Italians often define themselves first by their regional identity and second as Italians. Consequently, the standardization that has come with **globalization** has had far less effect in Italy than in many other countries. Traditional methods and grape varieties survive. The dazzling array of Italian wines available on the market is a painting that uses the full palette rather than employing only two or three colors.

Not surprisingly, wine reflects a wider set of Italian attributes. The Italian flair for style and fashion has spilled over into the wine industry. This can be seen in the packaging in particular—bottle shapes, labels, and even the overall dressing of the bottles have been influenced by Italian style. Inside the bottle, Italy has been on a quest for improving quality; the last 25 years have seen a huge shift from quantity to quality. After World War II, wine was seen largely as a calorie source in the Italian diet, and quantity was what was important. Since then, with wine as a widely available and accepted part of the diet, Italians have moved toward ever greater quality. Italy takes its food—and as a corollary, its wine as well—very seriously at every social level.

Market Structure.   Italy has a little more than 2 million acres under vine, third in the world after **Spain** and France. Many of the vineyards are too small to economically produce wine for sale (indeed, some are only large enough to supply a family's home winemaking needs), so numerous cooperatives have been established to pool the resources of local growers and make and sell their wine. Growers with larger vineyards or those in renowned **appellations** are more likely to make their own wine, which might be sold only at the **winery** itself or in local shops. Only the largest and most entrepreneurial producers aspire to market their wines nationally or internationally.

Production restrictions abound and there are strict agricultural regulations. Under **European Union** pressure, the total acreage is slowly shrinking by about 1 percent per year. Many appellations are currently closed for the purpose of adding new vineyards, and therefore planting rights for the most esteemed appellations have to be purchased from a current holder, much like a liquor license in many places in the **United States**. To further complicate the process, an official from the Italian government must approve all phases of a new winery project, and players from the municipality, the province, and the region all get involved along the way.

The system for wine distribution in Italy is the similar to what exists in **California**, where wineries use brokers to move their products through the distribution chain. At present, there are very few national **distributors** in Italy. Wineries appoint someone to represent them in a certain territory, paying a commission for placing their wines. This representative might have a few employees or may operate alone. Once the wine is sold, the onus is on the winery to get the wine to the buyer, which could be anything from a highway rest stop to a five-star restaurant. Wines travel in small case lots (typically six or more) by couriers from winery to destination. There are no credit laws in Italy, and it is not unheard of for restaurants to take six months to a year to pay. It is inevitable that Italy will need to move to a distribution system eventually.

By contrast, **importers** do exist in Italy, with a lot of wine being sold in **supermarkets** at all price points. Non-Italian wines are not significant, however, with the exception being **Champagne**. There are very few barriers; wineries, brokers, and importers can sell wine wherever they want, basically to whomever they want. They can sell from a shop, on the Internet, via direct mail, door-to-door, or in any other way they choose. There are no restrictions barring a producer from being, say, an importer, a distributor, a broker, or any other link in the distribution chain.

Challenges to the Italian Wine Industry.   When anything is taken to excess, it becomes a problem. In the case of the Italian *denominazioni di origine controllata* (DOC) **appellation** system, the Italian bureaucratic mind-set weighs heavily in the equation, and there is a lot of preservation of old traditions for preservation's sake, as when Chianti required white grapes in a **red wine**, mostly to protect the local farmers. Another problem is that DOC laws also insist on strict minimum and maximum percentages for the allowed grapes, thus limiting the winemaker's ability to produce the best possible wine from a particular vineyard. Bureaucracy also gets involved when Italians conduct regional **promotions** internationally that do not maximize available resources for those wines that have real market potential. Because the government does not require the participants to demonstrate marketability of the wines being promoted, money is wasted on non-export-worthy wines. It would be more effective if the government focused its funding on the *consorzi* (consortiums) that have high quality standards and a way to market the wines (for example, Brunello or Barbaresco), rather than sponsoring all producers equally.

Regions and Appellations to Watch.   Of all the regions in Italy, *Sicily* is probably the one with the highest potential for making profound wines right alongside good-quality, inexpensive wines. Yet Sicily has been more of a media darling (many **wine writers** have written about it and have stated that its wines are great) than a commercial success. One reason is that prices are often too high in Sicily, and this offsets its competitive advantages. One of the "hottest" areas for its future wine potential is Mount Etna, but Sicilians in general have yet to take advantage of their **terroir**, especially the dramatic temperature excursions between day and night. In addition, the emphasis on international varieties is not the way to go for Sicily. The world does not need another **Chardonnay**; it needs an alternative to Chardonnay (that is why **Pinot Grigio** has been so successful).

In the *Veneto,* there are close to 600,000 registered wine businesses, and this creates a skilled labor pool. Veneto producers have just the right combination of top-quality wines, such as Amarone, and well-made, good-tasting, inexpensive wines, such as Valpolicella, Lugana, Pinot Grigio, and Prosecco.

Chianti is a success because the producers there have worked out the bureaucratic system. Chianti is the most well-known Italian wine on the U.S. market, since it was the first to be imported into the United States. Tuscany has the added benefit of having spawned the iconic Supertuscan category, which producers embraced because these wines were so much better than what could be produced under antiquated appellation rules. Now, however, it is impossible for the **consumer** to pick up a Supertuscan and know what is inside the bottle. Producers in Tuscany want to make **quality wine**—that is not in question—but there is a gap in communicating this to consumers. Chianti Classico has climbed in quality, but the appellation is too broad. To take this appellation one step further, the wines in Chianti should be named, as they are in France, with the villages on the label: Greve, Castellina, Radda, and so forth.

To date, *Puglia* represents a missed opportunity. Here, the issue is the quality of the entrepreneurs. Given the quality of the wine and their high volume, the wines do not have the market penetration they deserve.

Finally, the *regional appellations*—IGT (*Indicazione Geografica Tipica*) Sardegna, IGT Sicilia, DOC Langhe, and so forth—are detrimental to the quality and image of Italian wine. In this instance, the Italians should take a page from the French: recognize the key varieties, define the appellation as a small geographic area, and trust the producers to do what they want. The grape varieties should also be on the wine's back label, eliminating the "math problem" that is inherent in so many Italian appellation laws. This would allow more freedom in the winemaking with more disclosure of grape varieties, in the same vein of disclosure in foods. While it is admirably apparent that Italians are passionate people, the appellation laws are a clear case of how Italy's passion for bureaucracy has gotten in the way.

Outlook.   While Italians will remain provincial in their drinking habits, this will slowly loosen up. Italy is an export-driven, export-minded country, and as such it has been very quick to embrace the emerging markets, such as India, China, and Korea. The trend in Italy is toward less globalization in wine, less oak, and backing off of experimentation with some of the international varieties. The trend toward lower yields and higher quality will continue and will allow Italy to remain one of the key players on the world's wine stage.

Leonardo LoCascio

Further Reading
FISAR (Italian Sommeliers Federation). www.fisar.com/index.asp.
Gambero Rosso. www.gamberorosso.it/portaleEng/Homepage/homepage.
Italian Trade Commission. www.italianmade.com/wines/home.cfm.

J

JAPANESE MARKET. *See* Asia

JOHNSON, HUGH (1939–)

Hugh Johnson is a revered **wine writer** in Great Britain who has perhaps done more than any other individual to boost interest in wine among Anglophone **consumers**. Johnson has written dozens of books since the 1960s, notably the annual *Pocket Guide to Wine,* published in its 32nd edition in 2008. Other highly regarded works include *The World Atlas of Wine,* now in its sixth edition and coauthored with **Jancis Robinson**, and *The Art and Science of Making Wine,* with James Halliday (rev. ed., 2007). Johnson was named to the Order of the British Empire in 2007.

K

KENDALL-JACKSON

Kendall-Jackson (K-J) Vineyards and Winery, headquartered in Santa Rosa, California, was founded by Jess Jackson in 1982 and became one of the largest **wineries** in the **United States**, with 2006 sales of 5.3 million cases. With a portfolio that focuses on premium wines, K-J's revenues of $927 million put it in fifth position by value. The company was restructured in 2006 to create Jackson Family Wines as a parent corporation for the Kendall-Jackson **brand** and other brands of the Artisans & Estates division. Jackson was an early proponent of cool-climate viticulture in **California**, especially in the Central Coast area. Jackson Family Wines owns more than 12,000 acres of vineyards in California from Santa Barbara to Mendocino, generally in cool areas along the coast or in higher elevations, as well as property in **Italy**, **Australia**, and **Bordeaux**.

The company sells several lines of wine under the Kendall-Jackson name, the lower tiers blending wine from multiple vineyards and the higher-priced lines coming from one or a few vineyards. It also sells wines under the Arrowood, Byron, Cambria, Cardinale, Freemark Abbey, La Crema, Matanzas Creek, and Murphy-Goode brands, among others. A new division called White Rocket Wine Company was created in 2006 with a mission of attracting new, young wine drinkers with unconventional wines and hip marketing.

KOSHER WINE

Judaism is the most wine friendly of the major **religions**—wine being an essential part of the Sabbath meal and especially the seder ritual at Passover—and also has some of the most detailed dietary laws, called *kashrut*. The intersection of these two facets of Judaism is kosher wine, wine that is kosher ("proper") for consumption. For Orthodox Jews and all who follow kashrut, the only wines that can be served are those that have been made in accordance with kosher procedures.

For a wine to be kosher, it must be made with equipment dedicated only to making kosher wine and must be under the supervision of a rabbi and touched only by Sabbath-observant Jews throughout the entire winemaking process from crush to bottling. The source of the grapes themselves is unimportant—grapes require no special treatment to be kosher—but after arrival at the **winery** and the beginning of processing, the equipment and personnel restrictions are absolute. Thus, making kosher wine is not something that can be done as a sideline or on a whim, but must be the sole focus of the winery.

Apart from the facility restrictions, kosher winemaking is not very different from standard winemaking. There are a few limitations on materials that can be used, forbidding any animal-derived products—which eliminates some yeasts and fining agents—but otherwise the winemaking is business as usual. Because kosher status derives solely from the conditions of production, it is conceivable to make any style or category of kosher wine.

During Passover, additional dietary restrictions come into force, although these generally do not affect winemaking. One exception is that making a wine kosher for Passover requires that no corn syrup be used as a sweetener—which is far from a normal winemaking procedure anyway, but is a technique used in some of the old-style sweet kosher wines, such as the powerhouses Manischewitz and Mogen David (owned by **Constellation Brands**, Inc., and the **Wine Group**, respectively), which must ensure that they use different sweeteners for Passover wines.

Once the wine is bottled and sealed, it requires no extraordinary handling to remain kosher through the time the bottle is opened. It may be moved, warehoused, trucked, and delivered by anyone and therefore can be handled like any other wine through the **import**, **distribution**, and **retail** channels. When the wine is served, however, it must again be opened, handled, and poured by Sabbath-observant Orthodox Jews to remain kosher.

This last requirement can be a problem, particularly in a **restaurant**, because the server may not be qualified to pour it as kosher wine, and in many jurisdictions it is illegal for customers to pour their own wine. This can also be awkward at home, for example, if non-Jews are invited to a seder. The solution in these situations is provided by *mevushal* ("cooked") wines, which are kosher wines that have been brought to or near the boiling point (thereby becoming unfit for use in idolatrous rituals and therefore safe for consumption by the faithful). Whereas this once might have meant a steaming cauldron over an open flame—resulting in a seriously changed flavor profile—it now generally means flash pasteurization, very briefly raising the wine to around 180°F and then rapidly cooled. Mevushal wines remain kosher regardless of who handles them. The flash pasteurization process has the added benefit of killing all yeasts and microbes in the wine and extending its shelf life, with minimal degradation in flavor.

Manischewitz is the largest kosher wine **brand**, and the largest kosher wine company is the Royal Wine Company, based in Bayonne, New Jersey, which reports selling more than a million cases of kosher wine in 16 countries. The large U.S. producers are based in **New York** and built their reputations on sweet, Concord-based wines. The last decade has seen an explosion of dry kosher wines from smaller producers in New York, **California**, and other states and from around the world. Israel, unsurprisingly, produces kosher wine, as does virtually every major wine-producing country. Kosher wines can now be found made from any of the major international grape varieties, as well as local varieties such as **Italian** Barbera or **South African** Pinotage.

Further Reading

Kosher Wine Society. www.kosherwinesociety.com/index.php?command=winearticles.

Rosen, Tzvi. "The Art of Kosher Wine Making." *Kashrus Kurrents,* www.star-k .org/kashrus/kk-thirst-wine.htm.

L

LABELS AS MARKETING

The design of wine labels is a bellwether of the wine industry's evolution commercially over the last century. As recently as 25 years ago, the wine **consumer** in a **retail** shop had a relatively small number of wines to choose from, both domestic and imported, and the labeling on those wine selections was fairly straightforward—provenance, vintage, producer, grape variety, and a few other technical details, with design playing a secondary role to content. Today, with a proliferation of **brands** from around the world, wine label design and content have become more strategic and relevant than ever in terms of driving consumer purchases. According to 2008 data, close to 43 percent of wine-buying consumers surveyed said that they are often influenced by the label and are open to innovative packaging in terms of prompting their choices. Many of these consumers, including the Millennials, are new to the world of wine, and design plays an even more prominent role in their choices.

Today's wine labeling—which spans the gamut from classic minimalist design to the ubiquitous "critter" or animal labels and everything in between—has built on the successes of past innovations. Perhaps most memorable and influential in the development of wine label design was Baron Philippe de Rothschild's revolutionary idea of taking the bottling, labeling, and maturing of his Château Mouton Rothschild out of the hands of the **négociants** in **Bordeaux** to his own property, assuming control in order to guarantee provenance. As part of this revolution, he commissioned various artists to create a design to grace the label with each new vintage. This became a much anticipated and sought-after release every year and featured artists as prominent as Salvador Dali and Marc Chagall. Often imitated today by such **wineries** as Taittinger, St. Supéry, Benziger Family Winery, and others, the wines are prized as much for their artistic renderings as for their content.

Label art is only part of the "power of the package" in **promoting** and selling wine. Distinctive elements of label shape, color, or design have also created such iconic labels as the striking signature yellow-orange ones on Veuve Clicquot

Champagne and the anemone Art Nouveau decal gracing the outside of the entire Perrier-Jouët fleur bottle. Both of these brands are immediately identifiable from across the room—a powerful way of translating the company image.

One thing that consumers apparently are instinctively attracted to on a wine label is the image of an animal. These "critter labels" have accounted for around one-sixth of all new wine brands in the past five years, and many have been highly successful. One such brand is Goats do Roam, from Charles Back of **South Africa**, which launched with not only a distinctive package and a goat on the label but also a fun play on words, an homage to the French Côtes du Rhone region. Early positive reviews by prominent **wine writers** such as **Jancis Robinson** established it as a wine made by a serious individual with a sense of fun and gave it legitimacy both inside and outside traditional wine circles. Its success and appeal were proven as it doubled its sales to 50,000 cases from the 2002 to the 2003 vintage.

Yellow Tail, from the Riverina region of **Australia**, is an even better example of the power of labeling. A phenomenon that captured the imagination of the mass wine consumer with its immediate cultural translation to Australia—at a price point that allowed for easy trial without heavy investment—Yellow Tail's label combined an Aboriginal-style wallaby image with an original styling of the brand name, and it became a huge success almost immediately. In 2001 when it launched, 200,000 cases were sold; in five years, it had reached over 10 million cases in sales worldwide.

The power of the label in terms of successful commerce in wine has also led to intense competition and litigation. A landmark case in the wine industry over labels was the 1997 battle between **Kendall-Jackson** Winery and E.&J. **Gallo**. In the famous Turning Leaf trade dress infringement lawsuit, proprietor Jess Jackson claimed that the label art for Turning Leaf too closely resembled that of his top-selling Vintner's Reserve and therefore caused consumer confusion at retail. The case went all the way to the federal level and came out in favor of Gallo. This case was the first of many wherein **appellations**, vineyard names, colors, and artwork have become proprietary in labeling and branding, causing wineries and trade organizations to file cease-and-desist orders at the very least and full-blown lawsuits when necessary.

Label designers these days have to navigate label laws both domestically and internationally. For instance, in Europe, nudity and beneficial health claims are allowed in label packaging, but in the United States, they are not. Thus, the 1993 Mouton Rothschild label featuring a reclining nude by the artist Balthus in Europe appeared in the United States with a large empty space where the drawing had been. In the United States, in technical compliance with **Alcohol and Tobacco Tax and Trade Bureau (TTB)** restrictions, designers address many design challenges by inverting the "back" and "front" labels. Mandatory labeling information is shown on a relatively inconspicuous "brand label," while artistic renderings and philosophical statements are made on what most consumers would consider the front label but is technically the back. In many Old World countries, appellational and consortium rules need to be adhered to and make it difficult to break tradition to market in a more consumer-friendly way.

In the future, some of the broader themes with respect to trends in labeling and packaging appear to be the use of environmentally sensitive labels, capsules,

closures, and **alternative packaging** as the wine industry aligns itself more closely with the green movement. Labels that translate a believable story behind the wine will become more commonplace. *See also* Fads and Fashions; Varietal Labeling.

Kimberly Charles

M

MARKETING. *See* Promotion

MECHANIZATION

Grape growing and winemaking resisted mechanization longer than many other industries, both because of a general consensus that handmade wines were superior and the fact that so many vineyards and **wineries** were family run. With the development of ever larger commercial operations and rising labor costs, combined with shrinking labor pools in many areas, mechanization has become accepted to a greater degree. Without it, the giant production facilities that account for a majority of wine sales would be impossible, and thanks to improved technology, even ultrapremium wines are now often taking advantage of partial mechanization. The primary goal is to use mechanization on jobs where it provides cost savings while maintaining or increasing quality.

In the Vineyard.   Depending on labor availability and the demands of the winery, the vineyard tasks that may be economically mechanized will vary widely by vineyard. The best machine for the job will vary with soil type, row and vine spacing, vineyard size, and topography. The machinery and mechanical tools most often employed include the following:

- *Grape harvesters:* A modern harvest machine will do the work of 20 pickers. Properly operated and in good mechanical condition, a harvest machine will do minimal damage to grapes, trellises, and next year's buds. Good harvest machines are expensive and require ongoing maintenance. The wineries that insist on hand harvesting are afraid their quality might be compromised by juice starting to ferment before it reaches the winery and by collection of MOG (material other than grapes); many also use ''hand harvested'' as a marketing tool. However, modern harvest machines treat berries more gently than ever and continue to improve on methods of removing MOG.

- *Pre-pruners:* A pre-pruner shows both economic and quality advantages in the vineyard. Its series of cutting blades chop canes into small pieces that drop off the trellis wires. Hand pruning requires many hours per acre to pull canes loose from the trellis, whereas a pre-pruner leaves just a few buds on each cane and makes it much easier for the hand pruners that normally follow to do a more accurate job of selecting their cuts.
- *Hedgers:* Wine regions that cannot get an adequate supply of hand laborers are moving toward the use of hedgers to do some form of box pruning, virtually eliminating the need for hand pruners. For those vineyards that top their canes to stop growth, trim the canes on the sides, or box-hedge instead of pruning, the hedging sickle bars mounted on the front of a tractor cut labor time to a quarter of that for handwork.

Other mechanical equipment that may be found includes wire lifters that mechanically raise wind wires as needed and are useful on large vineyards with trellis systems utilizing movable wires; machines that place and pick up bird netting, a very labor-intensive task on larger vineyards; and equipment for cultivating or removing weeds. The newest machines for leaf removal are much improved over earlier units that tended to damage vines and clusters. Research is even under way to use mechanical "sniffers" to analyze cluster ripeness.

In the Winery.   Where once everything was done by hands and feet, mechanization in the winery has become indispensable as a way of either reducing the need for labor or making tasks less arduous: forklifts move grapes and barrels; labor is reduced and quality improved by the use of sorting tables, destemmers, crushers, and presses; must pumps move grapes and wine with minimal damage; **temperature-control** equipment allows the winemaker to manage tank fermentations as well as storage conditions; punch-down machines that break up the caps during fermentation minimize a once-onerous job; modern lab equipment gives rapid and accurate test results; gyropalettes replace the grueling task of riddling for **sparkling wine**; bottling machines package wines much faster and more accurately than by hand; and temperature-controlled trucks move the wine from the winery to destinations far and wide.

While machines were initially relatively clumsy and detrimental to quality, each new generation of equipment has brought significant advances, and the most modern mechanical devices are now as effectual as humans, if not more so. Much of this improvement has come as a result of computerization. Computers control temperature and humidity in the cellars, and through the Internet even allow the winery to check temperatures and track wine shipments en route to markets. Modern computerized presses allow the winemaker to set complex programs to control the press process, although discussion still continues on the merits of the old basket press versus the modern bladder press.

Outlook.   The increased costs of labor and the ever-present threat of labor shortage will assure that both vineyards and wineries continue to watch the market for new machines that decrease costs without decreasing the quality of the wine. *See also* Information Technology; Profit and Profitability.

Norm McKibben

Further Reading

Greenspan, Mark. "Mechanization of Vineyards." *Wine Business Monthly,* November 15, 2007, www.winebusiness.com/ReferenceLibrary/webarticle.cfm?dataId=51977.

Justin R. Morris Vineyard Mechanization Symposium: Proceedings. Columbia: University of Missouri Extension, 2007.

MERLOT

Among red grapes, **Cabernet Sauvignon** may be the handsome, rugged leading man and **Pinot Noir** the seductive, mysterious prima donna, but Merlot is the versatile and talented supporting actor that gets somewhat less of the spotlight, yet pleases more of the audience more of the time. Less tannic than Cabernet and much deeper and darker in color than Pinot or Grenache, Merlot is an adaptable red wine that pairs well with hearty foods while being easier to drink by itself than many other reds. Its rich fruitiness and often silky texture have allowed Merlot to grow steadily in popularity, becoming the go-to red wine for many wine **consumers**.

Like Cabernet Sauvignon and its cousin Cabernet Franc, Merlot emerged from the vineyards of **Bordeaux** to the world stage, being taken around the globe by colonists, emigrants, and viticulturists to make a home in many places. It is still considered a "Bordeaux grape," however, and is in fact the workhorse variety of Bordeaux wines: 174,000 acres—54 percent of the vineyard land—in Bordeaux is planted with Merlot, particularly in Entre-Deux-Mers and the Right Bank. It usually makes up the major part of the blend in Bordeaux red-wine **appellations** outside the Médoc and Graves, including the general Bordeaux appellation itself, and Château Pétrus in Pomerol is famously made entirely from Merlot in most vintages. Merlot ripens earlier than Cabernet and is thus slightly more reliable in this climate.

Beyond Bordeaux, **France** has another 110,000 acres or so of Merlot, much of it in Languedoc-Roussillon. Altogether, France can claim roughly half of the world's 550,000 acres of Merlot vineyard land. The next largest producer, with about 64,000 acres, is **Italy**; there, the Veneto region has long been its home, followed by Sicily, which recently has overshadowed Friuli–Venezia Giulia in Merlot acreage. In the rest of the Old World, only Bulgaria, Moldova, and Romania in **Eastern Europe** and **Spain** have a significant amount of Merlot growing, but most **New World** countries include Merlot among their top red varieties. The **United States** has around 58,000 acres of Merlot vines. Most of this is in **California**, but a notable 10 percent is in **Washington**, which has demonstrated a particular affinity for this grape variety. Washington Merlots have a depth of character that is unmatched outside France.

Merlot is known for red and blue fruit flavors and aromas: plums, blueberries, red currants, black cherries, and the like. Its tannins are generally soft and only moderately astringent. The acidity and alcohol levels are site and vintage dependent. Bordeaux Merlots show higher acidity and firmer tannins, while New World Merlots are softer but higher in alcohol. Merlot is often a blending partner with Cabernet Sauvignon because it takes the hard edges off a young tannic Cabernet, while benefiting from the additional structure supplied by the Cabernet, and both mature elegantly with one another, especially after oak aging. This partnership is evident not only in Bordeaux-style blends (whether made in Bordeaux or else-where) but also in varietally labeled Merlots and Cabernets, which in most places can contain at least 15 percent of the other (25 percent in the United States) without having to mention it on the label.

Merlot has not yet quite become generic in the way **Chardonnay** has, but many casual wine consumers would be a little surprised to learn that "Merlot" is a grape name and not just another way of saying "red wine." In 2006, Merlot was the most purchased red **table wine** variety in the United States (second overall to Chardonnay), with a 13 percent market share, according to *Adams Wine Handbook 2007,* but strong Cabernet Sauvignon sales pushed Merlot down a notch in 2007. *Impact* data indicate that **varietally labeled** red Merlot sales in the United States amounted to 29.2 million cases (mc) in 2006, 36 percent of all red varietals, not counting 1.1 mc of red Bordeaux and 1.5 mc of "White Merlot" **rosé.**

Further Reading

Atkins, Susy. *Merlot: A Complete Guide to the Grape and the Wines It Produces.* London: Mitchell Beazley, 2003.

MONASTERIES

Monasteries are important in the history of wine production and viticulture because so many European vineyards were owned by Christian **religious** orders during the Middle Ages. Later, from the 1500s, religious missions were responsible for the spread of vineyards and wine production throughout Latin America and **California.** Both trends reflected the importance of wine in the symbolism and ritual of Christian churches.

The importance of wine in Christianity was a carryover from its significance in Judaism. Just as the grapevine was the most commonly mentioned plant in the Old Testament and became representative of the Jews, so wine assumed great prominence in Christianity. Christ's first miracle was to turn water into wine, and wine represents Christ's blood in the Christian communion. Because wine was needed for sacramental purposes, the Catholic Church fostered viticulture as Christianity spread throughout Europe and around the world. Some Church Councils, such as the Council of Aachen (816), decreed that every cathedral should have a vineyard. Vineyards owned by the Church, whether by parishes, bishops, or religious houses, produced far more wine than was needed for the purposes of communion. This was even more the case from the twelfth century, when the communion ritual was changed such that the priest sipped wine on behalf of the congregation, rather than the communicants themselves taking wine.

Because wine was consumed as part of the daily diet throughout medieval Europe, monastic vineyards produced wines for the monks' own consumption (Benedictines were permitted half a pint a day), for travelers lodging in the monasteries, and for commercial sale. The Abbey of St-Germain-des-Prés, near Paris, owned 750 to 1,000 acres of vines in 814, and the monks disposed of 640,000 liters of wine (the equivalent of 71,000 nine-liter cases) each year, most on the open market.

The extent of monastic vineyards varied greatly from region to region in Europe, but they tended to expand over time. Land planted in vines was sometimes bequeathed to religious orders, and knights heading off to the Crusades often made gifts of vineyards. In both cases, there was an expectation that grants of land, especially when planted with grapevines, would improve the donor's chances of salvation. In 1157, one Cistercian monastery received four acres of vines from a widow and her children so that the monks would pray for the soul of her dead husband.

It is often argued that monasteries preserved Europe's vineyards from the ravages of peoples such as the Goths, Visigoths, and Franks that swept into western Europe after the fall of the Roman Empire. The migration of these peoples, commonly termed the "barbarian invasions," is often portrayed as the destructive rampage of beer-guzzling brutes who had no appreciation for wine. Yet the laws introduced by Europe's new rulers frequently established penalties for damaging vineyards, and wine was quickly adopted as part of their culture. It is likely that established patterns of trading wine were interrupted by the arrival of these new peoples, but there is little evidence that vineyards were affected negatively.

Even if they were not necessarily the saviors of Europe's vines, religious orders and newly established parishes planted vineyards as Christianity spread through Europe from the fifth to tenth centuries, and monks such as the famous Dom Pérignon became dedicated viticulturists and winemakers. Monasteries were responsible for important developments in **grape growing** and winemaking, although the precise extent of their contribution has yet to be assessed. In **Burgundy**, for example, Cistercian monks are thought to have developed the idea of *terroir*, the total environment in which grapes grow. Land holdings in Burgundy were (and remain) very small, and quite distinct wines seem to have been made from vineyards separated by only a few yards. Monks also experimented with such viticultural practices as soil preparation, trellising, and pruning and with winemaking methods that included fermentation and barrel-aging. The Cistercian order, which had hundreds of abbeys, spread viticultural knowledge throughout Europe, including the important Kloster Eberbach in the Rhine district.

Because monasteries possessed vineyards over the long term and monks were among the literate elite, they were able to produce records of grape cultivation and wine production. Moreover, the continuity of monasteries favored the conservation of these records. For these reasons, monastic records of vineyards are more likely than secular owners' records to have survived, which might exaggerate the importance of monastic vineyards. But there is little doubt that monasteries fostered a scientific approach in many areas of their economic activities, and wine production figured large among them.

With the Protestant Reformation in the sixteenth century, monasteries in some wine-producing parts of Europe—notably in **Germany** and **Switzerland**—were abolished, and monks were released from their vows. Many took up commercial winemaking, while others who had been responsible for **distilling** spirits contributed to the start of the modern spirits industry in Europe. Some Protestant denominations contributed marginally to the demand for wine by reverting to the communion practice abandoned by the Catholic Church in which the laity participated in both the wine and the bread. Beginning with the French

Revolution (1789–1799), however, Church-owned agricultural land was seized by the state and sold to secular owners.

Just as the Reformation began in Europe, **Spain** began to colonize Latin America, and the Jesuit missions that accompanied the Spanish armies extended vineyards and wine production from Mexico to **Chile** between 1520 and 1560. Many of Chile's best wine regions were first put in production by the missions, and the Jesuits remained significant wine producers until they were expelled from many countries in the 1760s. Their missions were taken over by the Franciscans, and this order extended viticulture and winemaking into California in the 1770s. By the 1820s, the California missions were making wine commercially, and so important was the religious connection that California's workhorse grape was known as the Mission variety. The mission lands were secularized in the 1830s.

Rod Phillips

Further Reading

Johnson, Hugh. *The Story of Wine*. London: Mitchell Beazley, 1989.
Phillips, Rod. *A Short History of Wine*. New York: HarperCollins, 2001.
Seward, Desmond. *Monks and Wine*. New York: Crown, 1979.

MONDAVI, ROBERT (1913–2008)

Robert Mondavi was one of the most important American winemakers of the twentieth century. Mondavi was instrumental in creating a global market for **California** wine. He began working under his father at the family's St. Helena, California, winery and later the Charles Krug Winery after the Mondavis bought it, but in 1966 he left and started his own eponymous winery in Oakville, California. He was a tireless promoter of the quality and potential of California wine, traveling around the country and all over the world to **promote** not only his own wine, but also the **Napa Valley** and California's ability to make world-class wines. Mondavi pushed modern techniques, such as **temperature control** and **barrel** aging, as well as **varietal labeling**. He also believed strongly that wine was meant as an accompaniment for food, and he worked with restaurateurs and chefs wherever he went to make the connection of California wine with food, often pouring his own wines blind alongside European ones.

Mondavi endeavored to make high-quality wines at a variety of price levels, from the lower-priced, large-scale "Woodbridge by Robert Mondavi" line made in the Central Valley to the reserve wines made at the iconic, mission-style Oakville estate to the nearby joint venture with Baron Philippe de Rothschild, Opus One Winery. He also had joint ventures in Chile and with the Frescobaldi family in Montalcino, **Italy**. As an expression of his love of wine-and-food pairing, Mondavi provided the impetus and much of the funding for Copia: The American Center for Wine, Food, and the Arts in Napa.

The Robert Mondavi Winery went public in 1993 and was sold to **Constellation Brands**, Inc., in 2004. It is now part of Constellation's Icon Estates group.

Further Reading

Mondavi, Robert. *Harvests of Joy: My Passion for Excellence*. New York: Harcourt Brace, 1998.

Siler, Julia Flynn. *The House of Mondavi: The Rise and Fall of an American Wine Dynasty*. New York: Gotham, 2007.

MUST AND WINE ADJUSTMENTS

All producers want to make wine appealing to their **consumers**, no matter how different those appeals may be. Thus when they encounter grapes falling in some way below the standards they value, they adjust the must (unfermented juice), the wine, or both. Practical experience and tradition have no doubt evolved these techniques constantly through history. The breakthrough event was **Louis Pasteur**'s study of wine that discovered the role of microbes in its production, evolution, and degradation.

Two rules seem universal in regulations and attitudes regarding adjusting musts and wines. The first, that *local conditions are accommodated,* has two complementary parts: adjustments unlikely to be needed are prohibited (for example, acid addition in northern Europe and sugar addition in **California**), while those frequently needed for balanced, healthy wines are permitted (for example, sugar addition in northern Europe and acid addition in California). The second rule is that *actual additions to wines or musts* (except for ingredients that react and drop out) *are limited to components naturally occurring in them.* For instance, the addition of an organic acid such as tartaric is permitted, but the inorganic acids, such as sulfuric, are prohibited. Extraneous flavorings change a wine into a wine-based beverage of another category (as in the ''special natural wines'' in the **United States**). The idea of balancing deficiencies—within limits—in order to make a pleasing or traditional wine is accepted virtually everywhere, though embodiments of that idea vary with place.

Must Adjustments.   Actions may be taken in the **winery** to alter the unfermented or fermenting grape must in service of various goals, including the following:

- *To balance sugar.* The concentration of sugars in the must determines eventual alcoholic strength. To achieve desired style, adding sugars (as grape concentrate or as pure sugar, called *chaptalization*) is practiced in cooler climates; diluting sugars, usually with water, is practiced in warmer climates. Since yeasts have practical limits in their ability to ferment sugars, dilution is also a means to preclude unwanted residual sugar in wine.
- *To balance acidity.* Organic acids, a major element in the flavor of any wine, may be outside desired levels. Additions of native acids (most often tartaric, sometimes malic) are common in warmer climates, while deacidulation (with a carbonate substance that reacts with acids and falls out of solution) is sometimes practiced in cooler climates. Where a pH shift is needed greater than that available from acid addition, must (or wine) may be passed through ion-exchange systems.
- *To select or promote growth of microorganisms.* Yeasts are responsible for most of the transformation from must to wine, and certain bacteria are also very important. The nearly universal practice of adding some form of sulfur dioxide (SO_2) is,

among other things, a tactic to select preferred yeasts (*Saccharomyces*) or bacteria (*Oenococcus*). The nutrients required for their reliable and complete fermentation are often insufficient in musts and may be supplemented. These nutrients usually include some form of nitrogen and key amino acids. Other nutrients may be added to aid the growth of malolactic bacteria, or, by contrast, highly specific bacteria-lysing enzymes may be added to prevent or delay bacterial fermentation. Winemakers may add cultured yeasts or bacteria (selected by region or characteristic) or rely on microorganisms indigenous to their vineyard and winery. These techniques help producers select but also stabilize wine character.

- *To guard against or promote oxidative, reductive, or enzymatic reactions.* Enzymatic reactions, caused by the metabolism of yeast, are responsible for much of wine's flavor and aroma, both pleasing and problematic. Oxidation-reduction reactions also play a key role in the chemistry and biology of fermenting must. SO_2 affects both types of reaction. Exclusion of air (in fermentation vessels or transfer tools) as well as intentional oxygenation are key winemaking techniques to select and control these reactions as must becomes wine. Specific enzymes may be added to extract chosen compounds in the must, notably aromatic substances, tannins, anthocyanins (color), or polysaccharides (complex nonfermentable sugars). The addition of supplemental tannins may be seen as a balancing tactic, but is also part of an oxidation/reduction scheme.

Other refinements may be used to select character as well. Treatment of grapes arriving from the vineyard requires important choices, including whether or not they are destemmed, crushed, or inspected to sort out undesirable parts. Musts may be chilled or heated. During fermentation, they may be pumped over the "cap" of skins, punched into it, or pumped in and out of tanks (*delestage*). Temperature of fermentation, duration of skin contact, and the size, shape, and material of fermentation vessels are all choices that affect wine character.

Wine Adjustments.   Once the must becomes wine, further adjustments may be desired. *Balancing the wine* is arguably a goal that encompasses all wine adjustments. Encouraging or blocking malolactic fermentation, acidifying or deacidifying, and sweetening are the most obvious choices to balance flavor elements. There are other objectives for wine adjustments as well:

- *To guard against further microbial processes.* Adding SO_2, filtering or centrifuging, or treating with specialized, short-lived reactive substances (such as dimethyl dicarbonate) may be employed to stop further, unwanted microbial action (such as malolactic or *Brettanomyces* fermentations). These processes may be employed during aging or at bottling. As with techniques encouraging microbial processes, these preventatives work toward the stability and purity of the finished wine.
- *To "develop" the wine.* Aging wine in tanks or barrels (or aging with oak alternatives), oxygenating it (with racking or micro-oxygenation), extending exposure to the lees (settled grape and yeast solids), and blending lots are all tools that may develop a wine toward a profile chosen by the producer. Most of these techniques advance oxidation-reduction, enzymatic, or polymerization processes.
- *To remove unwanted substances.* Despite all care, wines often contain substances that are not wanted at all, or at least not in the concentrations found after fermentation. These may be filtered or centrifuged out (solids, yeast or bacterial cells),

"fined" out by adding a substance that binds and deposits them (tannins, pigments, aromas, metals), or removed with more specialized techniques such as reverse osmosis (alcohol or volatile acidity).

• *To make the wine more presentable for marketing.* Fining and filtration may simply make a wine more broadly acceptable for sale. Making a wine stable under hot or cold conditions (proteins or tartrates) is another common example of market preparation. Infusing or sparging of dissolved carbon dioxide, adjustment of SO_2 levels, or almost any "balancing" tool may be seen as a finishing touch to increase market appeal.

See also Dealcoholized Wines; Fortified Wine; Sulfites; Temperature Control.

Michael Havens

Further Reading

Boulton, Roger B., Vernon L. Singleton, Linda F. Bisson, and Ralph E. Kunkee. *Principles and Practices of Winemaking.* New York: Chapman & Hall, 1995.

Kenneth, Bruce W., C. Fugelsang, Barry H. Gump, and Fred S. Nury, *Wine Analysis and Production.* 2nd ed. New York: Aspen, 1999.

Peynaud, Emile. *Knowing and Making Wine.* New York: Wiley, 1984.

N

NAPA VALLEY

The Napa Valley is the most well-known wine region in **California** and possibly the most prestigious outside of Europe. Napa's outstanding reputation today results from the vision and determination of a number of legendary pioneers, consistent marketing and **branding**, a steady influx of wealthy investors, and high-quality grapes resulting from near-perfect growing conditions. While the region accounts for only 8 percent of California's vineyard acreage and a mere 4 percent of the total wine produced, Napa is the source for some of the most expensive and sought-after wines in the U.S. market.

The region, located north of San Francisco above San Pablo Bay, is named after the Napa River. The Napa Valley itself is some 30 miles in length and ranges from 1 to 5 miles in width. However, the term is often used loosely to encompass most of Napa County, including the higher elevations of the Mayacamas Range to the west and the Vaca Range to the east.

Napa is a complex growing region with a diversity of soil types, aspects, altitudes, maritime influences, and climatic patterns. The climate in Napa is essentially Mediterranean, but becomes more strongly influenced by maritime effects farther south in the valley. Growing conditions vary considerably due to differences in sun exposure between the east and west sides of the valley, diurnal temperature differences between the hills and valley floors, and the cool air and fog intrusion from the bay that enters the valley from the south each morning. Napa produces riper, richer wines with relatively **high alcohol content** when compared to Old World regions, such as **Bordeaux** and **Burgundy**.

Grapes were first planted in the Napa Valley by George Yount around 1836. The first commercial **winery** was Charles Krug Winery, which opened for business in 1861. By the early 1900s, there were more than 140 wineries in the Napa Valley, but they faced a number of challenges. Years of difficult economic conditions posed by the Great Depression, the outbreak of **phylloxera**, and the onset of **Prohibition** nearly ended all hopes that the Napa Valley would become a prominent wine region. A handful of wineries turned to the production of sacramental wines, however, and were able to survive.

After the repeal of Prohibition, Napa slowly recovered and built the infrastructure of a premium growing region. Two individuals who played an important role in the emergence of Napa as a great wine region were André Tchelistcheff and **Robert Mondavi**. Tchelistcheff's influence stemmed from the winemaking skill and experience he brought and shared with fellow producers in the 1960s and 1970s while working at Beaulieu Vineyard. Mondavi's profound impact stemmed from his tireless efforts in promoting his own winery, the Napa Valley generally, and wine as a **healthy** part of daily life.

The Napa Valley produces a range of wine grapes, the most important of which is **Cabernet Sauvignon**, which accounts for more than a third of the roughly 50,000 acres planted. Because of Napa's reputation, its Cabernet prices in recent years have exceeded $4,000 per ton, more than four times the California state average. **Merlot** just edges out **Chardonnay** for the number-two spot, and together they represent around 30 percent of grape acreage in the region. The balance is mostly **Sauvignon Blanc**, **Pinot Noir**, Sangiovese, **Syrah**, and Cabernet Franc. While **Zinfandel** played an important role in the history of Napa, it continues to decline, representing less than 2 percent of the annual harvest. In 2005, Napa produced more than 180,000 tons of grapes valued at over $500 million. As is customary in the **New World**, most wines rely on **varietal labeling**.

Today there are more than 325 wineries in Napa, producing some 8.5 million cases of wine and generating an estimated $2 billion in retail sales. The larger wineries include Beringer Vineyards, Sterling Vineyards, and Robert Mondavi Winery. Some of the smaller labels, often described as **cult wines**, produce quantities as small as a few hundred cases. Many of these wines sell at extremely high prices, ranging from $100 to $500 per bottle or more. The demand and high pricing for some of these wines has been created by scarcity and **ratings** as much as by actual wine quality.

Within Napa County are 15 American viticultural areas (AVAs): 5 on the valley floor, including Oakville, Rutherford, Los Carneros (shared with **Sonoma County**), and Stags Leap; 9 in the mountains and hills to the east and west, notably Howell Mountain, Diamond Mountain, Mt. Veeder, and Spring Mountain; and the large Napa Valley AVA, which covers almost the entire county. Additional AVAs, such as Calistoga, Pope Valley, and Coombsville, can be expected in the future.

Several associations play a vital role in the **promotion** of the Napa Valley as a premium region and a recognized brand. The Napa Valley Vintners association (www.napavintners.com) was successful in its legal battle with the **Bronco Wine Company** in requiring wines with Napa place names to contain a minimum of 75 percent fruit from the county. The Napa Valley Grapegrowers association (www.napagrowers.org) has led the movement for environmentally and socially **sustainable** agriculture, while Copia: The American Center for Wine, Food, and the Arts (www.copia.org) has helped promote Napa and the relationships among wine, food, and culture.

The scenic beauty of Napa, the idyllic lifestyle, and the prospect of producing world-class wine has attracted some of the most successful and wealthy individuals in the world. This influx of capital has helped to realize the great potential of the Napa Valley's vineyards and wineries, but it has also caused vineyard prices to nearly triple during the past decade; vineyard land in Napa now sells for between $50,000 and $275,000 per acre.

In the coming years, Napa will continue to set the standard for high-quality wine made in the **United States**. The high cost of production, particularly for vineyard property in Napa, will ensure that producers are forced to produce high-end wines. Wines made from Cabernet Sauvignon, Merlot, and other Bordeaux varieties will continue to define this region's greatness, while varieties such as Sauvignon Blanc, Pinot Noir, and Syrah will play a minor role.

Jay Youmans

Further Reading

Sullivan, Charles L. *Napa Wine: A History from Mission Days to Present*. San Francisco: Wine Appreciation Guild, 1994.

Walker, Larry. *The Wines of the Napa Valley*. London: Mitchell Beazley, 2005.

NÉGOCIANTS

The French word *négociant* means "merchant." Within the context of the wine trade, however, a négociant is typically much more than that. In most cases, négociants are wine merchants who buy grapes, must, or wine and then bottle and sell the wine under their own label. Négociants have long played an important role in the wine trade in the Old World, especially in **France**, and they have been growing in importance in the **New World** as well.

Although found throughout France, historically **Bordeaux** and **Burgundy** are among the most famous regions where négociants have wielded great power and influence. Within Bordeaux, the traditional role of the négociant was to purchase wine from a château, age it, bottle it, and then sell it under the château's name. As such, they were frequently referred to as *négociant-éleveurs* due to the important part they played in the *élevage* (postfermentation development) of the wine. At one point, most of the wine produced in Bordeaux passed through the hands of a négociant prior to reaching the **consumer**. However, due to the demand for château-bottled wine and the financial problems that occurred as a result of high prices and inflation in the 1970s, the role of the Bordeaux négociant has drastically changed since the 1980s. Presently, there are about 400 négociants in Bordeaux. Many function primarily as marketers of wine, but some now also own their own châteaux, and others have turned from the classified growths to creating their own less-expensive **branded** wines, blending wines sourced from all over Bordeaux.

Similarly, most Burgundy wine was once controlled by négociants. However, in Burgundy, the négociant concentrated on buying wine from growers, blending it, and bottling it under the négociant's own label. With so many small vineyards and different **appellations**, it made sense for growers to sell their wines (or grapes) to a négociant, who could then combine the smaller lots into larger, more commercially viable bottlings. Growers often did not have the means necessary to make wine themselves—some lacking enough volume to make vinifying the grapes a logical choice, others without the equipment, and most without the access to customers outside the local market. But as in Bordeaux, with the expansion of the global marketplace, there has been a push for growers to bottle and sell their own wines. While the approximately 250 négociants are still an essential part of the Burgundian marketplace, their role has shifted slightly in response to this trend. Many of the most important négociants, such as the houses of Louis Latour, Louis Jadot, and Bouchard Père et Fils, now have substantial vineyard holdings and produce wines not just from purchased grapes and wines but also from grapes grown in their own vineyards.

The traditional négociant, especially in France, has long been a slightly controversial figure. Due to the amount of blending that frequently takes place with a négociant-made wine, allegations of fraudulent practices have plagued various négociants over the years. Part of the reason that négociants have declined in numbers and popularity over time is the belief that wine bottled at a **winery** is less likely to have been adulterated. This is particularly important in classic regions where the quality and purity of the appellation is considered an intrinsic part of the wine. Yet as brands with broad-based appellations have grown in popularity, the négociant's skill in blending wines with the goal of creating a consistent taste has been responsible for a renewal of the négociant trade's esteem.

Increasingly, a modernized concept of the Old World négociant has been applied to the wine trade outside of Europe. The oversupply of grapes, especially in **California** and **Australia**, a drop in grape prices partly due to inexpensive production in **Chile** and **Argentina**, and improvements in **bulk wine** shipping have led to a wave of new négociant wines on the market. Effectively using the bulk wine market in addition to contracts with grape growers and wineries, a number of enterprising négociants, such as Don Sebastiani & Sons, Three Thieves, and A to Z Wineworks, have developed very successful brands with modern, eye-catching labels aimed at value-conscious wine buyers.

Furthermore, it is not just inexpensive wines that are finding their way into these négociant labels. When examining the costs inherent in making a bottle of wine, many producers—even those in the premium wine sector—can find it more financially advantageous to sell their grapes or wine rather than bottle and label it themselves. This has led to the appearance of a number of négociant wines made from grapes grown in premium appellations, such as the **Napa Valley** or the Barossa Valley, yet priced much lower than would be expected. However, given the dependence of so many négociants on the global bulk wine market, the question looms: What will happen to these new brands if the grape market starts to constrict? While many New World négociant brands have been warmly embraced by consumers, these négociants, like their Old World counterparts, will need to learn to adapt to any supply fluctuations, while still maintaining their quality standards, if they are to generate long-term success.

Given the variability of wine production around the world, it is difficult to assess the exact value or volume of négociant-produced wine. However, one has only to look at the dominant players in the world's major markets to recognize the importance of this segment of the wine trade. Yet those négociants who wish to be successful in the competitive market in the future will be marked by the ability to evolve, stay flexible, and respond quickly to the ever-changing global marketplace. *See also* Custom Crush Facilities; Futures; Virtual Wineries.

Sheri Sauter Morano

Further Reading

Brook, Stephen, ed, *A Century of Wine*. London: Mitchell Beazley, 2000.
Jefford, Andrew. *The New France*. London: Mitchell Beazley, 2006.
Loftus, Simon. *Anatomy of the Wine Trade*. New York: Harper & Row, 1985.

NETHERLANDS. *See* Dutch Market

NEW WORLD VERSUS OLD WORLD

In the wine gazetteer, "Old World" refers to those regions of the Earth that have been growing grapes and making wine from them continuously for hundreds or thousands of years—long enough to have made some definitive conclusions through trial and error about which grape varieties and winemaking techniques work best in their local conditions and which specific vineyard sites and parcels produce the best wine. In practice, this means Europe, from **Portugal** to **Greece** and central **Germany** to Sicily. There are older Old World areas in **Eastern Europe** and **Asia**, but these are usually not included because they are infrequently seen on the international market and the Communist governments that controlled most of these countries for much of the twentieth century severely disrupted whatever viticultural traditions had been built there.

The "New World," by default, is everything else, including not only the New World of the Age of Discovery—that is, the Western Hemisphere and Oceania—but also parts of Africa and Asia that have a relatively short wine history, such as **South Africa** and China. In general, serious winemaking in the New World dates back at most about two centuries, and in many places only a matter of decades.

The biggest difference between the two "worlds" is that Old World viticulture for the most part developed where the wine was needed and not necessarily where the grapes grew best. Transportation was much slower and more difficult in the Europe of a thousand years ago, and therefore **grape growing** and winemaking focused on areas close to population centers or with access to shipping, such as rivers and seaports. Soils were often poor, weather in some parts of Europe was harsh, and the topography could be challenging, but it was not feasible to bring wine in quantity from the Mediterranean coast to the cities of northern Europe, so wine was made in marginal climates as far north as possible as well as in the sunny south.

Growers in the Old World learned to grow grapes under difficult conditions and found that vines that were under stress from a demanding **terroir** often made some of the best wines, provided the fruit could ripen sufficiently before the onset of winter. Old World wines—especially those from the north, but even those from southern Europe, which is still far from tropical—tended to be high in acidity, low to moderate in alcohol, and medium bodied. They were identifiably different from one another due the combined factors of varying soils, climates, yeasts, and different strains and mutations of grape varieties, as well as region-specific winemaking techniques and equipment.

When winemaking established itself in the New World during the Age of Discovery and the **colonial era**, things were not much different at first. Grapes were planted near the newly established colonies and cities, regardless of growing conditions. However, almost all failed due to an inhospitable climate (whether too cold or too hot) or the effects of disease and pests, notably **phylloxera**. If it had not been for the **religious** requirement for wine to consecrate the Catholic Mass, viticulture would probably have nearly disappeared from the New World until fairly recent times. But eventually missionaries and immigrants found areas in **California**, **Argentina**, **Chile**, and **Australia** where the conditions favored viticulture, and it was here that the majority of the New World vineyards as we know them today were established.

In the hospitable environments of these New World regions, the troubles of frost, humidity, and phylloxera were largely absent, and grape growing proved relatively easy and even lucrative for growers close to metropolitan areas such as San Francisco or Buenos Aires. If there was a problem at all, it was that the grapes grew too well, tending to dissipate their flavor and character in heavy fruit crops, although this problem has been found to be manageable with proper vineyard management and other control techniques. Because the climate of these new vineyard areas tended to be quite warm and sunny compared to the Old World, the grapes ripened to a greater degree than was usually possible in Europe, resulting in wines that were higher in alcohol (or sugar), lower in acidity, and fuller bodied. These wines were considered to be in the "New World style"—rich, round, and robust compared to the complex, crisp, and elegant Old World–style wines made from the same grape varieties.

Flying winemakers have had an effect on narrowing the gap between these two nominal styles of wine. **Globalization** and the **information technology** revolution have fostered the sharing of winemaking techniques between them. **Climate change**, too, has contributed to the blurring of the once strong line between these two styles. The result is that it is becoming more and more difficult to pinpoint to a wine's origin in blind tastings.

Due to familiarity, availability, and perhaps lifestyle, many people in the New World naturally developed a strong preference for the New World wines, while residents of the Old World generally preferred their traditional wines. In modern times, of course, transportation is not as big an issue as it once was, and wines can be bottled at the source and then shipped around the world, or conversely shipped long distances as **bulk wine** and then bottled at the destination. Thus, **consumers** everywhere now have access to wines of both styles, and preferences have become more personal and a bit less societal.

In the New World, European wines have always had a following, but Old World producers have only recently seen their traditional home markets eroded by New World wines, especially from countries with aggressive export strategies, such as Australia. As a result, European winemakers have begun to experiment with making some of their wines in a New World style, particularly in warmer regions such as **Spain** and the south of **France**, perhaps using the **varietal labeling** that is common in the New World. These wines must often be designated as **table wine**, though, because the **appellation** laws for **quality wine** usually do not allow the nontraditional style to carry any higher designation. At the same time, many New World producers try to emulate Old World–style classics, using rigorous vineyard management, making **must and wine adjustments** in the **winery**, or searching out cooler growing areas.

In the **United States**, the dichotomy between the two worlds is apparent in consumption patterns that show distinct West Coast and East Coast palates. Being close to the source of most U.S. wines, consumers on the West Coast tend to strongly favor New World wines. In the largest state market, California, 82 percent of consumption is domestic, and a lot of the rest is from other New World countries, especially Australia. On the East Coast, historical patterns are more favorable for Old World wines, with Europe only a little farther away than California. In **New York**, itself the second largest wine-producing state, imports make up 42 percent of sales, with strong representation by Old World countries. *See also* Branding; Cult Wines; Flying Winemakers; Globalization; Global Wine Industry; High Alcohol Content.

NEW YORK

New York is one of the leading U.S. states in almost all categories of wine production and consumption, and New York City is the top city for the wine trade in the **United States**.

Although **California** dominates U.S. wine production, New York is the second largest wine-producing state. Its 29.3 million gallons of wine fermented in 2006—the equivalent of 12.3 million nine-liter cases (mc)—accounted for 4.4 percent of the U.S. total. With the addition of out-of-state wine, New York actually bottled 15.2 mc of still and **sparkling wines**, 6.7 percent of U.S. bottlings, in 2006.

There are three main winegrowing regions in New York: Long Island, the Hudson River Valley, and the Finger Lakes. All of these areas are plagued by vine disease brought on by high summer humidity, as well as the potential for damaging frosts and freezes in the fall and winter, although Long Island is moderated by the surrounding water and is therefore perhaps a more suitable growing area—its biggest problem may be the high cost of land. There are also many vineyards along the shores of lakes Erie and Ontario, but few of these produce wine grapes. As of 2005, the state had 31,000 acres of vineyards, including those for table grapes, juice, raisins, and wine grapes; the lion's share of the vineyard land is planted with Concord. Of the total grape harvest, about a third—48,000 tons in 2006—goes to making wine. Vinifera grapes make up about 10 percent of this; the rest is hybrids and native American varieties. Long Island is best suited for red grape varieties, while the Finger Lakes region relies on **Riesling**, Gewürztraminer, and various cold-hardy hybrids.

New York had 271 **wineries** as of 2006, accounting for 1 out of every 20 wineries in the United States. Many of these are small wineries that depend on **wine tourism** as much as wine sales for their income; only about two dozen make more than 20,000 cases per year, and two make more than a million cases annually.

Constellation Brands, Inc., is based in northwestern New York, where it began as Canandaigua Wine Company. The New York wine industry is represented nationally and worldwide by the New York Wine & Grape Foundation, whose tag line is *Uncork New York!*

New York State is the third largest wine market in the United States, after California and Florida. The 2006 consumption of 22.7 mc gave the state an 8.0 percent market share nationwide, according to *Adams Wine Handbook 2007*. It is the number-one consumer of imported wine, however, taking in about 9.5 mc, roughly an eighth of the wine brought into the United States from other countries.

New York City is the second largest U.S. city market for wine, after Los Angeles, and the largest for imported wine. Total wine consumption in the city was 9.6 mc in 2006, more than most states. When its entire metropolitan area is considered, including northern New Jersey and western Connecticut, New York City is the largest market in the United States: 26.5 mc, or 9.4 percent of the U.S. total, according to Adams.

Apart from the sheer volume of wine production and consumption in New York, the state and especially New York City are important to the U.S. wine industry as a national hub for the trade. Manhattan or its nearby vicinity is the home to many wine **importers** and trade associations; major wine **retailers**; wine, travel, and lifestyle periodicals and book publishers; **wine writers** and critics; **auction houses** with wine departments; **wine educators**; marketing and **promotion** agencies; broadcast, food, and travel television networks; and corporate headquarters for companies that buy large quantities of wine. In addition, the city is one of the fine-dining meccas of the United States, so it is a prestigious venue for wineries looking for exposure on highly regarded **restaurants**' wine lists. This concentration of wine expertise and resources makes New York City the site of many trade and **consumer** wine tastings and events and places it on the itinerary of most winemakers—whether from the West Coast or another country—who are on tour promoting their wines.

Further Reading

Cornell University, College of Agriculture and Life Sciences, New York State Agricultural Experiment Station. www.nysaes.cornell.edu.

New York Wine & Grape Foundation. www.newyorkwines.org.

NEW ZEALAND

On the world stage, New Zealand is a tiny producer, with just 68,000 acres in production and a total annual output of around 15 million nine-liter cases—less than half of 1 percent of overall global production—yet the country's profile in the international wine trade is soaring. New Zealand is a market leader in the premium sector of its key export markets, commanding a higher average bottle price than its competitors.

History.   Although the first New Zealand vineyard was planted in 1819, serious commercial production really began only near the end of the nineteenth century with the establishment of several high-profile wine estates. Early industry pioneers, many from what is now Croatia, established vineyards in West Auckland, within close proximity to the country's largest city. The temperance movement developed momentum and only narrowly missed enacting **Prohibition** in 1919, and this hampered the development of the wine industry for many years.

In 1973, Frank Yukich, then head of the country's largest wine producer, Montana Wines, took the bold step of purchasing 4,000 acres for a wine estate in Marlborough on the South Island. Montana's first commercial release of Marlborough **Sauvignon Blanc**, in 1980, was to prove a watershed for the New Zealand industry. The area's clear, cool nights and sunny, warm days resulted in a juicy yet pungent style of Sauvignon Blanc that met with wide appeal. In 1985, **Australian** winemaker David Hohnen at Cloudy Bay produced the first vintage of its iconic Sauvignon Blanc, and Cloudy Bay, along with other boutique labels from Marlborough, developed a huge following in the **British market** in the late 1980s and early 1990s.

The industry received another boost with the appointment of Australia's Dr. Richard Smart as the country's national viticultural scientist in 1982. Smart promoted better canopy management, principally through matching training systems to the site, as a means of producing riper fruit at commercial crop levels. For a short period in the mid-1980s, there was a serious oversupply of grapes, and the government sponsored a vine pull scheme. Fortunately, most of the vines removed were either in less favorable regions or were from higher-yielding but lower-quality varieties such as Müller-Thurgau.

Following Smart's departure in 1990 and the disbandment of the government viticultural center, primary research languished for several years. In 2004, the New Zealand government announced funding for a major six-year study into Sauvignon Blanc, bringing together wine companies, government researchers, and academics.

Industry. The New Zealand wine industry is characterized by a large number of small wineries and a handful of genuinely large-scale ventures. There are currently 576 registered wineries, but of these only nine produce more than two million liters (225,000 cases) of wine per annum. Nearly 90 percent of all wineries produce less than 200,000 liters (22,500 cases). The two largest companies, Pernod Ricard New Zealand and **Constellation** New Zealand, are both foreign owned. While only a couple of firms are listed on the local stock exchange (Delegat's and the New Zealand Wine Company), there are several other public companies, including a number of specialist vineyard management companies (for example, Oyster Bay Vineyards, Terra Vitae, and Seddon Vineyards).

Marlborough is by far the dominant wine region, both in producing area (54 percent of the national vineyard) and tonnage harvested (59 percent of the 2007 national vintage). The next biggest regions are Hawkes Bay and Gisborne.

Sauvignon Blanc is the most important variety, representing 41 percent of the planted area, but in tonnage terms more than 50 percent of the overall harvest in 2007. The next largest crops were **Chardonnay** (19 percent) and **Pinot Noir** (10 percent), both of which are important in **sparkling wine** production. Currently New Zealand is best known for its punchy, vibrant Sauvignon Blancs, although alternative styles of Sauvignon Blanc are emerging, employing natural yeast fermentations, barrel fermentation, lees aging, and malolactic fermentation.

The climate and soils suit high-quality Pinot Noir and Chardonnay production with the potential to compete with the best wines from **Burgundy**, although New Zealand Chardonnay has yet to establish its identity. Plantings of **Riesling**, **Merlot**, and **Cabernet Sauvignon** have remained static, even though the country produces fine examples of each. The current fad for **Pinot Gris** appears to be tailing off. Instead, other varieties are being experimented with, such as Viognier, Arneis, and even Albariño.

Nearly 60 percent of the country's production (8.5 million cases) is now exported, with that proportion set to increase even further as the world clamors for New Zealand's characterful, cool-climate wines. Export sales are accelerating, increasing 19 percent per annum over the past decade and 26 percent annually over the last five years. In 2002, the industry set an ambitious target of NZ $1 billion in export sales by 2010; having already reached NZ$767 million, that goal was revised upward to NZ$2 billion by 2015.

The largest single market, with nearly a third of that total, is the United Kingdom. Adding Australia and the **United States**, the top three export destinations account for around 85 percent of offshore sales. A wine has to pass a certification process to be eligible for export. Under recent legislation, exporting wineries must also adopt a Wine Standards Management Plan, which requires good record keeping and audit trails.

In 2001, New Zealand took a lead in the **closures** debate when a group of winemakers formed the New Zealand Screwcap Wine Seal Initiative to investigate changing over to screw caps. While there remain a small number of producers devoted to corks, more than 90 percent of New Zealand wine is now bottled under screw cap.

The New Zealand industry has set itself the goal of achieving 100 percent **sustainable** production by 2012. Currently 65 percent of the national vineyard area and 70 percent of overall wine production is processed under the Sustainable Winegrowing New Zealand scheme.

Environmental issues are critical to the country's wine industry, and with New Zealand's single largest wine market directly on the opposite side of the globe, producers have been forced to take carbon dioxide emissions and the concept of "food miles" seriously. Thus far, industry leaders have been reluctant to embrace the idea of **bulk** shipping for premium labels, and it looks as if glass bottles will remain in use for some time. However companies are working to reduce or at least measure their carbon footprints, with the New Zealand Wine Company becoming the first winery in the world to be certified as fully carbon neutral.

New Zealand Winegrowers (www.nzwine.com) is the main industry body, formed in 2002 by the merger of separate vineyard owners' and wineries' groups. Funding is by way of mandatory levies on grapes harvested and finished wine.

Challenges.   Availability of water for irrigation (and increasingly frost control) is a major limiting factor in the expansion of the New Zealand wine industry, especially in such drought-sensitive regions as Marlborough and Hawkes Bay. Labor is another huge concern. The industry has developed in sparsely populated rural regions, and creative solutions to the problem have had to be developed. Labor regulations have been tightened after several high-profile cases involving poor living conditions for workers.

New Zealand wine producers are also worried that the **exchange rate** will impact their **profitability**. The New Zealand dollar was first floated in 1985 and was at its lowest between 1986 and 2000, when export markets were first opening up. In early 2008, the dollar hit a postfloat high, and there are concerns that the industry growth is not sustainable at these levels.

Paul Tudor

Further Reading

Cooper, Michael. *Wines Atlas of New Zealand*. Auckland: Hodder Moa Beckett, 2002.

New Zealand Winegrowers Statistical Annual and *New Zealand Winegrowers Annual Report*. Auckland: New Zealand Winegrowers, annual.

NONALCOHOLIC WINES.   *See* Dealcoholized Wines

NURSERIES

As many as 99 percent of all new plantings in **California**, **Australia**, **New Zealand**, and Europe today are effected through the purchase of professionally grown nursery stock. This is driven by wineries' demand for specific grape varieties to meet their wine marketing needs.

In order to produce a certain variety, a rootstock suited to the vineyard site is chosen, taking into consideration the soil's potential vigor, water-holding capacity, and disease pressure (from fungi, nematodes, or insects such as **phylloxera**). Then the preferred varietal clone is grafted onto the rootstock as scion wood. This grafting can be done in the nursery or in the field.

Planting a vineyard is like any financial investment: the primary goal is to maximize return on investment. The professionally trained nursery operator will recommend the best rootstock–clone match for the climate, soil, pest and disease resistance, productive capacity, growth habit, and desired fruit characteristics.

One of the principal ways the nursery operator helps growers and vintners maximize their investment is by selling them clean and uniform plant material. Uniformity is of major importance to growers because it ensures lower cost of establishment, early first harvest, and uniformity of ripening, which is one of the fundamental quality parameters in the eyes of the winery.

There are some areas, such as **Washington** and **Chile**, where relative isolation, extreme weather, or lack of pests has allowed vineyards to be planted "own-rooted." In this case, growers will often propagate their own scion material without employing rootstock. However, the original source for the vines may still be a nursery.

Nurseries are often associated with local, state, or national quarantine programs to certify that the introduction and exchange of plant material is free of known pathogens (viruses, insects, and fungi). Some certification programs also serve to verify clonal origin of scions and rootstocks.

Grapevine prices have always been higher in the **United States** than abroad, although they have been static since the late 1980s as the value of the dollar has eroded. This means that entry of new nurseries into the U.S. market is unlikely. Interestingly, there has been little **consolidation** in the business. There remain three large nurseries in California, with a handful of small ones. The big three have been able to survive the highs and lows of the inelastic grower market by diversifying into other commodities, such as stone fruits and berries. European nurseries have also made inroads into the U.S. market. These nurseries opened up the Latin American market a few decades ago, but were unable to penetrate the lucrative U.S. market due to phytosanitary restrictions on importation of plant material. Now that this material is finally here, partnerships/agreements have been formed with U.S. nurseries for plant propagation.

The grapevine nursery business is a challenging one. It is cyclical in nature, and predicting appropriate production levels of the varieties required by the **grape-growing** industry is an inexact science. The popularity of a certain wine type is driven by **consumer** demand—trends that are difficult to forecast and frustrating to match when it takes five years to get the vineyard into full production.

An active debate within the nursery community surrounds the utilization of genetically modified organism (GMO) technology. While such plants could offer enhanced disease and pest resistance, their use is controversial. At present, they are in the experimental stage only and not yet commercially available.

Mark Chandler

O

OREGON

When wine people think of Oregon, they think of **Pinot Noir**—the grape has driven the state's wine reputation. Yet thanks to an industry-wide emphasis on quality, **sustainability**, innovation, and marketing, Oregon is increasingly recognized as a producer of many diverse wine styles and grape varieties.

By numbers, Oregon is one of the most important wine states of the **United States**, with the third largest number of **wineries** (over 350) and the fourth largest production volume (almost 1.75 million cases in 2006). Pinot Noir is the leading variety, with approximately 9,000 planted acres out of the state's total of 14,000, followed by **Pinot Gris**, **Chardonnay**, **Riesling**, and **Merlot**.

Oregon's geography naturally divides into cool-climate and warm-climate growing regions, giving the state unusual diversity in the kinds of grapes it can successfully grow. **Burgundian** and Alsatian varieties are most popular in the cooler-climate zones in the northwest of the state, while **Bordeaux** and Rhône varieties thrive in the warmer districts. A total of 16 American viticultural areas (AVAs) subdivide the state's winegrowing regions.

The Willamette Valley AVA, created in 1984, is the best-known and most economically important Oregon **appellation**. It encompasses the majority of the cool-climate **grape-growing** areas and is home to most of the state's Pinot Noir, Pinot Gris, Chardonnay, and Riesling production. This large appellation recently has been divided into six subappellations, each establishing a reputation for its own **terroir** based on important mesoclimate variations.

The Southern Oregon AVA, created in 2004, defines Oregon's largest warm-climate region and comprises four smaller appellations. Additional warm regions are located in the Columbia Gorge and eastern Oregon. Oregon shares with **Washington** portions of the Columbia Valley, Walla Walla Valley, and Columbia Gorge AVAs, and with Idaho a part of the Snake River Valley AVA.

The first modern vinifera vines in Oregon were planted in what is now the Umpqua Valley AVA by Richard Sommer in 1961. In 1965, David Lett moved to the Willamette Valley and planted that region's first Pinot Noir vines (after being told it was too cold and wet for them in Oregon), producing his first Pinot Noir wine in 1970.

Oregon's reputation got its first international boost when Lett's 1975 South Block Reserve from his Eyrie Vineyards placed second at a blind tasting in France. Skeptical Burgundian scion Robert Drouhin held a second tasting, with similar results. Intrigued, he established Domaine Drouhin Oregon in 1987, cementing the state's international reputation as a home for Pinot Noir.

The focus on quality Pinot Noir has been the key to Oregon's wine industry growth and the main determinant of the industry's economics. Successive waves of winemakers have come to the Willamette Valley and built a collective emphasis on low yields to improve wine quality, **organic** winegrowing to increase farmland sustainability, and careful site-matching to maximize fruit and wine character. These are all practices resistant to economies of scale.

Unlike neighboring Washington and **California**, there are no truly large wineries in Oregon. The biggest producers make less than 130,000 cases annually, and the industry average is probably close to 3,500 cases. Nearly all the state's wineries are family owned and operated, and many are now in their second generation of winemaking.

The fragmented nature of the industry, coupled with low yields, organic farming, hand production (there is very little **mechanized** farming in the state's wine industry), and hillside vineyards, has meant high labor and production costs and therefore high wine prices. Oregon Pinot Noirs are essentially boutique wines with limited availability, loyal customers, and prices that range from $35 to $75 a bottle.

However, some new business models are beginning to establish a lower entry price for good Oregon Pinot of around $20. A to Z Wineworks, for instance, was founded in 2002 on a **négociant** model, purchasing finished wines and blending them into its own **brand**. Because it has no investments in vineyards and does not do the winemaking, A to Z has been able to produce good-quality, lower-priced wines in quantity and has quickly grown to become Oregon's first or second largest producer.

Other wineries are planting larger vineyards, altering yields, and applying various technology and process economies to produce higher-volume Oregon Pinot Noir at lower prices. While the overall emphasis on small-production wines has not diminished, these new price-oriented efforts will likely gain momentum.

Renewed expansion in the state's warmer climate zones is also increasing the market viability of Oregon wine. In 1997, Earl Jones planted Tempranillo in the Umpqua Valley, and it has become one of the state's fastest-increasing varieties. **Syrah** has also proven to be a high-quality grape in all of the warm-climate appellations, and the market acceptance of Bordeaux-style blends is giving wineries new product and proprietary brand options.

Oregon's wine industry is heavily self-taxed in order to support the efforts of the Oregon Wine Board. This agency applies funds toward **promotion** programs to build demand and facilitate **distribution** of Oregon wine for all major markets, including Europe and **Asia**. A gauge of its success is the fact that Oregon's wine industry has a $1.5 billion economic impact and is vibrantly healthy and rapidly growing.

Cole Danehower

Further Reading
Oregon Wine Advisory Board. www.oregonwine.org.

ORGANIC GRAPES AND WINE

At its most basic, organic viticulture and winemaking involves growing grapes and producing wine according to the philosophy of using natural ingredients and methods in order to do the least possible harm to (and perhaps even provide benefit to) people and the environment. However, the specifics of what constitutes an organic product vary widely depending on who is doing the defining. Many **consumers** simply want a more **healthful** and environmentally friendly wine, but they are not in a position to verify whether a wine meets this nebulous goal. Therefore, various governments, advocacy groups, producer organizations, and trade associations have stepped in to certify which wines are worthy of being called organic—but with differing opinions on what ingredients, additives, techniques, and processes are acceptable in an organic wine.

Gaining certification can be an expensive and arduous process for a producer and may not have any validity in a different jurisdiction or market. Consequently, there are wines that are organic in one country but not in another, wines that are made with certified organic grapes but are not themselves organic, and wines that have been made by organic methods but have never been submitted for official certification as such.

Modern agricultural practices are highly efficient and have allowed production to increase in quantity, improve in quality, and spread to areas that have not traditionally been able to support agriculture. However, over time, some of the techniques and materials used can be detrimental to the environment and people's health. The organic movement strives to take a step back from the headlong rush toward progress, keeping many of the agricultural improvements but avoiding those that are harmful, while revisiting traditional techniques that have lost favor yet may be more viable over the long term.

One of the primary aims of the organic movement is to reject (or minimize as much as possible) the use of industrial chemicals and raw materials. These items are not part of the natural world—at least not in their synthesized form or concentration—and thus they upset the balance of nature. In the vineyard, that means fertilizers and pesticides, which cannot be confined to the vines and their attackers and end up contaminating nearby waters or killing off beneficial insects. In the **winery**, the focus is more on avoiding additives or techniques that could be unsafe for wine consumers. The alternatives to more common practices are more costly in terms of labor and/or expenditures, at least in the initial implementation, but provide benefits that make them worthwhile.

Often mentioned side-by-side in discussions of organic production are **biodynamic** and **sustainable** farming. Collectively these practices represent the ''green'' movement, and all have aspects applicable to grape growing and winemaking.

Organic Grape Growing.   Growing grapes of sufficient quality for winemaking requires some human intervention to ensure a disease- and pest-free, even-ripening, flavor-filled crop. Organic **grape growing** permits almost all the tricks of the viticultural trade—grafting, trellising, green harvesting, leaf pulling, drip irrigation, and so on—*except* the use of nonorganic (synthetic or artificial) fertilizers, pesticides, herbicides, fungicides, and similar chemicals. Such products have detrimental effects on the environment outside the vineyard and may also remain as residue in or on the grapes themselves and eventually find their way into the consumer's mouth. Therefore, organic grape growing requires growers to find other, less dangerous means of promoting plant growth and minimizing damage from pests and disease. The organic movement also generally forbids the use of genetically modified organisms (GMOs), insisting on vine improvement the old-fashioned way through the propagation of cuttings from selected vines (cloning).

Official certification as an organic vineyard typically requires a minimum of three consecutive years of organic practices. During this period, the grapes cannot be marketed as organic (or sold at higher organic prices), yet there is likely to be additional work involved and some crop loss due to the inability to use fertilizer and pesticides before the organic alternatives can take effect. This causes a financial barrier that dissuades many grape growers from going organic.

Organic Winemaking. If the only requirement for making organic wine was using organically grown grapes, there would be a lot more organic wine on the market. However, getting a wine certified as organic goes beyond viticulture to encompass the winemaking process as well, and many common winemaking techniques and materials are not approved for organic use. Understandably, organic grapes are a necessary starting point, but the techniques used in the winery must also be restricted to those that are not harmful to the environment (or to consumers), not overly manipulative, and generally "natural." One of the common enological techniques that is considered inappropriate for organic wine is the addition of **sulfites** as a preservative. Other prohibited ingredients include cultured yeasts and several fining agents, such as bentonite.

Official Standards. In the **United States**, the National Organic Foods Act was enacted in 1990. It gave the U.S. Department of Agriculture (USDA) the responsibility for setting standards for organic foods, including wine. The USDA created the National Organic Program (NOP), which maintains an official list of synthetic substances that are permissible in organic products and nonsynthetic (natural) substances that cannot be used. The USDA does not certify organic status itself, but rather accredits individual governmental and nongovernmental organizations to do the certifications. There are currently 55 certifying agencies in the United States, including many state agriculture departments and several private companies, and 40 abroad in 19 countries.

The NOP established four categories of more or less organic wines:

1. "100% Organic": as it says, everything used in production is organic.
2. "Organic": the wine contains no more than 5 percent nonorganic ingredients (and nothing forbidden for use in organic products).
3. "Made with Organic Grapes": the wine contains 70 to 95 percent organically grown grapes (and nothing forbidden).
4. Wines with less than 70 percent organic grapes may state the percentage of organic grapes, but cannot make any statement that the wine is organic.

For 100% organic and organic wines, the label must contain an ingredient list and a statement of which officially designated body certified the wine as organic; these wines may display the USDA Organic Seal.

Non-U.S. organic certification is not recognized in the United States, unless the certification is from one of the 40 USDA-accredited organizations. Without going through the process of U.S. certification, an imported wine cannot be labeled or marketed as organic regardless of its status in the country of production.

In addition to the USDA organizations, states such as **California** and **Oregon** have local bodies whose mission is to track and record statistics for all levels of responsible farming, as well as to support programs, disseminate information, and conduct education in the state.

In the **European Union** (EU), the standards for organic grapes and wine are generally comparable to those of the NOP, with only minor differences. Labeling practices are similar, although the EU allows wines to declare that they are in transition to organic status during the changeover period prior to certification, whereas the U.S. rules allow no such statement.

Outlook.   The larger and more globalized the wine world has become, the more the countervailing organic movement—one based on staying local—has grown. The number of organic vineyards and wines available worldwide represents a small portion of total production, but is on the rise. Sales of organic wines have risen sharply in recent years, doubling every few years—albeit from a small base. Sales of organic-grape wines reached $80 million in 2005, according to the Organic Trade Association. The European Union has most of the world's certified organic vineyards. They are most prevalent in the largest wine-producing countries, **Italy**, **Spain**, and **France**, which have a combined total near 215,000 acres, with Italy representing over half of that. Various EU countries still provide subsidies to those who convert to organic methods, and this is what has driven Italy's farmers to participate so wholeheartedly. **Germany**, the United States, **Argentina**, and **Chile** represent the next tier, with about 25,000 acres total.

From a short-term, strictly business standpoint, going organic may not make much sense, but from a longer-term or purely ethical view, it makes all the sense in the world. And with more and more people today getting interested in living a lifestyle that is healthier for both themselves and the planet, organic production is becoming a more rational business option even in the short term.

The costs of going organic and biodynamic are hard to pin down. Certification fees depend on the state of the farm before conversion, the size of the farm being converted, and the volume in sales of the entity involved—with costs being calculated on a sliding scale. Annual reinspection and certification fees apply and can range from a few thousand dollars up.

There are two main reasons for producing an organic (or made-from-organic-grapes) wine: a true belief in the merits of organic agriculture or a desire to capture part of the growing market for organic products (although the two motivations are not mutually exclusive). Among the true believers, the important thing is the philosophy, and certification is not necessary because the goal is being organic, not being *seen to be* organic. Marketers going after the organic customer may be less concerned with the philosophy than the label, and for them, certification of at least the grapes is essential. Regardless of the motivation, however, whether consumer or producer driven, the end result is beneficial for the environment and wine consumers. An important next step will be getting more wine-producing countries and regions to join together to offer organic certifications that consumers can trust and better understand.

Further Reading

Organic Consumers Association. www.organicconsumers.org.
Organic Trade Association. www.ota.com.
Organic Wine Journal. www.organicwinejournal.com.
USDA. www.ams.usda.gov.
Waldin, Monty. *The Organic Wine Guide*. London: Thorsons, 2000.

P

PARKER, ROBERT (1947–)

Robert Parker is the world's most influential wine critic. In 1978, Parker, then a practicing lawyer, launched his newsletter the *Wine Advocate* with the mission of providing unbiased reviews of wines to his readers. The publication took no advertising, allowing Parker complete freedom to write his candid opinions without fear of losing backers. As a simple way of summarizing his estimation of the wine's quality, he used a **rating** scale with a maximum value of 100 points. His opinions came to be valued by high-end **consumers** who had similar tastes in wine, and sales of wines Parker liked jumped, with a score of 90 or above usually translating into the wine quickly being sold out or markedly rising in price, or both.

The circulation of the *Wine Advocate* has continued to grow and is now reportedly in excess of 50,000. Its influence is far greater than that, however, as his reviews and scores are disseminated widely by suppliers, **importers**, **distributors**, **retailers**, and even **restaurants** that trumpet the wines they sell that have received praise from Parker. This has generated substantial controversy in the wine industry, as many consumers have skewed their purchases toward the high-scoring wines either under the assumption that they *should* like the wine or simply for the status symbol of owning and/or drinking ''Parker 90+'' wines. However, Parker's ratings are based on his own likes and dislikes—he has never claimed his scores represent everyone's objective ideal of wine quality—and Parker likes bold, fruit-driven, blockbuster wines. The weight given to his opinions has caused many winemakers to change their techniques to produce a wine that fits Parker's profile of a high-scoring wine, leading to the trends toward riper fruit, **higher alcohol content**, and earlier drinkability and away from more traditional Old World wine styles with moderate alcohol, higher acidity, and complexity gained by long aging.

Parker has authored several books, including multiple editions of his *Wine Buyer's Guide,* the seventh in 2008, and writes for various wine magazines. The *Wine Advocate* has expanded into the Web site erobertparker.com. Parker now limits himself primarily to reviewing wines from **France**, including his beloved

Bordeaux, and **California**, leaving the rest of the *Wine Advocate*'s critiques to collaborators.

Further Reading

McCoy, Elin. *The Emperor of Wine: The Rise of Robert M. Parker Jr. and the Reign of American Taste*. New York: Harper Perennial, 2005.

PASTEUR, LOUIS (1822–1895)

Louis Pasteur was the French scientist who turned winemaking from an art into at least partially a science and thereby laid the groundwork for making wine production into a business. Pasteur was a professor of chemistry at the University of Lille in 1856 when he began a study of the fermentation of wine and beer, a process that was well known but completely mysterious at the time. In the course of his research over the next decade, he showed that yeast was the cause rather than a by-product of fermentation and that bacteria were responsible for wine spoilage. He furthermore demonstrated that a process of rapid heating and cooling would kill the bacteria and prevent microbial spoilage—a process that became known as *pasteurization*. Pasteurization remains the most effective means for wine stabilization, and although the heating has some detrimental effects on the flavor and aroma, it is used on many high-volume wines. *Flash pasteurization*, using a very high but very brief heating of the wine, is a relatively recent development that has less noticeable ill effects on the wine and may become more widely adopted.

Pasteur published *Studies on Wine* in 1866. His later great achievements were in the field of bacteriology, including the development of an anthrax vaccine for sheep and the rabies vaccine for humans.

PERSONNEL

The employees who work in a wine business comprise the intellectual capital—the head, heart, and spirit—of the enterprise. In the wine industry, there are many different job positions that require various levels of education, experience, and skills. Beginning in the vineyard and moving through the wine value chain toward the end **consumer**, the following is a list of the key positions and major requirements.

Production.   The *vineyard manager* oversees all **grape growing** work within a vineyard or series of vineyards, including pruning, harvest, and vineyard maintenance operations. The position usually requires a B.S. in viticulture or a related field and/or prior experience working as a vineyard manager. Annual salaries range from $50,000 to $86,000. Reporting to the manager are full-time, part-time, or seasonal *vineyard workers,* possibly including *harvest interns* from universities or the public at large. Some vineyard operations may include *vineyard supervisors,* and larger operations may have a *vice president of vineyard operations/relations.*

The *winemaker* manages the wine production process within a **winery**, including working in partnership with the vineyard manager to determine the optimal time to harvest grapes, continuing through crush, fermentation, aging, bottling, and assisting in selling the wine. The position typically requires a B.S. in enology, fermentation sciences, or a related field and/or prior experience—commonly beginning as a *cellar intern,* then moving to *assistant winemaker* before becoming head winemaker. Large wineries will have multiple winemakers reporting to a *vice president of wine production.* Winemaker salaries range from $70,000 to $110,000. Some wineries may hire a *consulting winemaker,* who generally has years of winemaking experience and a track record for crafting award-winning wines.

Other positions within wine production include the *cellar master,* who works in partnership with the winemaker to manage cellar operations; *cellar workers,* who perform all of the manual work within the winery, such as punch downs, additions, racking, bottling, and many other operations; the *enologist,* who performs the chemical analysis on wines; *lab assistants,* who help the winemaker and/or enologist with wine analyses; and *cellar interns,* who are usually college students training to be winemakers.

Winery Administration.   The *chief executive officer* (CEO) or *general manager* (GM) of a winery is the top executive in charge of all operations, including production, marketing, sales, and accounting, and serves as the **brand** champion and spokesperson for the winery. This is more often than not the highest-paid position within the winery, with salaries averaging $140,000 to $350,000. Most such positions require a minimum of an MBA degree and extensive wine industry experience. Depending on the size of the winery, there may be a variety of people reporting to the CEO/GM. Frequently there is a *controller* or *chief financial officer* who is in charge of finance, accounting, and creating cost efficiencies in the winery. This person usually is required to have a B.A. or MBA in accounting or a related field and prior experience and is paid $85,000 to $115,000. Larger wineries will also have a *human resources director* to oversee the human resources (HR) or personnel function. Requirements generally include a B.A. in HR or a related field and/or HR certification plus experience, and salaries range from $85,000 to $110,000. Other administrative positions may include *director of information technology*, *facilities director, research and development,* and the support staff for all of the administrative functions.

The *vice president of winery marketing and sales* manages all **promotion** activities for the winery, including **distributor** and **retailer** relationships, as well as direct-to-consumer sales. Larger wineries will have separate vice presidents for marketing and sales, along with multiple departments, such as International Marketing/Sales. Requirements include a B.A. or MBA in marketing or a related field in addition to prior work experience (average salaries are $120,000 to $192,000). Reporting to the vice presidents may be *national account managers* ($65,000 to $105,000) and *sales* or *marketing reps* ($43,000 to $75,000). In addition, the *direct marketing/wine club* manager ($49,000 to $60,000), *tasting room manager* ($49,000 to $52,000), and *tasting room staff* ($24,000 to $32,000) generally report to the marketing/sales department. Finally the *vice president* or *director of public relations* ($50,000 to $85,000) and the *special events coordinator* ($40,000 to $43,000) may report to or partner closely with the marketing and sales team. All of these other functions normally require a college degree, with the exception of tasting room staff, who are often part-time workers paid an hourly wage.

Distribution.   A variety of personnel are involved in purchasing wine from wineries and selling, delivering, and servicing wine to retailers, including handling tax and documentation issues. Entry-level jobs as *distributor reps* may require a B.A. in sales or a related field and/or prior sales experience and wine knowledge. Salaries start low, with base pay of $29,000 to $40,000, but are usually supplemented by commissions. Seasoned reps and *regional managers* can earn $100,000 per year or more, with advanced positions as *director, special account rep,* or *vice president* earning much more. Positions as *importer, exporter, négociant,* or *broker* require extensive wine knowledge and good contacts.

Retail.   On-premise wine sales positions in **restaurants**, wine bars, and bars involve purchasing, merchandising, promoting, selling, and tracking wine sales in a restaurant or **hospitality industry** setting. A top position as *sommelier* at a high-end restaurant generally requires excellent wine knowledge, prior experience, and passing at least the Advanced Sommelier exam from one of the certifying organizations. Salaries range from $40,000 to $155,000. Other positions include *director of wine, wine buyer, wine sales rep,* and *bartender.*

In off-premise retail shops, wine sales entails purchasing, merchandising, promoting, selling, and tracking wine sales in a retail setting, whether a grocery store, **supermarket**, wine shop, or other retail outlet, such as Costco or Target. The major positions are *vice president of wine sales, wine director* or *manager, wine buyer, wine merchandiser,* and *wine sales rep.* Job requirements and salaries vary widely.

Wine Education.   *Wine writers* write articles, reviews, or books about wine. They often have at least a B.A. degree, along with extensive wine knowledge and excellent writing/teaching skills. Part-time wine writers can average $150 to $500 per article, whereas full-time writers for major wine journals are paid a regular salary. *Wine educators* generally teach in community colleges, universities, wine shops, restaurants, wineries, and private institutions and their income varies broadly.

Obtaining a Job in the Wine Industry.   In general, the most important requirements to obtain a job in the wine industry are wine experience and a passion for wine. The passion can be developed on one's own, but experience usually means starting from the bottom by obtaining a full- or part-time job in a wine shop or selling wine in a winery tasting room. This allows the individual to learn the business and to start networking with others in the industry. Another option is to return to school to obtain a wine degree or certificate. There are bachelor's and master's degrees in viticulture, enology, and wine business. There are also certifications in wine, as well as more rigorous private programs such as the Master of Wine and Master Sommelier.

Liz Thach

Further Reading

Cascio, Wayne F. *Managing Human Resources.* 7th ed. Boston: McGraw-Hill/Irwin, 2006.

Thach, Liz, and Lillian Bynum. ''Human Resources in the Wine Industry,'' in *Wine: A Global Business.* ed. Liz Thach and Tim Matz. Elmsford, NY: Miranda Press, 2004.

Thach, Liz, and Brian D'emilio. *How to Launch Your Wine Career*. San Francisco: Wine Appreciation Guild, 2008.

Tinney, Mary-Colleen. "2007 Salary Survey Report," *Wine Business Monthly,* October 15, 2007.

PHYLLOXERA

The phylloxera epidemic, which killed most of the vines in many of the world's most important wine-producing regions at the end of the nineteenth century, was a turning point in the history of wine and the wine industry. It led to a reorganization of vineyards in many parts of the world, ended some national wine industries and gave opportunities to others, and resulted in the modern situation where almost all of the world's vines are grafted onto phylloxera-resistant rootstock.

Phylloxera is a tiny yellow aphid, indigenous to North America, that feeds on the roots of grapevines. Native American vines are resistant to it, and when American vines were imported and planted in European vineyards for experimental purposes in the mid-1800s (before quarantine regulations existed), they carried phylloxera on their roots. Although insects of the genus *Phylloxera* were first identified in England, it was **France** that first experienced their devastating impact because of the country's important wine industry. Once in French soil, the phylloxera migrated from their American vine hosts to the nearby French vines, which had no immunity to them. Soon vines throughout the south of France began to die.

The problem was first noticed in France in the Rhône Valley in the early 1860s. Within 10 years, vast areas of French vineyards were wiped out, and by the early twentieth century, all the major regions, apart from **Champagne**, had been badly affected. The French government offered a reward for a solution, and various methods (including flooding vineyards and pumping sulfur into the ground) were tried. Eventually a solution was found: grafting French vines onto phylloxera-resistant American rootstocks, a procedure still carried out today throughout most of the world's wine regions.

From its initial impact in France, phylloxera spread to other countries in Europe, wreaking havoc in the vineyards of **Spain**, **Italy**, and **Germany**. But there was no steady spread across the continent: phylloxera reached **Portugal** in 1871, but was not noticed in Spain until seven years later and did not reach the Rioja region for another two decades after that, in 1901. It was recognized in Italy by 1870, **Switzerland** in 1874, and Germany by 1875, but not in **Greece** until 1898.

Meanwhile, the problem had spread well beyond Europe, as phylloxera-affected vines were shipped around the world. It was discovered in California (on European vines) in 1873, and by the 1880s it had cut a swath through **Napa** and **Sonoma** counties, as vineyard owners were slow to react. Phylloxera started killing vines in **Australia** in 1877, although important and extensive wine regions of South Australia were spared. **New Zealand** and **South Africa** were hit in 1885. The arrival of phylloxera in Peru in 1888 marked the beginning of the end of a large wine industry that had begun in the 1500s. **Chile**, however, was not affected, thanks to a combination of isolation and the country's sandy soils, which are apparently inhospitable to the aphid.

The effects of the phylloxera epidemic were enormous. Until vines were replanted on rootstock, wine production declined: by 1895, French wine production was less than a third of what it had been in 1875. Counterfeit wine (made from produce such as raisins and currants) became a problem. Many wine **consumers** in Europe turned to spirits, and Scotch whisky and aniseed-flavored drinks (such as pastis) began to enjoy strong sales. The devastation of Europe's vineyards and the decline in wine exports occurred just as **California**'s wine industry was taking off, and it gave Californian wines an opportunity to establish themselves in eastern markets before California, too, was affected by phylloxera. Similarly, the vineyards of Algeria and other French territories in North Africa expanded to produce wine for the European market.

Within Europe, the epidemic led to a wide-ranging reorganization of the wine industry. When vineyards were replanted in France, for example, marginal wine regions in the north were not replanted, and the center of gravity of the wine industry shifted south. More attention was paid to matching grape varieties to locations, and because of the need to regain lost markets, there was more emphasis on quality. It was only after the phylloxera epidemic that the French authorities began to implement the *appellation d'origine contrôlée* (AOC) rules. Since the early 1900s, they have governed viticulture and winemaking in France, by designating regions (*appellations*) and their permitted grape varieties, setting maximum yields, and providing for regular taste testing to ensure quality. French AOC rules became the model for wine law in other major European wine-producing countries.

The temporary collapse of the French wine industry also led to the migration of unemployed French winemakers to other parts of Europe and elsewhere, where they began to introduce French winemaking methods. In Spain's Rioja region, winemakers from **Bordeaux** modernized the wine industry and introduced barriques for aging. Rioja enjoyed an export boom until 1901, when it too was affected by phylloxera. By then, Bordeaux had been replanted with grafted vines and most of the French winemakers returned home.

Chile, where many French vines had been imported before the phylloxera epidemic struck France, found itself with vines that were older than those in France. One Bordeaux variety, Carmenere, was not replanted in Bordeaux after the phylloxera period, but was widely planted in Chile. Until the 1990s, these vines were thought to be a clone of **Merlot**, but they have since been identified as a distinct variety, and this "lost grape" has become Chile's signature variety.

The dislocation of production and trade in the all-important European (especially French) wine regions caused by phylloxera thus had wide-ranging implications. There has been a persistent search for suitable rootstock—phylloxera-resistant rootstock that is appropriate for the growing conditions in specific regions. One rootstock, AxR1, was widely used for grafting in California from the 1960s, but it proved to be vulnerable to a strain of phylloxera, and in the 1990s vast areas of vines on AxR1 roots in Napa and Sonoma counties had to be ripped out and replanted.

The great majority (about 85 percent) of the world's vines are now grafted onto American rootstock, but there are still sporadic outbreaks of phylloxera here and there. Chile and **Washington** are two of the best-known regions where grafting is not the norm.

Rod Phillips

Further Reading

Campbell, Christy. *Phylloxera: How Wine Was Saved for the World*. New York: Harper, 2004.

Ordish, George. *The Great Wine Blight*. London: Sidgwick & Jackson, 1987.

Phillips, Rod. *A Short History of Wine*. New York: HarperCollins, 2001.

PINOT GRIGIO/PINOT GRIS

One of the fastest-selling grape varieties in recent years has been Pinot Grigio, a light white wine that has become popular as an alternative to the ubiquitous **Chardonnay**, particularly in wine bars and **restaurants** by the glass. Relatively neutral, light bodied, and moderate in alcohol, with a name that has been relatively easy for **consumers** to pronounce and without the prominent oak aromas of many Chardonnays, Pinot Grigio has broken from the pack of secondary grape varieties to take a spot in the big leagues of production. It passed **Sauvignon Blanc** as Chardonnay's biggest competitor in U.S. sales in 2001.

Pinot Grigio has been grown throughout the north of **Italy** since the nineteenth century. The lightly colored (grayish, hence *grigio*) grape was once vinified as a red variety, and Santa Margherita **winery** claims to have been the first to ferment it without the skins, in 1961, resulting in the version so well known today. **Importer** Anthony Terlato of Paterno Imports brought Santa Margherita to the **United States** in the late 1970s and kicked off the **fad** that soon caught on in a big way with consumers looking for something white to order besides Chardonnay.

Italy produces about a third of the world's Pinot Grigio, with 16,300 acres under vine—still only a drop in the huge bucket of Italian vineyards, less than 1 percent of the total. It is most prevalent in the northeast in the regions of Trentino–Alto Adige, the Veneto, and Friuli–Venezia Giulia.

The grape did not originate in Italy, however, but rather in **France**, where it is known as Pinot Gris or sometimes Auxerrois. It is a sibling of **Pinot Noir**, but is no longer grown in **Burgundy** where it was first recorded. Pinot Gris is one of the major varieties in Alsace, where 5,600 acres are planted. There, it is often seen in both dry and late-harvest **dessert wines**. Alsatian Pinot Gris is fuller bodied, deeper colored, more aromatic, and more richly flavored than the typical Italian Pinot Grigio, although many small producers in Italy make similarly styled wines.

The demand for Pinot Grigio has not gone unnoticed in the rest of the world, and producers in several countries have been planting new vines or grafting Pinot Grigio onto existing rootstock to challenge Italy's dominance. This is particularly true in **California**, where Americans' thirst for Pinot Grigio has made it the fastest-increasing white variety, from zero to almost 8,000 acres in 20 years, averaging 25 percent annual expansion. There are also at least 5,000 acres growing in **Germany**—where the grape is called Grauburgunder or Ruländer—Moldova, and Romania.

Oregon has taken a liking to this variety as well, but the mostly small producers in Oregon prefer to emulate Alsace rather than the Veneto. They accordingly use the name Pinot Gris on the label, as do others in California and elsewhere who are willing to forgo the greater name recognition of Pinot Grigio and instead emphasize their goal of a fuller-bodied, sometimes oaked, wine style. Oregon has around 2,200 acres, roughly 15 percent of its total vineyard area.

Pinot Grigio/Gris sales in the United States remain very strong, with a 4 percent market share in 2006, according to *Adams Wine Handbook 2007,* making it the fifth most popular grape variety. Among white wines, **varietally labeled** Pinot Grigio/Gris was second, its 14.7 million cases (mc) representing 16 percent of all white varietals. Despite the efforts of California and Oregon, 10.5 mc were imports (94 percent of that from Italy), according to *Impact* data, up from just 3.7 mc in 2000.

It is hard to foresee how much longer Pinot Grigio can maintain its cachet, but it is likely that another decade hence will see the luster fading, as consumers tire of ordering Pinot Grigio like everyone else and seek out a new favorite. If the case of Pinot Grigio is a good lesson, the new sweetheart will come not from the established varieties, but from the ranks of relatively unknown grapes (or possibly a more familiar grape with an unfamiliar alternate name), positioned at just the right time and in just the right way to convince consumers that they have personally discovered a new wine that no one else knows about. In the meantime, Pinot Grigio/Gris will remain a juggernaut.

PINOT NOIR

Pinot Noir is the red grape of **Burgundy**, where it is capable of making the most elegant of **red wines**—velvety, extraordinarily complex, and ethereal. Pinot Noir is also one of the most finicky of grapes, and unlike some, such as **Cabernet Sauvignon**, that are happy almost anywhere, Pinot Noir under less than ideal growing conditions all too often produces thin, weedy, harsh wines. Nevertheless, the high points are so sublime that Pinot Noir lovers are willing to work through the forgettable ones to enjoy the great ones.

One example of a Pinot Noir lover, though a fictitious one, is Miles, Paul Giamatti's character in the 2004 movie *Sideways.* Miles waxes eloquent about Pinot Noir and has some unsympathetic words for Merlot in the Oscar-nominated film, and sales of Pinot Noir in the **United States** jumped up 16 percent in the first three months after the movie came out. Its market share continued to show double-digit annual growth through 2007, although Merlot appeared to be reclaiming lost ground as of 2008. Despite the spike in Pinot Noir sales, it is still a relatively small player on store shelves, with a 2 percent market share in the United States, according to *Adams Wine Handbook 2007.*

Pinot Noir originated in Burgundy, where it eventually displaced all other red grapes apart from a small amount of Gamay. There are now 26,500 acres of Pinot Noir in Burgundy, where its highest expression is found in the Côte de Nuits, especially in the *grand cru* vineyards. The **terroirs** with limestone soils favor Pinot Noir's development. Also on limestone, Pinot Noir's largest concentration (30,400 acres) is found just to the north in **Champagne**. There, along with its close cousin Pinot Meunier and **Chardonnay**, Pinot Noir usually forms part of the blend for the region's celebrated **sparkling wines**, adding richness, fruit flavors, and sometimes a hint of color (particularly in *blancs de noirs* and rosé Champagnes). Pinot Noir is used for that purpose in the majority of sparkling wines around the world.

France's 71,200 acres of Pinot account for somewhat more than a third of the global total of around 205,000 acres. The country with the next largest amount of acreage devoted to the variety (28,200) is neighboring **Germany**, where it is known as Spätburgunder. **Switzerland**, too, has substantial plantings of Pinot Noir, here called Blauburgunder. In **Italy**, the variety is Pinot Nero and is found mostly in the northeast.

The **New World** lags in Pinot Noir production, despite considerable interest in increasing output, particularly in reaction to the "*Sideways*" effect." The movie caught the industry flat-footed, and the sudden surge in demand drove the average price of Pinot fruit in **California** to more than $2,000 a ton (three times the price of Merlot). However, one problem facing winemakers with dreams of challenging, or at least matching, Burgundy's supremacy in Pinot Noir is that most New World winegrowing regions were established in areas with warm to hot climates—all the better to grow most wine grapes, but not Pinot Noir. Pinot becomes insipid if it loses too much acidity and becomes overripe. Thus, it is really suitable only for the coolest New World regions. **Oregon** and **New Zealand** are particularly well suited for quality Pinot Noir, and, in fact, it takes up almost two-thirds of the vineyard land in Oregon. In California, much of **Sonoma County**, the seaward side of the Central Coast region, and the Santa Barbara area are the best matches. In **Australia**, it is the southern coasts and Tasmania, and in **Chile**, the Casablanca and San Antonio valleys.

PORTUGAL

Twenty years ago, the Portuguese wine industry had fallen behind the major wine-producing countries despite its long wine tradition and the fact that Portugal is the land of one of the most famous wines in the world: Port. Portugal had been to a great extent a closed market for 50 years, with a dictatorship regime and an internal market (with huge per-capita consumption) that absorbed the major part of the production. Together, these two factors meant that Portuguese winemakers did not need to adjust to the outside world to sell their wines.

A lot has changed since the late 1980s. The Portuguese wine industry has developed at a fast and steady pace, launching wines to compete either in the entry-level market or among high-end expensive wines. Today, Portugal offers a full range of unique wines from several regions that the Portuguese believe are highly competitive. Portugal is definitely a "country of flavors."

Wines and Regions.   The most famous Portuguese wine is the **fortified wine** Port. The Port trade began in the seventeenth century when the English, cut off from the French wine industry, wanted to import more wine from the Iberian Peninsula, as they already did with Sherry. To make the wine capable of being transported to Britain, they decided to add spirits, creating a wine with a high residual sugar and **high alcohol content**. During the next centuries, numerous Port shippers entered the trade, and Port soon become a superstar in the world of wines.

Nowadays the Douro region produces not only Port but also **table wines** made from the same grape varieties, including Touriga Nacional, Touriga Franca, Tinta Roriz, and Tinta Amarela.

Vinho Verde is the major Portuguese white wine region. The cold granite soils of the north of Portugal, which has a very wet Atlantic climate, result in light white wines that have unusual acidity and are very aromatic. Vinho Verde offers various styles, from white to **red** and from very simple, fizzy wines to more aromatic and structured wines, especially those made from the Alvarinho variety. Other important varieties are the white Loureiro and Trajadura and the red Vinhão.

Less well known is Alentejo, which started to develop its wine industry within the last 20 years. Nowadays it is one of the most important wine-producing regions in the country, largely responsible for the development of Portuguese table wines. Alentejo has a very hot, continental climate and soils that are ideal to develop **quality wines**. It is renowned for producing red wines from such varieties as Trincadeira, Aragones (Tempranillo in **Spain**), Alicante Bouschet, and **Syrah** and white wines such as Antão Vaz and Arinto.

Other regions of great importance in Portugal include Palmela/Sado, Estremadura, Ribatejo, Dão, Beiras, Bairrada, and another famous fortified wine area, the island of Madeira.

Wine Industry.   Portugal today is the fifth largest wine source in Europe, producing 83.7 million nine-liter cases (mc) in 2006 from a little over 600,000 acres of vineyards. Port and Madeira accounted for about 13 percent of production, and nonfortified quality wines added another 34 percent. Two-thirds of Portuguese wine is red or **rosé**, and almost half comes from cooperatives.

Per-capita wine consumption in Portugal remains among the world's highest, so despite its relatively small population, Portugal is 11th worldwide in wine consumption. Domestic consumption of 52.2 mc in 2006, however, still leaves plenty of wine available for export, and in 2006, exports amounted to 32.5 mc, worth about €330 million. Fortified wines were 28 percent of this, and table wines (vinho de mesa and vinho regional) made up most of the rest, much of it sold as **bulk wine**. Interestingly, the largest export market for nonfortified wines was the former Portuguese colony of Angola, followed by **France**. Imports are negligible.

Challenges for the Portuguese Wine Industry.   The Portuguese wine industry is growing every day, but there is still a lot of work to be done. At present, there are still few Portuguese wine companies with real international dimension. Portuguese wines must differentiate themselves by the quality, the **terroir**, and the uniqueness of their flavors and not simply by volume. Furthermore, they must never underestimate the power of marketing—this has been the industry's main mistake in the last 10 years—and the need to create **brands** that are recognized all over the world.

There is no question that Douro, Alentejo, and Vinho Verde will lead, but other regions—some older, such as Dão, Bairrada, and Beiras, and some newer, such as Ribatejo and Estremadura—are also making some noise in the international markets. Even so, the challenge is enormous, and the Portuguese presence in the major wine markets still is not substantial. To change this, the producers must find a balance between the quality, quantity, and proper **promotion**.

The Portuguese are convinced that some major steps have been taken in the last five years. The quality is stable, the quantity is coming, and both the private and public sectors (for example, ViniPortugal, which promotes Portuguese wines abroad) are becoming more professional and aggressive. With all these factors together, Portugal will have a chance to compete with other wine nations on the strength of its tradition, quality, and uniqueness of the wines. *See also* Colonial Era; Fads and Fashions.

João Portugal Ramos

Further Reading

Metcalfe, Charles, and Kathryn McWhirter. *The Wine and Food Lover's Guide to Portugal*. Balcombe, England: Inn House, 2007.

PROFIT AND PROFITABILITY

From a purely financial outlook, *profit* is what differentiates a good business from a bad one. Profit equals *revenues* minus *expenses* (costs of doing business); in other words, it is the amount of money left over from sales after everything has been paid for. If this number is positive, the company is healthy; if not, it is in danger of being forced to close. Profit is typically reported in dollars (or the local currency) on a company's profit and loss statement.

Profitability is a somewhat more complex concept that relates to a firm's *ability* to generate a profit over time, taking into account the direction and rate of change of short-term profit levels, the volume of business, and the value of the company's assets. Profitability is usually stated in percentages.

Understanding the difference between these two concepts is fundamental to gauging the vitality of each segment of the wine market as well as understanding the profit margin from markups by each segment. The differences can be illustrated in the following hypothetical example of a bottle of winemaking its way through the U.S. market's three-tier system (scenarios and thus margins and profitability levels would vary in other markets with different structures).

Winery A, with approximately $2,000,000 in assets, makes 100,000 bottles of wine per year at an average cost per bottle of $5 for the grapes, packaging materials, direct labor, and equipment operation. In addition, there may be another $3 per bottle in fixed operating expenses and overhead, including administrative salaries, debt service, rents and leases, and the costs of **promoting** and selling the wine. The winery will try to sell its output to a wholesaler at around double its direct costs, or $10 per bottle, giving it a per-bottle *gross profit* of $5 and *net profit* of $2. Looking at aggregate figures with annual sales of 100,000 bottles, total revenues would be $1,000,000, gross profit (after subtracting the total direct costs of $500,000) would be $500,000, and net profit (after subtracting the combined direct and overhead costs of $800,000) would be $200,000, or 20 percent of revenue. Factoring in the winery's $2,000,000 in assets, the total profit of $200,000 divided by total assets yields a *return on assets* of 10 percent.

Following the wine farther down the supply chain, Wholesaler B purchases 10,000 bottles of Winery A's wine. Wholesalers or **distributors** typically take a profit margin of between 30 and 40 percent. In this example, Wholesaler B marks the wine up 35 percent, so it now prices the wine it bought from Winery A for $10 at $13.50 wholesale to be sold to **retailers** and **restaurateurs**. The distributor thus makes a gross profit of $3.50 per bottle or, after selling its full inventory, $35,000. Naturally, Wholesaler B also sells many other **brands**, so it may sell 1,000,000 bottles from various producers during the course of a year. If Winery A is typical, Wholesaler B has total gross profits of $3.5 million. Out of this, it must cover its costs, including shipping, overhead, marketing, sales and administrative salaries, and so forth. For Wholesaler B, this runs approximately $3 million, resulting in a net profit of around $500,000 (or $0.50 per bottle). Because the million bottles of wine cost $10 million, the profit is about 5 percent. In this representative example, the wholesaler has a much smaller *profit margin* than the winery, but makes 2½ times as much *net profit* overall due to its volume. Wholesaler B has around $5 million in assets (inventory, buildings, trucks, and so forth), giving it a return on assets of 10 percent, roughly the same as the winery.

Retailer C in turn marks the wine up another 35 to 50 percent. Winery A's wine, which the retailer bought from Wholesaler B for $13.50, might now sell to the **consumer** for $18.99, a markup of just over 40 percent. The retailer's profit margin is even slimmer than the distributor's because its overhead (salaries and rent) is relatively high, but a wine store that is properly merchandized and in a good location can do enough volume to have a substantial total profit. The retailer's return on assets is a bit higher because its assets (inventory) are smaller than the wholesaler or the asset-heavy winery. Depending upon volume, the retailer's profitability can increase to 12 to 15 percent.

Marketing affects profitability in that successful marketing plans and programs can help to increase demand and potentially raise the price consumers are willing to spend on the wine, thereby increasing profit. Promotion can add perceived value to goods and can sometimes allow a producer to achieve **cult** status, thus increasing profitability considerably. Price is based on a complex combination of factors: the firm's cost/profit objectives, what the market will pay, what the competition is charging, the price of available substitutes, and—very specific to wine—the time-to-market based on aging regimes. In international markets, fluctuating **exchange rates** and economic business cycles also affect price setting and ultimately profitability. Well-strategized price reductions can also increase volume and also ultimately profitability.

Successful players in the wine market recognize that each tier has its own profit structure and that volume can significantly affect profitability. Assets are often the most substantial in the production segment of the business, with retailing offering the best potential for a healthy return on assets and wholesaling generally providing the largest aggregate profits. *See also* Supply and Demand.

PROHIBITION

From 1920 to 1933, the **United States** enacted the legal ban on alcohol known as Prohibition—and the modern wine industry still encounters both legal and cultural obstacles that date back to that era. The seeds of Prohibition were sown in the nineteenth century, as a wave of **religious** enthusiasm swept across the country. As individuals went through conversions to become "born again," they simultaneously vowed to avoid moral vices such as dancing, playing cards, and the intemperate drinking of alcoholic beverages. Religious crusades promoting "temperance" also fit in well with the interests of the middle and upper classes, who thought that efficiency and self-discipline were virtues befitting an increasingly industrial society. Alcohol intoxication undermined American Protestantism's mission of saving souls and organizing them into well-regulated communities—particularly at a time when more and more non-Protestant immigrants kept arriving on the nation's shores. Temperance was thus not solely a moral or religious crusade, but also had elements of class hatred, ethnic prejudice, and a general fear of America's increasing pluralism.

The 18th Amendment to the U.S. Constitution, prohibiting the "manufacture, sale, or transportation of intoxicating liquors," went into effect in January 1920. The question of whether to include wine in the ban had been prominent throughout the public debate leading up to passage of the amendment. After all, wine was an integral part of Judeo-Christian tradition. The Bible endorses the consumption of wine, and wine had been central to Jewish and Christian worship for thousands of years. Proponents of total prohibition thus had to find ways to cast moral and religious suspicion on this very biblical beverage. Some Protestants argued that the Bible had been mistranslated and that the original text must surely have been referring not to wine but to simple, unfermented grape juice. Former Methodist minister Thomas Welch became so convinced that the consumption of alcohol blasphemed God that he perfected a process whereby grape juice could be boiled and filtered to remove the alcohol-producing yeast. The Welch Grape Juice Company was founded in 1869 to provide this simple grape juice.

American **wineries** had been producing 55 million gallons of wine (the equivalent of 23 million cases) per year just prior to the onset of Prohibition. Many of these wines were of exceptionally high quality and were helping to create a reasonably sophisticated **consumer** market. All of this came to an abrupt halt in 1920. Even though a few wineries were able to obtain licenses to produce wines for religious or medicinal purposes, most were gone forever. Wine production fell to just 3.5 million gallons annually.

Interestingly, the Volstead Act, which spelled out the terms of Prohibition, permitted the heads of households to make up to 200 gallons of wine per year for personal use. This explains the irony that during the 13 years of Prohibition, wine consumption in the United States actually grew, from 0.53 to 0.64 gallons per capita. Most of this wine was understandably of poor quality—made simply to be cheap and intoxicating.

The demand for alcohol endured, and the illicit consumption of bootleg liquor fueled organized crime and a widespread public backlash against the "Noble Experiment." Prohibition was repealed by the 21st Amendment in 1933, giving control over alcohol back to the states and local jurisdictions. However, by then, Prohibition had dealt the U.S. wine industry a staggering blow. Recovery after repeal was slow and difficult. Obstacles that had to be surmounted included the loss of winemaking talent, the disruption of vineyards, and the legacy of a patchwork of fairly arbitrary and inconsistent local laws that hampered the manufacture and inter-state distribution of alcoholic beverages. Even worse was the loss of a developed consumer palate for well-crafted wines. It was not until the 1970s that U.S. wine production reached its former levels, and still today state and local laws restrict the sale and transportation of alcohol more than any other food or beverage, while tacit suspicions about the morality of consuming alcohol persist within a sizable minority of Americans. *See also* Control States; Direct Shipping; Drinking Age.

Robert C. Fuller

Further Reading

Behr, Edward. *Prohibition: Thirteen Years That Changed America*. New York: Arcade, 1996.

Fuller, Robert C. *Religion and Wine: A Cultural History of Wine Drinking in the United States*. Knoxville: University of Tennessee Press, 1996.

Furnas, J.C. *The Life and Times of the Late Demon Rum*. New York: Putnam, 1973.

Rorabaugh, W. J. *The Alcoholic Republic*. New York: Oxford University Press, 1979.

PROMOTION

With so many wines available to **consumers** in the **global** marketplace, competition is often intense, and any producer that is trying to increase sales, or even defend its current market position, must engage in some form of promotion to sustain consumer interest. The main elements of marketing that are used to advance the sales of wine are advertising, sales promotion, and public relations. Still, there is such a wide range of specific strategies and tactics for promoting wine sales that it is impossible for even the largest companies to focus attention on all of them at the same time. Thus, choices need to be made, based on the company's philosophy and goals, to select the forms of promotion that are likely to be most cost-effective.

Promotion can be a significant cost factor, but when carried out properly, the return on investment can be very positive. The challenge is that it is notoriously difficult to measure the effectiveness of any specific avenue of promotion—indeed, at times, it is virtually impossible for the more esoteric forms. To add to the complexity, market conditions continuously change, so companies are forced to continually evaluate promotion efforts.

Types of promotions can be categorized based on what is being promoted, to whom it is being targeted, and which means are being employed.

Products Promoted.   Promotional activities can be narrowly or broadly focused. The narrower the focus is, the easier it is to see concrete results, but the less spillover there is for related products. On the other hand, a broad promotion can help sales over many product categories, but the benefits may be indistinguishable from many other market forces that are influencing sales at the same time and may not provide help to individual items that are struggling.

The most basic level might be characterized by a **winery** or **importer** focusing attention on a single specific wine, perhaps a new release or one for which sales have been flat. Introducing a promotional campaign for that wine would be expected to result in an immediate, measurable increase in sales of that wine, but would not necessarily improve the sales of other wines from the same producer. To have a more general effect, the promotion may provide support for the complete line of wines, a **brand**, or the winery as a whole. Such a promotion is likely to help several different wines within the company, but the benefit will be diffused over the product line; it may help sales overall, but not in the places where it was most needed.

There are even larger canvases for promotional campaigns, moving beyond a single company to promote an entire category of wine—for example, there have been campaigns focused on wine regions, styles, grape varieties, and so on. Such crusades are normally waged by issue-specific organizations and are aimed at positioning their constituent group as well as gaining mindshare among buyers. Wine regions may be supported by groups of regional producers, as in the case of the **Napa Valley** Vintners or the Consorzio Vino Chianti Classico, or by governmental or semiofficial organizations, such as Wine **Australia**. "Wine Country" businesses or associations that benefit from **wine tourism** are often involved in regional promotion as well. Other trade and consumer groups boost various types of wine: **organic wine** being promoted by the Organic Trade Association, for instance, or wines made from the **Zinfandel** grape variety by the Zinfandel Advocates & Producers association.

A promotional goal could even be as broad as advancing the industry as a whole. The wine industry engaged in a modest general self-advancement campaign in some markets in 1999 with the slogan "Wine. What are you saving it for?" but other industries, notably the beef and milk boards, have sponsored more effective campaigns of this sort.

Targets of Promotion.   The primary target of advertising campaigns is usually the end user of the product—in this case, the wine consumer. This type of "pull" strategy, directed right at consumers, is used by producers with the goal of increasing demand. Various media are available, including magazines, TV, radio, and, of course, the Internet. The *Wine Spectator,* the *Wine Enthusiast, Wine & Food,* and *Gourmet* are popular print outlets used by wineries and wholesalers for targeting consumers. Campaigns in these publications generally promote individual brands or wines, typically by extolling the sensory attributes of the wines or the lifestyle the advertiser hopes to associate with drinking them. Broader campaigns may attempt to increase public awareness generally or to raise the profile of a company or category, heightening interest in (or possibly reducing resistance to) a wine product among even nondrinkers; for example, **sparkling wine** producers may advertise in a brides' magazine to link their products with weddings and the inevitable toasts to the happy couple. Given the sensitivities about alcohol, however, wine advertisers need to take care to avoid a backlash in countries and regions with large populations who are morally or **religiously** opposed to alcoholic products.

Another important target of promotional activity is the trade. Advertising in such trade publications as *Wine Business Monthly* or *Nation's Restaurant News* may encourage more on- and off-premise wine **retailers** to carry specific wines, for example. In addition, there are many more direct promotional approaches, such as incentives that are designed to persuade sales representatives to sell, or wine buyers to order, more of a particular product. For companies that provide services and goods to wineries and other members of the industry—say, **barrel** makers, **bulk wine** brokers, or designers of point-of-sale software—the trade is likely to be the only target for promotion, through such channels as advertising and possibly discounts on volume purchases or free goods offered by suppliers to retailers.

Means of Promotion.   The most effective campaigns identify one or more target market segments that have high priority and match the type of promotion to the audience. The target segments may be differentiated based on geography or demographics, and the campaign can go after a segment that is already predisposed to the wine (for example, French or Italian wines in **New York** City) or one that is considered to be an underserved but potential growth market (twentysomethings or **women**, for instance).

The most visible form of promotion is advertising. The wine industry spent about $130 million on wine advertising in the **United States** in 2006. Almost $100 million of this went for print ads, 76 percent in magazines, 16 percent in newspapers, and 8 percent on billboards. The remainder was spent on broadcast ads, more or less evenly split between television and radio. Over the last 20 years, wine companies have drifted away from advertising on television, but with the rise of cable TV, several wine producers are exploring this medium now that they believe they have the chance to target specific segments again. Internet advertising of wine was estimated at just $3 million in 2006, down 75 percent from 2005.

In 2006, the largest wine advertiser was **Gallo**, spending $24 million over all its brands, but the largest individual brand was **Yellow Tail**, which spent $10 million on advertising after doing no advertising at all for its first few years on the market. Even though the sparkling wine category is less than 5 percent of total U.S. wine consumption, it accounted for almost 20 percent of all advertising in 2006.

There are many other avenues for promotion, however. Companies may choose to try connecting with consumers through direct mail, special events, **wine clubs**, or tastings. Specific consumer-focused sales promotion activities include discounted pricing programming for periods of time (subject to local regulations), point-of-purchase displays, sweepstakes, and logo-imprinted giveaways. Giving away free samples, a popular sales promotion in many other consumer goods industries, is not used nearly as much in the wine trade because of legal restrictions, but wineries and some retail establishments with proper licensing use this tool extensively. During holidays, certain producers will use price packs (often two for the price of one) or premiums (for example, glasses packaged with a bottle of Champagne) as a means to entice consumers to buy.

Another strategy is to target opinion makers, especially **wine writers** and **sommeliers**, hoping to impress them sufficiently that they will speak highly of the wine or brand to large numbers of consumers. Along the same lines, wineries participate in many different **festivals, trade shows, and competitions**, looking for awards and high **ratings** that will give their wines significant favorable exposure. Both trade- and consumer-oriented shows or tastings are popular around the world— Vinexpo, Vinitaly, and ProWein are just a few of these major events that have both trade and consumer elements. Such events frequently have **wine education** sessions for consumers or the trade, although these can often be sales pitches couched in a quasi-seminar setting.

Since consumers cannot buy what they cannot find, it is vital to suppliers that their wines appear in a sufficient number of retail and **restaurant** outlets. Encouraging sales from the **supply** side, they may try to get importer or **distributor** sales representatives more interested in placing the wine, and wine buyers and sales staff more interested in moving it, by offering various types of sales incentives— trips, giveaways, or cash. Alternatively, they may simply offer temporary discounts on the wholesale price of the wine to the retailer; if the retailer chooses to pass the savings along to the consumer, the wine becomes more attractively priced on the shelf, and if not, the retailer's increased **profit** margin gives an added incentive to sell more wine, perhaps by setting up eye-catching displays or running staff contests. State and local laws may prohibit some of these possible forms of promotion, however, but whatever means are used, the ultimate goal is to push the product through the supply chain.

The wine industry has seen an increase in the use of public relations (PR) to help build brand awareness and to promote the perceived lifestyle benefits of drinking wine. PR uses messaging techniques to reach buyers in many of the same media outlets as paid advertising, but placements are free. In-house PR departments or external PR agencies work to create and disseminate positive stories about products and brands to generate favorable publicity. In the wine industry, winery owners are also heavily publicized and in some instances have achieved star status among wine drinkers. In addition, many wine companies also rely on the Web as a PR conduit to build positive relationships with their customers. As advertising rates have increased significantly and the ad channels have become more cluttered, many segments of the industry have turned to PR as a more targeted way of spending their promotion dollars, and PR can be an effective image- and brand-building tool.

All media of promotion cut into a supplier's profit, whether through direct expenditure, as in the case of advertising, or loss of revenue, as when taking a price cut. In addition, vast amounts of wine are given away as samples for tasting to sales personnel, writers, and potential buyers, as well as for donations to charitable causes. However, when properly executed, the returns outweigh the expenses, and the promotional activities bring in sales well in excess of their cost. *See also* Consolidation; Labels as Marketing.

Further Reading

Hall, C. Michael, and Richard Mitchell. *Wine Marketing: A Practical Guide.* Oxford, England: Elsevier, 2007.

Kotler, Philip, and Gary Armstrong. *Principles of Marketing.* Upper Saddle River, NJ: Pearson/Prentice Hall, 2008.

Moulton, Kirby, and James Lapsley. *Successful Wine Marketing.* New York: Springer, 2001.

Wagner, Paul, Janeen Olsen, and Liz Thach. *Wine Marketing and Sales: Success Strategies for a Saturated Market.* San Francisco: Wine Appreciation Guild, 2007.

Q

QUALITY CONTROL

Quality control (QC) and its partner quality assurance (QA) are methods of ensuring that the wine produced at a **winery** is safe for consumption and of uniformly high quality, and both are an essential part of doing business in the modern world. Typically, these functions have a relatively low profile unless there is a problem, but because a major problem can ruin a business (and in rare cases, cause harm to the public), they are an important safeguard against trouble.

Quality assurance is a business's overall plan for achieving appropriate quality standards.

Quality control is the enactment of that QA plan. These interrelated activities are designed to trace a wine's progress from inception in the vineyard and winery, through bottling, **bulk** handling, and storage (if applicable), and onto the shelf so that the wine reaches the **consumer** in the condition the winemaker intended while at the same time meeting the consumer's expectations.

The following factors are normally included in the QA plan:

1. *Establishing the criteria for overall wine quality.* The wine must meet the winery's standards for taste, aroma, color, and so forth. "Typicity" may also be a requirement in Old World **appellations**.
2. *Absence of faults and contaminants.* The wine must be hygienic, safe, and without obvious problems. Possible deficiencies include visible faults, such as protein haze, sediment (in a young wine that should not have any), or oxidative browning; aroma faults, such as **cork taint**, excessive acetaldehyde, acetic acid, and so on; and the related category of tastable faults. Contaminants are very rare, but could include measurable pesticide residues from the grapes, or broken glass, cork dust, or other debris from a bottling line problem.
3. *Stabilization.* The wine should be secure from any unwanted chemical or microbiological changes happening in the bottle during storage. *Cold stabilization* is a normal procedure to reduce or eliminate later tartrate crystal deposits in the bottle, as is *fining* (adding inert particulate matter to a wine in tank that collects other large molecules and particles as it falls to the bottom) to remove excessive

phenolics that may cause browning or proteins that might cause a haze. Sterile filtering, addition of sulfur dioxide and/or sorbic acid, and pasteurization are possible methods for dealing with yeast and bacteria that could cause refermentation in the bottle, especially in wines with moderate levels of residual sugar or low acidity.

4. *Legal requirements.* The wine must meet legal standards in order to be salable. These standards may come from local or national governmental authorities or from a body that oversees specific appellations. Examples include legal limits on certain components or ingredients in the wine, such as **sulfites**, volatile acidity, and so forth.

5. *Traceability.* Measures must be taken to ensure that any problems discovered later with a particular bottle of wine can traced back through the entire supply chain and winemaking process to find the source of the problem, identify other bottles that might have the same problem, and segregate those that are free from problems.

QC programs tend to be voluntary in the **New World**, under the assumption that the marketplace will force suppliers to maintain high quality, whereas in the Old World, a QA plan is mandated—which, in turn, makes it a requirement for New World producers with intentions of exporting to Europe. Some of the most notable components in QA plans used for identifying potential problems and monitoring for them include the following:

- Hazard Analysis and Critical Control Points (HACCP, pronounced *hass*-up) is a widely used system created by the National Aeronautics and Space Administration (NASA) to maintain quality for space launches. Under a winery's HACCP plan, the entire winemaking process is analyzed to determine the specific *critical control points* (CCPs) at which problems are most likely to occur or to be recognizable, and then procedures are designed to monitor these CCPs for deviations from defined limits of safe practice. HACCP procedures are mandatory in the **European Union**, but not in the **United States** where they were devised. Nevertheless, many wineries around the world, including some in the United States, follow HACCP procedures voluntarily, especially those producing large volumes of wine or shipping product to foreign markets.

- ISO (International Standards Organization) 9000 is a demand-side system driven by customers—for example, a **supermarket** chain. The ISO 9000 documents describe in detail the safety requirements, level of quality, and general characteristics for various products, including wine, that the customer is willing to accept from producers or suppliers. An outside auditing body is then engaged to test the product and verify that it meets the stated performance requirements.

- ISO 14000 is an environmental management system for reducing harmful environmental impact.

- Total Quality Management (TQM), developed in Japan, is basically a philosophy of all workers and managers pursuing safety and quality at every step of a process.

The advantages of QA/QC procedures are obvious—especially to any winery that has ever had a serious quality issue that resulted in a public relations scandal or costly product recall. The procedures establish confidence that the wine is safe and at an acceptable quality level for sale, avoiding damage to the **brand** name or the reputation of the business, harm to consumers, and potential lawsuits. A good QC program gives a winery the ability to quickly identify and correct problems before they leave the facility or compromise larger quantities of wine. Many supermarkets and other large purchasers insist on winery QA/QC programs to limit their own liability, so they are a prerequisite to large-volume sales. The downside is that there can be considerable expense at a large winery for monitoring equipment, QA staff, consultants, and so on, the benefits of which may never be seen. Still, as global trade continues to grow, as the wine industry's impact on the environment continues to be a concern, and as consumers continue to be interested in full disclosure in food labeling, QA/QC systems will become more and more important worldwide.

QUALITY WINE

In the **New World** in general, the term *quality wine* has no specific definition and simply refers to "good wine"—whatever that might mean to the speaker. In particular, **wineries** are free to market their products as quality wines without needing to demonstrate any precise characteristics (**Canada** is one exception, where the Quality Wine Alliance has attempted to give meaning to the term). In the **European Union** (EU), on the other hand, *quality wine,* or its equivalent in other languages, has a strict legal definition that carries specific requirements that separate quality wine from other wines.

EU regulations have brought together the patchwork of national wine legislation that existed before the European economic union by defining a general system into which most national systems fit. In 2008–2009, with the implementation of the Common Market Organization for wine, existing national appellation laws were being rewritten in accordance with a new EU system that will recognize only Protected Designation of Origin (PDO) regions for quality wine. These new laws were to be in place by August 2009.

The existing European structures are typically depicted as a "quality pyramid" with **table wines** as the broad base and quality wines forming the tip of the pyramid. In the umbrella EU scheme, only the top level—designated VQPRD (*Vin de Qualité Produit dans une Région Déterminée*) or, in English, QWPSR (Quality Wine Produced in a Specified Region)—is officially "quality wine." To achieve this recognition, a wine must meet a list of standards that stipulate the place of origin or **appellation**, grape varieties used, **grape-growing** and winemaking techniques, and quality tests for the finished wine.

Individual European wine-producing countries interpret the EU legislation for their own wine industry, and most have simply adapted their traditional systems to the EU template. In many countries, there are two traditional designations that meet the EU standards for quality wine. Thus, in **Italy**, both DOCG (see the sidebar on the next page for definitions of acronyms) and DOC wines are considered VQPRD—that is, quality—wines. The lower levels in the Italian system, IGT and *vino da tavola,* are not technically quality wines because they are not required to meet as rigorous a set of standards, even though many excellent and very pricy "Super Tuscans" fall into these latter categories.

The proportion of quality wine to table wine varies from country to country. In **France**, about 55 percent of production is quality wine (AOC or VDQS). In **Germany**, by contrast, more than 98 percent of the wine produced typically achieves one of the two VQPRD designations, QmP and QbA.

EU laws also recognize subcategories of quality wine for **sparkling wine** (VSQPRD/QSWPSR), **fortified** or "liqueur" wine (VLQPRD/QLWPSR), and other special types. In **Portugal**, quality wine makes up 47 percent of production, but this can be broken down further to 13 percent VLQPRD, mainly Port, and 34 percent nonfortified VQPRD wines.

Because no New World regions spell out winemaking procedures to the degree the European Union does, no wines from outside the EU meet the European criteria for quality wine—regardless of their excellence, reputation, or price. Non-EU wines are officially either "Wine from a Designated Region," if they are from an approved wine-producing area such as the **Napa Valley**, or just "Wine."

Several professional **wine education** organizations that offer certifications require prospective candidates to evaluate quality levels as part of the certification process, but each has its own parameters of exactly what defines quality. These differentiations are primarily for legal, statistical, and/or evaluative purposes, however, because **consumers** ultimately decide the quality and value of any wine.

National Designations for Quality Wine

In the **European Union** (EU), the following categories are established by national wine laws and recognized by the EU as *quality wine* (with the theoretically highest-quality category—the one most stringent regulations—listed first). Within each country, the categories are listed in nominal descending order of quality, based on the stringency of regulations and oversight.

- Austria: Districtus Austriae Controllatus (DAC); Prädikatswein; Kabinett; Qualitätswein
- Bulgaria: Controliran or Vina s Garantirano i Kontrolirano Naimenovanie na Proizkhod, Vina s Garantirano Naimenovanie na Proizkhod
- Czech Republic: Jakostní Víno s Přívlastkem, Jakostní Víno, Víno Originální Certifikace (VOC)
- France: Appellation d'Origine Contrôlée (AOC), Vin Délimité de Qualité Supérieure (VDQS)
- Germany: Qualitätswein mit Prädikat (QmP), Qualitätswein bestimmer Anbaugebeite (QbA)
- Greece: Onomasía Proeléfseos Eleghoméni (OPE), Onomasía Proeléfseos Anotéras Piótitos (OPAP)
- Hungary: Minőségi Bor
- Italy: Denominazione di Origine Controllata e Garantita (DOCG), Denominazione di Origine Controllata (DOC)
- Luxembourg: Appellation d'Origine Contrôlée (AOC)
- Portugal: Denominação de Origem Controlada (DOC), Indicação de Proveniencia Regulamentada (IPR)
- Romania: Vin de Calitate Superiorară cu Denumire de Origine Controlată şi Trepte de Calitate (DOCC), Vin de Calitate Superiorară cu Denumire de Origine Controlata (DOC)
- Slovakia: Akostné Víno s Prívlastkom, Akostné Víno
- Slovenia: Vrhunsko Vino Zaščiteno Geografsko Poreklo, Kakovostno Vino Zaščiteno Geografsko Poreklo
- Spain: Denominación de Origen Calificada (DOCa), Denominación de Origen (DO), Vino de Pago, Vino de Calidad con Indicación Geográfica (VCIG)

R

RATINGS AND SCORES

The practice of critics rating wine is increasingly important in the world of wine. In large part, this is because of the increased choice being offered to **consumers**, but a further contributing factor is that many drinkers are now more demanding and see wine not as a commodity, but rather as a lifestyle beverage.

While in the past consumers eager to drink high-quality wines might have placed themselves in the hands of a trusted merchant or bought simply by reputation or habit, they are now "empowered" and want to make their own choices, guided by information sources of their own choosing. And at the higher end, the ranks of wine collectors—people who buy, cellar, and frequently trade fine wines—have swelled globally.

The growing demand for the best fine wines has seen their prices soar, and with more buyers chasing the same group of classic wines, buyers sometimes have to choose and pay for their wines as **futures**, before they are even bottled (*en primeur*)—a practice that has spread from the classic regions of **Bordeaux** and **Burgundy** to encompass the Rhône and vintage Port as well. The role of the critic in acting as a gatekeeper is therefore more important than ever.

The modern era of wine criticism (distinguishing wine *critics,* whose primary role is to rate individual wines, from **wine** *writers*, who seek to inform readers, drawing them into the world of wine, without necessarily focusing on specific products) began with **Robert Parker**, the dominant wine critic of the last 25 years. Parker began his career as a lawyer, but developed an interest in wine that eventually spawned a newsletter, the *Wine Advocate.* Parker's 100-point scoring system resonated with consumers, who found it a handy shortcut through the complex world of wine. It was the 1982 vintage in Bordeaux that saw Parker's first great triumph. While many fellow critics gave the vintage a lukewarm reception, Parker broke ranks and declared it a great success—a decision that the market and other expert tasters later ratified. Parker's views quickly became trusted by both consumers and the marketplace. In recent years, such has been the extent of his influence in Bordeaux, the most significant fine wine region, that the châteaux have even withheld opening prices until Parker has published his initial scores on the wines. Without doubt, an essential part of the modern en primeur campaign is the release of Parker scores. The near dominance of Parker in this region has actually opened the door for others: because his scores have such a strong bearing on prices, collectors are now on the lookout for wines that he has missed but that other critics have spotted, because this is the last refuge for value for money wines.

While he remains the dominant force in wine criticism, Parker's scores are not the only wine ratings with some influence. The *Wine Spectator* is the most widely read wine magazine in the **United States**, and its scores, also on a hundred-point scale, have considerable influence in the United States, less so elsewhere. Michel Bettane, a critic who also made his name with the 1982 vintage, is important in **France**; **Spain**, **Germany**, **Austria**, and **Portugal** also possess critics who have some influence on their domestic markets. And there are critics specializing in areas where the *Wine Advocate* has less influence, the most noteworthy of which is Allen Meadows who covers the wines of Burgundy in his subscription newsletter.

There are several advantages to critical ratings. First, they offer busy but affluent wine collectors a "helicopter ride to the top," a shortcut to the "best" wines. They allow someone who does not have the experience or ability to taste young wines with accuracy to have confidence in his or her purchasing decisions. They allow new wine buyers to trade up and spend a lot of money, safe in the knowledge that they are not going to end up with duds. Even where collectors have experience, they do not usually have the opportunity to taste the top wines at the very early stage where purchasing decisions need to be made to secure an allocation, so when it comes to futures, buyers have no option but to trust either the views of critics or the reputation of the producer. Perhaps most importantly, it is likely that the presence of such an influential critic as Parker has acted as a catalyst in the expansion of the whole fine wine sector by creating interest in the world's great wines and then guiding cash-rich but time-poor collectors to some of the best.

One further positive aspect of the Parker phenomenon is that it has created an opportunity for ambitious new producers. Within a few years of their debut vintage, wineries that have assembled a string of high Parker scores can be catapulted to stardom and achieve high prices for their wines in a way that previously was not possible without a long track record. The fact that this sort of "kingmaking" exists has given existing producers a reason to raise their game, as well as encouraging new producers to aim high.

However, critics have themselves become the focus of criticism. The first is that Parker, with his powerful influence on the wine trade, has led to a homogenization of styles in the fine wine areas where he has greatest influence. He is criticized for having a personal preference for big red wines that are concentrated, with rich fruit and considerable new oak influence. Because of his influence on prices, producers are placed under subtle pressure to adopt winemaking styles that result in the sorts of wines that achieve critical acclaim.

The second criticism is a conceptual one, regarding the reduction of a wine to a number. Some ask whether it is useful to see wine merely in terms of a score, as this ignores the important stylistic distinctions that make up the diversity of wine. These certainly are not recognized by scores, which, alone, seem to indicate that a single universal standard can be applied to wine. Many wineries that in the past have made wines that exhibit regional typicity have modified their style such that they now make wines with less regional influence, but which are more likely to gain high scores.

But these criticisms could be leveled at any critic with a broad following, and it seems unfair to take just one critic to task largely on the basis that he has been highly successful at what he does.

The Parker era will shortly draw to a close, and as yet, no single critic looks placed to fill his shoes. It seems likely that there never will be another Parker. Instead, his role will be taken by a multitude of critics, each with a smaller sphere of influence. In addition, communication among individual wine lovers facilitated by the likes of Internet wine discussion boards and CellarTracker will help fill some of the void that remains.

Jamie Goode

Further Reading

Clemens, Scott. "What the Ratings Really Mean and Why We Need Them." *Wine Business Monthly,* December 15, 2004, www.winebusiness.com/ReferenceLibrary/webarticle.cfm?dataId=36266.

Franson, Paul. "How Different Publications Rate Wine." *Wine Business Monthly,* December 15, 2004, www.winebusiness.com/ReferenceLibrary/webarticle.cfm?dataId=36264.

Tish, W. R. "Ten Reasons We All Lose When Numbers Dominate the Marketplace." *Wine Business Monthly,* December 15, 2004, www.winebusiness.com/salesmarketing/webarticle.cfm?dataId=36265.

Veseth, Michael. "Wine by the Numbers." American Association of Wine Economists, April 13, 2008, www.wine-econ.org/2008/04/13/wine-by-the-numbers.aspx.

RED WINE VERSUS WHITE WINE

Over most of the history of wine, the world's appetite has been mostly for red wine. This is undoubtedly due to the fact that until modern **temperature control** equipment became available, white wines—unless **fortified** or infused with preservatives such as pine resin or herbs—did not last very long before oxidizing. Red wines, although no one knew exactly why, did not oxidize as quickly, and their stronger flavors masked the off-odors even after they started to turn.

Once glass bottles, cork **closures**, and oak **barrels** came into use for wine, along with better sanitization and sulfur preservatives, white **table wines** began to be more competitive with reds, but tastes still ran toward red wines. As late as 1970, **consumers** in the **United States** were drinking 50 percent red to 25 percent white, the other 25 percent being **rosé**.

In the late 1970s, especially in the United States, a cultural shift took place, with society becoming more interested in an active lifestyle and **healthy** living, and white wine—with its often lower alcohol levels, cleaner appearance, and livelier taste—seemed to fit better into the social scene. As a result, white wine sales soared, leaving reds far behind. At the peak of this **fad** in 1985, white wines dominated reds 62 percent to 20 percent. Predictably, such a swing could not be sustained, and red wines slowly regained their popularity, helped considerably by the publicizing of the **French paradox**, showing that red wines were actually healthier for people than whites. Since 1999, the two categories have been almost equal. In the table wine category, Americans in 2006 drank 44.5 percent white, 43.4 percent red, and 12.1 percent rosé. Red wine is a clear favorite over white in most other countries of the world, however.

The major difference between red wines and white wines, besides color, is the skins. Red wines are made with them, whites without. The reason is that the chemical compounds that make the skins of red grapes (also often called black grapes, although their color can range anywhere from pink to red to purple to inky black) a different color from white grapes (which are really green) can endow a red wine with beneficial characteristics. White grapes, lacking many of these compounds, profit far less from skin contact and can, in fact, pick up unwanted flavors from too much of it.

Red grapes, and therefore red wines, contain much higher concentrations of *polyphenols* (also called *phenolics*) than their white or rosé counterparts. One important group of polyphenols is the *anthocyanins,* which are the substances that actually introduce the red, blue, and purple colors to both grape and wine. Another is *tannins,* which are largely responsible for the longevity of red wines. Polyphenols have been shown to have antioxidant properties—removing free radicals from the body—that may have significant health benefits, such as lowering the likelihood of coronary artery disease, colon cancer, and other diseases. Red grape skins also contain numerous flavor compounds that are fundamental to the enjoyment of a wine.

While white wines cannot match reds in these health claims based on polyphenols, both white and red wines by definition contain alcohol (ethanol), which also has many potential health benefits, along with a long list of potential risks for those who drink too much too often. Furthermore, many people find that crisp or fruity white wines are more pleasant for drinking on their own without food, and whites usually match better with lighter foods, such as fish, chicken, game fowl, and vegetarian fare, than reds do. And most sweet **dessert wines** are white. Thus, red and white both have a place, depending on the circumstances. *See also* Grape Growing; Varietal Labeling.

RELIGION

Wine, more than any other beverage, is connected with a long cultural heritage that bestows an intimate association with religious worship and celebratory ritual.

Ancient Religions.   The religious use of wine probably dates back to well before 4241 BC, the year that the Egyptians began marking time with a calendar. The Egyptians believed that wine was to be enjoyed not only in life but in the afterlife as well, and thus ancient tombs have been found to contain copious supplies of wine vases and whole vineyards decorously painted on the walls. The god Osiris and goddess Hathor were variously identified as the patrons of wine and were honored on a monthly "Day of Intoxication."

Wine, along with olive oil, provided the ancient **Greeks** with a precious export commodity that they could use to trade in the Mediterranean world. Wine became the focal point of Greek social life and was lavishly praised by Greek poets as the veritable fountain of civilized life and thought. The god Dionysos was hailed as the giver of all good gifts and the patron of wine. Dionysos was said to offer ecstasy, spiritual vision, and wild intoxication to his devotees, who would unite with him through ritual wine intoxication.

Other early religions developed mythical accounts of the creation of wine from the body of a primordial divine being. An Iranian legend, for example, recounts how wine originated from the blood of the ritual sacrifice of a primordial bull. Each year's crushing of grapes was thereby said to reenact this sacrificial slaughter, and the resulting wine was consequently thought capable of bestowing the bull's strength, energy, and vital force upon those who consumed it. This belief has its parallels in many other religions, not the least of which is Christianity's belief that those who drink sacramental wine take Christ's essential nature and his very blood within their own bodies.

Judaism.   Wine was not a luxury in **ancient Mediterranean** culture. It was a staple of everyday life, drunk by people of all classes and all ages. It is thus not surprising that wine permeates the Judeo-Christian cultural heritage. The Bible attributes to Noah the first cultivation of grapes and making of wine. After the Flood had receded and the inhabitants of the Ark had disembarked, Noah became "the first tiller of the soil. He planted a vineyard; and he drank of the wine, and became drunk" (Gen. 9:20). Jewish scripture goes on to depict wine as a sign of God's blessing (Gen. 27:28; Deut. 7:13; Zech. 9:17). What most commended wine to biblical writers was its ability to alter moods and to raise a person's spirits. Wine produces a "gladdening of the heart" that enriches human life (2 Sam. 13:28; Esther 1:10; Ps. 104:15; Eccles. 9:7).

To this day, Judaism considers wine to be a symbol of joy. Wine is almost always present when Jews celebrate family or religious events, such as weddings, the weekly Sabbath meal, Purim, or the annual Seder dinner that commemorates Passover. The traditional Jewish toast before drinking wine is "L'Chaim!" (To life!), expressing reverence for the sanctity of human life. In keeping with *kashrut*, the Jewish dietary laws, Orthodox Jews and many others drink only **kosher wines**.

Christianity.   Given the importance Jews place on wine, it is not at all surprising that the first public miracle performed by Jesus occurred at the wedding at Cana where he turned water into wine so that the celebration might continue (John 2:1–11). As a Mediterranean Jew, Jesus made the drinking of wine a central act in forging fellowship among his followers. The Christian sacrament of communion illustrates how fully the subtle pleasures of wine drinking were associated with the religious urge to find union with God.

Throughout the Middle Ages the Christian Church was the repository not only of reading and writing but also of the valued skills of winemaking. Parcels of land were bequeathed to Catholic **monasteries**, which in turn transformed them into some of Europe's most productive vineyards, providing the Church with its sacramental wine as well as enabling clergy to enjoy some of the benefits of luxury and comfort. Priests and monks perfected many of the fermentation and bottling techniques still used today. The most famous of all monk vignerons is undoubtedly the

Frenchman Dom Pérignon, whose skills as a cellarmaster remind us how fully the Christian tradition has promoted the production of **quality wines** both for the celebration of Mass and for daily living.

The intimate association of wine with religion carried over to the American colonies. The Pilgrims, for example, used wine to celebrate their first Thanksgiving in 1623. Protestants who shudder at the thought of drinking alcohol did not live in colonial New England. The Puritans embraced the mood-elevating properties of alcohol, as is exemplified in the Congregationalist preacher Increase Mather's remark that alcoholic drink is "a good creature of God." On North America's other coast, Father Juan Ugarte led a small group of Jesuit priests from Mexico into today's **California** as early as 1697. They immediately planted grapes so that they would have a reliable supply of wine for celebrating Communion. Missions were eventually built in San Diego, Los Angeles, Santa Barbara, Monterey, and San Francisco—becoming the nucleus of California's famed wine-producing regions.

Today, wine remains an integral part of the Catholic and Eastern Orthodox Mass, poured with every celebration of the rite, often daily, at parish churches, cathedrals, shrines, abbeys, and monasteries worldwide. Wine is also a feature of many Protestant Communion services, although these are typically held far less often, and in some denominations unfermented grape juice has been substituted for wine. Many Protestant sects frown on or actively oppose the consumption of alcohol, including wine, continuing the revivalists' drive against intoxication that led to America's experiment with **Prohibition** in the 1920s. The largest such group is the Southern Baptists, which is a large factor in the notably low per-capita wine consumption of the American South.

Other Major Religions.   Wine is absent in the world's second largest religion, Islam, owing to the Muslim ban on alcoholic beverages. However, the proscription of wine was not one of Muhammad's original concerns. The Quran speaks positively of wine, one verse praising it as one of the signs of Allah's grace unto humanity: "And of the fruit of palm trees, and of grapes, ye obtain an inebriating liquor, and also good nourishment." Another verse lists "rivers of wine, a joy to those who drink" as being among the pleasures the faithful might look forward to in paradise. However, Muhammad was later sufficiently outraged by the drunken excesses of his followers to condemn the drinking of wine. Commentaries on the Quran relate how Muhammad's companions held drinking parties that led to their failure to observe ritual prayer. A verse from the Quran made this prohibition explicit: "O true believers! Surely wine and gambling... are an abomination, of the work of Satan; therefore avoid them, that ye may prosper."

Although the use of intoxicants is forbidden within Buddhism, wine is closely connected with religious attitudes in most of **Asia**. In contemporary Japan, for example, rice wine (sake) is commonly placed on the family altar. Wine is intimately associated with rituals and ceremonies honoring the *kami,* or divine beings, and there are large casks of sake located at most of the major Shinto shrines. For the same reason, it is also present in Japanese wedding ceremonies for the toasts that the bride and groom make to one another and is used in ceremonies such as the dedication of a new home or building.

Throughout Chinese history, wine has been associated with religious offerings. Even today, wine is placed on altars in businesses or **restaurants** in honor of the god of prosperity or other protective deities. On Chinese New Year and other holidays, wine is offered to ancestors as a token of the indissoluble union of family ties. On the holiday known as the "Spring Sweeping of the Graves," wine is brought to the ancestral burial grounds and first offered to the spirits before being consumed by the living.

Robert C. Fuller

Further Reading

Adams, Leon. *The Wines of America*. Boston: McGraw-Hill, 1990.

Fuller, Robert C. *Religion and Wine: A Cultural History of Wine Drinking in the United States*. Knoxville: University of Tennessee Press, 1996.

Hyams, Edward. *Dionysus: A Social History of the Wine Vine*. New York: Macmillan, 1965.

Seward, Desmond. *Monks and Wine*. London: Mitchell Beazley, 1983.

RESTAURANTS

The on-premise trade has always been a key sector for the wine industry. From huge chains with hundreds of units that sell a handful of wines in massive quantities to white-tablecloth venues whose wine lists are dozens of pages long, the on-premise sector is frequently where most people taste a wine for the first time.

Almost all restaurants in the **United States** above the fast-food level carry wine, with a few exceptions such as locations in "dry" counties, operations too close to a church or school to get a license (local liquor laws differ), and those self-styled

Top 10 U.S. Restaurants Chains with Wine Programs, 2007

Rank among All Chains	Restaurant	Number of Units	Food & Beverage Sales ($ Billions)
11	Applebee's Neighborhood Grill and Bar	1,930	4.70
12	Chili's Bar & Grill	1,146	3.73
16	T.G.I. Friday's	854	3.05
17	Outback Steakhouse	948	3.03
19	Olive Garden	582	2.62
20	Red Lobster	682	2.58
30	Ruby Tuesday	926	1.75
35	The Cheesecake Factory	131	1.25
53	Romano's Macaroni Grill	237	0.78
55	P.F. Chang's China Bistro	152	0.76

Source: Restaurant & Institutions, www.rimag.com/info/CA6521551.html.

family restaurants that adhere to a post-**Prohibition** belief that wine does not belong at the table with children.

There were slightly more than a quarter-million on-premise outlets selling wine in the United States in 2006, according to the *Adams Wine Handbook 2007*. Collectively, they sold 63.8 million cases of wine, a six-million-case increase over the previous year and a figure that has been constantly on the rise since 1998. The on-premise sector has also been steadily increasing its share of total wine sales relative to off-premise **retailers**, according to Adams, reaching 50 percent of total wine dollar revenue in 2006.

According to the Washington, D.C.–based National Restaurant Association (NRA), wine continues to grow in popularity among all the full-service restaurant segments. The NRA's 2008 Restaurant Industry Forecast reported that 71 percent of fine-dining operators said their customers are ordering more wine by the glass than they were two years ago. Full-service operators across all segments also were more likely to indicate that domestic wine was growing in popularity compared with imported wine.

The NRA also conducted an Internet survey in October 2007 of 1,282 members of the American Culinary Foundation, asking them to rank food and beverage items as "hot," "passé," or "perennial favorite." **Organic wine** was ranked as hot by 60 percent of respondents, **red wine** by 43 percent, white wine by 37 percent, and **sparkling wine** by 27 percent. Only 17 percent of respondents ranked wine-and-food pairing and **sommeliers** as hot alcohol-related trends, one percentage point lower than beer-and-food pairing.

Branding and the Cash Cow.   The on-premise sector is where producers and **importers** generally try to introduce their high-end or allocated **brands**. Both major and boutique wine brands are acutely aware of the importance of placing their brands in top-ranked and well-respected restaurants. Many **cult** and low-production wines are sold only in the on-premise arena and often by a specially trained, separate sales staff. The continued focus on restaurants is driven by a concern that top wines could lose prestige if sold in low-end retail shops and **supermarkets**.

Wine has historically been among the most lucrative sales categories for restaurants, with markups generally running two and a half to three times the wholesale cost of the bottle. The more expensive the wine, the gentler the markup typically is. Wines by the glass are usually priced at the wholesale price per bottle, or that plus a dollar, the idea being to recoup the purchase price on the first glass. By comparison, spirits markups are similarly high, if not higher, while food markups have tended to run lower. A successful high-end restaurant will generally make approximately one-third of its **profits** from its beverage program, which includes wine, spirits, perhaps beer, and sometimes nonalcoholic drinks. Many restaurants and bars, due both to big markups and savvy wine buying, can attribute an even greater percentage of their revenues to their beverage programs.

The old system of markups is gradually changing with the influx of new restaurants aimed at wine lovers that offer a greater selection of well-priced wines. They are also offering innovative **promotions** on off-nights—for example, half-price on wines under a certain price, or a glass-and-a-half-size "carafe" pour—that help them sell more wine at a more advantageous price.

Top 10 Independent U.S. Restaurants for Wine Sales, 2007

Restaurant	Location	Food & Beverage Sales ($ Millions)
Tao Las Vegas	Las Vegas	66.6
Tavern on the Green	New York	37.6
Joe's Stone Crab	Miami	29.7
Smith & Wollensky	New York	28.7
Tao Asian Bistro	New York	26.8
Old Ebbitt Grill	Washington, D.C.	21.5
Gibsons Bar & Steakhouse	Chicago	20.8
Fulton's Crab House	Lake Buena Vista, Florida	20.7
SW Steakhouse	Las Vegas	20.5
Bob Chinn's Crab House	Wheeling, Illinois	20.4

Source: Restaurant & Institutions, www.rimag.com/article/CA6554058.html.

The mix of total restaurant wine sales, which used to rely heavily on by-the-glass sales, is steadily shifting to greater bottle sales in most types of establishments as **consumers** are drinking more, appreciating value, and being permitted to take home unfinished bottles in more and more states. On the other hand, most bars still reap the bulk of their sales from mixed drinks.

Allowing customers to bring their own wine can also generate a profit. Corkage fees—the charge for opening, providing stemware, and serving a patron's bottle—can range from $5 to $50, depending on the restaurant and the market. Some restaurants offer a no-corkage BYOB night to fill seats and increase revenue on traditionally slow nights such as Sunday or Monday. Most fine restaurants discourage customers from bringing their own wines, with exceptions being made for regular customers and those who bring, and share, exceptional bottles. Restaurants in wine-producing areas such as **California** and the Pacific Northwest tend to be more accepting of customers bringing their own wines.

Wine Lists.   All restaurants need to offer some well-known brands, varietals, and regions on their lists. Most sommeliers will then build out their list to support their favorite producers, work with their chefs' foods, and suit their price range. Some high-end restaurants seek out wines that they can carry exclusively, or buy only from **wineries** or importers with whom they have a relationship. This is why working the field continues to be essential for producers, importers, and **distributors**.

Chain restaurants, like hotels, may want to have all or a majority of their wine lists be identical in all markets. Sourcing wine for multiple locations in numerous states can be challenging, however. In the United States, all importers and producers are required to sell their products through a wholesaler, and no one wholesaler is yet a national presence. Although much **consolidation** is occurring, the country's largest distributor is in only slightly more than half the states. Each individual state functions as a separate division, so while the same company might carry a brand in multiple states, it is likely that the chain will have to deal with several different distributors of that brand to service all of its locations.

Food and beverage directors looking to create uniform wine lists, or core lists of brands that all outlets are mandated to carry, in multiple states have to choose from brands that are available nationally. Because relatively few brands are large enough to have distribution in so many states, this makes it quite difficult for small, low-production wines to gain access to a list at chain and even some smaller multiunit restaurants.

Buyers and Their Challenges.   Large chain restaurants generally have a corporate buyer who has a strong sense of what wines sell in the chain's outlets, knows what is distributed locally, and has established relationships with key wholesale partners. These buyers are primarily looking for nationally available brands, value, reliable delivery, and supplier support.

Smaller establishments, such as boutique hotels, may have an on-premise food and beverage manager and a sommelier, both of whom will have a say in choosing the wines for the list. They are often looking for unique wines to distinguish their establishment, a dependable wholesaler that will sell and deliver regularly in small quantities, and attention to service and detail.

At a single-unit restaurant, the general manager or chef may be responsible for the wine purchasing. In a small operation were everyone wears so many hats, the wine buyer may look to a small group of trusted local wholesalers and producers who understand the restaurant's style and food and can make suggestions that will fit well even if the buyer cannot taste through them all.

Restaurants of any size continue to face a number of business hurdles related to wine. Every professional in the restaurant business wants to make sure the wine being served was stored, delivered, and maintained in temperature-controlled conditions. Yet not all wholesalers have refrigerated delivery trucks, and not all restaurants have sufficient appropriate storage areas. Storage alone, climate controlled or not, is often a challenge for smaller operations.

Keeping by-the-glass wines fresh is also a continual challenge. Many restaurants gas or Vacu Vin their open bottles at the end of the day, and it is also common to record the date the bottle was opened.

Finally, personnel and training are potentially troublesome areas. Inexperienced servers, who are often not even of legal drinking age, may be unable to identify oxidative notes on wines or even corked wines. In the United States, they also tend not to view working in a restaurant as a full-time career, which can lead to frequent staff turnover. *See also* Hospitality Industry; Personnel; Wine Education.

Liza B. Zimmerman

Further Reading

Cheers. www.adamsbevgroup.com/magazines.asp.

National Restaurant Association. www.restaurant.com.

Nation's Restaurant News. www.nrn.com.

Restaurants & Institutions. www.rimag.com.

Santé. www.santemagazine.com.

Wine & Spirit. www.wine-spirit.com.
Wine Business Monthly. www.winebusiness.com.

RETAILERS

Retail sales, also known as off-premise sales, have been the backbone of the American wine industry for as long as alcohol sales have been legally allowed. When **Prohibition** was repealed in 1933, the federal government gave states the right to regulate the sale of alcohol within their borders. Many of the Prohibition-era laws still remain active in the United States, and the result is a national patchwork of conflicting laws determining where, when, and how **consumers** can buy wine and other alcoholic beverages.

The most notable of the Prohibition-era regulations is the still-obligatory "three-tier system," which requires that alcohol producers (the first tier) sell their goods to wholesalers (the second tier), who then **distribute** the product to retailers, **restaurants**, and other outlets (the third tier). Most states allow private companies to distribute and sell alcohol, but there are 18 **control states** that act as wholesalers and sometimes retailers of alcoholic beverages. The control is usually limited to spirits, however, and wine and beer are frequently more widely available.

With some exceptions, **wineries** must go through the three-tier system in order to get their wines to consumers. Off-premise retail is the largest wine sales channel in the **United States**, ahead of on-premise sales (restaurants, bars, the **hospitality industry**, and so forth) and direct-to-consumer sales from wineries (a channel available in most states, though some are excessively restrictive or have given access only to small wineries).

Segment Size.   The off-premise retail channel in the United States accounts for 75 to 80 percent of wine sales by volume and 50 to 60 percent by dollar value, according to research by the Nielsen Company, which tracks retail wine sales. For 2007, this equates to sales of 235 to 250 million cases (mc) worth $15 to $18 billion.

Nielsen's TDLinx division counted 149,486 U.S. off-premise sales locations in 2007, up 3.8 percent (5,495 stores) over 2006. Retailer types vary significantly in many ways, including their size, their variety (also called assortment) of wines available, and the consumer objectives of the store. The largest category is *convenience stores,* with 73,374 outlets in 2007, followed by *liquor stores,* with 39,306 sites. *Grocery stores* account for 26,280 wine sales locations, while 6,323 *drugstores* sell wine. *Mass merchandisers* sell wine at 1,990 locations, and there are 806 *club stores* with wine on their racks.

Even this does not tell the whole story, as Nielsen does not track all wine retailers. There are many more off-premise sales outlets than these figures reflect, including an unknown number of independent and high-end wine shops and Internet retailers. Many of these locations offer premium and luxury, small-production wines that cannot be found in larger outlets.

Retail Outlets.   Attitudes toward wine assortments are changing throughout the retail segment. Retailers recognize that the wine category is incredibly popular and offers steady growth even as other categories falter. Furthermore, retailers are interested in attracting the highly desirable wine consumers into their stores.

In states where it is legal to sell wine in the food, drug, and mass-market channels, wine is the 15th largest category in dollar sales (up from 21st in 2001) and is among the highest growth segments of any consumer goods product. Between 2006 and 2007, wine sales grew by 7.5 percent to reach a value of $5.3 billion—only four other categories grew more. Wine has also jumped above six categories it trailed in 2001, including pet food, ice cream, and cookies.

Many retail outlets have historically relied on volume sales of wines aimed at less-sophisticated wine consumers. The most popular wines sold at most retailers tend to be low-priced, large-format **brands**, such as five-liter boxes, 1.5-liter bottles, or wines priced at less than $8. The reasoning is due in large part to logistics. Individual stores in the largest retail segments are usually part of regional or national chains. Only mass-produced wines have enough volume to meet the demands of large retailers such as the Kroger Co.; SuperValu, Inc.; or 7-Eleven, Inc. Small premium- and luxury-priced brands are generally sold only by independent, dedicated wine retailers, where filling volume needs is less of a concern.

In mixed-goods retail environments such as **supermarkets**, mass merchandisers, and warehouse clubs, wine buyers spend much more than nonwine consumers. In a food store–specific analysis by Nielsen, the average customer basket size without wine was $38.13; with wine, the checkout total leapt to $68.52. And wine alone did not account for the $30 difference (Nielsen found the wine itself added an average of $13)—wine buyers were also more likely to purchase other premium products elsewhere in the store.

Retailers such as these feel that having a wine department enhances the store's image and appeal. Wine buyers are a large, affluent consumer segment that is likely to seek out a variety of wine products at different price points. Consumers have also recently trended toward higher-priced wines; in food, drug, and liquor stores, the highest growth rates by price segment are all $10 and above.

Within the grocery store channel, the subgroups showing the strongest growth in wine sales are the natural/gourmet stores and the limited-assortment segment. At natural/gourmet stores, wines are a natural fit. The top brands in these venues are vastly different from most other large retail categories. Nine of the top 10 brands in 2006 did not appear in the top 10 wines of any other large channel. These wines are generally from premium, mid-priced brands, and many are made with **organic** or **sustainable** practices. Limited-assortment outlets, on the other hand, are succeeding for a far different reason. These discount chains are aimed at budget-conscious consumers willing to forgo some variety for the sake of cost, including in their wine choices.

In response to the American consumer's newfound wine affinity, some retailers have focused on offering higher-quality (and usually higher-priced) wines in a more intimate and personalized environment. California-based Safeway, Inc., for example, has remodeled many stores' wine departments to make the section more inviting. Physical changes—such as wooden shelves, soft lighting, and stylish floors—differentiate the section from the rest of the store. Cultural changes, such as offering wine tastings and hiring in-store wine stewards, are giving supermarket shoppers the hands-on experience they might normally expect only from an exclusive wine shop.

Two Notable Retailers.   Costco Wholesale Corporation, a warehouse store that claims to be the largest wine retailer in the United States, has a unique approach to its wine program. First, there is a core set of well-priced wines that can generally be found at every Costco location. The company also maintains a fine wine program that is designed to cater to local preferences by offering lower-volume, higher-quality wine choices. Costco's regional buyers are given full control over wine assortments in their stores and can offer as little as a single case of wine in one store location. These buyers develop strong relationships with **importers**, distributors, and wineries, giving them access to wines that may not be available to other retailers. Because the fine wine program is based more on quality than quantity, the assortment changes frequently.

One of the most unique wine retailers in the United States right now is the Wine Library, a New Jersey–based wine store that has grown its business using the unique personality of principal Gary Vaynerchuk to take advantage of Internet-based opportunities. Vaynerchuk hosts a daily Internet show at www.TV.WineLibrary.com, tasting wines that are available on the store's Web site and at its retail location. The show attracts more than 60,000 viewers per day and has earned Vaynerchuk attention from popular talk shows, news programs, and magazines.

Internet Retailing.   Vaynerchuk's success underscores the changing retail landscape. Many brick-and-mortar wine shops or small chains are moving to a business model mixing on-site and online sales. A limited number of states allow retailers to ship wine directly to consumers, at least within state lines. An industry lobbying organization called the Specialty Wine Retailers Association was formed in 2006 to protect and expand these laws. Retailers have many of the same issues with **direct shipping** that wineries had prior to the 2005 *Granholm v. Heald* Supreme Court ruling, which found that states could not discriminate against out-of-state wineries with regard to in-state wine deliveries. Despite the lobbying group's efforts, retailers have also had mixed results in lawsuits trying to extend the *Granholm* decision to wine merchants.

Though complicated laws restrict some **e-commerce**, savvy retailers can navigate through the legal compliance issues to establish a strong Web presence in addition to their physical location. While direct sales may be on the horizon for large grocery chains, that segment has so far largely ignored Internet wine sales opportunities.

Mary-Colleen Tinney

Further Reading
Beverage Dynamics. www.adamsbevgroup.com/magazines.asp.
Harper's. www.talkingdrinks.com.
Wine Business International. www.wine-business-international.com.
Wine Business Monthly. www.winebusiness.com.

RIESLING

The Riesling grape, with its long history, its extraordinary ability to reflect the **terroir** where it is grown, and its capacity to age and develop well beyond what its deceptively precocious youth would suggest, has earned its spot as one of the world's great wine grapes. Riesling's fortunes have waxed and waned over time as economic conditions and **consumer** tastes have changed. There is seemingly a disconnect between its prestigious position as a great wine grape (often considered one of the top three or four most important white varieties) and the kind of broad appeal and mass popularity of other highly regarded grapes, such as **Chardonnay**, **Sauvignon Blanc**, and **Cabernet Sauvignon**. While it may be on the rise, Riesling is still somewhat of a niche player.

Also known as White Riesling, Weisser Riesling, Johannisberg Riesling, and Rhine or Rhein Riesling, this variety is a cold- and frost-resistant and early-ripening grape. It has high natural acidity, but in warm climates it can ripen so early that it loses its acidity. These characteristics make it a natural match for cooler regions, notably Germany, Alsace, and **Austria**, where harvest can extend into October and November, and even later for select sweet wines. Riesling has tight bunches of small berries and as a result is susceptible to botrytis. While this presents problems with regard to managing the grape in the field, it is also responsible for some of the world's best sweet **dessert wines**.

Riesling is generally produced as a monovarietal and is rarely made in a style where oak plays a major role. Cool fermentation in stainless steel or larger neutral wood is the norm. It has an excellent ability to convey the characteristics of the terroir where it is grown, with soil and climate conditions captured and expressed in differences of aromas and flavor that are noticeable, albeit sometimes subtle. Its naturally high acidity and extract are cited as playing a role in its ability to age and develop so well, and the acidity is also important in the raciness of its dry versions and for creating balance in its sweeter styles, allowing them to carry their high residual sugars while remaining fresh and lively on the palate.

Regions. Germany is the largest grower of Riesling, with 60 percent of all plantings worldwide—about 52,000 acres of some 86,000 acres total. It is planted in most German wine regions and is produced in nearly every style, including **sparkling** Sekt. The sweet versions are typically in the QbA (*Qualitätswein bestimmer Anbaugebeite*) or higher *Prädikatswein* **quality wine** category. Dry Riesling is on the rise in Germany, driven by domestic and international demand. *Trocken* and *halbtrocken* ("dry" and "half-dry," respectively) Rieslings are up from 16 percent of total production in 1990 to 28 percent in 2006. Requirements for trocken wines are based on capping the maximum amount of residual sugar in the wine, measured in relationship to total acidity. Trocken wines are generally several degrees higher in alcohol than their sweet counterparts because more of the sugars have been converted during fermentation.

Riesling was planted throughout **Germany** in the Middle Ages, and by the late 1800s, it was as highly sought after and as popular and expensive as the top **red wines** from **France**. During the twentieth century, the grape lost ground to earlier-ripening and more easily grown varieties; in the 1930s, the Rheingau was planted only 57 percent to Riesling compared to 78 percent today. Riesling's fortunes continue to fluctuate, but there are encouraging signs. Its plantings increased from 19.7 percent of total vineyard area in Germany in 1980 to 21.3 percent in 2007, a period when total white wine-grape plantings were falling relative to red. During this time, it traded positions with Müller-Thurgau to become the most widely planted grape in Germany. The Deutsches Weininstitut reports that demand for German Riesling in the **United States** resulted in a 10 percent increase in value and a 2 percent increase in volume of exports in 2007 over 2006 and describes the U.S. market as dynamic.

Elsewhere in Europe, Alsace in France is another major producer of Riesling with a long history and a reputation for high quality. It is the most widely planted grape in Alsace at more than 20 percent of the total plantings, 8,500 acres in 2006. Most Riesling in Alsace is dry, ranging from minerally and steely to lush and weighty. The late-harvest Vendange Tardive and Sélection de Grains Nobles designations are the exceptions and have considerable sweetness. Austria also has a very good reputation for Riesling given its relatively small area planted of 4,000 acres, representing less than 3 percent of its total vineyard area. Austrian Rieslings are mainly made in a dry style. In addition, **Italy** and several countries in **Eastern Europe** have plantings of Riesling.

In the **New World**, **Australian** Riesling has lost ground in the recent past, being overtaken by Chardonnay in 1992 and other grapes since, and it is best known for the dry styles produced in Clare and Eden valleys. Total acreage has been in transition, with just over 10,000 acres in 2006. **New Zealand** is a relatively minor player with 2,200 acres of Riesling in 2006, but it has several areas showing promise due to favorable climate and soil conditions.

On the North American continent, Riesling is grown in many U.S. states, as well as in **Canada**. **Washington** has the most, with 4,400 acres planted and more going in; given its northerly latitude and cooler climate, the variety shows signs of promise and expansion here. **California** has grown Riesling since the late nineteenth century, but today it is a small percentage of the total, with only about 2,200 acres planted. However, since 2000, there has been a noticeable resurgence, with tons crushed rising by 46 percent. Acreage in other states is minimal. Canada, although relatively new to the business, has shown promise with Riesling, especially for ice wine.

Outlook.   Riesling sales have shown dramatic improvement in the United States, with Nielsen data indicating that the variety doubled in sales between 2006 and 2008. Yet while Riesling seems to be coming back into vogue, it still has a number of issues that play a role in keeping this great wine grape from being more widely embraced. Difficulty in communicating levels of sweetness and style, complex and ever-changing wine laws, confusing labeling, and the associations made between Riesling and inexpensive mass-produced sweet wines all play a role. The preference for dry wines as the current fashion may hurt Riesling in some ways, but at the same time open the door for continued growth in the dry styles.

There are continued efforts to **promote** and increase consumer awareness for Riesling. Specialty **importers** such as Terry Theise and Rudi Wiest in the United States have been tireless promoters and have met with success in their market. Riesling's versatility with a wide range of cuisines makes it a favorite of restaurateurs, **sommeliers**, and **retailers**, even if they often have to lead their clients to the wines by the hand. There are a number of organizations that are engaged in the promotion of Riesling as well, including the Deutsches Weininstitut (www.deutscheweine.de), the newly formed International Riesling Foundation, and grower organizations such as the VdP (Verband Deutscher Prädikatsweingüter), including the Grosser Ring and Charta, which impose winemaking standards that are stricter than the existing laws in the interest of producing the finest wines possible.

Riesling's future success will in large part depend on the consumer and, in turn, will require finding a way to communicate its unique and individual style, sweetness level, and sense of place efficiently, without making it too complex and at the same time without making it so simple as to become meaningless.

Christopher Cree

Further Reading
Price, Freddy. *Riesling Renaissance*. London: Mitchell Beazley, 2004.

ROBINSON, JANCIS (1950–)

Jancis Robinson is a prolific wine author, critic, judge, and educator, perhaps best known in Britain as wine columnist for the *Financial Times* and worldwide for editing the definitive wine reference, *The Oxford Companion to Wine,* now in its third edition (2006). She has more than a dozen other books to her credit, including *Jancis Robinson's Wine Course* (rev. 2nd ed., 2006), *Jancis Robinson's Guide to Wine Grapes* (1996), and with **Hugh Johnson**, the latest version of *The World Atlas of Wine* (6th ed., 2007). She has also hosted numerous television and radio programs and has an informative and continuously updated Web site, www.jancisrobinson.com. Robinson is highly regarded for her scholarship and approachable writing style. She earned her Master of Wine in 1984 and was awarded the Order of the British Empire in 2003.

ROSÉ

Whether called pink, rosado, rosato, Weissherbst, chiaretto, blush, or even ''white,'' rosé wines are a popular transitional category between white and **red wines**. They are prized by aficionados for their white-like crispness and refreshing quality and their extra layer of flavor from the red side of the equation, as well as for their beautiful color. For many red wine lovers who cannot bring themselves to drink white, rosés fill the need for a lighter, more revitalizing wine during the hot days of summer. Dry rosés can act as an intermediate step for the white wine drinker moving toward red wines, and the sweeter versions often represent an entry-level drink for people who are first learning to appreciate wine.

Rosés are made, at least for local consumption, almost everywhere red wine is made. There are many ways to make a pink wine, but the most traditional and generally most successful way is by following the usual red winemaking process until shortly after fermentation has begun and then separating the skins from the juice and finishing the fermentation like a white wine. This allows only a fraction of the pigmented compounds from the red grape skins to leach out into the juice, giving it a distinctive but light touch of color. Depending on the length of skin contact and the grape variety involved, the resulting wine can be anywhere from a pale salmon hue to a bright, transparent ruby red. Because most flavor compounds are found in the skins as well, the depth of flavor in the wine will roughly match the depth of color.

The other primary method for making a rosé is by blending red and white wine, although this is not permitted everywhere. It is also possible to make a pale rosé by vinifying a *tenturier*, such as Alicante Bouschet, a grape variety that has some color in the pulpy flesh of the grape.

In some instances, the rosé wine may be merely a by-product of the winery's procedures for extracting the maximum color in its red wines. Some quantity of juice may be drained off red wine during the early stages of maceration or fermentation to increase the ratio of skins to juice and produce a deep red wine. The juice taken off the skins will have some color and can be used to make a rosé.

Because rosés are made from ripe grapes in essentially the same way as a white wine, the alcohol levels usually average between 11 and 13 percent, depending on the climate. The minimal skin contact ensures very low levels of tannin. Sweetness varies from completely dry to semisweet; this difference is not always apparent from the label, although the terms *blush* and *white*—as in "white **Merlot**"—are usually reserved for the sweeter styles.

Rosés are made in many European wine regions and are the specialty of some **appellations**. Tavel and Bandol in the south of **France**, for example, are well known for their rosés, as is the central Loire Valley. **Spain** and **Italy** also produce substantial quantities of rosé wines. In most cases, European rosés are fermented dry, and they may include any of the red grapes grown in the region of production. Grenache, Mourvèdre, **Syrah**, and **Cabernet Sauvignon** are some of the better-known varieties used, but the list is quite long.

Rosé **sparkling wines** are also fairly widespread, although they represent only a small fraction of the sparkling wine market (although if Blanc de Noirs, which often has a slight tinge of pink color, is included, the proportion is more significant). Given the celebratory and romantic reputation of sparkling wine, rosés are considered by many to be the height of fashion, and rosé **Champagnes** can be among the most expensive and sought-after styles. Although many white sparkling wines contain some portion of red grapes, the rosé versions are generally made by blending still red wine into the base wine before the second fermentation. This is one of the few instances in Europe where this is permitted. In Champagne and similar wines, the red grapes are **Pinot Noir** and Pinot Meunier; in Cava, Pinot Noir and Garnacha (Grenache).

In the **New World**, rosés are more likely to be semisweet, although dry rosés are becoming more widespread. Rosés are usually either **varietally labeled** with a well-known red grape variety or simply called "Blush." Blush wines in three-liter bottles or five-liter boxes are among the best sellers in the economy price tier. The blush category was created when **Zinfandel** growers in California's Sierra Foothills region needed a market for their grapes in the days when white wines were all the rage in the 1970s. The resulting "white Zinfandel," created and still dominated by Sutter Home Winery, became a huge force in the U.S. market that remains significant today.

By the 1980s, blush/rosé had carved out a 25 percent share of the U.S. market for itself, slowly rising to its peak of 32 percent in 1990. Since then, according to *Impact,* the category has been in decline, but it still registered around

12 percent of all table wine sales in 2006. Most of this is of the sweeter blush variety, with white Zinfandel alone accounting for 8 percent of U.S. **table wine** sales; 97 percent of rosé wine consumption in the United States is domestic.

Despite—or perhaps because of—the popularity of the sweet blush style, many **consumers** who consider themselves serious wine drinkers have tended to shun not only blush but all rosé wines, yet this group is starting to realize the merits of the dry style. Coupled with the white Zinfandel drinkers who are easing their way toward appreciating red wines, dry rosés have begun to see greater interest and acceptance, as evidenced by solid growth in the thin sliver of the U.S. pie claimed by imported rosés—in the range of 30 percent a year for the past few years. At the same time, the **British market** has seen rosé sales shoot from next to nothing up to around 6 percent of total sales. In France, rosé is one of the few categories of wine that is increasing in sales, reaching almost 12 million cases annually.

The convergence of trends favoring dry wines, moderate alcohol, **healthy** anthocyanins, and new alternatives to the usual wine offerings bodes well for continued increases in market share. Dry rosé is hot, and growth in the sector should remain strong for some time to come. *See also* Must and Wine Adjustments; Trinchero Family Estates.

S

SAUVIGNON BLANC

Sauvignon Blanc is one of the great white wine grape varieties, often overshadowed by the less temperamental **Chardonnay** and temporarily challenged by the upstart **Pinot Grigio**, but among the two or three favorite white wines of most **consumers**. Sauvignon Blanc has the advantage of providing more depth of flavor than either of those competitors, while providing more range of flavor than **Riesling**. Thus, it is one of the international varieties that is grown in most wine-producing countries and has many devotees worldwide.

Sauvignon Blanc—sometimes called simply Sauvignon—originated in **France**, where it is closely associated with two regions. The variety is the primary white grape of the southwest corner of France, including **Bordeaux**. There, it is the junior partner of Sémillon in the great sweet **dessert wines** of Sauternes and Barsac, among other similar botrytis-elevated wines. However, it takes the starring role in the dry white wines of Bordeaux, such as Pessac-Léognan, Graves, and Entre-Deux-Mers, as well as many other whites of Southwest **appellations**. The other French bastion of Sauvignon Blanc is in the Loire Valley, especially its upper reaches in central France. It can be found in Touraine and other districts farther downriver, but it is most famous in Pouilly-Fumé and Sancerre, which many consider the highest expressions of Sauvignon Blanc.

There are 62,200 acres of Sauvignon Blanc vines planted in France—17,000 in the Loire, 15,700 in Languedoc-Roussillon, 12,400 in Bordeaux, and the rest mainly scattered throughout the south and southwest. This represents about a quarter of the Sauvignon Blanc planted worldwide. The wines of Sancerre and Pouilly-Fumé are noted for their austere, mineral-slate character, while those of Bordeaux and the south tend to be somewhat richer with more citrus flavors, but still with high acidity.

Since leaving its homeland, Sauvignon Blanc has traveled widely around the globe, settling in many places. Interestingly, the country that has become most closely identified with the variety in recent years could not be any farther from France: **New Zealand**. In the late 1980s, Sauvignon Blanc was recognized as one of the most promising grapes in New Zealand and Cloudy Bay's Sauvignon Blanc made a big splash internationally, especially in the **British market**. Over the past decade, New Zealand and Sauvignon Blanc have become almost synonymous to many wine lovers, and by 2002, Sauvignon Blanc had moved ahead of Chardonnay as the country's primary grape variety; it now takes up more than 26,000 acres, or about 41 percent of all vineyard land in New Zealand. Here, it makes a much different wine from any French version; in fact, its combination of grapefruit, gooseberry, and tropical fruit is quite distinct from Sauvignon from anywhere else.

The global acreage devoted to Sauvignon Blanc could now exceed 200,000 acres. Apart from France, the variety is not prominent in Europe except in **Italy**'s Alto Adige and in **Eastern Europe**, where there may be as much as 40,000 acres. In the **New World**, besides New Zealand, Sauvignon Blanc is important in **South Africa** and **Chile**, both with about 21,000 acres; the **United States**, with 14,400 acres in **California** and another 1,000 acres in **Washington**; and **Australia**, with almost 10,000 acres. Wines from any of these countries can range from insipid—when overcropped or overripe—to exciting, often with grassy, herbaceous aromas and moderate acidity. Sauvignon Blanc is occasionally oaked like a Chardonnay, but it does not blend its flavors nearly as well with the oak's vanillins.

Sauvignon Blanc was the seventh most purchased **table wine** variety in the United States in 2006. U.S. sales of Sauvignon Blanc wines amounted to around 8.4 million nine-liter cases (mc), including white Bordeaux and other nonvarietally labeled French Sauvignon Blancs, giving it a 9 percent market share among white varieties, according to *Impact*. Imports accounted for 1.6 mc of this total, with 1.4 mc of the imports coming from New Zealand.

Further Reading

Atkins, Susy. *Sauvignon Blanc: A Complete Guide to the Grape and the Wines It Produces.* London: Mitchell Beazley, 2003.

SCANDINAVIAN MARKET

The four Nordic countries Sweden, Denmark, Finland, and Norway are often considered a single market, although the differences among them are quite large. While Denmark is a free market, the others are dominated by state monopolies responsible for all **retail** sales. There are companies active in more than one market, but only one mayor player, V&S Group (now owned by Pernod Ricard), is working in all four markets.

The structure of all three monopoly markets is the same. Wines are offered to the monopolies through local **importers** in response to tenders sent out from the monopoly. Wines are selected after a blind tasting, and a fixed margin based on the purchase price is added by the monopoly, making the pricing structure of these markets highly transparent. The purchasing procedure makes entry into the monopolies' shelves extremely difficult, but once there, the opportunities of gaining high sales volumes are very good.

Per-capita consumption of wine is steadily increasing in the three monopoly markets. The Danish market is more stable, but also has the highest rate. In fact, with over 44 liters per adult consumed, Denmark has the highest figure of any non-wine-producing country in the world. Finland has the lowest consumption of the three monopolies, with 18 liters per adult.

In volume terms, Sweden has the largest market and the largest growth, equating to 16.4 million nine-liter cases (mc) of **table wine** in off-premise retail in 2007, up 5.7 percent from 2006. Denmark is next at 11.6 mc, followed by Norway (6.3 mc) and Finland (5.4 mc). On-premise sales figures are not as easily obtained as the off-trade figures, but **restaurants** and bars represent a comparatively small fraction of total sales in most of the countries. This segment represents 21 percent in Denmark, but it is just 13 percent in Norway and not more than 10 percent in Sweden and Finland.

All the Scandinavian countries show a dominance of **red wine**, which represents more than 70 percent of the total table wine sales in Denmark and Norway, although a more modest 54 percent in Finland and 61 percent in Sweden. The major trading partners differ between the markets. While Denmark and Norway are more traditional, with **France** as the most popular country of origin, Finland and Sweden are more oriented toward the **New World**, with **Chile** and **Australia** the most popular.

Sparkling wine is growing faster than any other wine category, showing two-digit growth in all countries. In Denmark, the growth was over 25 percent in 2007, while the figures for Finland, Sweden, and Norway were 20 percent, 15 percent, and 14 percent, respectively.

Characteristic for all markets is an unusually high market share for wines in **alternative packaging**, such as bag-in-box and to some extent Tetra. In Sweden, 55 percent of all wine sold is bag-in-box; with Tetras selling another 9 percent, little more than a third is sold in bottles. The market share for bag-in-box is increasing fast in the other countries as well and is now 52 percent in Norway, 33 percent in Finland, and 25 percent in Denmark. Many wine producers, such as Australian market leader **Foster's**, are now producing boxes exclusively for the Scandinavian markets.

Ulf Sjödin

Further Reading
Alko (Finnish monopoly). www.alko.fi.
Systembolaget (Swedish monopoly). www.systembolaget.se.
Vinmonopolet (Norwegian monopoly). www.vinmonopolet.no.

SHANKEN COMMUNICATIONS

M. Shanken Communications, Inc., the publishing group of Marvin Shanken, includes the leading **consumer** wine magazine in the **United States** and two of the alcohol beverage industries' leading trade publications. Shanken is the CEO and publisher, and the company's headquarters are in New York City.

The *Wine Spectator* is the most widely read U.S. wine magazine, with paid subscriptions in the 400,000 range and total readership estimated at more than 2 million. *Wine Spectator* **ratings** and reviews are highly influential among wine buyers and consumers, and **retailers** routinely cite them in shelf talkers and advertising. The magazine was founded in 1976 and purchased by Shanken in 1979; the online version Winespectator.com was inaugurated in 1996.

Impact and *Market Watch* are trade publications for the wine, beer, and spirits industries. Shanken also publishes *Food Arts,* a trade magazine for **restaurants** and the **hospitality industry**, as well as *Cigar Aficionado.*

SHIRAZ.   *See* Syrah/Shiraz

SOMMELIERS

The rough translation of the French term *sommelier* is one who performs wine service in a **restaurant**. The profession developed in parallel with the first true restaurants in Paris in the late eighteenth century. At that time, it was the sommelier's role to know the restaurant's wine cellar and cuisine intimately and to help diners select the best possible wine to pair with the menu and the diners' tastes. The sommelier would then open, taste, and serve the bottle to his guests. Eventually, the sommelier's responsibilities grew as wine lists were created, allowing customers to make their own choices. But the sommelier's role remained essentially the same, as few patrons were well enough informed to choose ideal wines independently.

Today, restaurants are becoming increasingly casual, and the formal dining establishments of old have practically disappeared. Many restaurants that do have a wine program have chosen not to employ a sommelier, thus placing the onus of wine selection on the customer with a greater or lesser degree of assistance from the server. But there is a resurgence of upscale restaurants that have large wine cellars and extensive wine lists. These establishments usually employ a sommelier, whose responsibilities include not only maintaining the cellar and serving the guest but also stocking the bar inventory and every other beverage the restaurant offers. This new generation is also entrusted with the education of the restaurant's waitstaff in wine service, the wines of the list, spirits, and food-and-wine pairing. Thus the actual time spent on the floor selling wine to guests is but a fraction of the overall responsibilities of the modern sommelier. In that context, less than 1 percent of restaurants today have true sommeliers, even though a talented sommelier can add hundreds of thousands of dollars in sales to the bottom line of a restaurant with a fine wine program.

Becoming a sommelier requires extensive **wine education**, knowledge of restaurant operations, and considerable time spent working the floor of fine dining establishments. This expertise comes from concentrated studies and certification programs, as well as years of on-the-job experience. While there are no restrictions on who can call themselves sommeliers, there are several organizations that offer training and certification for those seeking a career as professional sommeliers. The leading organization is the Court of Master Sommeliers, based in the United Kingdom. Its program offers four levels of instruction and examinations: the Introductory Sommelier Course, the Certified Sommelier Examination, the Advanced Sommelier Course and Examination, and the Master Sommelier (MS) Diploma. There are currently 136 Master Sommeliers in the world, with 94 in the **United States**. Other American sommelier organizations include the International Sommelier Guild and the American Sommelier Association.

With increasing wine consumption in the United States over the last few years, more restaurants are expanding their wine lists and wine-by-the-glass programs, necessitating the staffing of dedicated sommeliers. This is a trend that will continue with increased **consumer** awareness of wine and wine's integral part in the fine dining experience, and thus the role of professional sommeliers will continue to grow in importance and influence.

Tim Gaiser

Further Reading

Julyan, Brian. *Sales and Service for the Wine Professional*. 3rd ed. London: Cengage Learning EMEA, 2008.
Sommelier Journal. www.sommelierjournal.com.

SONOMA COUNTY

Sonoma County, **California**, is regarded as one of the world's premier wine regions. It is known for the large diversity of grapes grown within its borders and for its high-quality wines. Russian settlers in Fort Ross planted the county's first wine grapes soon after 1812, but **grape growing** really began in earnest when Spanish missionaries arrived in 1823 and planted vineyards a year later at the Mission San Francisco Solano in what is today the town of Sonoma. These original vineyards provided the cuttings used by Gen. Mariano G. Vallejo and other early settlers to start many new vineyards. By the time California became a part of the **United States** in 1850, grape growing and winemaking within the county were flourishing.

However, it was a Hungarian self-proclaimed count, Agoston Haraszthy, "the Father of California Wine Industry," who put Sonoma County on the path to becoming a premier wine region. Sent by state legislators, Haraszthy traveled through Europe collecting grape cuttings and returned with more than 100,000 from 300 French, German, Italian, and Spanish varieties. Many plants grown from these cuttings eventually found their way into vineyards across the state. Haraszthy is also credited with starting the state's first premium **winery** in 1857, Buena Vista Winery, which still exists today (as Buena Vista Carneros Winery) as the longest-operating winery in California. Immigrants from **Italy** and **Germany** continued to arrive in Sonoma County in the latter half of the nineteenth century, bringing their winemaking traditions with them. Many current wineries, such as Foppiano Vineyards, Gundlach Bundschu Winery, Sebastiani Vineyards & Winery, Seghesio Family Vineyards, and Simi Winery, trace their origins to these early settlers.

Even though **phylloxera** wiped out many vineyards in the 1870s, they were quickly replanted on rootstocks, and by 1920, the wine industry in Sonoma County was thriving. **Prohibition** soon thereafter closed down most of county's wineries, leaving only a few who made wine for religious purposes, although grape growers prospered during this time by selling grapes to home winemakers. The revival of the wine industry after Repeal was a slow process, but by the 1970s, renewed investment in vineyards and wine technology stimulated the growth that led Sonoma County to become a leader in the premium wine segment.

From these beginnings, Sonoma County has emerged as an important area for grape cultivation. As of 2006, 60,300 acres, about 5.7 percent of available land in Sonoma County, was planted to wine grapes. **Chardonnay** is the primary variety, with 15,800 acres, followed by **Cabernet Sauvignon** with 12,100 acres and **Pinot Noir** with 11,000. **Merlot**, **Zinfandel**, **Sauvignon Blanc**, and many other varieties are also planted in the county. The total crush in 2006 was 233,000 tons—60 percent red and 40 percent white—worth $430 million.

Today there are more than 350 wineries located within Sonoma County, annually producing more than 30 million gallons of wine, the equivalent of 12.6 million cases, or a little more than 6 percent of the total for the state. Revenues in 2005 were close to $2.5 billion, and wine contributed more than $8.2 billion to the local economy.

The primary factor that distinguishes Sonoma County from many other viticulture regions is its compelling diversity. Sonoma County's bucolic geography features inland valleys, wetlands, rolling hillsides, and mountain ranges. Water plays a vital role in shaping the many microclimates, as the Pacific Ocean, the Russian River, and San Pablo Bay wield a mighty influence on the weather. An abundance of distinct soil types and various growing conditions provide near-perfect conditions for the many varieties of wine grapes that are grown.

As well as belonging to the North Coast American Viticultural Area (AVA), Sonoma County is home to an additional 13 AVAs. While many grape varieties are grown in each of these AVAs, the warmer areas of Alexander Valley, Knights Valley, and Sonoma Valley are known for their Cabernet Sauvignon, Merlot, and Sangiovese. In the cooler regions of Green Valley, Russian River Valley, Carneros, and Sonoma Coast, Chardonnay and Pinot Noir thrive. Dry Creek Valley and Rockpile have earned a reputation for their exceptional Zinfandel wines.

A group of prominent trade associations, such as the Sonoma County Vintners, Sonoma County Winegrape Commission, Sonoma Valley Vintners & Growers Alliance, Russian River Wine Road, and others representing the various AVAs, support the marketing of Sonoma County wines. While each group's mission varies slightly, the overriding goal of these groups is to build awareness for Sonoma County wines and enhance the prestige of the Sonoma name, which they do by organizing and promoting wine **festivals** and events, attending trade shows, and developing promotional materials to support their members.

Janeen Olsen

Further Reading
Sonoma County Vintners. www.sonomawine.com.
Sonoma County Winegrape Commission. www.sonomawinegrape.org.

SOUTH AFRICA

South Africa is a relative newcomer to the international wine trade, but has the potential for tremendous growth if the country's producers can band together the way **Australia**'s have to pursue an export strategy. The country is already the eighth largest wine-producing nation, with an output of 9.4 million hectoliters, or 104 million cases (mc), in 2006.

Despite its newcomer status, South Africa is arguably the most senior of the **New World** countries, having had a commercial wine industry for more than four hundred years. However, for most of that time, it has been a relatively closed market. When the industry first developed in the seventeenth century during the **colonial era**, South Africa served as a victualing stop for trade ships traveling around the tip of Africa between Europe and the ports of the Orient, and a small export business with the **Dutch market** developed, built mainly around sweet **fortified** and **dessert** wines, including the famous Constantia. The economics of exporting wine at such a distance from potential markets (with intense competition much closer to them) were unfavorable, though, and South African winemaking instead focused on supplying the Dutch and English colonists locally.

Years later, when exporting over long distances became more commonplace, South Africa found itself disconnected from the outside world, being shunned for its apartheid racial policies, and thus was unable to join other New World countries that were making their mark in the **global wine industry**. Only after the transfer of power to multiracial democratic rule and the end of apartheid in the early 1990s did South Africa have the opportunity to compete, but having been untouched by competition for so long, its wines were not up to international standards. To remedy this, the South African winegrowers initiated a radical program to update their industry. A huge replanting scheme replaced the majority of mediocre grape varieties with international varieties, and **wineries** received new equipment and technical expertise from abroad that had not been available to them before. The results have been nothing short of stunning, and South Africa is quickly gaining recognition and respect among **consumers** around the world.

The South African wine industry is based in the south and west of the country, which is drier than the eastern parts. The first vineyards were planted in Cape Town, but as that area became more urbanized, they were planted farther afield, first in Paarl and Stellenbosch and later in the Breede River Valley, Olifants River, and Klein Karoo. The more recent developments have been along the southern coast at such places as Walker Bay and Cape Agulhas, where cool-climate grapes thrive. The Wine of Origin (WO) system, which has been in place since 1973, designates geographical indications for production and labeling purposes. It currently lists (in order of decreasing size) 5 regions, 21 districts, and 56 wards.

South Africa's vineyard area has been increasing steadily for two decades. As of 2007, the country had 311,000 acres under vine, including 252,000 acres of wine grapes, a 17 percent increase from 10 years earlier. This fails to show the scale of the upheaval that has taken place, however. In the 1997–2007 time frame, more than 110,000 acres of less desirable grape varieties were uprooted and replaced by international varieties, changing the entire complexion of the industry. Some 53 percent of the vines are now less than 10 years old. Until 2004, most of the new vines were red varieties, but the pendulum has now swung back the other way and whites represent three-quarters of the newest plantings.

White wines account for about 70 percent of South Africa's 104-mc output. The largest production is of Colombar (**California**'s "French Colombard"), which alone is almost one-fourth of the country's wine volume; it is used for blending, **distillation**, and locally for a light white wine. The other high-volume variety, at 21 percent of production, is Chenin Blanc, locally known as Steen, which is South Africa's most widely planted variety. For exports, the more important varieties are the international favorites, including **Cabernet Sauvignon** (approximately 7.2 mc produced annually), Shiraz (**Syrah**; 6.6 mc), **Chardonnay** (6.4 mc), **Sauvignon Blanc** (6.2 mc), and **Merlot** (5.0 mc). In addition, South Africa produces around 4.7 mc of its unique Pinotage variety.

Domestic consumption amounts to about 35 mc per year, and that is expected to rise slowly as consumption increases in the townships, where the formerly disenfranchised black population is getting better access to wine than in the past. Imports into South Africa total 3 mc or less, almost all of which is **bulk wine**.

With output far in excess of consumption, South Africa has substantial capacity for exports. Exports have been increasing rapidly and in 2007 were essentially equal to domestic consumption at approximately 35 mc, up 16 percent from 2006 (around 25 mc worth of wine is distilled annually, as well). Almost 40 percent of the exports went out as bulk wine, and 21.2 mc were in bottle or, increasingly, **alternative packaging**. The **British market** was by far the largest destination for exports (9.7 mc, three-quarters of it in bulk), followed by **Germany** (6.6 mc). The Dutch and **Scandinavian** markets were significant, as well. Exports to the **United States** totaled 1.3 mc, 85 percent of which was bulk wine.

Further Reading

S.A. Wine Industry Information & Systems. www.sawis.co.za/sawisportal/.
South African Wine Industry Trust. www.sawit.co.za.
Wines of South Africa. www.wosa.co.za.

SPAIN

Spain has been among the top wine-producing countries for centuries and yet is considered by many to be one of the world's most exciting new wine regions. The reason for this dichotomy has to do with the fact that historically most Spanish exports have come from a handful of **appellations**—notably Rioja, Sherry, and Cava—that were long on tradition and short on innovation, but within the past two decades, wines of a much wider spectrum of styles have appeared on the world market from several other areas in Spain, and even the well-known regions have been reinvigorated with more modern winemaking and export **promotion** activities.

Spain's enological history goes back to the Phoenicians in the **ancient Mediterranean**, who brought vines to ports on the eastern coast. The **Greeks** and Romans followed, establishing colonies and cities. Wine became a part of the culture, grown in every part of the country. When the Islamic Moors controlled most of the Iberian Peninsula from the eighth to fifteenth centuries, wine continued in production, as the Moors did not prevent Christians and Jews from drinking it, and a lively export trade with England developed. After the expulsion of the Moors, the English took control of most of the wine trade in the southwest, creating the **fortified** Sherry wine that is known today to better export it to England and her **colonies**.

When **phylloxera** struck the vineyards of **France** in the 1860s, many French winemakers migrated across the Pyrenees into Spain to make wine, and the influx of expertise from **Bordeaux** helped to raise the bar of quality for the wines of Rioja to a world-class level—until phylloxera found Rioja at the turn of the twentieth century. By the time the industry had had a chance to replant and recover, the Spanish Civil War had left Francisco Franco in charge of the country as dictator, and international trade diminished. Only after the end of Franco's long rule in the mid-1970s did Spain reawaken. As democracy returned to the country and Franco's suppression of the regional cultures of the minority peoples of Spain (notably the Catalans, Basques, and Galicians) was lifted, a general renaissance led to the development of modern winemaking in many places in Spain, but particularly in the autonomous regions of the north: Rias Baixas in Galicia, several areas along the north coast in Basque Country, and throughout Catalunya, including Priorat and Penedès.

Spain is a fairly large country, slightly smaller than France, but entirely within the temperate zone where grapes can be grown successfully. As of 2006, it had 2.9 million acres of vineyards, by far the most of any country in the world. Due to the low planting density and yields, however, Spain is only the third largest wine producer, after France and **Italy**. In 2006, the country produced 38.2 million hectoliters of wine, the equivalent of 425 million nine-liter cases (mc). The majority of production is in Castile–La Mancha province in the center of the country. Apart from the vast swaths of the undistinguished Airén and Bobal grapes, the most widely planted grape varieties are Garnacha (Grenache), Tempranillo, and Monastrell (Mourvèdre).

The basic **quality wine** designation in Spain is the *denominación de origen* (DO). A higher categorization, *denominación de origen calificada* (DOCa), has been granted only to Rioja (in 1991), Priorat (2001), and Ribera del Duero (2008). *Vinos de pagos* are outstanding single-vineyard estates. *Vino de calidad con indicación geográfica* (VCIG) is a new quality-wine category set up for probable future DOs. About 35 percent of production is quality wine, including Cava and Sherry. The lower levels include *vino de la tierra* (regional wine) and *vino de mesa* (**table wine**).

Per-capita consumption, which has been steadily declining, has dropped to 34 liters (or about 39 liters per adult), about half its level 20 years earlier. Total consumption in 2006 was about 152 mc, roughly on par with the Chinese market for fifth globally. More than 115 mc was used for **distillation** into brandy or ethanol, but this still left a substantial amount available for export.

Spanish producers exported 159 mc in 2006 (rising to 170 mc in 2007), putting Spain in a position to usurp France's accustomed position as the world's second largest wine-exporting country (after Italy). Of this, more than 81 mc went out as **bulk wine**, along with 14 mc of unfermented must. The value of the wine exports was €1.63 billion (increasing to €1.83 billion in 2007). The primary recipient of Spanish exports is France, but because 80 percent of this is inexpensive bulk wine, France falls behind the United Kingdom, **Germany**, and the **United States**, which all bring in much more bottled wine, in terms of sales value. Russia is another big customer for Spanish bulk wine. The United States is currently Spain's biggest growth market, with sales increasing more than 20 percent a year. U.S. imports totaled 6.5 mc in 2007, almost half of which was still, quality wine and 20 percent was Cava **sparkling wine**.

With such large production and falling domestic consumption, imports are not a major category in Spain. Recent years have seen around 3 mc imported.

Spain's marquee regions are Rioja, Cava, and Sherry. Rioja, straddling the provinces of La Rioja, Basque Country, and Navarre, is best known for its **red wines**, made from a Tempranillo-led blend that can include Garnacha, Graciano, and Mazuelo. White Riojas, which account for about 15 percent of production, can contain Viura, Malvasia, and Garnacha Blanca. The region has 141,000 acres of vineyards, with an average annual output of around 28 mc. In 2006, Rioja sales reached a record 29 mc.

Cava is Spain's traditional-method sparkling wine. The Cava DO is discontinuous, with segments throughout the country, but 85 percent of the production comes from the Penedès area in Catalunya. The traditional grapes used—primarily Macabeo, Xarel-lo, and Parellada—do not overlap with those of **Champagne**, but the laws have recently been amended to allow the use of **Chardonnay** and, for **rosé**, **Pinot Noir**. Sales of sparkling wine—most of it Cava—in 2007 were about 18.2 mc, of which 70 percent was exported.

Sherry is the classic fortified wine made in the Andalusian region around Jerez. Sales of Sherry have been shrinking, falling to 6.1 mc in 2007. The domestic market has remained relatively stable at 1.5 mc, but exports have dropped almost 20 percent since 2003. Two-thirds of the exports go to the British and **Dutch** markets.

Spanish wine imports will continue to represent a growth area in the United States in the next five years. With the recent trend toward unoaked white wines, Galicia's Albariño has enjoyed great popularity. Spain's venerable Priorat region, back from a near-century of neglect, now produces some of the country's more internationally styled and high-priced wines from Garnacha that have been popular with wine critics, garnering off-the-charts **ratings**. The wines of Ribera del Duero, though smaller in production volume than Rioja, are Rioja's equal in reputation. Even La Mancha, once relegated to the "wine lake" category, with its relatively inexpensive land, is now attracting winemakers from inside Spain, as well as international investors and winemaking consultants. As Spain continues to exploit its favorable mix of high elevation, dry days and cool nights, low yields from indigenous varieties, and a talented winemaking pool, its star will continue to rise on the international stage. *See also* Fortified Wine.

Further Reading

Federación Española del Vino. www.fev.es [Spanish only].

Jeffs, Julian. *The Wines of Spain*. Rev. ed. London: Mitchell Beazley, 2006.

Read, Jan. *The Wines of Spain*. Rev. ed. London: Mitchell Beazley, 2005.

Wines from Spain. www.winesfromspain.com.

SPARKLING WINE

The sound of the celebratory *pop* from a chilled bottle of sparkling wine is a ubiquitous feature of parties and commemorations of all kinds, from graduation parties to ship christenings to sports championship celebrations—and, of course, New Year's festivities. The pop comes from carbon dioxide (CO_2) trapped under pressure in the wine, which, when opened, erupts into a myriad of bubbles. Some wines—described variously as *pétillant, frizzante,* or just "fizzy"—are bottled with a little CO_2 remaining in them to add some zip and freshness, but truly *sparkling* wine is the version with 5 to 6 atmospheres of pressure, a heavier bottle to withstand the pressure, and typically a mushroom-cork-and-cage **closure**.

Production.   **Champagne**, where the concept was developed, is the definitive quality standard for all sparkling wine, and deservedly so. The region has worked hard to preserve and protect its quality by subscribing to a stringent set of criteria required for every bottle allowed to carry that **appellation**. Nevertheless, an increasing number of high-quality sparkling wine producers around the world strive to emulate—and in some cases achieve—Champagne's quality for half or even a third of the cost.

What makes Champagne unique is a combination of factors involving the selection of grapes (**Chardonnay**, **Pinot Noir**, and/or Pinot Meunier), the unique **terroir**, the skillful art of blending, and the time expended for aging on the lees in the bottle to gain greater complexity. Sparkling wine that is made and aged in the same bottle in which it is sold, like Champagne, is referred to as *méthode traditionnelle* (traditional method) or the equivalent in other languages. For these wines, the bubbles are created naturally by a secondary fermentation within the bottle. This is a costly and exacting process, although the introduction of **mechanization** has made it far less labor-intensive than it once was. The traditional method is also used for **Spanish** Cava, as well as nearly all upper-end sparklers from the **New World**.

There are other, less expensive methods for making sparkling wine that are used in other places. The *Charmat, tank,* or *cuve close* process performs the secondary fermentation in a pressurized tank before bottling. This is used for such sparkling wines as **Italian** Prosecco and **German** Sekt. These wines are fruitier and display fresher primary aromas of the grape because of their minimal aging on the lees. The *transfer method* mainly describes transference of méthode traditionelle wine into unique bottle sizes, such as half-bottles, magnums, or larger formats. The least expensive sparkling wines are achieved by simple *carbonation* of still **table wine**.

Consumption.   With so many sparkling wine options in the market today, the **consumer** can choose from many styles and a range of price points to fit any budget. The U.S. thirst for sparkling wine has averaged 12.7 million nine-liter cases (mc) for the last decade—including a spike of 14.9 mc in 1999 for the millennium celebrations. The trend in the last five years has shown slow but steady growth, although it has not kept pace with the increase of wine consumption overall, falling to just 4.7 percent of total wine sales. Much of the decline, however, has been at the lower end of the spectrum, and revenues from sparkling wine sales continue to rise. The top states for sparkling wine consumption, according to *Adams Wine Handbook* data, are **California**, Illinois, **New York**, Florida, and Texas.

More bottles of sparkling wine get popped during the holiday season than at any other time of year. Nearly a third of all sparkling wine sales take place in December.

With Champagne imports into the **United States** close to surpassing a record 2 mc, there remains a steady interest in bubbles. **Women** especially are driving figures for per-capita consumption. As a result, sparkling wine as a category is on the rise in **restaurants** and bars, which are capturing full potential with by-the-glass options. Restaurateurs are reintroducing consumers into the category with a heightened sense of interest and discovery. Crisp and clean with lower levels of alcohol than many modern table wines, sparkling wines represent something new that can be paired with a generous range of foods.

The opportunity to enjoy a glass of great fizz is not restricted to Champagne itself. Sparkling wines from **France**, most notably *crémants* from Alsace, the Loire Valley, and Limoux, are gaining traction in the market. Cavas from the Penedès in Spain offer tremendous flavor and complexity at one-third the price of entry-level nonvintage Champagne. In the U.S. market, virtually all imported sparkling wine (37 percent of total sparkling wine sales) comes from France, Italy, or Spain, although **Australia** is beginning to edge into the market. With the dollar steadily decreasing in value, however, American consumers are seeking alternatives closer to home. In the United States, there are excellent examples of traditional-method sparkling wines originating from many regions, including California's Anderson Valley, **Napa Valley**, and **Sonoma County**; **Oregon**; **Washington**; and New Mexico.

Trends.   Sparkling wines today are starting to be promoted not only as a luxury offering but also as a creative mixer for many wine-based cocktails. The **consolidation** of **brands** through the numerous reshufflings of corporations has created a synergy among wine and spirits brands to promote new recipes on the cocktail scene. Martini & Rossi Asti Spumante is the base for Amaretto di Saronno liqueur splash with sour mix. LVMH (Moët Hennessy Louis Vuitton) has global **promotions** showcasing Domaine Chandon's affinity for the perfect sparkling Kir Royale heightened with Chambord. Sparkling wines are quickly becoming a popular alternative wine base to many recipes beyond Bellinis and Mimosas. They are popping up on many hotel- and chain-driven programs, as well as savvy **cruise line** menus where a guest's license to celebrate and indulge is being quenched. As a result, it has become more common to find packaging of single-serve 187-ml bottles used for by-the-glass programs in lounges and bars than just as the option in hotel minibars.

Pink and even red sparkling wines are becoming popular. One of the best-selling wines at Walt Disney World's Epcot International Food & Wine Festival is Brachetto d'Acqui, a red sparkling wine from Piedmont, Italy. Off-dry to sweet, this bright strawberry and raspberry sparkler is a favorite refresher by the glass itself and when paired with a bite of dark chocolate. **Rosé** still wines are popular and trendy, and sparkling wine producers should take note that the consumer is looking for these styles by the glass.

Global warming's effects are starting to be noticed and may shake things up in the sparkling wine world. Cool-climate viticulture is a requirement for harnessing the desired acidity levels in grapes to be used for sparkling wine. Historically, one would not dare to suggest that Champagne could have a rival for its terroir and unique **grape-growing** conditions. However, it is hard to dismiss the fact that running through Sussex and Surrey in southeast England are chalky soils that closely match the terrain within Champagne itself. **Climate change** leading to rising temperatures in Champagne may call into question whether this is still the area for producing the best sparkling wine. Certainly southern England, along with other chilly environments, such as Tasmania in Australia, Central Otago in **New Zealand**, British Columbia in **Canada**, and parts of Germany, are areas to watch in the years ahead as their sparkling wine quality will only improve thanks to consistently warmer temperatures.

It may come as no surprise that sparkling wine can originate from all major wine-producing regions. However, one may not be as familiar with grapes grown in **Greece** that are used to produce delicate floral sparkling wines of distinction. The Athiri grape is especially favored to produce bright examples from the island of Rhodes. In addition, the popular Moschofilero is a rising star, used in many blends and giving off hints of rose petals. Not far away, several countries of **Eastern Europe** that have long histories of sparkling wine production are poised to greatly expand their exports to the West.

John Blazon

Further Reading

Barrie, Susie. *Champagne and Sparkling Wines: A Complete Guide to Sparkling Wines from Around the World.* London: Mitchell Beazley, 2004.

Stevenson, Tom. *World Encyclopedia of Champagne and Sparkling Wine.* Rev. ed. South San Francisco, CA: Wine Appreciation Guild, 2003.

SULFITES

Sulfites are a never-ending source of interest and generally unwarranted concern by **consumers**, who assume the fact that wine labels carry the warning ''Contains Sulfites'' means that sulfites are something unnatural and dangerous. They attribute various maladies, particularly headaches, to the presence of sulfites and search out wines that do not have any. In fact, sulfites are natural and highly useful, almost essential, in the winemaking process as a preservative; thus, there are very few wines without sulfites. They *can* be dangerous—to asthmatics who are highly sensitive to them. Otherwise, sulfites are harmless.

Sulfites are chemical compounds that contain the sulfite ion SO_3. *Sulfur dioxide,* SO_2, is equivalent, because in the presence of water, H_2O, it forms *sulfurous acid,* H_2SO_3, which readily dissociates into hydrogen ions and SO_3. This reaction can go the other way as well, releasing SO_2 into the wine. It is the sulfur dioxide that is important in winemaking, because its presence has several beneficial effects, including lessening oxidation (which creates off-odors and turns wine brown) and killing unwanted yeast and bacteria that might otherwise spoil the wine.

Sulfur was used at least as far back as the **ancient Mediterranean** period to help preserve foodstuffs and wine. It is used in vineyards to retard fungus and disease on grapes and vines, especially in humid conditions. Sulfur, often in the form of sodium metabisulfite powder, may be sprinkled or sprayed on newly harvested grapes or added to freshly crushed grape must to prevent the early initiation of fermentation. Further, it is frequently added to a finished wine—especially one with residual sugar—to ensure that yeast or bacteria do not start a secondary fermentation in the bottle. This is often an important step in **quality control**.

Wines can be made without adding sulfur, and **organic wine** is prohibited from having sulfur added. Without this important preservative, however, other methods, such as sterile filtering, must usually be used to eliminate bacterial spoilage, and earlier oxidation is likely. Nor does this mean that such a wine is necessarily sulfite-free, because some sulfites are typically produced by normal chemical processes during fermentation. A study presented at the 1995 Organic Grape and Wine Symposium reported that in trial fermentations with no added sulfur, yeast produced up to 41 parts per million (ppm) of sulfites.

In the **United States**, the maximum permissible concentration of sulfites is 350 ppm, and any wine (domestic or imported) with more than 10 ppm—the smallest amount that current tests can detect—must display the sulfites warning. The **European Union** (EU) has essentially the same rules (since 2005) except that the ceiling is lower; EU maximums range from 160 ppm for dry **red wines** to 260 ppm for sweet white **dessert wines**. The European Union has designated sulfur dioxide as approved food additive E220 (various sulfite compounds are E221–E228), which may be seen on some food labels.

In general, wines contain on average about 80 ppm of sulfites. At levels approaching the maximum, the sulfur in the wine becomes noticeable and unpalatable. However, most people have no ill effects from the sulfites in wine—or in other foods in which sulfites are routinely employed as preservatives, such as dried fruits and many fruit juices. Sulfite allergic sensitivity is essentially limited to asthmatics, of whom 5 to 10 percent are sulfite sensitive. While there is something as yet unidentified in red wine that does seem to cause headaches in some people, no correlation has been found between sulfites and headaches, and because white wines tend to have more sulfites than red wines do, sulfur is not implicated in red wine headaches.

SUPERMARKETS

For grocery retailers looking for a category that offers **profitable** growth opportunities, enhances their image, and contributes to bigger baskets at the checkout counter, there is one product that answers all these needs: wine. Supermarket chains such as Tesco and Sainsbury's in the United Kingdom and Aldi in **Germany** have long recognized this and are among the largest wine **retailers** in the world.

In the **United States**, not every state allows the sale of alcohol in grocery stores, but in the 30-plus states where it is not prohibited, selling wine alongside groceries has proven to be a highly successful strategy. Annual sales of wine by the 26,000-plus wine sellers in the grocery channel have moved past the $5 billion a year mark, ranking wine 15th out of 120 categories in supermarket sales. Considering only the states where wine is legally sold in grocery stores, wine ranks eighth—ahead of such staples as cereal, soup, eggs, ice cream, and detergent. Though beer ranks higher than wine in terms of overall sales in the grocery channel, wine shows the greatest growth in recent years.

Positive Aspects of Supermarket Wine Sales.   With these numbers, and the fact that almost all consumers visit grocery stores, it is clear that the grocery channel, in all of its different variations, offers a powerful opportunity for **wineries** and **distributors** to reach the **consumer**. Today's consumer desires convenience and value. Stocking wine on grocery store shelves directly answers these needs: the convenience of a one-stop shop and the attractive pricing resulting from the enormous buying power of supermarket chains.

Wine is an attractive product from the grocery retailer's point of view because it draws customers who want the upscale image wine offers. Different segments within this channel—conventional supermarkets, limited assortment stores, small grocery stores, supercenters, and specialty stores—attract different consumers. For each segment, market intelligence on the habits of their customers is essential to help them develop the most attractive selection for their base.

Supermarkets serve a practical purpose: to sell groceries. Offering wine for sale alongside groceries attracts more affluent customers and provides them with the convenience of one-stop shopping. And it pays off at the checkout counter. People who buy wine at the grocery store tend to buy a basketful of groceries as well, increasing the total spend by an average of $30 each trip—of which only about $12 is attributable to the wine itself.

In response to the growing appeal of the wine category, U.S. supermarkets are adjusting their offerings with a nod to the consumer's desire for variety. In 1999, less than 2,000 wine **brands** were sold. By 2007, that number had doubled. The dominance of the top 10 brands during that time shrank from one-third of all dollar spending to just over one-quarter, a further testament to the consumers' thirst for variety.

Beyond the conventional supermarket, such specialty grocery stores as Trader Joe's and Whole Foods Market adopt wine as a "destination" category, frequently offering unique vintages available only in their stores. Private-label wines, or wines exclusive to a single organization, are growing in importance, though are still relatively small compared to Europe, or even to other private-label categories in the United States. Since these wines are generally not labeled with a store or retailer identifier, consumers often would not know it is an "exclusive" label. Some specialty grocery stores further differentiate themselves from competitors by offering wine classes at their stores.

"Bigger box" stores such as Wal-Mart and Target also recognize the demand for wine. For this segment, operating as a wine merchant is still an underdeveloped area, but one that offers fuel for growth. In fact, wine was the fastest growing category for Wal-Mart Stores, Inc., in 2007. Because of their considerable reach, these retailers could significantly expand wine-buying opportunities for consumers.

Negative Aspects.   Although supermarkets tend to offer excellent values on the wines they stock and their wine assortment is growing, critics point out that the combination of high volumes and low margins required for entry into this sales avenue often restricts the range of choice available to the consumer. Furthermore, storage conditions in some supermarkets are less than ideal, and whereas there is almost always an employee who can discuss meat or produce at a grocery store, the same can rarely be said about the wine department.

Thus, while the grocery channel is a formidable competitor among wine-selling outlets, there is still reason for the local liquor store and wine shop to exist. Lack of shelf space will always be an issue in supermarkets, allowing more specialized wine shops to differentiate themselves through their variety of offerings from smaller producers, less familiar places of origin, and uncommon grape varieties that lack the visibility of the big brands with the power to stake out space in the supermarket. The personalized service offered by a local wine shop and their more intimate knowledge of the consumer is an additional advantage.

Looking Forward.   Across all segments in the grocery channel, wine is a dynamic category that has great potential for growth. While the number of people buying wine remains relatively constant, the category continues to benefit from consumers who increase the number of purchases and buy at higher price points than in the past. Innovations in varieties continue to keep the category fresh. **Alternative packaging** and **closures** that answer the consumer's need for convenience, including screw caps and three-liter boxes, are becoming more prevalent. Marketing designed to focus on the social aspects of wine consumption or to appeal to the consumer's interest in knowing more about wine could be used to enhance sales in stores.

For grocery retailers, a well-planned assortment of wine can be leveraged to attract desired consumer segments. For a truly effective strategy, retailers have to develop accurate consumer profiles at the local level to understand who their customers are and then use that market intelligence to adopt the strategies that best address their needs. Though a complex task, pairing the right wines with food in the grocery channel can be highly successful. *See also* British Market; Bulk Wine/Juice Trade; Globalization; Labels as Marketing; Wine Clubs.

Danny Brager

Further Reading
Supermarket News. http://supermarketnews.com.

SUPPLY AND DEMAND

Supply and demand are economic concepts that describe the two sides of a market transaction. The supplier has incentives to supply more quantity of a good as price increases, while the quantity demanded is inversely related to price. When the price in a market is too high, more is supplied than demanded, and pressure builds on the price to fall. For example, overplanting **Cabernet Sauvignon** pushes prices for that variety down. The reverse is also true: if a price is relatively low, excess demand will drive it up. An example of this is the penetration strategy used by **Chile** and **Australia** in the U.S. market, coming in at relatively low prices and gaining market share as price slowly rises. A market comes to *equilibrium* when the quantity supplied equals the quantity demanded, that is, where no shortage or surpluses exist.

Producers are driven by *profit* incentives, maximizing revenue above cost. **Consumers** are driven by *utility* incentives, the total satisfaction from consuming a good or service less the cost of purchasing it. As prices initially rise from a relatively low level, revenue and profit increase. As prices continue to rise, however, the increase in revenue peaks and then reverses as the quantity demanded declines.

Supply. **Wineries** in principle directly determine the supply of wine. Wine supply should follow grower incentives, within the restrictions of climate and geography. For example, when the demand for **red wine** increased after the **French paradox** was publicized (describing the **health** benefits from drinking red wine), some growers decided to pull out white varieties and plant more red grapes. However, vineyard changes are slow processes, as it takes between three and five years to receive a viable crop from new plantings, and the original investment in the plantings is lost when pulled. Grape supply is also tied to labor availability and weather. A bad harvest can change the market quickly, as can a change in labor prices. In addition, wine, like other alcoholic beverages, is a highly regulated product with much government intervention. The **European Union**, for example, is introducing subsidies to grape growers to reduce their vineyard area in order to artificially raise prices as supply decreases.

Wine supply anecdotally has a 10-year cycle. At the beginning of the cycle, an excess supply of a given wine-grape variety appears, driving prices down. A recent oversupply in Australian grapes due to large government subsidies, for instance, caused Australian wine prices to fall. In contrast, **Pinot Noir** prices have slowly risen and continue to grow due to a reduction in plantings and areas that can support Pinot Noir grapes.

Supply is bifurcated between grape production and wine in the bottle. The winery must view these as distinct processes; the vineyard is agricultural, and the winery is a manufacturing endeavor. Winery costs depend on **barrel** prices, **bulk wine** costs, wages, bottle and cork prices, transportation, boxes, labeling, and other manufacturing expenses. A change in any of these costs can change wine prices for consumers.

Once the wine is produced, suppliers face another cost: compliance. The level of compliance depends on the country in question. In the **United States**, the 21st Amendment allows for a federalist approach to regulating alcohol sales and taxes: each state dictates how wine is sold within it, making every state a little different. Some states are "reciprocal": their taxation and shipping laws are the same, and they act like a wine union of sorts. The market between **California** and Colorado is an example of a reciprocal agreement where **direct shipping** is possible. In contrast, **New York** is a state where supplying wine has long been monopolized by specific **distributors** through state laws; an outside supplier of wine must sell to a state-licensed distributor in order to supply the New York market.

Demand. Wine demand, in many ways, is more simple than supply. Demand for wine shifts based on consumer trends: for example, the 2004 movie *Sideways* sparks a sudden interest in Pinot Noir; new health reports about the benefits of antioxidants cause consumers to shift toward red wines. Much of this is due to what is known as *hedonic demand,* where demand is driven not so much by price but by the marketing of the wine characteristics or quality level. Hedonic demand is now the way academics view and study wine demand, although there is some debate over whether this affects the *elasticity* of demand—how responsive the quantity demanded is to a price change—or whether wine quality changes the amount demanded at every price.

For the winery, **promotion** has become a focal activity in producing and selling wine, and it affects the winemaking process—perhaps necessitating handpicking rather than **mechanical** harvesting, which in turn drives up wine prices. The wine's regional aspects, the so-called **terroir**, affect the price of wine. How specific the wine's designation is—region, **appellation**, or vineyard—can change the wine's characteristics. A vineyard-designated wine is an attempt to differentiate one product from another that is produced from a larger, less distinctive viticultural area, and thus to be able to charge a higher price based on greater hedonic demand.

Wine is sold at different price points, based on perceived quality, and a host of third-party appraisers exist to guide wine consumers in their choices. Famous publications include the *Wine Spectator* and the *Wine Advocate*. Many blogs and other Web sites are now devoted to wine quality discussions in an attempt to minimize the chance of choosing a poor-quality wine. Price points have developed as a way of quality tiering, where most wine consumers assume that paying a higher price for a wine begets higher quality. Tasting scores and their effects on demand are a thread that needs more research.

Demand theory suggests that there are issues of substitutability and complementarities that are both internal and external to the wine industry itself. Food-and-wine pairing has become a way to both market and tie wine purchases to other consumption. Acting as complements, wine is sold not on its own merits, but on the synergistic effects of these pairings. This is especially true in **restaurant** sales. On the substitutability side of demand, wine consumers face choices of purchasing **sparkling**, **fortified**, or **table wines**, whites, **rosés**, or reds, and then substituting different varieties within these groups. This is especially true in red wines, where Cabernet Sauvignon, **Merlot**, Pinot Noir, **Zinfandel**, **Syrah/Shiraz**, and other red varieties battle for shelf space and consumers. Perhaps a larger issue is competing with other beverages, especially beer and soda. For wineries everywhere, the challenge of displacing other beverages in the American diet is likely the largest long-term issue regarding the U.S. wine market.

Outlook.   Three trends are evident in the wine industry concerning market forces. First, supply is to become more **global**; even China is investigating the possibilities of an export wine industry. Second, the American consumer will likely remain the focus of global wine supply, despite the many competitors both inside and outside of the wine industry. Finally, the pricing and markets for wine are likely to become ever more driven by perceived quality rather than supply of grapes or overall consumer ability to purchase. The manipulation of consumer tastes and preferences by wineries will continue to be the driving force in selling wine.

Robert Eyler

Further Reading

Buccola, Steven T., and Loren VanderZanden. "Wine Demand, Price Strategy, and Tax Policy," *Review of Agricultural Economics* 19 (1997): 428–40.

Combris, Pierre, Sébastien Lecocq, and Michael Visser, "Estimation of a Hedonic Price Equation for Bordeaux Wine: Does Quality Matter?" *Economic Journal* 107 (1997): 390–402.

Lecocq, Sébastien, and Michael Visser, "What Determines Wine Prices: Objective vs. Sensory Characteristics," *Journal of Wine Economics* 1 (2006): 42–56.

Wittwer, Glyn, Nick Berger, and Kym Anderson. "Modelling the World Wine Market to 2005: Impacts of Structural and Policy Changes," Centre for International Economic Studies, January 2001, www.adelaide.edu.au/cies/papers/0102.pdf.

SUSTAINABILITY

Sustainable winegrowing is defined as wine-grape growing and winemaking practices that are sensitive to the environment (environmentally sound), responsive to the needs and interests of society at large (socially equitable), and economically possible to implement and maintain (economically feasible)—otherwise known as the "three *E*'s" of sustainability.

The philosophy of sustainability is that vineyards and **wineries** should preserve natural resources and build close relationships with employees and communities while at the same time enhancing the quality of their products. Using sustainable winegrowing practices, vintners and growers

- help reduce water and energy use,
- minimize pesticide use,
- build healthy soil,
- protect air and water quality,
- recycle natural resources,
- maintain the surrounding wildlife habitat,
- provide employee education,
- communicate with neighbors about vineyard and winery operations, and
- ensure high-quality grapes and wine.

Our Common Future, a groundbreaking 1987 report from the United Nations World Commission on Environment and Development, describes sustainable development as "development that meets the needs of the present without compromising the ability of future generations to meet their own needs" and serves as the basis for many current sustainability definitions and initiatives. Since the late 1980s, the terms *sustainability, sustainable development,* and *sustainable agriculture* have been widely used in the governmental, nongovernmental, and private sectors.

Since the mid-1990s, the wine industries in **Australia**, the **European Union**, **New Zealand**, **South Africa**, **Switzerland**, and parts of the **United States** have created voluntary programs to help define and promote sustainability in their respective winegrowing regions. In 2006, the International Federation of Wines and Spirits (FIVS—Federation Internationale des Vins et Spiritueux), an international trade association for all sectors of the alcohol beverage industry, announced the Global Wine Sector Environmental Sustainability Principles, which "satisfy the triple bottom line of economic, environmental and social sustainability" and are incorporated into these international efforts.

The **California** Sustainable Winegrowing Program, launched in 2002, was the first statewide program of this type and has been widely adopted by the California's vintner and grower community. The program provides leadership in the path to sustainability and gives the California wine industry a unique advantage in the **global** market. A comprehensive workbook and educational workshops provide practical, how-to information on sustainable winegrowing. Using the workbook, participants self-assess their vineyards and wineries and voluntarily contribute data to measure adoption of sustainable practices. Statewide Sustainability Reports document results, identify strengths and opportunities for improvement, and set goals to increase adoption of sustainable practices. As of fall 2007, more than 1,300 vintners and grape growers—who produce more than 60 percent of California's wine and farm over half of the vineyard acreage—have analyzed their operations during more than 100 self-assessment workshops. Some 5,000 have participated in another 100 or so educational workshops targeting specific practices, such as energy efficiency and air and water quality.

Many of the international programs provide a similar framework for improving environmental, social, and economic performance in vineyards, with some also incorporating winery operations. Through the Sustainable Winegrowing New Zealand program, for instance, more than 360 vineyards and 40 wineries have been accredited using a positive-points self-audit scorecard. As of the 2005–2006 harvest season, more than 90 percent of South Africa's wine-grape producers had signed up for the Integrated Production of Wine system, which utilizes guidelines that cover sustainable practices for both vineyards and wineries. The Australian Wine Industry Stewardship program provides a national framework for viticulture research and environmental programs and, as of 2007, involves 40 wineries and includes a grower survey addressing natural resource issues with a winery practice survey to be added in the future.

While no single "sustainable" label or set of standards exists for wine, there is a growing number of national and regional certification programs, and increasingly wineries communicate their sustainable practices to **retailers** and **consumers**. "**Organic**" and "**biodynamic**" are two certifiable production methods that fall under the broader framework of sustainable winegrowing. Grapes used in wines labeled as organic or "made with organically grown grapes" were farmed without synthetic fertilizers, pesticides, or fungicides for a period of at least three years; wines labeled as organic do not have **sulfites** added to prevent spoilage. In addition to following the organic tenets, biodynamic grape growers treat the vineyard as a complete ecosystem. These categories are not mutually exclusive.

By adopting sustainable practices, vintners and growers are able to conserve money and resources and improve relationships with employees and neighbors. Although marketing was not the impetus for sustainability programs in the international wine community, retailers and customers around the world are increasingly demanding products that are produced in an environmentally and socially responsible manner, particularly in Europe, Japan, and the United States. Because of their proactive efforts in sustainability, winegrowers are poised to continue to be environmental stewards and good neighbors while producing high-quality wines for generations to come.

Allison Jordan

Further Reading

Australian Wine Industry Stewardship. www.wfa.org.au/awis1.htm.

California Sustainable Winegrowing Alliance. www.sustainablewinegrowing.org.

Dlott, Jeff, Kari Birdseye, Joe Browde, John Garn, Allison Jordan, Clifford Ohmart, Karen Ross, and Ann Thrupp, eds. *Code of Sustainable Winegrowing Practices Self-Assessment Workbook.* 2nd ed. San Francisco: California Sustainable Winegrowing Alliance, Wine Institute, and California Association of Winegrape Growers, 2006.

FIVS Global Wine Sector Environmental Sustainability Principles. www.fivs.org.

Integrated Production of Wines in South Africa. www.ipw.co.za.

Nigro, Dana. "Green Revolutionaries." *Wine Spectator* (June 30, 2007): 56–88.

Sustainable Winegrowing New Zealand. www.nzwine.com/swnz.

SWITZERLAND

Switzerland is a wine-loving country, ranking among the top 10 in per-capita wine consumption at 43.5 liters per adult in 2006, outpacing even **Spain**. In 2006, Switzerland consumed 31.3 million nine-liter cases (mc) of wine, a figure that has been very slowly falling for several years. The preference is decidedly for **red wine**, which accounts for two-thirds of consumption; 4.6 percent is **sparkling wine**, while still white and **rosé** wine represent less than 29 percent.

The country lies far enough south in central Europe for winegrowing, but the proportion of steep terrain and high elevations of the Alpine nation limits the amount of cultivatable land available for all agricultural uses. There are 36,800 acres under vine—less than in the **Napa Valley**—in no less than 658 designated **appellations** (designated AOC [*appellation d'origine contrôlée*], GUB [*geschützten ursprungsbezeichnungen*], or DOC [*denominazione di origine controllata*], depending on the language of the canton). Three-quarters of the vineyard acreage is in the Francophone western part of Switzerland, mainly around Lake Geneva in the Vaud and along the Rhône River in the Valais. Only about 7 percent of the vines are in the Italian-speaking Ticino canton to the south. At least 200 grape varieties are recorded, but by far the most widely planted grapes are **Pinot Noir** (aka Blauburgunder; 30 percent of vineyard acreage) and the white Chasselas (29 percent), followed distantly by Gamay (11 percent) and **Merlot** (6.7 percent).

Domestic wine production in Switzerland in 2006 totaled 11.2 mc, 53 percent of it red. Because this is not much more than a third of the demand, the country imports about 20 mc per year, making it the tenth largest wine-importing country in the world. Its primary trading partners are **Italy**, **France**, and **Spain**; in 2006, they exported 5.2, 4.2, and 3.1 mc of wine to Switzerland, respectively. Very little **New World** wine is imported. Because of the high demand at home, not a great deal of Swiss wine leaves the country—only 290,000 cases in 2006.

Further Reading

Swiss Wine. www.swisswine.ch.

SYRAH/SHIRAZ

Syrah is a venerable grape variety from the Rhône Valley in **France** that has rather suddenly moved from a small niche category to a global darling that is being planted everywhere. It has demonstrated promise in many locations, but it is still too soon to tell where it will thrive and whether **consumers** will flock to Syrah as they have to **Merlot** and **Pinot Noir** before it.

Until fairly recently, Syrah was an almost unknown grape variety, at least by that name. It was grown in any quantity only in two places. One was its birthplace in the Rhône Valley, where in traditional fashion, the wine was named after the region and not the grape. Thus, Côte Rôtie and Hermitage, both Syrah wines, had excellent reputations, and other Rhône wines that had at least some Syrah in them, most notably Châteauneuf-du-Pape, were well known, but only the cognoscenti knew the grape's name. The other home of Syrah was **Australia**, where it had been imported in 1832. There, however, it was called not Syrah but either Shiraz—under the misapprehension that it was native to the area around Shiraz, Persia—or Hermitage.

Syrah originated in the Rhône Valley centuries ago as a natural crossing of two little-known vinifera varieties and became the primary grape of the northern Rhône. Eventually it was transplanted into the southern Rhône as well and then throughout the south of France. When the *appellation contrôlée* system was established, it was listed as an allowed variety in most of the appellations of Languedoc-Roussillon and Provence. Still, there were less than 7,000 acres of Syrah in France in 1970.

When **varietal labeling** became commonplace in the **New World** in the 1970s, Syrah began to emerge from the shadows, slowly gaining a following among consumers who liked big **red wines** but were looking for an alternative to **Cabernet Sauvignon**. It was introduced into **California** in 1971 (although other grapes there had been misidentified as Syrah for decades) and began to expand its international presence with plantings in **Argentina** and **South Africa** as well. Even in France, Syrah began to appear in ever-increasing numbers of varietally labeled *vins de pays* (country wines). French plantings had reached 70,000 acres by 1990.

Today, France remains the primary source of Syrah, with 172,000 acres under vine. This represents almost 8 percent of the vineyard area of France, more than Cabernet Sauvignon, but considerably less than **Merlot**. More than 55 percent of the Syrah is found in the Languedoc region, much of it for varietal wines, and only 8 percent in the northern Rhône.

Shiraz in the 1970s was underappreciated in Australia and found itself used in sweet and **fortified wines** or blended into the more highly regarded Cabernet wines, although there were notable exceptions, including the most famous Australian wine, Grange—then known as Grange Hermitage and made from 100 percent Shiraz—which was launched commercially in 1952. As tastes began to shift in the 1980s, Shiraz's potential as a source of serious red wine became clear, and Shiraz plantings in Australia increased rapidly, up to 15,000 acres by 1990, before the big wine boom in Australia began.

Though just one of many important grape varieties in France, Shiraz is the flagship grape of the Australian wine industry. With almost 100,000 acres by 2006, Shiraz made up almost a quarter of Australia's vineyard acreage. It is the most widely planted variety in Australia, even though in 2007 it dropped to second place behind **Chardonnay** in harvested tonnage. More importantly, the country had firmly established Shiraz as a household word in the U.S. and **British markets** and had created a direct link between "Shiraz" and "Australia" in many consumers' minds. Although Chardonnay and Shiraz are close in production figures, people much more readily identify Australia with Shiraz. Of the 21.6 million cases (mc) of **table wine** Australia exported to the **United States** in 2006, Shiraz was the largest segment, with a 37 percent share. Globally, Australia exported about 56 mc of Shiraz in 2003.

The third largest producer of Syrah is Argentina, which has about 29,000 acres, followed by the United States. California alone has around 18,000 acres, and **Washington** adds a respectable 2,800. In the United States, producers usually label their wine as Syrah, although there are a few who use Shiraz, either because their vines are cuttings from Australian vineyards or simply to be identified more closely with the popularity of Australian Shiraz. The other large grower of Shiraz is South Africa (20,700 acres), but the variety can be found in at least experimental plantings in virtually every country that grows wine grapes.

Americans consumed 10.5 million cases (mc) of varietally labeled Syrah/Shiraz in 2006, which represented about an eighth of all red varietals. Of this, 8.6 mc were imports, 93 percent of which were from Australia.

Particularly in the southern Rhône Valley, Syrah is also used as the basis for some excellent **rosés**, which are often quite hearty and deeply colored thanks to Syrah's characteristics.

T

TABLE WINE

There are a variety of definitions for the term *table wine,* depending on the context. In casual conversation, it refers to wines suitable for the dinner table—relatively dry, still, moderate-alcohol wines—as distinguished from those that are seen as having more specialized purposes, including **sparkling**, **fortified**, **dessert**, aromatized, and aperitif wines. However, *table wine* also has legal definitions that arise in business discussions.

The **Alcohol and Tobacco Tax and Trade Bureau (TTB)** of the U.S. Department of the Treasury defines *table wine* (also known as "light wine") as "grape wine having an alcoholic content not in excess of 14 percent by volume" [27 CFR Part 4, sec. 4.21(a)(2)]. Further delving into the definition of *grape wine* adds the restrictions that table wine be nonsparkling, not aromatized, and of at least 7 percent alcohol by volume (abv). Thus, the TTB definition approximates the informal meaning of the term except that it specifically delimits what constitutes moderate alcohol. Anything over 14 percent abv (up to 24 percent where the spirits begin) is officially *dessert wine.*

With the recent **high alcohol content** trend—where growers let their grapes hang on the vine longer, developing ever higher potential alcohol, while waiting for full physiological ripeness of the grapes—it is not uncommon for wines from hot, sunny regions to move out of the table wine category. This distinction is more than mere semantics, because the TTB tax rate for dessert wine is half again as much ($1.57 per gallon, compared to $1.07) as for table wines.

Using the TTB terminology, U.S. consumption of table wine in 2006 was 258 million cases. This represented 91.2 percent of total U.S. wine consumption.

In the **European Union** (EU), *table wine* has two official and somewhat contradictory meanings. First, "table wine" is the nomenclature for all EU wines that do not qualify as **quality wine**. This does not necessarily mean that the wines are poorly made, but only that they were not made under the strict rules required for designation as "quality wine"—perhaps the wine came from a region not

---

National Designations for Table Wine

In the **European Union**, the following categories are established by national wine laws and recognized by the European Union as table wine. The higher category of "table wine with geographical indication" is shown in italics.

- Austria: *Landwein,* Tafelwein
- Bulgaria: *Regionalno Vino,* Trapezno Vino
- Cyprus: *Topikos Oínos* (TO), Epitrapezios Oínos (EO)
- Czech Republic: *Zemské Víno,* Stolní Víno
- France: *Vin de Pays* (VdP), Vin de Table (VdT)
- Germany: *Deutscher Landwein,* Deutscher Tafelwein, Tafelwein
- Greece: *Topikos Oínos* (TO), *Onomasía katá Parádosi* (OKP), Epitrapezios Oínos (EO)
- Hungary: *Tájbor,* Asztali Bor
- Italy: *Indicazione Geografica Tipica* (IGT), Vino da Tavola (VdT)
- Luxembourg: *Vin de Pays* (VdP), Vin de Table (VdT)
- Portugal: *Vinho Regional* (VR), Vinho da Mesa (VdM)
- Romania: *Vin de Calitate Superioară* (VS), Vin de Masă (VM)
- Slovakia: Révové Vína Stolové
- Slovenia: *Deželno Vino,* Namizno Vino
- Spain: *Vino de la Tierra* (VdT), *Vino Comarcal,* Vino de Mesa (VdM)

---

currently recognized as a fine-wine **appellation**, used grape varieties not permitted for the local area, or was made in an atypical style.

EU regulations break the table wine category into two groups—which is where the second meaning of the term confusingly comes into play. Nonquality wines that are produced in large winegrowing districts or Protected Geographic Indications (PGIs) are designated "Table Wines with Geographical Description." These are wines that are generally typical of a broad region, but lack the specificity, **terroir**, or history or fail to follow the rigorous **grape-growing** and winemaking procedures required of quality wines. Examples include **Spain**'s *vino de la tierra* and **France**'s *vin de pays.* Other nonquality wines that are not made within a single authorized zone are simply "Table Wine," or the local-language equivalent—*vinho de mesa, Tafelwein,* and so forth.

To illustrate the opportunity for misunderstanding, consider the proportion of **Italian** table wine. Quality wines (DOCG and DOC) comprised 31 percent of Italian production in 2006, so table wines accounted for 69 percent. However, because 27 percent of Italian production was at the IGT level (Table Wines with Geographical Description), *vini da tavola*—literally, table wines—made up just 42 percent. Then again, using the TTB definition or just a more commonsense one, more than 90 percent of Italian wines are table wine.

TEMPERATURE CONTROL

High temperatures, and to a lesser extent cold temperatures, can wreak havoc with grapes and wine at any stage from vineyard to glass, and temperature control is therefore an important consideration for every segment of the wine industry.

In brief, high temperatures accelerate the biochemical reactions that take place in grapes and wine, often changing the character of the wine dramatically, for the most part in undesirable ways. Abnormally cold temperatures can also cause problems, though these are usually not overly damaging to the wine. Depending on where it occurs and when it is recognized, temperature damage is likely to result in a significant financial loss for someone, or if it makes it into the marketplace undetected, it can seriously hurt the **winery**'s reputation among **consumers**.

In the vineyard, the temperature, for the most part, is out of the control of the grape grower. The grower can do little beyond adjusting trellising, pruning, and irrigation of the vines to manage the temperatures dealt by nature. The primary exception is in frost prevention. In cool climates or unusually cool weather in moderate climates, grapes may be left on the vine quite late in the season to allow them to ripen as much as possible. This runs the risk of frost damage as winter approaches, but up to a point, the grower can protect the grapes. Wind machines can circulate the air above the vineyard to avoid the development of cold pockets in low-lying areas, while smudge pots and other types of heaters, or even open fires, may be used to warm the vineyard enough to prevent frost from forming. In more serious cold snaps, water may be sprayed on the vines from sprinklers; the water freezes into an icy coating around the grapes and acts as insulation from the colder air.

Harvesting the grapes is the first point at which temperature control becomes a major issue in most vineyards. In most **grape-growing** regions, harvest takes place in late summer or early fall, when it can still be quite warm and sometimes genuinely hot. Grapes cut from the vines and then transferred into larger containers for movement to the winery (with some grapes inevitably bursting and releasing juice in the process) can begin to oxidize and ferment quickly in warm temperatures. Among the remedies for this problem is keeping the grapes as cool as possible to minimize chemical reactions and the growth of yeast. In modern vineyards in hot climates, grapes are routinely harvested **mechanically** at night when temperatures are lowest. It is also possible to place the harvested grapes immediately into a refrigerated container for shipment (grapes may have to travel for hours across **Australia** or **Washington**, for example, before reaching the winery). Some growers use dry ice to cool grapes in transit.

In the winery, it is equally important to keep the grapes and juice as cool as possible after arrival to prevent fermentation from starting too early—especially when a period of settling or soaking with the skins is desired before the onset of fermentation. Later, it is also important to keep the wine from getting too warm as it sits in the tanks or **barrels**. The most crucial period of temperature control in the winery, however, is during fermentation.

Yeasts generate a lot of heat during the fermentation process—enough that they can actually kill themselves off through overheating, resulting in an incomplete (stuck) fermentation. Moreover, the temperature of the fermenting wine has a major effect on the characteristics of the finished wine: lower temperatures tend to retain substantially more aromatics and fruit flavors of the grapes—a feature that may be desirable or undesirable depending on the style of wine being made. Thus, winemakers need to use temperature control techniques to keep the fermentation at the desired temperature level. In a modern winery, this is usually achieved by fermenting in temperature-controlled tanks—stainless-steel tanks that have a surrounding jacket through which chilled fluid can be pumped to draw off excess heat (or on occasion, heated fluid to warm the tank's contents); similar results can be achieved in other tanks with a temporary insert of a cooling coil into the fermenting juice. Other techniques include running cool water over the outside of a tank. Using air-conditioning to cool the entire tank or barrel room may be sufficient to keep the wine cool after fermentation.

Another common procedure in the winery is cold stabilization. This involves chilling a wine, generally a white wine, to around 20°F (−7°C) for an extended period to cause excess tartaric acid in the wine to crystallize out of solution—so that it will not happen later in the bottle. This is often done in temperature-controlled tanks, although the traditional Old World method is simply to allow the cellar to be chilled by outside air during the winter.

After fermentation and cold stabilization, the wine should ideally remain at a "cool cellar temperature"—the 50s°F (10°C-15°C)—until consumed. In this temperature range, wines intended for early drinking will lose little of their freshness, and those intended for aging will mature at an appropriately slow pace. Occasional short excursions out of this temperature range will not affect the wine noticeably, but long periods at warm room temperatures or higher, or frequent large temperature variations, will prematurely age the wine. In addition, at very warm temperatures, the volume of the liquid in the bottle will expand to the point where it may push up the cork, leak wine, and let in some air—potentially ruining the wine or at least making the bottle unsalable. Cold temperatures are less hazardous, but may result in unsightly tartrate crystal buildup in the bottle (where it can often be mistaken as broken glass by consumers), and freezing should be avoided.

Keeping the wine at cellar temperature after leaving the winery requires attention to each step of storage and transport. Every time the wine is moved—from winery to **distributor** to **retailer**—temperature must be considered, and if necessary, refrigerated or at least insulated transport should be used. When the wine is exported to a distant market, whether as **bulk** or bottled wine, the potential for trouble multiplies. Refrigerated transport, whether in a ship's hold, railcar, or tanker truck, is critical, and the temperature control must be maintained throughout any stopovers en route. This is a particular concern for businesses engaged in **direct shipping** and **e-commerce**, because the shipment, though usually not of long duration, is often out of their control.

Storage conditions at the winery, distributors' warehouses, and most fine wine shops are usually optimized for the wine, since the inventory is these businesses' major asset. In retail outlets where wine is just a sideline—including many **supermarkets**, liquor stores, and casual **restaurants**—temperature conditions are less likely to be appropriate for wine storage, due to lack of space, customer comfort considerations, or lack of awareness of the problem. It is not uncommon in a small restaurant for wine to be stacked next to the oven or on top of cabinets near the ceiling just to get it out of the way. Once wine is purchased and taken home by a consumer, storage conditions can range from ideal to appalling. Most consumers are aware that white wines are usually served chilled and reds at a cool room temperature, but many do not realize the harm they can do to the wine by storing it in a warm place.

Temperature control can add substantially to the cost of making or selling wine, but it is crucial. Allowing a wine to get overheated can substantially lower the odds that the wine will be enjoyed when finally served—and therefore be bought again. It is important that everyone in the wine industry spread the gospel of temperature control to their colleagues, customers, and fellow consumers so that wines have a chance to be judged on their own merits and not in a diminished condition due to poor handling. *See also* Climate Change; Quality Control.

TERROIR

On the simplest level, *terroir* refers to the natural environmental parameters that define the agricultural potential of a zone or unit of land, with the implication that these conditions cannot be easily modified by human intervention. Yet, terroir can come to life and be expressed in a finished product only through the management provided by winegrowers and winemakers. Site and process are thus symbiotically intertwined, yet separate.

In the 1990s, a debate arose regarding the meaning and merits of terroir. Some question the relevance of nature-based terroir, maintaining that the outcome is largely the product of winemaking. The debate is complicated by the inability to prove with empirical precision the relative contributions of the many factors that determine the attributes of wine. The most widely accepted definition of *terroir* is a multidisciplinary or holistic one such as that adopted by UNESCO (the United Nations Educational, Scientific and Cultural Organization) in 2005. This interpretation refers to terroir as a delimited geographic space founded on the interaction between a natural milieu and human factors. Terroirs, in this view, are living, dynamic spaces that produce original, recognizable products.

Natural components of terroir include climate, topography, and soil. *Climate* encompasses temperature, precipitation, humidity, and wind and is the most important single factor determining the suitability of a site. Temperature, which has a critical role in the vine's functioning, has been assessed and modeled by numerous scientists. Precipitation and seasonality are fundamental to **grape growing**. Numerous **New World** vineyards are planted in regions with hot summers and inadequate rainfall, while many classic European wine districts experience more marked seasonal temperature variance along with sufficient (at times, excessive) precipitation during the growing season.

Topography has direct and indirect influences. Vineyards on slopes have improved drainage and receive heightened solar radiation and warmth, which may be critical to ripening in marginal climates. Altitude brings progressively lower temperatures, and cooler, elevated sites have attracted growers in hot regions.

Soil should be subdivided mentally into surface soils and deeper geologic features. Wines of all qualities and styles are grown on a wide diversity of soil types around the world. The role of soil is nonetheless the most controversial of all terroir components. Consensus exists on the importance of the soil's physical structure, particularly with reference to regulation of water supply to the vine. This has greater relevance in regions where rain falls while the vine is in leaf, such as **Bordeaux** and **Burgundy**, than in arid New World regions where hydration is controlled by irrigation technology. Despite claims by wine tasters, no correlation has been scientifically proven between soil chemistry and specific organoleptic features of wines.

Natural factors notwithstanding, it is a basic truth that wine would not exist without human intervention. The expression of terroir can be disguised or altered by technological practices, such as clones, trellising, irrigation, additives, cultured yeasts, methods to concentrate juice or wine, and wood treatments. At the same time, holistic terroir is a universal concept with global relevance. It is now generally accepted that great wines everywhere result from the optimum marriage of cultivar(s) and site, combined with vineyard management and winemaking techniques that allow a terroir "footprint" to be expressed.

The identification of unique outstanding terroirs has engendered schemes to protect those place names from fraud and competition. Terroir therefore serves to underpin the market potential of wines and to add value. **France**'s *Appellation d'Origine Contrôlée* (AOC), introduced in the 1930s, is the modern model for such legislation. Classic European terroirs codified by law include Chablis, Saint-Émilion, Sauternes, **Champagne**, and Hermitage in France; Rioja and Ribera del Duero in **Spain**; and Chianti Classico and Barolo in **Italy**. The New World's less restrictive schemes—such as the American viticultural areas (AVAs) of the **United States** and **Australia**'s Wines of Geographical Indication—are also, in principle, terroir based, recognizing such terroirs as the **Napa Valley**, the Russian River Valley in **Sonoma County**, Coonawarra in Australia, and Marlborough in **New Zealand**.

With continued global warming, some classic regions may exceed the range of optimum maturity for cultivars presently mandated by appellation laws and may find that some currently prohibited varieties become viable. Areas whose commercial potential is presently restricted may be able to produce marketable wine styles. Persistent drought coupled with depleted water supplies (in aquifers and snowmelt, for example) may shift the comparative advantage away from irrigation-dependent regions. If sea levels rise significantly (by 15 feet or so), celebrated Bordeaux terroirs like Châteaux Latour and Lafite Rothschild could be partially submerged, and local climatic changes will affect many low-lying vineyards. Thus **climate change** holds the potential to reconfigure present-day terroir and redefine the competitive landscape.

Roger C. Bohmrich

Further Reading

Bohmrich, Roger. "Terroir: Competing Perspectives on the Roles of Soil, Climate, and People." *Journal of Wine Research* 7, no. 1 (April 1996): 33–46.

Pott, Aaron. "The Ancient Roots of Terroir." *Wines & Vines* 85, no. 5 (May 2004): 77–80.

Tate, A.B. "Global Warming's Impact on Wine." *Journal of Wine Research* 12, no. 2 (August 2001): 95–109.

Wilson, James E. *Terroir*. Berkeley: University of California Press, 1998.

TRADE BARRIERS

Barriers to trade are external factors that inhibit or block firms' abilities to do business with each other as they attempt to operate in other countries, provinces, and states. Barriers to trade created by economic, regulatory, and cultural factors are very common in the wine industry.

Economic Barriers.   Economic barriers to the wine trade often take the form of tariffs and import duties, unfavorable **exchange rates**, and trade discounts and **promotions** that occur within the **distribution** channel. When such barriers exist, the **winery** must somehow cover the additional costs imposed. In the worst cases, it faces the difficult decision of either increasing the price of its wine to a level that **consumers** may not be willing to pay or reducing the company's earnings to such a low level that the business is no longer an attractive proposition.

Most wine is taxed through tariffs or duties when it crosses national borders. Governments can also tax wine when sold across state borders within the **United States**. Countries sometimes sign trade agreements to reduce or remove those tariffs. For example, in 2004 **Chile** and the United States signed a free trade agreement that is to be phased in over the next 12 years and will remove all tariffs on traded products. Numerous other groups of nations around the world have signed similar pacts. These agreements benefit the wineries from the participating countries, while at the same time making it more difficult for producers located in countries not party to the agreements to compete with their exports. In the absence of such an agreement, tariffs may be used in political maneuvering, as when the United States instituted a 200 percent punitive tariff on European wine during a dispute over agricultural subsidies in 1992—risking a quid pro quo tariff against U.S. wine exports.

Currency **exchange rates** are another economic factor that often create trade barriers. Exchange rates fluctuate over time, giving some countries cost advantages over others. For example, when the dollar was strong against many foreign currencies in the early 2000s, importing wine into the United States was easier because the imports were relatively cheap. However, exports from **California** suffered during this time as they became more expensive than competitors in foreign markets. By 2007, with the dollar falling against major currencies, the situation had reversed: The weaker dollar was helping create an upswing in exports from the United States, and although the volume of wine imported into the United States did not decrease, the prices **importers** charged inched higher.

Business practices within the distribution channel for wine can also create economic barriers to entry. The majority of wine sold in the United Kingdom is heavily discounted by **retailers**, creating a situation where many wineries have found it difficult to earn a **profit**. Unless a company's cost structure and pricing strategies can absorb these additional discounts, companies may find that exporting to this competitive market is no longer profitable. Even at the world's largest wine firm, **Constellation Brands**, Inc., executives are concerned over the lower earnings they must accept in the **British market** due to trade promotion practices.

Regulatory Barriers.   Regulations governing wine and the wine trade exist to protect consumers and to ensure that firms abide by accepted business practices and pay taxes. One important area where regulatory issues differ among countries is allowable winemaking practices. While it is reasonable to expect that countries should have laws that protect consumers against adulteration and fraud in wine, there is not always agreement among regulatory bodies on how best to prevent these nefarious practices. For example, in some wine-producing regions with warmer climates, acidification is routinely used to produce more balanced wines, whereas in other areas, this practice is illegal. Chaptalization is another controversial practice, allowed in some cooler growing areas, such as **Germany**, but forbidden in most others. In order to standardize winemaking practices among producers, the **European Union** has signed recently agreements with **Australia**, Chile, and the United States. Now when wines are exported to another country, the exporter must provide documentation that the winemaker has followed acceptable practices.

Laws concerning labeling can also present trade barriers to foreign producers. In the United States, the term *reserve* on a label is considered a marketing term and has no legal definition, whereas in Europe, its use imposes strict requirements involving aging that a wine must meet. If wines from other countries do not meet these requirements, they must change their labeling, which in turn can impact the intended **brand** positioning within a market. Until recently, the use of famous geographical names on wines coming from other regions was common. Now agreements between countries protect such **appellations** from use by producers outside the specified region.

Regulations on wine sales within the United States are complicated and are different in every state, creating for many firms a significant if not insurmountable barrier to trade. In most cases, the use of wholesalers or distributors—the three-tier system—is mandated by law. Wine importers, as well as domestic producers located in another state, must obtain licenses for each of the 50 states where they intend to sell their wines. They must comply with myriad state laws and pay taxes in every state if they seek nationwide distribution. In some states, the wine can be sold directly to retailers and consumers, whereas in other states, state-owned monopolies conduct and oversee all wine sales. Given the complexity and cost of complying with the regulations, most wine firms limit their wine sales to only a few promising markets.

Cultural Barriers.   Culture plays an important role in shaping consumers' wine-drinking preferences and therefore can also act as a trade barrier for marketers of wine. The most obvious cultural barrier would be the inability to sell wine in places where the dominant **religion** forbids alcohol consumption. In some wine markets, consumers strongly prefer local wines, even when the law permits and even encourages imports. In **France**, for example, many consumers drink wines produced only in their local area—never those from other French regions, let alone other countries. This loyalty to locally produced wines is not unique to France and can be found in many major wine-producing countries, the United States being a notable exception to this cultural pattern.

Culture can also shape the perceptions that consumers hold about wine-producing regions. Many consumers associate Mexico with the production of tequila, not wine, although wine producers in the Baja California region of Mexico are attempting to change these negative perceptions. It is still difficult to convince consumers to accept wines from new areas that have not yet earned a reputation for their wines, no matter how good the product actually tastes. Many new wine-producing areas, such as China and India, may initially encounter these cultural barriers to trade. *See also* Direct Shipping; E-Commerce; Globalization; Global Wine Industry.

Janeen Olsen

TRINCHERO FAMILY ESTATES

The sixth largest wine company in the **United States**, Trinchero Family Estates is the parent of Sutter Home wines, the world's 10th largest **brand**, with sales of 8.2 million cases (mc) worldwide and 7.7 mc in the United States in 2006. Trinchero's total U.S. sales for all brands in 2006 amounted to 9.3 mc, or 3.2 percent of the U.S. market, with a value of $612 million. The company is based in St. Helena, California, at the Sutter Home property purchased by Mario Trinchero in 1947. Sutter Home Winery was a typical small **Napa Valley** winery in 1968 when it began making **Zinfandel** wine from grapes grown in the Sierra Foothills region of **California**. In 1972, current chairman and CEO Bob Trinchero, Mario's son, started selling a small amount of *saignée* runoff **rosé** wine from the Zinfandel production. This wine proved extremely popular, and "White Zinfandel" was born. Sales skyrocketed and pushed Sutter Home into a leading position in national sales by the mid-1980s. The name of the company was changed to Trinchero Family Estates in 2000.

TTB. *See* Alcohol and Tobacco Tax and Trade Bureau (TTB)

U

UNITED KINGDOM. *See* British Market

UNITED STATES

The United States ranks as the world's third largest wine market, after **France** and **Italy**. Sales of all wine in the U.S. market totaled $30 billion in 2007. In addition, the United States is the world's fourth largest wine producer, third largest wine importer, and sixth largest wine exporter.

Consumption. The U.S. wine market has been growing steadily since 1994, reaching 745 million gallons—the equivalent of 313 million nine-liter cases (mc)—in 2007, up from 288 mc in 2006. The United States now represents about 11 percent of global wine consumption. Thus, although currently ranking only 37th in the world in per-capita wine consumption at 11.43 liters, the U.S. market is forecast to become the world's largest volume wine market by 2010.

Where formerly wines under $6 per 750-milliliter bottle dominated the U.S. wine market, today this segment represents less than one-third of wine dollar sales, although it still is some 60 percent of the volume. Sales in this segment have been flat for several years. Wines selling for more than $15 per bottle account for another third of wine sales revenues; although only about 8 percent of volume, they are the fastest growing segment of the wine market. Wines priced between $8 and $15 per bottle—especially between $10 and $15 per bottle—are now the heart of the U.S. wine market.

These sales trends reflect the American **consumers**' growing preference for higher-quality, premium-priced products—in wine as in many other products. North America is the only large wine market in the world where demand for wine over $10 per bottle is a major and growing market segment—and is thus the target market for all the world's wine producers. As a consequence, the United States may already be the world's largest wine market in dollar terms.

Chardonnay and **Cabernet Sauvignon** dominate U.S. wine consumption. **Merlot** is the third most popular variety, although its sales have been nearly flat since

Top 10 Wine-Producing States, 2006

Rank	State	Production Gallons (millions)	Production Cases (millions)
1	California	592.4	249.1
2	New York	29.3	12.3
3	Washington	20.1	8.44
4	Oregon	4.16	1.75
5	Florida	1.76	0.74
6	New Jersey	1.68	0.71
7	Kentucky	1.25	0.53
8	Ohio	1.15	0.48
9	Virginia	0.98	0.41
10	Missouri	0.90	0.38

Source: Alcohol and Tobacco Tax and Trade Bureau.

2005. Rapid growth continues to be seen in alternative white wines, including **Pinot Grigio**, **Sauvignon Blanc**, and **Riesling**. **Red wine** claims a slightly larger market share than white. **Pinot Noir**'s sales continue to be strong, but have slowed somewhat from the extraordinary growth seen in 2005 and 2006. Americans are also exploring various Mediterranean varietals and red **Zinfandel**, although **Syrah** sales have been sluggish and the grape appears to be in surplus.

Imports.   Imports have claimed an increasing share of the U.S. market and now represent about 31 percent of all wine sales. Imports into the United States totaled about 87 mc in 2006. Italy has consistently led import volumes, while France consistently leads in import value. However, France's imports have declined most years over the past decade and remain below their peak levels of the 1990s, although some recovery has been seen since 2006. **Australia** is the second largest source of imports by volume, third by value, nearly quadrupling sales over the decade, although growth has slowed significantly in the last year. **Spain** and **Chile** rank fourth and fifth in import value. Imports of Spanish wine have more than doubled over the decade, accelerating in recent years, while Chile's sales of wine into the United States have been static or declining through most of the period. There has also been a significant increase in imports of foreign **bulk wines** for bottling in the United States. Such imports of foreign bulk wines increased by 110 percent in 2006.

Production.   Producing 230 mc of still and **sparkling wine** in 2006—plus 28.5 mc of **vermouth**, **wine coolers**, and other special wines, and 42 mc for **distillation**—the United States is responsible for almost 10 percent of the world's wine production from 5 percent of the total vineyard acreage. **California** produces 86 percent of the U.S. still and sparkling wine.

The United States ranks sixth in the world for planted vineyards, with 934,750 grape-bearing acres, of which half is wine grapes. Dramatic expansion of vineyard acreage through the 1990s led to a severe grape surplus from 2001 to 2004, capped by the extraordinarily large harvest of 2005, largely due to nearly 50 percent higher yields. The surplus, along with winery **consolidation** and the growing difficulty in obtaining grape contracts from producers, has discouraged planting since 2001.

The number of **wineries** in the United States doubled from 2,688 in 1999 to 5,426 in 2006. The majority (2,447 in 2006) are in California, followed in number by **Washington**, **Oregon**, and **New York**. There are now wineries in every state. Some 88 percent of the U.S. wineries produced less than 12,500 cases of wine in 2006, with many producing less than 5,000. There has been active consolidation among larger wineries, as they seek to increase economies of scale and also to move toward the faster-growing higher-price segments.

The number of wine labels and **brands** coming to market continues to multiply. The **Alcohol and Tobacco Tax and Trade Bureau** (**TTB**) of the Treasury Department, which regulates beverage alcohol at the federal level, reported in 2007 that it had registered more than 90,000 labels from all countries. The Nielsen Company reports at least 13,861 active wine stock-keeping units (SKUs) in U.S. grocery and drug chain channels—the largest number in any category in these stores. The proliferation of brands creates relentless pressure on wineries to increase quality and restrain prices.

The U.S. place-of-origin system is managed by the TTB, which has sole authority to define and approve place-of-origin designations, although states can add further guidelines and restrictions. The place of origin for a U.S. wine can be "United States" (or "American wine"), a state or a multistate **appellation** (up to three states), a county or a multicounty appellation (up to three counties), or a TTB-recognized delimited **grape-growing** area referred to as an American viticultural area (AVA). The AVA concept was first formalized in the United States in 1978.

Sales and Distribution.   The traditional structure of the U.S. wine industry was dictated by the 21st Amendment to the U.S. Constitution, which gave each state the authority to regulate alcoholic beverages within its borders. Under this structure, alcoholic beverage producers, licensed at both state and federal levels, sell their products to **distributors**, themselves licensed at both levels. The distributors then sell the product to a licensed **retailer** ("off-premise") or **restaurant**, bar, or hotel ("on-premise") venue, which then sells the product to the consumer.

This structure is typically described as the "three-tier system." Although also licensed by the federal government, distributors are state based and function under state-defined structures. There are no nationwide distributors. For distribution purposes, the United States is effectively 51 different entities (including the District of Columbia). State laws may restrain the establishment of new distributors through "franchise" or domicile laws and other regulations, although many of these regulations and laws are being challenged in federal courts. Similar laws and regulations may limit winery opportunities to reach markets in several states.

Importers are treated as producers in terms of distribution and are obligated to sell their products through licensed distributors, although some importers also have distribution licenses. "Tied house laws" generally prohibit producers from also holding distribution licenses and distributors from holding on-premise retail licenses.

Thus, the producer traditionally has limited contact with the final consumer or even the venue selling the product and is dependent on the distributor in each state to move its wine. Distributors are generally free to choose which wine products to carry in their portfolios and how to market them.

Eighteen states (plus two counties in Maryland) currently have state monopolies over some aspect of alcohol beverage retailing or wholesaling and are therefore called "**control states**." Most of these jurisdictions control spirits only; in just five states (plus the two Maryland counties), the government maintains control over wine wholesaling, and in only one, Pennsylvania, is wine completely controlled by the state at the retail level. Several control states operate monopoly liquor stores that also sell wine. The remaining states allow wine to be sold in grocery stores and in some cases convenience stores. About one-quarter of the U.S. population lives in control states.

Exports. U.S. wine exports, 95 percent of them from California, reached a record high $951 million in 2007 on a volume of 50.3 mc, up 8.6 percent and 12 percent, respectively, from the previous year. About half of U.S. wine exports are shipped to the **European Union**, accounting for $474 million, with the **British market** being the primary European destination, followed by Italy and **Germany**. **Canada** was the largest non-European market, and the second largest single country, at $234 million. It was followed by Japan, **Switzerland**, and Mexico. Bulk wine is a growing share of U.S. wine exports.

While the United States, unlike most other wine-producing countries, does not have a national export market **promotion** and subsidy program for wine, the Foreign Agricultural Service of the U.S. Department of Agriculture does provide assistance to exporters and has funded, along with industry, the Wine Institute California Wine Export Program, developed and operated by the advocacy organization for California's wineries. This program focuses on "educating the foreign wine trade and media about the quality and range of California wines" through tastings, trade shows, trade and media visits and publications, analysis of foreign markets, data on market entry, and advocacy for the removal of **trade barriers** for U.S. wine exports. Various regional organizations and some state-level agencies also provide promotional support through trade shows, visits, and collateral.

Overall government support for the wine industry has been minimal. Total funding for grape- and wine-related research and education in 2005 was approximately $42 million, primarily from state-level programs.

Trends and Outlook. Key trends in the U.S. wine market include the following:

- growth of winemaking arrangements, including **custom crush** and **négociant** arrangements, providing alternatives to the extremely high capital costs of establishing new wineries
- growth of private-label wines, still a relatively small segment of the U.S. wine market
- continued growth of **wine tourism** and "destination wineries"—visitor-driven wineries—across the country
- parallel expansion of winery direct sales as a **profit** center for wineries, particularly in response to the continuing consolidation of the distribution channel, along with continuing legal challenges to barriers to winery **direct shipping**
- expansion of wine offerings, in terms of number of SKUs and volume, and rising price levels for these offerings in the retail channel in parallel with the emergence of new wine retailing formats

- accelerated consumer interest in exploring new tastes, flavors, and origins of foods—as well as wines—with an accompanying lack of brand or regional loyalties, a preference for brand variety, and a generally more experimental attitude toward both wine and food, especially among the younger generation
- continued proliferation of brands and small wineries across the United States, even as the larger wine groups continue to consolidate
- growing professionalism of this still-small U.S. industry, although somewhat constrained by the growing scarcity of viticulture and enology professionals and the clouded outlook for skilled vineyard workers

Overall, the future for wine in the United States is quite positive. Wine remains the "affordable luxury" and "special experience" that the American consumer continues to seek, even in the face of an economic slowdown.

Barbara Insel

Further Reading
American Journal of Enology & Viticulture. www.ajevonline.org.

Cass, Bruce, and Jancis Robinson, eds. *The Oxford Companion to the Wines of North America.* New York: Oxford University Press, 2000.

U.S. Alcohol and Tobacco Tax and Trade Bureau. www.ttb.gov.

WineAmerica: The National Association of American Wineries. www.wineamerica.org.

Wine Business Monthly. www.winebusiness.com.

Wine Institute. www.wineinstitute.org.

V

VARIETAL LABELING

Varietal labeling, at its simplest, is the practice of using the name of the grape variety on a wine label as a descriptive term. This kind of labeling, mainly associated with **New World** wines, was introduced in America in the late 1930s as a way of distinguishing wines of higher quality made predominantly from a single grape variety and was embraced by other New World countries, especially **Australia** and **New Zealand**.

In the **United States**, Maynard Amerine of the University of California at Davis and wine **importer** Frank Schoonmaker were early advocates of varietal labeling. After the repeal of **Prohibition**, Amerine began urging growers to plant better grape varieties and to put the name of the dominant variety on the label—but only if that varietal imparted its unique character to the wine. A little later, Schoonmaker realized that American wines would become important on the international market as a result of World War II, when the supply of European wine dwindled. He advocated the use of varietal labeling to assure **consumers** that American wines were honestly made, honestly labeled, and of high quality. Today, U.S. laws state that most wines must contain 75 percent or more of the stated variety in order to bear the name of that variety on the label, an increase over the 51 percent standard of the early 1940s.

This was a departure from the way wines traditionally had been labeled. Before then, most wine traded in the world came from European wine regions, where the demarcated region of origin has generally been the recognized and legal way to label wine. The wine laws of the **appellation** would state which grape variety or varieties could be in the bottle, but this was not generally permitted to be written on the label, thereby **promoting** the distinctiveness of the wine region and its **terroir** over that of the grape variety (exceptions include **Germany** and **Austria**, numerous **Italian** appellations such as Montepulciano d'Abruzzo that carry a grape name as part of the appellation, and a few small regions such as Alsace and Trentino–Alto Adige that underwent complete transformations due to war). In most European countries, grape varieties appeared only on the labels of country wines (for example, *vin de pays*), not on **quality wines**. In particular, the vin de pays wines of **France**'s Languedoc-Roussillon region widely used and benefited from varietal labeling. Today, however, the practice is slowly being adopted by several Old World countries and is even being introduced in such stalwart regions as **Burgundy** and **Bordeaux**, albeit slowly.

The consumer-friendly nature of varietal labeling is one of its positive attributes. Just by reading the label, one knows what is in the bottle and thus has a good clue as to the wine's characteristics. Varietal labeling has also made it easier for wines from unknown regions or countries to gain immediate acceptance in the market if they prominently display familiar varietal names.

The primary downside of varietal labeling, especially in the New World, is that it diminishes the importance of the sense of place or terroir—which is precisely the reason that Europeans have resisted allowing grape varieties on the wine label. Another drawback is that it demeans wines made from blends of grapes in the style of some of the best Old World wines, such as Bordeaux, Châteauneuf-du-Pape, Rioja, Chianti, and **Champagne**. For this reason, winemakers have introduced proprietary names such as Opus One and Le Mistral for high-quality blended wines and even founded the Meritage Association for producers of wines made in the classic Bordeaux style.

Despite the fact that there are some distinct disadvantages to adopting varietal labeling into the existing structure, France is moving to do just that. Since 2005, following a VinExpo study showing how much of the wine market France has lost to New World competition, the French have been allowing the use of the grape name on the label of quality wines. Some producers adopted the practice even earlier, but it has not yet come into widespread use. Most of the wines that do opt to label with the variety fall within the $5 to $15 price bracket, which has sparked opposition from producers in Languedoc-Roussillon, whose value-priced vin de pays wines have been allowed to state varietal names since the 1980s. Since a vast portion of the French wine surplus is attributed to these Languedoc-Roussillon producers, added competition in the value-priced varietal market is not necessarily welcome.

Before varietal labeling exerted influence on growers to plant popular varieties, the most widely planted wine grapes in the United States were **Zinfandel**, Alicante Bouschet, and Carignan. The first of the "fighting varietals"—the top-selling varietal jug wines during the 1970s wine boom—were **Cabernet Sauvignon**, Zinfandel (mainly white Zinfandel), and **Chardonnay**. Today, Chardonnay, **Merlot**, and Cabernet Sauvignon drive 40 percent of U.S. wine sales. **Pinot Grigio** is quickly gaining in popularity and sales, as is **Pinot Noir**, although, being more difficult to grow, it is still in relatively short supply. On the international market, **Sauvignon Blanc**, **Riesling**, and **Syrah/Shiraz** are also big players among the top varietals. *See also* Branding; European Union; Labels as Marketing.

Mollie Battenhouse

VERMOUTH

Vermouth is a classic example of an aromatized wine, flavored with various herbs, including wormwood, *wermuth* in German, which gives its name to the product. It is also a type of **fortified wine**, its alcohol volume raised to 16 to 17 percent through the addition of grape spirits. It is made in two general styles—Italian (red and sweet) and French (white and dry)—although both are actually made in many countries. Annual consumption worldwide is estimated at 25 million nine-liter cases (mc). Major producers include Cinzano, Lillet, Martini & Rossi, Punt e Mes, and Noilly Prat.

In the **United States**, vermouth is a small category; according to *Adams Wine Handbook 2007,* the 1.8 mc of vermouth sold in 2006 represented just 0.6 percent of total U.S. wine consumption. Of this, a slight majority, 940,000 cases, was imported, more than 90 percent of it from **Italy**. Domestically produced vermouth, primarily from E.&J. **Gallo** Winery, accounted for 48 percent of sales. Vermouth has declined as a category from 2.4 mc at the beginning of the 1990s and is more popular as a cocktail ingredient, particularly for the recently trendy martini, than as an aperitif wine.

VIRTUAL WINERIES

In the most general terms, a virtual winery is a **brand** without a **winery**. In the 1980s, most domestic wines were made in a brick-and-mortar winery that usually bore the same name as the one on the label. Today, faced with the considerable capital outlay and the special skill set required to build and operate a wine production facility, many aspiring vintners are forgoing the traditional chateau altogether. Brand owners are also realizing that in the increasingly Web-centric world economy, market share can be gained and kept without maintaining an overhead-heavy tasting room. Add to that the fact that virtual wineries can create award-winning wines at a decent cost of goods sold, and it makes sense that a successful brand no longer has to have a physical home.

There is some controversy, however, about what a virtual winery is *not.* Most in the industry agree that a virtual winery is not simply a **négociant**; négociants typically buy finished **bulk wine** on the spec market, and though they may blend and bottle the wine, they are opportunistic buyers and have no control over their raw material. Some small brand owners—who often prefer to be called "micro-wineries" or "micro-vintners"—also want to distance themselves from well-heeled wine enthusiasts who pay thousands of dollars for a **barrel** of wine to be produced on their behalf at an increasing number of purpose-built "boutique urban wineries." Subtle shades of meaning aside, most industry members would agree that a virtual winery produces at least one commercially distributed brand, has its own management and winemaker (who may be a consultant), does not own bonded winery premises, and controls all of the winemaking decisions.

As the numbers of bonded wineries in the **United States** increase, so, in general, do the number of virtual wineries. In 2007, a survey conducted by *Wine Business Monthly* found 4,850 bonded grape wineries and 1,161 virtual wineries in the United States. **California** had the largest number of virtual wineries (853), with **Oregon** (73), **Washington** (40), and **New York** (20) following. These numbers fluctuate as players enter and exit the market—in 2007, 95 virtual wineries received bonded premises.

The industry itself has changed to accommodate what might be called the "pay for play" revolution. Whereas 20 years ago no one thought of building and staffing a winery for the express purpose of renting out tank and barrel space, today there are more than 30 of these **custom crush** wineries on the West Coast. Satellite services have also sprung up to serve this growing industry segment; niche distributors, mobile bottlers, and cooperative tasting rooms enable the virtual winery to get its goods to market.

As the average brand life has shortened and wine **consumers** seek new, trendy, and more esoteric wines, it may make more and more sense for companies to focus on virtual brands rather than on traditional estate-based stalwarts. Brands that are not wedded to specific vineyards, **appellations**, or physical wineries are often more nimble, can capture better **profit** margins, and can respond more quickly to market demands. In today's "virtual winery" world, it seems wiser to first develop a salable brand, get product on the market, and only then—if the brand seems to have longevity—build a physical winery and visitor center.

Alison Crowe

Further Reading

Rauber, Chris. "Wine, without the Vine." *San Francisco Business Times,* May 28, 2004, www.bizjournals.com/sanfrancisco/stories/2004/05/31/story6.html.

Schneider, Sara. "Virtual Vineyards." *Sunset,* www.sunset.com/sunset/food/article/0,20633,1149908,00.html.

Tinney, Mary-Colleen. "Number of US Wineries Tops 6,000." *Wine Business Monthly,* February 2008.

W

WASHINGTON

Washington State is the second largest producer of *Vitis vinifera* wine in the **United States**. What drives Washington's growth and impact in the U.S. market is lower land and grape prices for high-quality fruit compared with **California** and a growing market awareness of the region derived from its positive, increasing recognition for quality in the wine press and trade.

Background and History.   The state's winegrowing history dates back to 1825, when vines were planted by the Hudson's Bay Company at Fort Vancouver, although serious viticulture began only with the introduction of native American and hybrid varieties later in the nineteenth century. **Grape growing** proved to be very difficult in western Washington due to the cool, wet climate and in eastern Washington because of the lack of rainfall and harsh winter frost pressure. The expansion of irrigation projects in the Columbia Valley of eastern Washington in the early twentieth century opened the region to large-scale agriculture, including vineyards.

Washington's importance today results primarily from the extraordinary contributions of early producers such as W. H. Bridgeman, who took a chance on vinifera in eastern Washington in the 1930s. In the 1940s and 1950s, Dr. Walter J. Clore of Washington State University confirmed that vinifera could grow there, provided there was adequate water and careful attention to winter frost protection. He encouraged producers to plant vinifera and is today considered by many the "father of Washington winegrowing."

Physical Factors.   Virtually all of Washington's wine grapes grow on the eastern side of the Cascade mountain range within the greater Columbia River Valley. The maritime climate of western Washington produces large amounts of rain and snow, but eastern Washington lies in the rain shadow of the Cascades. Consequently, the region has very low rainfall (6 to 12 inches annually), very hot and dry summers, and very cold, frost-prone winters—an ideal continental climate.

The Columbia Valley's location between 45° and 46° north latitude contributes to conditions more like **Burgundy** or **Bordeaux** for growing grapes than California, including about an hour more sunlight per day during the summer ripening period and lower temperatures heading into the harvest period. Combined, these factors allow for excellent fruit maturity with better acidity and less propensity for overripeness compared to more Mediterranean latitudes or locations, such as the **Napa Valley**. Frost in the late spring and early fall and hard freezes during the winter are always a concern, however.

Massive volcanic eruptions millions of years ago created deep, rocky, basaltic parent rock formations. Between 8,000 and 15,000 years ago, multiple cataclysmic floods washed over the region from east to west, carving out the gorges, including the Columbia River channel, and leaving behind massive amounts of sand, silt, and gravel as top soil. Strong winds over time have also contributed a light, powdery soil with good drainage capacity. These sandy, silty soils on top of rock have low fertility, require irrigation, and do not permit the spread of **phylloxera**. Virtually all of Washington's vinifera vines are grown on their own roots.

Aspects of the Washington Wine Industry.   The first "modern" **wineries** in Washington began in 1967, with the founding of Chateau Ste. Michelle Winery (parent company founded in 1934) and Associated Vintners (now Columbia Winery) near Seattle. Moderate but steady growth over the last 25 years has seen the winery count rise from these two to more than 530. Most of this increase has been in smaller wineries making between 2,000 and 15,000 cases a year. The Ste. Michelle Wine Estates group, the largest producer in the state, accounts for two-thirds of the wine produced—5 million cases out of the nearly 8 million cases produced in the state in 2007.

The total Washington wine-grape production in 2007 was 127,000 tons; this represents about the same amount produced in Napa County alone—just 4 percent of total California production. While Washington production and acreage are large compared with other states, all of Washington's 31,000 acres could fit within the Napa Valley American Viticultural Area (AVA). But costs in Washington are lower than in California. In 2006, the average Washington **Cabernet Sauvignon** price was $1,260 per ton, compared to $3,000 to $4,000 for **Sonoma County** and Napa fruit. Washington **Chardonnay** and **Merlot** averaged $780 and $1,100 a ton, respectively, only about a third of the price in Napa. Based on critical reviews, the quality of the wines produced in Washington is equivalent to those of California, albeit in a different style that many find more similar to European wines than Californian ones. Indeed, there are a growing number of European producers and winemakers who have entered into joint ventures or built wineries in Washington for that reason, as well as cost issues, including Piero Antinori, Ernst Loosen, Christophe Baron, Gilles Nicault, and others.

Excellent press and the recognition that certain varieties, such as **Riesling**, Cabernet, Merlot, and **Syrah**, reveal a unique regional character in Washington have given the state a distinctive "voice" in the market. Washington's market share lies mainly in the premium and higher levels. Its wines represent approximately 3 percent of the total U.S. wine production and revenue. Notably, Washington is the largest producer of fine Riesling in the United States, with sales growth exceeding 20 percent for the last two years. With 4,400 acres, the grape is now second only to Chardonnay in plantings of white varieties.

Syrah, according to many producers, represents the state's future signature wine. Eastern Washington's similarity in climate and geology to the northern

Rhône Valley in **France** has inspired a surge in production of Syrah in the last several years. Prior to 1986, there were only 95 acres of Syrah in the state; now there are nearly 3,000, and the price per ton is nearly equal to Cabernet.

The Future.   Washington's image as a clean, "green" environment, combined with its scenic beauty, contributes strongly to the state's ability to increase the reputation and market penetration for its wines. There is some room for vineyard growth, but this is strictly regulated by availability to an increasingly stressed water supply system. Provided that land prices do not escalate dramatically, Washington will continue producing very good quality affordable wines, while increasing its capability for making world-class wines as vineyards mature and experience grows.

The strength and steady vision of the state's largest and finest producers, along with the enthusiasm of its iconic smaller wineries, continue to encourage new markets to open their doors to Washington's distinctive and flavorful wines. The Washington Wine Commission actively supports the industry, has done much to help guide development of the AVAs—now nine in number—and assists with marketing Washington wines internationally, particularly in Japan and **Canada**.

Joel P. Butler

Further Reading

Hall, Lisa Shara. *Wines of the Pacific Northwest: A Contemporary Guide to the Wines of Washington and Oregon.* London: Mitchell Beazley, 2001.

Washington Wine Commission. www.washingtonwine.org.

WINE BARS. *See* Hospitality Industry; Restaurants

WINE CLUBS

The term *wine club* encompasses several types of organizations, ranging from social groups to small informal retail operations to large businesses that sell everything under the sun, including wine. Wine clubs are multifaceted, come in an array of sizes, and have their own personalities and quirks.

Social wine clubs date back to nineteenth-century England. These originally were class-based, high-society groups, with membership normally for gentlemen only and strictly by invitation. Today, however, wine clubs come in all shapes and sizes and for all societal groups. They may be relatively well established or completely informal. Some clubs meet monthly, others quarterly, and some have no set schedules. They may meet in members' homes or in **restaurants**. Usually there is a theme for each meeting—for example, wines of **France**, **Sonoma Chardonnays**, **sparkling wines**, southern **Italian** reds, and so on. The group may charge membership dues or share the cost on a pay-as-you-go basis. One of the main goals of most social wine clubs is to taste many wines for a reasonable cost. Often food and wine are paired.

Social wine clubs are very popular. Around the country and the world, clubs such as the International Wine Society, the Confrérie de la Chaîne des Rôtisseurs, and the Vintners Club in San Francisco have left their imprint on **wine education** and wine tasting. These clubs are by invitation only and have dues and assessments; frequently one has to purchase a fraction of the cellar. Some clubs go under such catchy names as the Society of the Black Glass, Les Amis du Vin, the Purple Foot Society, and Noble Rot. Social clubs usually emphasize fun and wine appreciation, sharing costs and lacking formal rules.

Warehouse clubs are a retailing phenomenon that have brought a form of wine club to the shopping center. Led by Costco, Sam's Club, and BJ's Wholesale Club, these membership stores have entered the big-box retailer segment with a bang. In fact, Costco is the largest wine retailer in the **United States**—and not only of inexpensive everyday wines: it is also the largest seller of first-growth **Bordeaux** and of Dom Pérignon **Champagne**. Still, warehouse clubs tend to be discounters of wines, and as a result, many smaller, **cult**, and ultrapremium **wineries** tend to avoid this form of retailing.

Another type of club that has burst onto the scene in recent years is the *Internet wine club.* This is a form of **e-commerce**, a retail outlet usually with no brick-and-mortar storefront that specializes in regular recurring purchases—two wines a month, a case every other month, and so forth. Some examples include the Discount Wine Club, California Wine Club, International Wine Club, Wine of the Month Club, Basement Wines, and many others. Most of these have a specific focus, such as French, **Californian**, or **Australian** wines, and they also offer **promotions**, discounts, and new releases. Many offer unique selections that are not readily available at traditional beverage retailers. However, in many states, **consumers** cannot buy wine directly, because Internet wine clubs fall under **direct shipping** restrictions. In the economic downturn of 2008, wine clubs have seen a drop in patronage, with some members deciding to opt out of the automatic shipments.

Wineries themselves have carved out a similar niche, with their own *winery wine clubs* becoming an integral part of their retail tasting rooms and Web sites. These clubs may have several levels of membership, sending customers two or four or six bottles of a specially selected wine at predetermined intervals. They may or may not charge a membership fee in addition to the cost of the wine and shipping. Additional benefits might include discounts on wine merchandise or special invitations to winery activities. This is a way for wineries to sell small or unusual wines, new releases, reserve wines, and experimental lots.

Some wineries believe wine clubs account for as much as two-thirds of the **profitability** of their tasting rooms. Through direct mail and the Internet, wineries can reach customers who may never visit or see their winery. Wine clubs have even started member rewards programs like those of **airlines** and restaurants.

Other groups—such as alumni associations, nonprofit organizations, and trade associations—have also formed wine clubs. KDFC, San Francisco's classical music radio station, has a wine club that partners wine with various pieces of music. The Lodi-Woodbridge Winegrape Commission has a club that promotes various wines from Lodi, California.

Shields Hood

WINE COOLERS

Wine coolers are an almost extinct category of beverage that became a **fad** in the 1980s. They were originally a carbonated mixture of wine with various fruit juices, intended as an alternative to beer that was simpler, more refreshing, and less alcoholic (at about 6 percent alcohol by volume [abv]) than most wines. They sprang to prominence with the California Cooler **brand** and through the marketing of the Bartles & Jaymes brand by E.&J. **Gallo** Winery. The majority were made in **California**, and after the **United States** imposed a 100 percent tax on imports of wines under 7 percent abv in 1989, the U.S. market became almost exclusively California based.

U.S. consumption of wine coolers grew sharply in the early 1980s, according to *Adams Wine Handbook* data, reaching a maximum of 53.6 million cases, 22 percent of total U.S. wine consumption, in 1987. Consumption fell below 10 million cases in 1995 and below 1 million in 2003. As of 2006, consumption was down to 250,000 cases, 0.1 percent of total U.S. consumption. However, after a tax increase on wine in 1991, almost all "wine coolers" switched to using malt-based alcohol rather than wine.

WINE EDUCATION

The subject of wine is a complex one and is beyond the capacity of any individual to master without outside assistance. Certainly wine can be enjoyed on a personal basis without academic, rigorous study, but to truly understand the world of wine or to be a professional in any aspect of the wine industry requires a more or less formal wine education. This course of education can be accomplished on one's own using books, periodicals, DVDs, Internet sources, and personal exploration or in a group setting under the guidance of a wine educator.

Wine educators form an intriguing and eclectic group that encompasses **wine writers**; university professors in viticulture or enology programs; in-house educators at **wineries**, **import** houses, **distribution** companies, and **retail** establishments; **sommeliers** in **restaurants**; sales staff at wine shops; independent wine educators who run classes; and many more, including more experienced friends and colleagues. In the broadest sense, a wine educator is anyone who teaches someone else about wine, and therefore virtually everyone who works in the industry is a wine educator.

There are two major segments to the wine education field: consumer education and professional education, with specialties in both areas. Although there is plenty of overlap between these segments, those who teach consumers generally focus on wine appreciation, including information about wine regions and styles, grape varieties, label reading, and individual producers and wines that will enhance a consumer's enjoyment and selection of wines. The role of professional wine education is to provide training to winemakers, grape growers, and others working in production and/or sales, marketing, and financial management. This training concentrates more on technical aspects: critical tasting and analysis, the science of winemaking, sales techniques, specific portfolios of wines, and so forth.

Consumer wine educators range from the local **wine club** hosting the odd monthly informal tasting to seriously busy types, such as Kevin Zraly, who run

Wine Education Programs

The following is a sampling of wine education programs. All are conducted in English.

Degree Programs (Wine Business)

BEM (Management School Bordeaux), Wine MBA Programme; Bordeaux, Adelaide, and London
www.bem.edu/en/programmes/mba/wine-mba

Sonoma State University, Rohnert Park, California
www.sonoma.edu/winebiz/

University of Adelaide, Waite Campus, Adelaide, S.A., Australia
www.agwine.adelaide.edu.au/agribus

Degree Programs (Viticulture and/or Enology)

California State University, Fresno
www.csufresno.edu/catoffice/current/enoldgre.html

Cal Poly, San Luis Obispo, California
www.cafes.calpoly.edu/departmentsandmajors/majors/wineandviticulture.asp

Charles Sturt University, Wagga Wagga, N.S.W., Australia
www.csu.edu.au/faculty/science/wfs/

Cornell University, Ithaca and Geneva, New York
www.grapesandwine.cals.cornell.edu

Oregon State University, Corvallis
wine.oregonstate.edu

University of Adelaide, Roseworthy and Waite Campuses, S.A., Australia
www.agwine.adelaide.edu.au/wine

University of California, Davis
wineserver.ucdavis.edu

Washington State University, Pullman and Richland
wine.wsu.edu/education.html

Degree Programs (Hospitality/Restaurant/Beverage Management)

Florida International University, North Miami
hospitality.fiu.edu

Johnson & Wales University, Providence, Rhode Island; North Miami, Florida; Denver, Colorado; Charlotte, North Carolina
www.jwu.edu/hosp

New England Culinary Institute, Montpelier and Essex, Vermont
www.neci.edu/hotel-restaurant-management

University of Denver, Denver, Colorado
daniels.du.edu/hrtm.aspx

University of Nevada, Las Vegas
hotel.unlv.edu

University-Level Certificate Programs

Boston University, Boston, Massachusetts
www.bu.edu/foodandwine/wine_programs/index.html

Virginia Tech, Blacksburg
www.vtwines.info

Certification and Diploma Programs

American Sommelier Association, New York, New York
  www.americansommelier.com
American Wine Society, Lawrenceville, Georgia
  www.americanwinesociety.org/web/judge_certification.htm
Association of Italian Sommeliers, California Branch, Los Angeles
  www.sommelieronline.us
Court of Master Sommeliers, American Chapter, Napa, California
  www.mastersommeliers.org
Court of Master Sommeliers, London
  www.courtofmastersommeliers.org
Institute of Masters of Wine, London
  www.mastersofwine.org
International Sommelier Guild, Coral Springs, Florida; Hamilton, Ontario, Canada
  www.internationalsommelier.com
Society of Wine Educators, Washington, D.C.
  www.societyofwineeducators.org
Sommelier Society of America, New York, New York
  www.sommeliersocietyofamerica.org
Wine & Spirit Education Trust (WSET), London
  www.wset.co.uk

Online Courses and Certifications

Parker & Zraly Wine Certification Program
  www.erobertparker.com/newSearch/wine_certification.aspx
Wine Australia
  www.wineaustralia.com/USA/Default.aspx?tabid=2558
Wine Spectator School
  www.winespectatorschool.com/wineschool/

Other Noteworthy Programs

Bordeaux Wine School, Bordeaux, France
  ecole.vins-bordeaux.fr/anglais/
Copia: The American Center for Wine, Food, and the Arts, Napa, California [WSET certifications]
  www.copia.org
Harriet Lembeck's Wine & Spirits Program, New York, New York
  212-252-8989
International Wine Center, New York, New York [WSET certifications]
  www.internationalwinecenter.com
Kevin Zraly's Windows on the World Wine School, New York, New York
  www.windowswineschool.com
Spanish Wine Academy, Spain and Portugal [WSET certifications] and traveling worldwide
  www.thewineacademy.com

numerous series of classes that are oversubscribed every session. Others write books or articles in consumer or trade periodicals that convey wine knowledge to others.

Degree programs in viticulture and enology exist in all major wine-producing countries of the world. These are often complemented by executive-level business programs aimed at winery managers, sales and marketing executives, and finance and human resources personnel who work in all aspects of the wine trade. In response to the ever-growing **global wine industry**, the most comprehensive curriculum to debut in recent years, with its first graduating class in January 2002, is the Wine MBA based in **Bordeaux** and run in a consortium fashion among top universities in several countries. The online world has made inroads into wine education, as well. Culinary schools have gotten into the act, too, offering wine courses for credit as part of the curriculum, with courses being taught by in-house wine education instructors, often supplemented by guest lecturers from the trade. All of this has led to an improvement in wine quality due to better education in production and marketing segments.

Thirty some years ago, when the U.S. wine industry was beginning to take off and Riunite was the top-selling wine in the country, the official job title of "wine educator" was almost nonexistent. Wine information was disseminated through various channels, typically sales. Today, at least one person is wholly dedicated to this role at all major wine companies, if not teams scattered throughout various divisions. As an ever-growing wine world continues to refine its wines and its practices and a consuming public continues to be interested in wine and fascinated by its complexities, the need for professional wine educators continues to grow.

In the **United States**, a group of academics and wine professionals formed the Society of Wine Educators (SWE) in 1974. Its mission is to advance wine education through professional development and certification. This was perhaps the first group to use the term *wine educator* in its title, although there were other organizations with similar goals already established in Europe. Three of the most notable were the Wine & Spirit Education Trust (WSET), the Institute of Masters of Wine (MW), and the Court of Master Sommeliers (MS), all formed in Great Britain. The WSET was founded in 1969 to provide high-quality education and training in wines and spirits among professionals in the **British market**. The MW organization, whose mission is to promote the highest level of educational achievement for the wine industry, held its first exam in 1953, while in 1969 the MS Court was established to encourage improved standards of beverage knowledge and service in hotels and restaurants. Each of these four organizations confers its own certificates, diplomas, or credentials to those who successfully meet its criteria, including passing a written and/or practical examination.

Today there are at least a hundred organizations around the world that declare their mission to be wine education, plus another several hundred that are engaged in some sort of wine education activity. The vast majority of these are targeted to consumer education. The range of wine education offerings include accredited courses at colleges, independent wine classes, interactive Web sites, radio and television programs, books, magazines, newsletters, tasting events, wine associations and trade bureaus, specialized wine education consultancies, wine region tours, seminars at festivals, and courses offered as part of in-house training at importers and distributors. As well, on-premise and off-premise retail outlets, wine clubs, and other tasting affinity groups from wineries offer programs.

Challenges.   The growth of the global wine industry—new consumers in both established markets and new markets developing around the world, different styles and origins of wines appearing in the market continually, and consumers trading up to higher-quality offerings—requires more and better education for the industry's professionals. As the demand for education increases, challenges have developed for this segment of the industry.

Despite the many certification programs offered in the United States in particular, there are no real barriers to entry as a "wine educator," so the quality of instruction is uneven. Anyone can hang out a wine educator shingle and start offering classes to the public, as there is not enough public awareness of the professional certifications and not enough certified trainers to go around. This is much less true in the United Kingdom, where there are many more MWs and tens of thousands of people with some level of certification from the WSET. In the United States, SWE has stepped up the number of testing opportunities for its Certified Wine Educator (CWE) and Certified Specialist of Wine (CSW) credentials, and the WSET is becoming more active (it now offers courses and examinations in 39 countries), with courses in some two dozen North American locations.

One issue that used to be more prevalent in consumer education than it is today is the sales pitch disguised as education. With too few wine educators available, sales staff or marketing people were often assigned the task of conducting seminars, which then came off as thinly veiled advertisements for a particular **brand** or producer. Consumers generally were dissatisfied with this tactic, and most professional organizations now frown upon this practice.

The cost of organizing a wine education program, whether for consumers or the trade, varies based on the level of offerings. Expenses can include the educators' own time and/or salaries for assistants; costs of acquiring existing study materials or creating new study guides, CDs/DVDs, and testing components; research materials; online programming; wines for tasting; glassware and associated supplies; and more. Time is perhaps the most underestimated factor. The rule of thumb in training—and wine education is no exception—is that it takes 10 hours of preparation for every hour of quality instruction or seminar delivery time. The key to making training cost-effective is to be able to reuse essentially the same material several times. However, many higher-level programs are customized and require special focus each time, which adds to their cost.

In the corporate setting, proving a net positive effect on the bottom line— showing the relationship of wine education to sales, **promotion**, and **profitability**— to justify a wine education program is challenging. Sales training programs can be designed to track with general educational offerings, but the vagaries of the marketplace often intercede, making it hard to keep momentum. Nevertheless, most people understand that there is a relationship between a better educated sales force and increases in wine sales, and the challenges come in negotiating the exact trade-off of time spent off the street with the investment in a better-trained team.

A continuing problem in wine education is a lack of training or experience in pedagogy—basic teaching skills. A love of wines and a deep knowledge of them are not sufficient to be a wine instructor. Unlike oration, education is not about the presentation of material as much as it is about the effective communication of the information by others. Professional wine educators need to understand the value of spending time on both learning about wine and learning about teaching.

Outlook.   The outlook for wine education—at least for the near term—is very positive. Trends will include the continued prominence of the sommelier as a tastemaker and guru for restaurant goers at all levels. As younger wine drinkers and professionals join the industry, more wine schools will pop up offering innovative online programming featuring celebrity educators, such as the recent Full Circle Wine Solutions entrant into the game started by two former Beam Wine Estates executives, Evan Goldstein and Limeng Stroh. Cultural shifts in the workforce will drive the need for more accessible programs, for example, the Spanish-language WSET program at the International Wine Center in **New York**. As **globalization** provides an increased number of wine offerings and penetration into new geographic and demographic markets continues, the United States will continue to professionalize its wine education segment. Consumer tastes will continue to broaden and refine, and the need to get the word out will only increase. The challenge to professionals will be to unravel the mystery of wine just enough to make it intriguing without demystifying the beverage to the point of making it uninteresting.

Further Reading

Court of Master Sommeliers. www.mastersommeliers.org.
Institute of Masters of Wine. www.masters-of-wine.org.
LocalWineEvents.com. www.localwineevents.com.
Society of Wine Educators. www.societyofwineeducators.com.

WINE GROUP, THE

The generically named Wine Group is a conglomerate that ranks as the world's third largest wine company. The corporation was founded in 1981 to purchase the wine portfolio owned by the Coca-Cola Company, most notably the Franzia **brand**. Aggressive pricing and the use of bag-in-box **alternative packaging** helped to propel Franzia to the highest-volume brand by the late 1990s. Today, Franzia is the largest brand worldwide, selling 24.0 million nine-liter case equivalents (mc) in 2006, 22.8 mc of that in the **United States**—a 7.8 percent market share—at an average retail price of just $1.85 per 750 milliliters, according to data from *Impact*.

Another of the original Wine Group brands was Mogen David, a **New York**–based winemaker well known for **kosher wine**, as well as for its **fortified** MD 20/20. Other brands acquired by the Wine Group along the way include Concannon, Corbett Canyon, Foxhorn, and Glen Ellen. For 2006, the company's brands collectively sold 41.9 mc globally and 36.6 mc in the **United States**. This gave the Wine Group a 12.6 percent share of the U.S. market by volume, placing it third behind E.&J. **Gallo** Winery and **Constellation Brands**, Inc., although it was fourth in revenues (behind **Foster's Group**) at $1.05 billion.

The Wine Group's market share grew considerably in 2008 when it bought the Almaden and Inglenook brands from Constellation. Together, Almaden and Inglenook had U.S. sales of 11.7 mc in 2006 and will thus give the Wine Group one-sixth of the U.S. market and second position behind Gallo. The Wine Group's CEO is David Kent, and its headquarters are in San Francisco, with operations in several locations in **California** and New York.

WINERIES

While there are many crucial segments that make up the wine industry, none is more important or fundamental than the winery. Wineries are where the magic happens—grapes come in one door, alchemy takes place, and the storied elixir called wine flows out the other door. Without them, there would be no wine industry, and thousands of people around the world would be, if not out of jobs, at least doing something quite different and probably not as satisfying. And millions of people would be without one of life's greatest pleasures: a well-deserved glass of wine. This is not to say that running a winery is easy or even **profitable**, however. In the end, it is a business that depends on selling its product at a profit, and in too many cases, adverse market conditions, high overhead, inefficiencies of operations, unfortunate strategic decisions, and other factors—often largely beyond the winery's control—conspire to make that impossible.

Wineries exist at the central node of a complex network of businesses and individuals that supply raw materials and equipment to the winery or help in one way or another to get the wine into the hands of **consumers**. There is no reliable global count of wineries, but some idea of the numbers worldwide can be gleaned from the example of the **United States**—producer of 7 percent of the world's wine—where there were 5,958 commercial wineries in 2007. Winemaking facilities range in size from a home winemaker's back room to industrial operations the size of small cities. Many could not fill a shipping container with their entire yearly output, while a few make millions of cases a year. The vast majority of wineries are found in the same regions where wine grapes are grown, but thanks to the miracles of refrigeration, some exist far away from their sources.

The idealized model of a winery is a beautiful estate or chateau comprising several acres of vineyards, with the winery facility located in the middle of them. This winery harvests its own grapes; brings them into the winery; makes, ages, and bottles its wine; and ships it off to market. Of course, the type of grand winery that usually comes to mind is inevitably one that was built, and usually continues to operate, with a fortune raised in some other field of endeavor, such as banking or technology, rather than from the wine business.

There are many other models, of course. In the modern world of business specialization, almost every facet of the process can be farmed out to specialists. In fact, a **virtual winery** can be pieced together by delegating all aspects of the winemaking process: buying grapes, using a **custom crush facility**, hiring a consultant winemaker, using a mobile bottling line, renting warehouse storage space, and selling to a **négociant**.

Other models of wineries include small operations run by an individual or a family. These may parallel the idealized model, although on a more modest scale.

Such a winery might produce 1,000 cases of wine from its three acres of vines. At the other end of the spectrum are industrial facilities that are like science-fiction versions of the idealized models. Looking more like refineries than wineries, these plants have numerous huge outdoor tanks and spiderwebs of pipes, hoses, and cables. The largest winery in the world, E.&J. **Gallo** Winery, makes more than 60 million cases of wine a year at its four major **California** facilities. Another type of winery is the cooperative, where smallholders pool their output to take advantage of the economies of scale to compete in the big leagues.

The primary input to a winery is typically grapes, freshly harvested from its own or others' vineyards. The **grape-growing** segment of the industry is widely acknowledged as being the cornerstone of winemaking: it is impossible to make top-quality wine with mediocre fruit. Thus, quality-driven wineries—if they do not control their own vineyards—strive to develop strong relationships with growers in order to guarantee the finest raw materials for the style of wine they produce. In many cases, due to distance from grape-growing regions or desired **terroirs**, insufficient volume from their own vineyards, or merely convenience, wineries buy juice from grapes that have been harvested, crushed, and/or pressed elsewhere. The **bulk wine** and **juice trade** caters to this market.

The winery staff may range from one to hundreds of people, but for any given batch of wine, there is usually a single person who is considered the *winemaker*. Whether alone or with a team of assistants and helpers, this person is primarily responsible for the decisions that go into the creation of the wine and often its maturation as well. In medium-size and larger wineries, there is normally a cellar staff responsible for day-to-day care of the wine and the winery equipment; the staff's leader is the *cellar master*. The winemaking process may be aided by greater or lesser degrees of **mechanization**, from the crusher-stemmer and wine press to the bottling line.

Other members of the winery's staff, depending on the size of the operation, may include administrative staff, tasting room staff responsible for at-winery sales to consumers, and personnel in charge of **promotion**, **direct shipping** to customers, a **wine club**, and local sales to **restaurants** and **retailers**, where permitted.

A few wineries, especially makers of **cult wines**, are small enough or popular enough that they are able to sell their entire annual output to consumers from the winery itself. Others are not interested in consumer sales at all and sell their wine to négociants or other wineries in bulk. Most, however, rely on middlemen to get their wine into the hands of consumers. **Distributors** represent the wineries in various markets and help to find on- and off-premise sales outlets for the wine. In addition, wines that cross national borders generally require an **importer** or agent to receive the wine and may have an exporter as well.

Wineries that produce wines in the ultrapremium and luxury strata generally rely on **ratings** from wine critics, medals and other recognition from **festivals** and competitions, and favorable reviews by **wine writers** to keep demand high. Others that compete for a broad consumer base look for widespread distribution to the retail trade or to large-volume purchasers such as chain restaurants, **supermarkets**, **airlines**, **cruise lines**, and the **hospitality industry**.

New wineries open all the time, but the expense of starting a winery from scratch is formidable, especially in highly sought-after areas such as the **Napa**

Valley or Tuscany. In other less well-known regions, the entry costs may be lower, but the increased difficulty of finding a market makes profitability just as difficult to achieve. Thus, many wineries operate at a loss for years before either finding a niche, changing hands, or closing. One solution has been **consolidation**, which has brought some unprofitable wineries into larger groupings that are able to share resources and thereby cut costs. In the **New World** especially, it is possible for wineries to stay profitable by altering their wine styles and even grape varieties to keep up with new **fads and fashions** in consumption, but in many regions, particularly in the Old World, **appellation** laws, traditions, or climatic conditions may foreclose that option, and wineries must focus on making the best wine they can and be prepared to periodically ride out difficult times. *See also* Wine Tourism.

Further Reading
Appellation America. wine.appellationamerica.com.
Practical Winery & Vineyard. www.practicalwinery.com.
Vineyard & Winery Management. www.wvm-online.com.
WineAmerica: The National Association of American Wineries. www.wineamerica.org.

WINE TOURISM

Wine tourism can be defined as the pursuit and enjoyment of wine and wine-related activities while traveling. It is a subset of the larger phenomenon of culinary tourism—the search for unique and memorable eating and drinking experiences while traveling—which also includes gourmet tourism (high-end experiences), beer tourism, spa cuisine, and so on. At the **grape-growing** end of the business, wine tourism is also related to agritourism.

Development of Wine Tourism.   The act of enjoying local food and drink while traveling is as old as civilization itself. **Ancient Mediterranean** soldiers and merchants traveled far from home and often partook of the local cuisine, which often included wine. Travel was an essential part of the education of young gentlemen in the seventeenth to nineteenth centuries, particularly among the British, who embarked on the "grand tour" of continental Europe and learned much about wine. After World War II, Western Europe became a popular destination with Americans who could afford the cost and time for international travel. All visitors must eat, and because wine is such an integral part of European culture, with European travel came more of a formal introduction to wine.

In 1976, when **California** wines bested French wines in the "Judgment of Paris" blind tasting, the world's attention was suddenly focused on California as a wine producer. That notoriety, combined with the other allures of the state, helped to attract droves of tourists and to formalize the activity now called "wine tourism." The **Napa Valley** is now the number two tourist destination in California, just after Disneyland.

The Wine Tourism Experience.   Today, wine tourism has grown to encompass a wide range of experiences for a wide range of **consumers**: **winery** visits, dining out, stays in bed-and-breakfasts among the vineyards, and even picking grapes or helping out in the winery cellar ("voluntourism"). Part of the appeal of wine tourism is that it is a romantic activity. Wine tourism fosters a permanence of memories, because all five senses are involved. The hands-on activity appeals to current consumer demands for interactive learning experiences. And naturally, the lubricating effects of alcohol must have some effect on the positive impression of the overall wine tourism experience.

Wine tourism takes many forms. Some wine tourists prefer day-trips to local wineries, such as those visiting Napa and **Sonoma** from San Francisco. Others prefer longer stays in other countries, as seen by the hordes of international tourists that descend upon Tuscany each summer. Still others prefer guided wine tours, which are offered to many destinations around the globe.

Some wine tourists seek the road less traveled and the wineries less visited. They may look for smaller producers who may not be open to the public or take visitors by appointment only. Others are drawn to the glamour or opulence of the larger estate wineries in California, châteaux in **France**, or villas in **Italy**.

Economic Impact. The wine tourism experience is largely about adding value to a commodity—the grape and its end product, wine. Visitors meet the winemaker—often a celebrity of sorts in culinary circles. They may visit the winery's gift shop to take home memories of their trip. They may buy food if there is a **restaurant** or on-site catering or may tour the grounds. Some meeting planners may hold a special meeting or event at a winery. The wine tourists may support the winery's special causes, such as a charity or the **sustainability** movement. In addition, the winery may be one stop within a larger food and wine trail. The sum of these experiences is that the goal of business-savvy wineries is to harness maximum spending by each winery visitor.

A 2007 study commissioned by the International Culinary Tourism Association (ICTA), along with initial findings from **Australia**, California, and **Canada**, shows that wine tourists tend to be better educated and have more disposable income than average tourists. The study confirms that some consumers choose a destination solely or largely because of specific food and drink to be found there. The more popular destinations in California, **New York**, Italy, and France are becoming overrun and losing much of their cachet, and now lesser-known destinations, such as Hungary, Slovakia, and **New Zealand**, are afforded an excellent opportunity to secure a part of the economic pie.

When tourists buy a $10 bottle of wine directly from the source, the winery gets the full amount, whereas if that same bottle is sold to a restaurant or **retailer**, the winery retains only around two-thirds of the sales price, or if sold through a wholesaler/**distributor**, just half. Jim Trezise, executive director of the New York Grape & Wine Foundation, reports that wine sales make up only 80 percent of what the visitors spend at the wineries. The remainder is spent on souvenirs, accessories, food, and other items. Most importantly, tourists also purchase meals and often stay overnight in the area, further contributing to the local economy. Additional expenditures may include culinary education and classes, spa treatments, cultural activities such as theater and performing arts, sporting pursuits, and higher-end recreational activities such as hot air ballooning or horseback riding. According to a recent study by MKF Research, wine tourism generates $3 billion within the **United States** alone, providing employment for 50,000 people.

Outlook.   Many European wine regions are currently suffering from extremely high prices due to demand and the strong euro, as well as oversaturation of their small venues by large number of tourists. This is creating consumer demand for differentiation and setting the stage of success for **New World** wine destinations such as **South Africa**, Australia, **Chile**, and **Argentina**.

Erik Wolf

Further Reading

Great Wine Capitals Global Network. www.greatwinecapitals.com.

Hall, C. Michael, Brock Cambourne, Liz Sharples, and Niki Macionis. *Wine Tourism around the World*. Oxford, England: Elsevier, 2000.

International Culinary Tourism Association. www.culinarytourism.org.

Wolf, Erik. *Culinary Tourism: The Hidden Harvest*. Dubuque, IA: Kendall/Hunt, 2006.

WINE WRITERS

The role of wine writers is the same as that of other journalists: to provide honest and accurate information, to report on trends, and to analyze and synthesize data to make their subject easier for readers to understand. Wine writers act as honest brokers between producers and **consumers**, providing varying amounts of **wine education** and/or wine **ratings** that allow consumers to make sense of the bewildering array of wines there are to choose from. Oftentimes, this gives them the confidence to step out of their comfort zone and try a new wine. Without wine writers, new or small producers or regions would have an even harder time breaking into the market.

Some writers focus on telling stories, some on explaining details, and some on describing specific wines (these are often referred to as *wine critics*), but all add to the body of knowledge available to help consumers find a good wine—either by writing directly for consumers or by adding to the literature for the trade. The following is a cross-section of some of well-known wine writers and critics and their major works.

History.   Wine writers today are expected to be neutral and not tied to any single company or **brand**, but this was not always so. In the 1950s, wine writers were all in the trade. It was understood that writing was one way they sold their wines. When they wrote about them, they told their readers what they were supposed to taste like and how to use them and encouraged their readers to become customers, and no one thought there was anything wrong with that. One of the earliest commercial wine writers was André Simon, a Pommery **Champagne** salesman who founded the International Wine & Food Society in London. Other famous writers were in the trade in England, for example, Harry Waugh, Michael Broadbent, MW (Master of Wine), and John Avery, MW. Nowadays, however, writers who have affiliations are no longer trusted. In addition, there is so much personal uncertainty about what to buy that ratings have become the name of the game—a numbers game.

Books.   The range of wine books is very broad. There are scholarly forays into wine-related themes, such as *1855: A History of the Bordeaux Classification* by

Dewey Markham, Jr. (1998); Paul Dolan's *True to Our Roots* about **phylloxera** (2003), and historical tomes like *Wine and War: The French, the Nazis, and the Battle for France's Greatest Treasures* by Donald and Petie Kladstrup (2002). Pairing food and wine has also become a hot topic. *Wine Style* by Mary Ewing-Mulligan, MW, and Ed McCarthy, CWE (Certified Wine Educator) (2005) and *What to Drink with What You Eat* by Andrew Dornenburg and Karen Page (2006) are helpful guides.

The writers who produce reference books have the satisfaction of knowing that their readers continually depend on their books. One major writer in this genre is **Jancis Robinson**, MW. Consider her *Vines, Grapes & Wines* (1986) and its update *Guide to Wine Grapes* (1996), listing every known grape, complete with pseudonyms; *Vintage Time Charts* (1989), an original look at the way wines age; the excellent collection of maps of wine regions in the *World Atlas of Wine,* whose fifth edition (2001) was coauthored with **Hugh Johnson** (author of the first four editions); and the mammoth *The Oxford Companion to Wine,* now in its third edition (2006).

Not to be overlooked are books by writer/educators: *Exploring Wine: The Culinary Institute of America's Guide to Wines of the World* by Steven Kolpan, Brian H. Smith, and Michael A. Weiss (2nd ed., 2002) and *The Wine Bible* by Karen MacNeil (2001). Kevin Zraly's *Windows on the World Complete Wine Course* (2007) and *American Wine Guide* (2008) are also major references.

The writing team of Ewing-Mulligan and McCarthy has written *Wine for Dummies,* selling more than a million copies and translated into 24 languages, now in its fourth edition. Their other books in the series include *White Wine for Dummies, Red Wine for Dummies, Wine Buying Companion for Dummies, French Wine for Dummies,* and *Italian Wine for Dummies,* and they are working on more regions. McCarthy was the solo author of *Champagne for Dummies.*

Periodicals and Newspapers.   Every wine periodical must include ratings to sell their publications. Ratings are found in *Decanter,* the *Wine Spectator, Wine & Spirits,* the *Wine Enthusiast,* the *International Wine Review, Quarterly Review of Wines, Beverage Dynamics,* and lots more. The *New York Times* tasting panels, initiated by Frank J. Prial and followed by Eric Asimov's tasting panels and Internet blog, and Dorothy J. Gaiter and John Brecher writing in the *Wall Street Journal,* provide even more updates, along with a lot of reader interaction.

Newsletters.   The phenomenon of **Robert Parker**, biographied in Elin McCoy's *The Emperor of Wine* (2006), parallels—or has caused—the great surge of interest in wine in the **United States**. His small, rather personal newsletter, the *Wine Advocate,* appeared to burst on the scene with the outstanding 1982 vintage in Bordeaux. The confluence of a great vintage at still "reasonable" prices with an easily understandable rating system for purchasers catapulted Parker to the forefront. Before him, if any system was used at all, it was the 20-point "Davis System" from the University of California, Davis, which was actually a system for **California** winemakers who were trained to look for flaws. When Parker started rating wines on a 100-point system, everyone could understand what a 95 meant. Shortly thereafter, other publications that had been using other numbering systems switched over to the 100-point system. The fact that no wine was ever rated below a 50, effectively turning the 100-point system into a 50-point system, did not seem to matter.

It was not just the public who latched on. Retail store owners who were tired of writing advertising copy for their wines simply forgot about the words and put down the numbers from Parker or, later, from the *Wine Spectator*. Retailers stopped seeing salesmen and tasting wines—all they needed was a price list and Parker numbers to make a purchase.

A few trusted newsletters do describe a wine with words: Stephen Tanzer's *International Wine Cellar,* started in 1985, is respected, as is his blog at graperadio.com. Another reliable newsletter, more specific to **Pinot Noir**, is Allen Meadows's *Quarterly,* which has been published for more than 25 years.

Web Reviews.   In an effort to get people to trust their own opinions and to be less rating-number dependent, Ed McCarthy's winereviewonline.com is updated every two weeks with easy-to-understand reviews. More reviews of top wines can be found on Jancis Robinson's Web site www.jancisrobinson.com, a paid membership site. As wine consultant for British Airways and a member of the Royal Household Wine Committee that chooses wine for Buckingham Palace, she is often the first to taste important new releases. Other popular wine Web sites include www.drvino.com, hosted by author Tyler Colman, and the frequently quoted "Nat Decants," an online wine newsletter from Natalie MacLean. Wine reviews can also serve as third-party endorsements for **wineries**.

A Unique Column.   *New York Times* writer Howard G. Goldberg writes small. But in his weekly wallet-sized column for the "City" section, he selects one wine for his "Wine under $20" piece. He believes that the public should be able to locate the wines he reviews, which is not always the case with other columnists. Before he writes up a wine and names a **retail** source, he makes sure that the store has at least three cases on hand, with backup at the **distributor**. The retailer must also maintain the price quoted in the near term. One review of a Rioja sold 3,000 cases very quickly.

Outlook.   The emphasis for wine writers will continue to evolve with time and technology, but as new regions emerge, old ones change, and different types and styles of wine appear, there will always be a need for wine writers to investigate, explain, and interpret these developments to professionals and consumers alike.

Harriet Lembeck

WOMEN

Women play critical roles in all aspects of the wine business, from production to consumption. Though viticulturists, winemakers, and winery executives are still largely male, the increasing presence of females in vineyards, cellars, and boardrooms comes at a time when **consumer** interest in wine is peaking.

With more than 300 million cases consumed yearly in the **United States** and more American adults choosing wine over beer as their alcoholic beverage of choice, wine is becoming part of this country's culinary culture. There has also been a shift in behavior from sipping the occasional glass on a special occasion to enjoying it more regularly with meals, including purchasing more while dining.

Much of this growth has been due to women, who make up almost 58 percent of U.S. wine consumers, more than 45 million strong.

Collectors are still seen as primarily male, but among consumers even those categorized as high-end wine drinkers skew female—no surprise when considering that women bring in at least half of the household income in the majority of U.S. households and influence more than 80 percent of dollars spent.

Women's preferences in wine are generally like those of men. Like men, women drink more red than white or blush wine, for example. The gender divide is not about what is in the bottle, but how women *approach* what is in the bottle. A vinous male/female equation is balanced out by the way the sexes communicate about wine and integrate it into their respective lifestyles. Women more often choose wine for gatherings, as gifts, and to enhance a social experience. Females tend to gravitate toward information about food-and-wine pairing and entertaining with wine. They view a glass of wine as a relaxant to transition from workday stress to home life. Women also generally approach wine from an experiential standpoint: their interests lie not in how well a wine scores in a wine publication but in how good the wine tastes and where and with whom it is enjoyed.

When it comes to women's buying habits, they fall on the adventurous side of the scale, with value playing a strong role. Women buy both expensive and inexpensive wines, but they are highly concerned with perceived value, whether the wine costs $5 or $50. Recommendations from friends and family tend to weigh heavily in the selection process, as does a bottle's visual appeal.

With the realization of females' household buying power, wine companies have become more aggressive about specific gender **promotion** initiatives, and programs marketing directly to women have had some success. **Brands** made specifically to appeal to females through taste and style have launched to mixed results.

Creative packaging and in-store point of sale displays, along with advertisements placed in women's magazines and participation in female-focused events from the food world to fashion circles, have proven popular. With targeted magazine ads, winery collateral material such as brochures, **wine clubs**, and Web sites aimed at empowering women, marketing to the female consumer segment will continue. Due to growing consumer confidence, strong purchasing power, and the expanding importance of females in the industry, the future roles of women in the wine world will continue to grow. *See also* Health; Labels as Marketing.

Leslie Sbrocco

Y

YELLOW TAIL

One of the most remarkable success stories of the past decade, Yellow Tail is a **brand** created by John Casella of Casella Wines, in the Riverina area of New South Wales, **Australia**, in 2000. Intended from the start as an export-oriented brand for the U.S. market, Casella worked with **importer** William Deutsch of W. J. Deutsch & Sons, Ltd., to introduce a **Chardonnay** and a Shiraz that featured an attractive **label** with a wallaby and the name rendered intriguingly as [yellow tail], along with a fair price and good quality. From 225,000 cases in 2001, sales grew stunningly over the next several years, impelled almost entirely by word of mouth and favorable press. Yellow Tail sold 4.3 million cases (mc) in 2003 and was up to 8.1 mc in 2006, making it the largest imported brand in the **United States** with retail sales of $671 million. By itself, Yellow Tail represented almost 11 percent of all imported wine sales and over 34 percent of Australian wines sold in the United States. The line has expanded to 18 **varietally labeled** wines, including 5 in a reserve range, and a **sparkling wine**, and the company now exports to Europe, as well as selling domestically in Australia. Its global sales in 2006 reached 10.5 mc, the world's sixth largest brand. Deutsch & Sons, which also imports 750,000 cases of Georges Duboeuf wines from **France** per year, is based in White Plains, New York.

Z

ZINFANDEL

Although some of its mysteries have been solved, including the fact that it did not originate in North America, the inscrutable Zinfandel is still considered by many to be America's great domestic wine grape. Grown in **California** for more than a century and a half, this red grape variety was the workhorse of the pre-**Prohibition** California wine industry and was widely planted. After Prohibition, many cuttings from established wine regions in Europe were brought to California to establish new vineyards, but Zinfandel did not seem to be among the varieties grown in the Old World. Thus, it (and to a lesser extent, Petite Sirah) became known as an American grape. It was prized for producing hearty, deeply colored, flavorful **red wine** and was often the backbone of the blended red wines of the day. With the eventual dominance of **varietal labeling** later in the century, Zinfandel suffered from its lack of a connection with a famous European region and was overshadowed by the likes of **Cabernet Sauvignon**, though it remained one of the top varieties grown in California and had a small but loyal following as a varietal.

In the mid-1970s, Zinfandel's fortunes took a turn when a semisweet **rosé** wine made from juice drawn off of fermenting red Zinfandel became hugely popular almost overnight, introducing "white Zinfandel," a **fad** that remains an important category of U.S. wine sales today. Suddenly, there was great demand for Zinfandel grapes for varietally labeled wine. This gave the variety sufficient name recognition such that, when American consumers began shifting their interest away from white wines and back toward reds, "serious" red Zinfandel began to get the credit it deserved.

Today, Zinfandel is the fourth most purchased wine-grape variety in the **United States**. In 2006, according to *Impact* data, Zinfandel sales totaled 23.5 million nine-liter cases (mc), 83 percent of which was white Zinfandel. The 4.0 mc of red Zinfandel accounted for 5 percent of varietally labeled **red wines**, while Zinfandel continued to rule the blush category with an 86 percent share of varietal rosés. Both the white and red versions have smaller but important exports, especially to the **British market**. Sales of red Zinfandel in **bulk** are also doing well.

Although many wine regions are experimenting with Zinfandel, almost all of the variety's **New World** plantings are in California, where there were 49,700 acres in 2005. **Sonoma**, Mendocino, and San Luis Obispo counties, the Central Valley around Lodi, and the Sierra Foothills region are home to much of the vineyard land. There are a few hundred acres in other states. The variety is **promoted** by the Zinfandel Advocates & Producers (ZAP).

In the Old World, it turns out that there is a substantial amount growing in **Italy**, though not under the name of Zinfandel. After years of speculation, Dr. Carole P. Meredith of the University of California at Davis proved through DNA testing that Zinfandel was not a mutation that had spontaneously developed in North America, but was in fact essentially the same as both the Primitivo variety of Puglia in southern Italy and Crljenak Kastelanski of Croatia, with the latter apparently being the source of both Primitivo and Zinfandel. Throughout Italy, there are perhaps 30,000 acres of Primitivo, mainly in Puglia. Croatia's version was apparently largely wiped out by **phylloxera**, but is being replanted now that its connection with Zinfandel is known.

Though genetically identical, Primitivo and Zinfandel have different characteristics. In fact, some new plantings in California are using Primitivo rather than Zinfandel for the former's earlier and more even ripening and higher natural acidity. Under **European Union** laws, Primitivo can be—and in many cases, is being—labeled and marketed as Zinfandel, but under **Alcohol and Tobacco Tax and Trade Bureau (TTB)** rules, the two are considered distinct grape varieties for labeling U.S.-made wines. *See also* Trinchero Family Estates.

Appendix A

International Wine Data

A case equals 9 liters.

ARGENTINA

Wine market	Historically self-contained, becoming a major exporter
Known for	Malbec
Population	39.5 million (2007)
Vineyard area	550,000 acres (2006)
Wine production	170 million cases (2007)
Wine consumption	123 million cases (2006)
Wine imports	Negligible
Wine exports	56 million cases (2007)

AUSTRALIA

Wine market	Highly export oriented
Known for	Shiraz
Population	21.1 million (2007)
Vineyard area	417,000 acres (2006)
Wine production	159 million cases (2006)
Wine consumption	51 million cases (2006)
Wine imports	4 million cases (2006)
Wine exports	87 million cases (2007)

AUSTRIA

Wine market	Largely self-contained, with balanced moderate imports and exports; EU member
Known for	Grüner Veltliner
Population	8.3 million (2007)
Vineyard area	125,000 acres (2006)
Wine production	25 million cases (2006)
Wine consumption	27 million cases (2006)
Wine imports	7.8 million cases (2005)
Wine exports	7.5 million cases (2005)

BELGIUM

Wine market	Importer; EU member
Known for	Historically beer drinking, but becoming more wine friendly
Population	10.5 million (2007)
Vineyard area	Few hundred acres
Wine production	11,000 cases (2006)
Wine consumption	31 million cases (2006)
Wine imports	32 million cases (2006)
Wine exports	Negligible

BRAZIL

Wine market	Historically self-contained, with growing import sector
Known for	Large potential market
Population	187 million (2007)
Vineyard area	215,000 acres (winegrapes, 2006)
Wine production	24 million cases (2006)
Wine consumption	39 million cases (2006)
Wine imports	6 million cases (2006)
Wine exports	390,000 cases (2006)

BULGARIA

Wine market	Highly export oriented; EU member
Known for	Only significant exporter to West during Soviet period
Population	7.6 million (2007)
Vineyard area	168,000 acres (2006)
Wine production	20 million cases (2006)
Wine consumption	4 million cases (2006)
Wine imports	1.4 million cases (2006)
Wine exports	12 million cases (2006)

CANADA

Wine market	Net importer; mostly government monopoly
Known for	Ice wine
Population	33.3 million (2008)
Vineyard area	22,000 acres (2006)
Wine production	10 million cases (2006)
Wine consumption	42 million cases (2006)
Wine imports	32 million cases (2006)
Wine exports	800,000 cases (2006)

CHILE

Wine market	Highly export oriented
Known for	Good-quality, low-priced exports, bulk and bottled
Population	16.6 million (2007)
Vineyard area	482,000 acres (2006)
Wine production	94 million cases (2006)
Wine consumption	26 million cases (2006)
Wine imports	Negligible
Wine exports	48 million cases (2006)

CHINA

Wine market	Self-contained, with a crash program of modernization; three-tier system
Known for	Huge potential market; Hong Kong as hub of Asian wine trade
Population	1.32 billion (2007)
Vineyard area	650,000 acres (winegrapes, est. 2006)
Wine production	135 million cases (2005)
Wine consumption	150 million cases (2006)
Wine imports	12 million cases (including bulk, 2006)
Wine exports	Negligible

DENMARK

Wine market	Importer; EU member
Known for	Only open market in Scandinavia
Population	5.5 million (2007)
Vineyard area	None
Wine production	None
Wine consumption	20 million cases (2006)
Wine imports	21 million cases (2006)
Wine exports	None

EUROPEAN UNION

Wine market	Open internal trade among 27 member states; coordinated wine laws
Known for	Majority of world's wine production, consumption, and trade
Population	491 million (2008)
Vineyard area	9.6 million acres (2006)
Wine production	1.98 billion cases (2006)
Wine consumption	1.59 billion cases (2006)

FRANCE

Wine market	Net exporter; EU member
Known for	Heart of wine production; Bordeaux, Burgundy, Champagne
Population	64.1 million (2007)
Vineyard area	2.2 million acres (2006)
Wine production	581 million cases (2006)
Wine consumption	367 million cases (2006)
Wine imports	58 million cases (2006)
Wine exports	163 million cases (2006)

GERMANY

Wine market	Net importer; EU member
Known for	Riesling
Population	82.3 million (2007)
Vineyard area	252,000 acres (2006)
Wine production	99 million cases (2006)
Wine consumption	222 million cases (2006)
Wine imports	147 million cases (2006)
Wine exports	35 million cases (2006)

GREECE

Wine market	Self-contained, with growing export sector; EU member
Known for	Indigenous grapes; Retsina

Population	11.1 million (2007)
Vineyard area	277,000 acres (2006)
Wine production	44 million cases (2006)
Wine consumption	36 million cases (2006)
Wine imports	Small
Wine exports	3.4 million cases (2006)

HUNGARY

Wine market	Largely self-contained, slight net exporter; EU member
Known for	Tokaji, Bull's Blood
Population	10.0 million (2007)
Vineyard area	200,000 acres (2006)
Wine production	36 million cases (2006)
Wine consumption	33 million cases (2006)
Wine imports	2.0 million cases (2006)
Wine exports	7.6 million cases (2007)

INDIA

Wine market	At the initial stages of development
Known for	Huge potential market
Population	1.17 billion (2007)
Vineyard area	Few thousand acres
Wine production	530,000 cases (2005)
Wine consumption	610,000 cases (2006)
Wine imports	100,000 cases (est. 2005)
Wine exports	Negligible

ITALY

Wine market	Net exporter; EU member
Known for	Indigenous varieties and styles
Population	59.1 million (2007)
Vineyard area	2.1 million acres (2006)
Wine production	594 million cases (2006)
Wine consumption	304 million cases (2006)
Wine imports	18 million cases (2004)
Wine exports	200 million cases (2006)

JAPAN

Wine market	Net importer, largest in Asia; three-tier system
Known for	Sake
Population	128 million (2007)
Vineyard area	550,000 acres (2006)
Wine production	12 million cases (2005)
Wine consumption	28 million cases (2005)
Wine imports	17 million cases (2006)
Wine exports	Negligible

MOLDOVA

Wine market	Highly export oriented
Known for	Bulk wine exports
Population	3.8 million (2007)
Vineyard area	363,000 acres (2006)

Wine production	27 million cases (2005)
Wine consumption	2.3 million cases (2005)
Wine imports	Negligible
Wine exports	27 million cases (2005, before Russian embargo)

NETHERLANDS

Wine market	Importer; EU member
Known for	Strong import market
Population	16.4 million (2007)
Vineyard area	Less than 1,000 acres (2006)
Wine production	90,000 cases (2006)
Wine consumption	39 million cases (2006)
Wine imports	46 million cases (2006)
Wine exports	Negligible

NEW ZEALAND

Wine market	Net exporter
Known for	Sauvignon Blanc
Population	4.2 million (2007)
Vineyard area	68,000 acres (2007)
Wine production	15 million cases (2006)
Wine consumption	9.7 million cases (2007)
Wine imports	4.7 million cases (2007)
Wine exports	9.4 million cases (2007)

PORTUGAL

Wine market	Historically self-contained, moving toward greater export orientation; EU member
Known for	Port, Vinho Verde, indigenous varieties
Population	10.6 million (2007)
Vineyard area	615,000 acres (2006)
Wine production	84 million cases (2006)
Wine consumption	53 million cases (2006)
Wine imports	10 million cases (2006)
Wine exports	33 million cases (2006)

ROMANIA

Wine market	Largely self-contained, slight net exporter; EU member
Known for	Cotnari
Population	21.4 million (2007)
Vineyard area	526,000 acres (2006)
Wine production	56 million cases (2006)
Wine consumption	62 million cases (2006)
Wine imports	Negligible
Wine exports	5.6 million cases (2002)

RUSSIA

Wine market	Net importer; three-tier system
Known for	Large-scale, low-priced bulk imports; sparkling wine
Population	142 million (2007)
Vineyard area	173,000 acres (2005)
Wine production	50 million cases (2006)

Wine consumption	120 million cases (2006)
Wine imports	80 million cases (2006)
Wine exports	Negligible

SOUTH AFRICA

Wine market	Historically self-contained, becoming a major exporter
Known for	Pinotage
Population	48.6 million (2007)
Vineyard area	252,000 acres (winegrapes, 2007)
Wine production	104 million cases (2006)
Wine consumption	35 million cases (2006)
Wine imports	3 million cases (2006)
Wine exports	35 million cases (2006)

SPAIN

Wine market	Net exporter; EU member
Known for	Rioja, Cava, Sherry
Population	45.1 million (2007)
Vineyard area	2.9 million acres (2006)
Wine production	425 million cases (2006)
Wine consumption	150 million cases (2006)
Wine imports	3 million cases (2006)
Wine exports	159 million cases (2006)

SWEDEN

Wine market	Importer; EU member
Known for	Systembolaget national monopoly
Population	9.1 million (2007)
Vineyard area	None
Wine production	None; small production from bulk wine and juice imports
Wine consumption	16 million cases (2006)
Wine imports	16 million cases (2006)
Wine exports	Small volume of re-exports

SWITZERLAND

Wine market	Net importer
Known for	Chasselas
Population	7.5 million (2007)
Vineyard area	37,000 acres (2006)
Wine production	11 million cases (2006)
Wine consumption	31 million cases (2006)
Wine imports	20 million cases (2006)
Wine exports	290,000 cases (2006)

UNITED KINGDOM

Wine market	Importer; supermarket driven; EU member
Known for	Major wine importer; London as center of world wine trade
Population	60.8 million (2007)
Vineyard area	2,000 acres (2006)
Wine production	281,000 cases (2006)
Wine consumption	130 million cases (2006)
Wine imports	141 million cases (2006)
Wine exports	Negligible

UNITED STATES

Wine market	Largely self-contained, but with sizable imports and exports; three-tier system
Known for	California, especially the Napa Valley and Sonoma
Population	303 million (2007)
Vineyard area	475,000 acres (winegrapes, est. 2006)
Wine production	230 million cases (2006), not including special wine categories and distillation
Wine consumption	288 million cases (2006)
Wine imports	87 million cases (2006)
Wine exports	50 million cases (2007)

WORLD

Population	6.67 billion (2007)
Vineyard area	19.6 million acres (2006)
Wine production	3.18 billion cases (2006)
Wine consumption	2.67 billion cases (2006)

Appendix B

Conversions

Volume
1 standard bottle = 750 milliliters (ml) or 25.36 fluid ounces (fl. oz.)
1 liter = 1,000 ml or 0.264 U.S. gallons (gal) or 33.82 fl. oz.
1 gallon = 3.79 liters or 128 fl. oz.
1 standard case = 9 liters or 2.38 gal
1 hectoliter (hl) = 100 liters or 26.4 gal
1 million cases (mc) = 9 million liters or 90,000 hl or 2,378,000 gal

Area
1 acre = 0.405 hectares (ha)
1 hectare = 2.47 acres
1 square kilometer (sq. km) = 0.386 square miles (sq. mi.)
1 square mile = 2.59 sq. km

Length/Distance
1 foot = 0.305 meters (m) or 12 inches
1 meter = 3.28 feet (ft) or 39.37 inches
1 kilometer (km) = 0.62 miles
1 mile = 1.61 km

Weight
1 pound = 453.6 grams or 16 ounces
1 kilogram = 2.205 pounds

Selected Bibliography

Adams Wine Handbook 2007. Norwalk, CT: Adams Beverage Group, 2008.

Amerine, Maynard A., and Vernon L. Singleton. *Wine, an Introduction*. Berkeley: University of California Press, 1977.

Barr, Andrew. *Drink: A Social History of America*. New York: Carroll & Graf, 1999.

Broadbent, Michael. *Michael Broadbent's Vintage Wine*. New York: Harcourt, 2002.

Cass, Bruce, ed. *The Oxford Companion to the Wines of North America*. Oxford: Oxford University Press, 2000.

Clarke, Oz, and Margaret Rand. *Oz Clarke's Grapes and Wines: The Definitive Guide to the World's Great Grapes and the Wines They Make*. Orlando, FL: Harcourt, 2007.

Foulkes, Christopher, ed. *Larousse Encyclopedia of Wine*. New York: Larousse, 1994.

Gabler, James M. *Wine into Words: A History and Bibliography of Wine Books in the English Language*. 2nd ed. Baltimore: Bacchus Press, 2004.

Goode, Jamie. *The Science of Wine: From Vine to Glass*. Berkeley: University of California Press, 2005.

Johnson, Hugh. *The Story of Wine*. London: Octopus, 1989.

Johnson, Hugh, and Jancis Robinson. *The World Atlas of Wine*. London: Mitchell Beazley, 2006.

Julyan, Brian. *Sales and Service for the Wine Professional*. 3rd ed. London: Cengage Learning EMEA, 2008.

Lukacs, Paul B. *American Vintage: The Rise of American Wine*. New York: Houghton Mifflin, 2000.

Margalit, Yair. *Concepts in Wine Technology*. San Francisco: Wine Appreciation Guild, 2004.

Moulton, Kirby, and James Lapsley. *Successful Wine Marketing*. Gaithersburg, MD: Aspen, 2001.

Peynaud, Émile. *The Taste of Wine: The Art and Science of Wine Appreciation*. 2nd ed. New York: Wiley, 1996.

Pinney, Thomas. *A History of Wine in America*. 2 vols. Berkeley: University of California Press, 2005.

Robinson, Jancis. *Vines, Grapes, and Wines*. New York: Knopf, 1986.

————, ed. *The Oxford Companion to Wine*. 3rd ed. Oxford: Oxford University Press, 2006.

Stevenson, Tom. *The Sotheby's Wine Encyclopedia*. 1st American ed. New York: DK, 2007.

————. *Wine Report 2009*. New York: DK, 2008.

Thach, Liz, and Tim Matz, eds. *Wine: A Global Business*. Elmsford, NY: Miranda Press, 2004.

Wagner, Paul, Janeen Olsen, and Liz Thach. *Wine Marketing and Sales: Success Strategies for a Saturated Market*. San Francisco: Wine Appreciation Guild, 2007.

Web Sites

American Journal of Enology & Viticulture. www.ajevonline.org.

Decanter. www.decanter.com.

Harper's. www.talkingdrinks.com.

Jancis Robinson's Purple Pages. www.jancisrobinson.com.

Journal of Wine Research. www.tandf.co.uk/journals/carfax/09571264.html.

Quarterly Review of Wine. www.qrw.com.

Wine & Spirit International. www.wineandspirit.com.

Wine & Spirits. www.wineandspiritsmagazine.com.

Wine Business International. www.wine-business-international.com.

Wine Business Monthly. www.winebusiness.com.

Wine Enthusiast. www.winemag.com.

Wines & Vines. www.winesandvines.com.

Wine Spectator. www.winespectator.com.

Index

The main entries for the indexed subjects are shown in boldface.

About the Editors and Contributors

The following abbreviations are used:

CWE	Certified Wine Educator
DWS	Diploma, Wine & Spirit Education Trust
MS	Master Sommelier
MW	Master of Wine
WSET	Wine & Spirit Education Trust

Geralyn Brostrom, CWE, is the vice president of education for Winebow, an importer and distributor of fine wines. As a Georgetown University–certified trainer, her specialization is in wine education. She has served as executive director and director of education for the Society of Wine Educators and has experience in all segments of the wine industry.

Jack Brostrom is a book editor with a long interest in wine that began early in his Navy career. Among other wine-related projects, he drafted the 2008 update to the Society of Wine Educators' *Study Guide* for the Certified Specialist of Wine program. He has worked in wine retail and production in Pennsylvania and Washington.

Alberto Antonini is a renowned consultant to wineries in several Italian regions and many other countries, including Argentina, Australia, Chile, Portugal, Romania, South Africa, and the United States. He is the founder of the Matura consulting group in Vinci, Italy.

Mollie Battenhouse is the wine director at Domaine53, a private wine club. She graduated from the Culinary Institute of America and later worked as the wine and training director at Best Cellars and as sommelier at the Tribeca Grill, both in New York City. She currently teaches wine classes through the International Wine Center.

Thomas Belelieu is the general manager of the Whitehall Hotel in Chicago and was formerly the wine director at Walt Disney World. He was the founding chairman of the Sommelier Guild of Canada and served on the Board of Directors of the Society of Wine Educators.

John Blazon, MS, is a veteran of 25 years in the food and beverage industry. At Walt Disney World Parks and Resorts he manages the wine programming and vision. He became the 59th U.S. Master Sommelier in 2004 shortly after receiving *Santé* magazine's 2003 Wine Professional of the Year award.

Roger C. Bohmrich, MW, is managing partner of Millesima USA, a retail entity based in New York. He has been in the wine trade for more than 30 years and was previously a senior executive with a major U.S. wine importer, where he managed an extensive portfolio from France and other countries. He was the founding president of the Institute of Masters of Wine (North America).

Danny Brager is vice president and group client director for the Nielsen Company, where he leads the Beverage Alcohol Client Service team, supporting more than 150 manufacturer and wholesaler clients in the beer, wine, and spirits industries, providing business information, analysis, and insights. He is a frequent speaker on wine trends at many client and industry events.

Bartholomew Broadbent is the cofounder and CEO of Broadbent Selections, an importer of fine wine, and also produces his own Broadbent Port and Madeira in Portugal. He is a prolific lecturer and serves on numerous tasting panels and at wine competitions around the world. Among his many achievements and honors, he is a cavaleiro of the Confraria do Vinho do Porto.

Joel P. Butler, MW, is the director of education for Ste. Michelle Wine Estates. He became one of the first two resident American Masters of Wine in 1990 and is a vice president of the Institute of Masters of Wine (North America). He also acts as a wine judge and has written for numerous publications, including the *Los Angeles Times* and the *Independent on Sunday* (London).

Jean-Louis Carbonnier is president of Carbonnier Communications, a New York City–based marketing and public relations consultancy that specializes in terroir wines and foods. Before that, he was the U.S. representative of the Comité Inter-professionnel du Vin de Champagne (CIVC). He serves as Champagne consultant to *Wine News* magazine.

Laura Catena, M.D., is vice president of Bodega Catena Zapata and owner of Luca Winery, both in Mendoza, Argentina. She was the editor of *Mendoza: Our Terroir* (2002).

Mark Chandler is the executive director of the Lodi Winegrape Commission and farms 175 acres of winegrapes in the Lodi appellation. His previous experience includes winemaking and marketing management, and he is past president of the Society of Wine Educators.

Rebecca Chapa, DWS, CWE, has taught wine classes for consumers with her own company, Wine by the Class, since 2001, and founded her San Francisco–based consulting company, Tannin Management, in 1999. She is an adjunct instructor at the Culinary Institute of America and teaches WSET classes at Copia in Napa.

Kimberly Charles, DWS, is a marketing communications professional with an agency in San Francisco that specializes in wine & spirits public relations (www.charlescomm.com). Prior to founding her firm in 2003, she was communications director for E.& J. Gallo Winery and was public relations director at Kobrand Corp. in New York.

Mary Ellen Cole is cellar master of the Los Angeles International Wine and Spirits Competition at the Los Angeles County Fair.

Amy Cortese is a freelance journalist based in New York. She has written about wine for such publications as *Business Week, Conde Nast Portfolio, The American,* and the *New York Times*.

Christopher Cree, MW, is the owner of 56 Degree Wine, a retail wine shop in Bernardsville, New Jersey, and founder of Wine Experts, LLC, a consulting business developing wine events, education programs, and travel for nonprofit, corporate, and private clients.

Alison Crowe is the winemaker at Plata Wine Partners, LLC, based in Napa, California. She has made wine at Chalone Vineyard, Bonny Doon Vineyard, and Bodegas Salentein in Argentina, among others. She is a frequent contributor to *Wine Business Monthly*, pens the popular "Wine Wizard" column for *WineMaker* magazine, and is the author of *The Wine Maker's Answer Book*.

Cole Danehower, copublisher and editor-in-chief of *Northwest Palate* magazine, received the James Beard Foundation Journalism Award for his wine writing in 2004. His writing on Oregon wines has appeared in *Wine & Vines,* the *San Francisco Chronicle,* and *The Oregonian* and at AppellationAmerica.com.

Michael J. Decker, D.Phil., is Maroulis Professor of Byzantine History and Orthodox Religion in the Department of History at the University of South Florida. His publications include the forthcoming *Tilling the Hateful Earth: Agriculture and Trade in the Late Antique East*.

Steve Dorfman is a partner of the Ciatti Company, wine and grape brokers. He formerly served as senior vice president and chief winery officer of the Brown Forman Corporation.

Chris Dowsett is the resident winemaker for Artifex Wine Company, a small custom crush facility in Walla Walla, Washington.

Andrea Englisis, DWS, is co-owner and vice president of Athenee Importers, a family-owned and -operated import company established in 1974 specializing in wines from Greece and Cyprus.

Robert Eyler, Ph.D., is a professor of economics and director of the Center for Regional Economic Analysis at Sonoma State University. His areas of specialization include wine industry economics.

Patrick Farrell, M.D., MW, CWE, is the CEO of Inventive Technologies/BevWizard, Inc. A board-certified internist and ophthalmologist, he was the first physician to become an MW. He has lectured and written frequently about wine and health topics, including in *Wine and Society* and *The Professional Wine Reference*.

Doug Frost, MS, MW, is a Kansas City–based author and educator. He has written three books: *Uncorking Wine* (1996), *On Wine* (2001), and *The Far from Ordinary Spanish Wine Buying Guide* (2nd ed., 2007). He is the wine and spirits consultant for United Airlines and writes about wine and spirits for many national and international publications.

Robert C. Fuller, Ph.D., is Caterpillar Professor of Religious Studies at Bradley University in Peoria, Illinois. Among his 12 books on modern American religion is *Religion and Wine: A Cultural History of Wine Drinking in the United States* (1996).

Tim Gaiser, MS, is the director of education for the American Chapter of the Court of Master Sommeliers, as well as a contributing editor for *Fine Cooking* magazine and an adjunct professor for the Rudd Center for Professional Wine Studies at the Culinary Institute of America at Greystone in Napa Valley. He has developed wine education programs for several restaurants, winery schools, and wine distributors.

Jamie Goode, Ph.D., a scientist by training, is a wine writer and technical journalist specializing in the science of wine. He has a weekly column in British national newspaper the *Sunday Express,* and his book *The Science of Wine* was published in 2006 by University of California Press. He hosts the informative website and blog at www.wineanorak.com.

Patricia Guy worked in the wine trade in New York and London before moving to Verona, Italy, in 1991. She writes about Italian wine, food, and culture for magazines in several countries and teaches tasting to wine professionals, including enology students of the University of Verona's Wine Department. Her most recent books include *Matching Wine with Asian Food.*

Suzanne Haley, CWE, is the California/Oregon/Washington portfolio manager for Stacole Fine Wines in Florida. She was the founding director of the Washington Wine School in Washington, D.C., and the editor of *Uncorked* magazine from 2003 to 2006.

Michael Havens, Ph.D., founded Havens Wine Cellars in Napa Valley in 1984. He has consulted for several small Napa wineries, more recently in South America, pioneered in winemaking techniques (micro-oxygenation), and was the first New World producer of the Albariño variety.

Shields Hood, CWE, is an experienced sommelier, retailer, and distributor who represents several small wineries and importers with marketing and sales support. He is a past president of the Society of Wine Educators.

Barbara Insel is the president and CEO of Stonebridge Research Group, LLC, a market intelligence firm that provides business advisory services for the wine industry. She was formerly the managing director of MKF Research, LLC, where she led many of the wine industry's major research projects.

Gregory V. Jones, Ph.D., is a professor in the Department of Environmental Studies at Southern Oregon University in Ashland, Oregon. He is a research climatologist and is considered to be one of the world's foremost authorities on climate, viticulture, and wine, giving hundreds of presentations internationally and writing numerous book chapters, reports, and articles on wine-related issues. He also conducts applied research for the winegrape industry in Oregon.

Margie Ferree Jones is an associate professor at the Collins School, California State Polytechnic University, Pomona, where her responsibilities have included teaching international wine and hospitality marketing. She also serves as a steward for the Los Angeles County "Wines of the World Competition."

Allison Jordan is executive director of the California Sustainable Winegrowing Alliance and communications programs manager at the Wine Institute. Previously, she served as vice president and acting executive director of Resource Renewal Institute, a San Francisco–based environmental organization.

Willi Klinger is the director of the Austrian Wine Marketing Board. He has held top positions in all wine distribution channels from retail to export. He is also lecturer at the University of Natural Resources and Applied Life Sciences in Vienna.

Edward M. Korry, CWE, is department chair of Beverage and Dining Service at the College of Culinary Arts, Johnson and Wales University, Providence, Rhode Island. Korry serves as the chair of the Education and Outcomes Committee of the Alcohol Task Force at Johnson and Wales and is on ServSafe Alcohol Review Committee.

Harriet Lembeck, CWE, is chairman of the New York Wine Press, a wine-writer group, and is president of the Wine & Spirits Program, which presents classes in wine and spirits appreciation. She has written the 6th and 7th editions of *Grossman's Guide to Wines, Beers and Spirits,* is a contributor to *Beverage Dynamics* magazine, and served as wine director of the New School for 15 years.

Leonardo LoCascio is the president and CEO of Winebow, Inc. Named one of the most influential wine personalities of the last 20 years by Robert Parker in 1998, he imports 60 prized Italian producers as Winebow's Leonardo LoCascio Selections. He is also a partner with the Allegrini family in two Tuscan estates, in Bolgheri and Montalcino.

Dewey Markham, Jr., is the author of *Wine Basics* (1993) and *1855: A History of the Bordeaux Classification* (1998). He has lived and worked in Bordeaux since 1993.

Norm McKibben is a managing partner in Pepper Bridge Winery, Artifex Wine Company, Seven Hills Vineyard, and Les Collines Vineyard in the Walla Walla appellation. He has also served as chairman of the Washington Wine Commission and a member of the Oregon Wine Board.

Richard Mendelson, J.D., is an attorney with the law firm of Dickenson, Peatman, and Fogarty in Napa, California, specializing in alcoholic beverage law and land use planning for wineries and vineyards. He teaches about wine law at the law schools of UC Berkeley, Aix-Marseille, and Bordeaux, as well as at UC Davis, and is a past president of the International Wine Law Association.

Sheri Sauter Morano, MW, is the spokesperson for Wines of France. She has been an MW since 2003 and wrote her dissertation on the potential impact of liberalized direct shipping on the three-tier system.

Stephen A. Mutkoski, Ph.D., is the Banfi Vintners Professor of Wine Education and Management at Cornell University. He has authored *The Wine Professor* series and two distance-learning courses: "Foodservice Management Systems: Issues and Concepts" and "Foodservice Management Systems: Operations," published by eCornell.

Philippe Newlin is the tasting director at *Wine & Spirits* magazine. He also teaches wine classes at Columbia Business School and contributes to Devour.tv.

Janeen Olsen, Ph.D., is professor of marketing in the Wine Business Program at Sonoma State University, where she teaches courses in wine marketing and the global marketplace for wine. She is a coauthor of *Wine Marketing and Sales: Success Strategies for a Saturated Market* and has spoken on a variety of wine-related topics at symposiums and conferences worldwide.

Jennifer D. Pereira, AIWS, CWE, has been an instructor at Johnson & Wales University in Providence, Rhode Island, since 2003, teaching both degree courses

in wines and spirits as well as WSET certificate courses to local industry professionals. In addition, she manages a small vineyard in the Berkshires, contributes
articles to national media, and has over 20 years in the food and wine industry.

Rod Phillips, Ph.D., is professor of history at Carleton University, Ottawa, Canada,
where he teaches courses on the history of food and drink. His books include
A Short History of Wine (2000), and he writes for the wine press in Canada, the
United States, and the United Kingdom.

João Portugal Ramos is the winemaker at Monte da Caldeira winery in Estremoz,
Alentejo, Portugal. As a consulting enologist, he has played a relevant part in the
development of some notable Portuguese wines across a wide variety of regions.

Jamie Ritchie is a senior vice president of Sotheby's and head of Sotheby's Wine
Department in North America. He was responsible for starting Sotheby's wine
sales in New York in 1994. As a respected authority on the wine market, he has
been regularly featured in the *Wall Street Journal, New York Times, Los Angeles
Times, Forbes,* and the *Wine Spectator*.

Leslie Sbrocco is an award-winning author, writer, speaker, wine consultant, and
television host. She has written two books, *Wine for Women: A Guide to Buying,
Pairing and Sharing Wine* (2003), which won the coveted Georges Duboeuf
Best Wine Book of the Year award, and *The Simple & Savvy Wine Guide* (2006).

Bruce Schneider is the third generation of his family to work in the wine industry.
He has expertise as a winemaker (Schneider Vineyards, North Fork of Long
Island) and branding and marketing consultant to domestic and foreign wine
producers. As senior managing director at RF Binder Partners, he oversees the
U.S. offices of Wines of Germany and Wines of Chile.

Ulf Sjödin, MW, is the wine manager of V&S Group in Stockholm, Sweden,
responsible for wine quality and strategic pricing on the Swedish, Norwegian,
and Finnish markets. In 2007 he became the first Swedish Master of Wine.

Robert W. Small, Ph.D., is professor emeritus of the Collins School at California
State Polytechnic University, Pomona. He served as the head of the Hospitality
Management Program beginning in 1987 and then dean. He taught courses on
food and beverage management and wines, spirits, and beers. He has served as
chairman of the Los Angeles County Fair Wine Competition since 1998.

Jan Stuebing Smyth is the regional director of Wine Australia in the United States,
based in New York. She worked with Food and Wines from France in the early
1980s, a Napa Valley winery in the late 1980s and was an international importer
in the early 1990s before joining the Australians in 1996.

Liz Thach, Ph.D., is a management and wine business professor at Sonoma State
University in the Wine Business Center, where she teaches in both the

undergraduate and new Wine MBA programs. In addition, she has consulted for more than 20 wineries. She has published numerous wine articles and two books: *Wine: A Global Business* (2004) and *Wine Marketing and Sales* (2007).

Mary-Colleen Tinney is a writer and editor at *Wine Business Monthly* magazine. She has extensively covered the retail market, writing a monthly column analyzing. She has also covered the direct-to-consumer channel, regional news, and wine marketing.

Paul Tudor, MW, is an independent wine writer, educator, and industry consultant based in Auckland, New Zealand.

Barry Wiss, CWE, is vice president of communications and trade relations for Trinchero Family Estates. He has 25 years' experience in hospitality and education and is a certified sommelier.

Erik Wolf, the president and CEO of the International Culinary Tourism Association and president of the International Culinary Tourism Institute, is internationally recognized as the founder of the culinary tourism industry. He holds an M.A. in travel marketing and international communication and has more than 20 years of experience with a variety of travel industry companies.

Jay Youmans, MW, is a 30-year veteran of the wine industry and has been involved with marketing, distribution, importation, brand development, brand building, and education. He passed the MW exam in 2004, winning the Viña Errazuriz Award for the outstanding paper on the business of wine.

Liza B. Zimmerman, DWS, is a San Francisco–based wine writer and the principal of a wine events business, Liza the Wine Chick. Formerly the managing editor of Shanken Communications' *Market Watch,* her writing now appears regularly in *Wine Business Monthly, Caviar Affair, In the Mix,* and Fodor's, among other publications.